MISTRESS
OF THE HOUSE

MISTRESS OF THE HOUSE

Great Ladies
and Grand Houses
1670–1830

Rosemary Baird

Weidenfeld & Nicolson
LONDON

First published in Great Britain in 2003
by Weidenfeld & Nicolson, a division of
the Orion Publishing Group Ltd
Orion House
5 Upper Saint Martin's Lane
London, WC2H 9EA

A CIP catalogue record for this book is available
from the British Library.

ISBN 0297 83078 3

Printed and bound by Butler & Tanner Ltd,
Frome and London

CONTENTS

LIST OF ILLUSTRATIONS

Front Cover:
Unknown Lady Seated in front of a House, by Thomas Gainsborough, *c.* 1750. © Yale Center for British Art, Paul Mellon Collection, USA/Bridgeman Art Library

Colour Plate Sections:

Unknown Lady Seated in front of a House, by Thomas Gainsborough, *c.* 1750. © Yale Center for British Art, Paul Mellon Collection, USA/Bridgeman Art Library

Mariage à la Mode: The Marriage Contract, by William Hogarth, 1743. National Gallery, London/ Bridgeman Art Library

A Tea Party at Lord Harrington's House, by Charles Phillips, 1730. © Yale Center for British Art, Paul Mellon Collection, USA/ Bridgeman Art Library

The Mall in St James's Park, by Thomas Gainsborough, *c.* 1783. © The Frick Collection, New York

Weston Park, Shropshire. © The Trustees of the Weston Park Foundation, UK

Lady Wilbraham, by Sir Peter Lely, *c.* 1662. The Trustees of the Weston Park Foundation, UK/ Bridgeman Art Library

Marble Hill, Twickenham. © English Heritage Photographic Library

Henrietta Howard, later Countess of Suffolk, by Charles Jervas, *c.* 1724. © English Heritage Photographic Library

Marble Hill, engraved after Augustin Heckell, 1749. © English Heritage Photographic Library

Marble Hill: the Great Room. © English Heritage Photographic Library

Marble Hill: table by William Kent. © English Heritage Photographic Library

Firle Place, West Sussex: fox table. © Firle Estate Trustees

The Earl & Countess of Upper Ossory at Ampthill Park, Bedfordshire, by Benjamin Killingbeck, 1777. Ackermann and Johnson Ltd, UK/Bridgeman Art Library

View of Arlington Street from Green Park, watercolour by J. Whittock, 1848. © The British Museum

Louise de Keroualle, by Sir Peter Lely, *c.* 1671. © Althorp

Goodwood House, West Sussex: cabinet given to Louise de Keroualle by King Charles II. © Trustees of the Goodwood Collection

The Château de la Verrerie, Aubigny. © Comte Béraud de Vogüé

Ham House, Middlesex: the Jacobean north façade of 1610. © The National Trust Photographic Library/ Nick Meers

Elizabeth Murray, Lady Tollemache, later Countess of Dysart and Duchess of Lauderdale, by Sir Peter Lely, painted *c.* 1648. © The National Trust/ Ham House, Richmond, Surrey

Ham House: the modified south front. © The National Trust Photographic Library/ William R. Davis

Ham House: original hanging in the Queen's Antechamber. © The National Trust Photographic Library/ Bill Batten

Ham House: ebony table with silver mounts and caryatids. © The National Trust Photographic Library/ Bill Batten

Lady Caroline Fox, later Lady Holland, in masquerade costume, by William Hoare of Bath, *c.* 1750. © Trustees of the Goodwood Collection

Holland House, Kensington, *c.* 1850, lithograph. © Trustees of the Goodwood

Collection

Lady Louisa Lennox, by Allan Ramsay, c. 1759. © Private Collection

Mary Blount, Duchess of Norfolk, English School, 1730s. Reproduced by kind permission of Their Graces The Duke and Duchess of Norfolk, Arundel Castle

St. James's Square, engraving, c. 1752. © Yale Center for British Art, Paul Mellon Collection, USA/ Bridgeman Art Library

The Music Room, Norfolk House. © V&A Picture Library

Ugbrooke Park, Devon: the Norfolk House bed hangings. © Clive Boursnell/ Country Life Picture Library

Mary Blount, Duchess of Norfolk, holding an embroidery bodkin, by John Vanderbank, 1730s. © Clive Boursnell

Ugbrooke Park, Devon: cockatoo from the Norfolk House bed hangings. © Clive Boursnell/ Country Life Picture Library

Worksop: the Gothic Farm. © Rosemary Baird

Pediment for Worksop Manor, designed by Mary, Duchess of Norfolk. © Rosemary Baird

Worksop Manor, Nottinghamshire, by William Hodges, 1777. Reproduced by kind permission of His Grace The Duke of Norfolk, Arundel Castle

Audley End, Essex, late eighteenth-century watercolour based on earlier engravings by Henry Winstanley. © English Heritage Photographic Library

Audley End, Essex: the Countess of Portsmouth's rebuilt gallery. © John Bethell/ Bridgeman Art Library

Audley End, Essex: the Fish Room, now called the Saloon. © English Heritage Photographic Library

Audley End, Essex. © English Heritage Photographic Library

Alnwick Castle, Northumberland, by Canaletto, 1752. Private Collection/ Bridgeman Art Library

Views of Alnwick Castle, by J. Bell, 1770s. © Collection of the Duke of Northumberland

Syon Park, Middlesex, by Canaletto, 1749. © Collection of the Duke of Northumberland

Northumberland House, London, by Canaletto, 1752. Private Collection/ Bridgeman Art Library

Sandleford Priory, Berkshire. © Michael Lyons

View from Sandleford Priory, by Edward Haytley, 1744. © Collection of Mr and Mrs Thomas Gibson

Sandleford Priory: the ceiling of the Octagonal Drawing Room, by James Wyatt. © Michael Lyons

Hill Street, London: the Zephyr ceiling by James 'Athenian' Stuart, painted in 1767. © Clive Boursnell

Joseph Bonomi: Design for the Great Room at Montagu House, 1790. © RIBA Library Drawings Collection

Saltram House, Devon, from the southeast. © The National Trust Photographic Library/ Rupert Truman

Saltram House, Devon: proposed design for Lady Catherine Parker. © Chris Vile/
The National Trust, Devon and Cornwall Region
Theresa Parker with her son, John, later 1st Earl of Morley, by Sir Joshua
Reynolds, 1772–5. © The National Trust Photographic Library/ Rob Matheson
Saltram House, Devon: some of Theresa's collection of black basalt vases. ©
Clive Boursnell
Saltram House, Devon: the Saloon, or Great Room. © The National Trust Photo-
graphic Library/ Andreas von Einsiedel
Jane, Duchess of Gordon, in Elizabethan costume, by Sir Joshua Reynolds, c.
1775. © Trustees of the Goodwood Collection
Gordon Castle, Morayshire, engraving. © Trustees of the Goodwood Collection
Jane, Duchess of Gordon, with her son, George Marquis of Huntly, by George
Romney, 1778. Scottish National Portrait Gallery, Edinburgh, Scotland/ Bridge-
man Art Library
Kinrara: the house built by Jane, Duchess of Gordon for her own occupation. ©
Private Collection
Belvoir Castle, Leicestershire. © Paul Barker/ Country Life Picture Library
Fire at Belvoir Castle, English School. © Reproduced by kind permission of His
Grace The Duke of Rutland
Elizabeth, Duchess of Rutland, at Belvoir Castle, by George Sanders, c. 1817–20.
© Reproduced by kind permission of His Grace The Duke of Rutland
Elizabeth, Duchess of Rutland, at Belvoir, by George Sanders and John Ferneley,
c. 1820. © Reproduced by kind permission of His Grace The Duke of Rutland
Lancaster House, The Mall, London. © Mark Fiennes/ Lancaster House
Belvoir Castle: the Elizabeth Saloon. © Paul Barker/ Country Life Picture Library

For Peter

AUTHOR'S PREFACE

'Never underestimate the domestic power of women.' These words, spoken to the author some twenty years ago, were the starting point for many thoughts about the importance of women in their own homes, and, specifically, in grand houses. Various writers have been interested in the history of everyday life at all levels in historic houses,[1] and in documenting the daily routine of servants and their domestic duties,[2] but much more needs to be said about the achievements of the lady of the house. This book goes against the current trend in historic house visitor interest by investigating the drawing room rather than the kitchen, the gilded interiors rather than the nursery. It considers the extent to which women have played a part in the creation of those interiors, and the magic touch that brings together a whole house and its intricate workings. It is not a feminist study so much as a look at the particular symbiosis between a woman and her house.

A date range of 1670–1830 has been selected in order to cover some of the greatest and most beautiful of English country houses. All were newly fashionable in their day, from the handsome domestic-looking red-brick and stone classical hybrids that sprang up after the Civil War, through the Palladian houses of the early eighteenth century, to the lighter classical interiors of Robert Adam and the sophistication of the early Regency style. Reference is also made to earlier houses that were refurnished in the taste of the day.

Whom to choose from among the women who built, decorated and ran them, and which of the houses? Obviously the availability of evidence is a constraint: many houses were created by owners who left neither diaries nor letters, portraits nor topographical views. Often it is assumed that the husband was the patron, because his name would appear on bills, but it may equally have been his wife. Of the women who are known to have been builders, decorators and collectors, Mrs

Montagu begs for a study all of her own. Much has been written about her as a literary critic and as a bluestocking, and she appears as a patron in works on James 'Athenian' Stuart, Robert Adam and James Wyatt, but the full range of her patronage has by no means been covered. Of others, such as Mary Blount, Duchess of Norfolk, who was the driving force behind the creation of two magnificent houses; Elizabeth Seymour, Duchess of Northumberland, who restored the dilapidated Alnwick Castle; and Elizabeth Howard, Duchess of Rutland, an obsessive builder, despite much verbal recognition of their importance in their ancestral homes, there is far more to be said, much of it gleaned from contemporary documents. Often such women were celebrated in their own lifetime, but little may have been heard of them since. Sometimes too they are not well known outside their locality; both statements are true of the Countess of Portsmouth at Audley End.

Often just a different way of thinking about houses stimulates new findings. This is certainly so with women such as Elizabeth Murray, Duchess of Lauderdale; Caroline, Baroness Holland at Holland House; and Theresa Parker at Saltram. Despite much coverage of her life, the patronage of Louise de Keroualle, Duchess of Portsmouth, has hardly been recognised, while a full biography of Jane, Duchess of Gordon, is long overdue. Not only have many new discoveries about them been made, but the juxtaposition of all these powerful personalities also builds up an interesting comparative picture.

It was not intended at first to include such a large number of duchesses, but those selected had emerged as particularly fascinating and daring individuals, with the opportunity to make an impression on the very largest houses. Although some already came from quite a grand background, not one could ever really have foreseen the demands of being a duchess. In the words of the present Duke of Richmond, no ducal wife can anticipate the task ahead of her, unless she herself has grown up as the daughter of a duke. Many duchesses, and especially those in this book, are therefore women who rose to a challenge.

Conversely, the achievements of certain great chatelaines are mentioned here largely for context and comparison. They include women such as Sarah, Duchess of Marlborough at Marlborough House and Blenheim; the superb Henrietta Howard, Countess of Suffolk at Marble Hill; Alice Sherard, Lady Brownlow at Belton; and Elizabeth,

Countess of Home at 20, Portman Square, all of whom have been written up recently enough, and with sufficient attention to letters and accounts, to make further investigation superfluous.[3] Georgina, Duchess of Bedford is the latest claimant to this list, for the house that she built at Endsleigh in Devon rather than for her relatively minor additions at Woburn Abbey.[4] The work at Welbeck Abbey in Nottinghamshire of Henrietta Cavendish-Holles, Countess of Oxford and Mortimer, and the great-great-great-granddaughter of Bess of Hardwick, has also been ably portrayed, with additional findings pending.[5]

Often one must be grateful to an owner for being a conservator rather than a mover: these people get little recognition for their good taste. The brash and bossy Elizabeth, wife of Henry, 3rd Baron Holland, has already been well documented for her complete renovation of Holland House in the Regency period; it is felt that the lesser-known work of her predecessor Caroline, Lady Holland, is therefore more deserving of investigation. Women gardeners are not included except where their talents also extended to the house: they are due a whole study in their own right.

In recent years some finely calculated treatises have sought to make all sorts of measurements and definitions about the eighteenth century.[6] While this book draws on the results of this admirable historical method, which counts numbers of divorces, of lady painters, of peeresses of the realm and of everything it can, it does not aim to give any more than an overview. The life of each individual lady of the house had similarities with those of her contemporaries, and differences. The aim is simply to draw attention to a very popular subject, that of the great classical era of English house building and decorating, but in a different way. The primary sources are both literary and visual: diaries and letters, novels, plays, poems and theses, together with portraits and landscapes, miniatures and watercolours, sculpture and porcelain.

I am grateful to many country house owners, to the National Trust and its representatives, and to curators, archivists and experts who have given so generously of their own knowledge: many of the latter are acknowledged for specific contributions in the endnotes. The staff of many County Record Offices and of the British Library, especially the Rare Books Room, and of the London Library, have been superbly professional, as has Carolyn Garner at the Huntington Library in California. I am especially grateful for time, help, hospitality and access to: the Duke and Duchess of Rutland, Lord and Lady Clifford of Chudleigh, Comte and Comtesse Béraud de Vogüé, the Hon. Mrs Townshend, Major General Bernard Gordon Lennox, Major and Mrs Robin McLaren, Mr & Mrs Brian Farr, Mr & Mrs Henry Farr, Sue Baumbach, Clare Baxter, Deborah Gage, Eileen Harris, Brian Howes, Gilly Lehmann, Lee Martin, Evelyn Pritchard, Kenneth Quickenden, Dr John Martin Robinson, Katherine Sharp, Annabel Westman; Pauline Leach and HSBC Republic Bank (UK) Limited; Peter Sanders-Rose and the Govenors of St. Gabriel's School, Sandleford Priory; the Royal Over-Seas League, London; the Headmaster and Governing Council of Stonyhurst College and the Trustees of Weston Park; and for their patient support, to Kathryn Bellamy and Wendi Nicholson.

For special permission to publish from documents, my acknowledgements are additionally to the Duke of Norfolk, the Duke of Northumberland and the Trustees of the Goodwood Collection.

For inspiring me to embark on this project and for their encouragement throughout, my thanks are both to the Earl of March and Kinrara, and to my heroic husband, Peter Andreae.

Chapter 1

THE FEMININE TOUCH

'What were country houses for? They were not originally, whatever they may be now, just large houses in the country in which rich people lived. Essentially they were power houses – the houses of a ruling class...Basically people did not live in country houses unless they either possessed power...or were making a bid to possess it.'

Mark Girouard, *Life in the English Country House*, 1978

In the eighteenth century Britain was run by its landowners, for whom the acquisition of estates was a bid for power rather than for privacy. Land was the only certain basis of power, because of the support systems it created. In the seventeenth and eighteenth centuries, when a woman married, she married not just a person but a way of life; for the fortunate, this meant being conjoined in a situation based on land or property. The aristocracy preferred to keep to its fairly close circle, admission to whose serried ranks was procured by ownership of forests and farms, as well as by titles and honours, intellect and beauty. The gentry in turn liked to be associated with their local landowners. Fields were not necessarily farmed exclusively for profit: in the eighteenth century it was advantageous to have tenants who not only brought domestic rents but also electoral votes.

Through their own fortunes and connections, heiresses and women of the aristocracy assisted their husbands in fulfilling their social and political ambitions. As mistress of a great house, a wife would have the means to help her husband make his way in public life. Such was the case with Lady Caroline Lennox, who married not fortune but ambition: as he climbed, her husband Henry Fox, the politician, acquired Holland House, from which he gained both further status and a location for political entertaining near to London. Gentlemen who established a power base in the country, but also spent some months in town, could be given royal and political appointments. By this route, an ambitious landowner might in due course become a peer and create a dynasty. At Stowe the large Temple-Grenville family developed their political skills and their house and landscape park simultaneously, making it the bastion of Whiggism and the fashionable meeting place of their political allies.

Fortunes were often created from politics, as achieved by all three sons of George Grenville, Marquis of Buckingham, as well as from Court appointments.[1] The notion of royal and government service as a public duty and not for personal financial gain is a later, nineteenth-century ideal. Earnings from political sinecures often funded estates, which drew attention to the success of the owner, thereby bringing him further honours and promotion. Houghton in Norfolk was created by Sir Robert Walpole as a part of his political ascent, and Hagley Hall in Worcestershire was transformed by Lord Lyttelton from the revenues of his relatively junior post as Royal Cofferer. The law also continued to be a source of considerable wealth: Belton House in Lincolnshire owed its origins and development to successful careers in both law and politics by the Brownlow family.

Without a great house at its centre, land had little purpose in the display of wealth and power. Whereas the medieval house had tended to develop outwards in stages from the central hall, the pervasion of classical influences in the seventeenth century meant that older houses were often demolished, and new houses were built as complete entities according to the latest fashion. From the times of the Elizabethan prodigy houses – created specifically to impress the monarch, with the intention of persuading her to visit – the homes of the very wealthy became great showcases in which to display status and learning through art, notably portraits and tapestries, carved furniture and flamboyant silver. By the mid eighteenth century ancestors shared the walls with personalised paintings of favourite horses and dogs, while a wider dimension of learning gained on the grand tour was revealed through views of Venice and Rome, and by biblical and classical scenes. At this date, interiors, furniture and fittings were not designed for a specifically country location, but followed the latest London fashions. Town and country life fed each other. Often the greatest works of art were kept first in the London house: as the eighteenth century progressed, more and more were removed to the country.[2]

While most great houses in England were created by the 'Bachelor Duke' or the 'Architect Earl', a number were built by women, most notably, in the sixteenth century, by the redoubtable Bess of Hardwick. Other women who built great houses are included in this book. Often it was the men who made the initial decisions on the interiors, though the celebrated patronage of the Countess of Home at 20, Portman Square, in London, shows us a woman who was perfectly able so to do. The combination of the creation of houses and their smooth running was special to women; however, in many earlier houses it is their role in the creation that has not always been recognised. At Saltram House in Devon, although Theresa Parker made most of the decisions, she felt that she must give the credit to her husband: similarly, the influence and achievement of many talented wives has gone unsung. As collectors of art works too, it is true to say that men predominated. However, the many exceptions have never been noted cumulatively: even when lady collectors were documented recently,[3] the impression that remained was that their main acquisitions were porcelain, shells and botanical specimens.

Refurbishment was a different matter. Sarah, Duchess of Marlborough was fearless in her execution of the building works at Blenheim Palace. Unfortunately, she never liked Blenheim and after her husband's death she completed the rich, dark interiors grudgingly, as a tribute to him.[4] Sometimes it was a question of making the best of an ancient and unfashionable family seat. In either case, for many women the creation of a great house became her life's work. From dadoes to doorknobs, furniture arrangements to picture hangs, it was she who made the choices. Out of sheer practical necessity, women acquired far more furniture than they have hitherto been credited for, and were often involved in commissioning portraits and in buying prints.

In the building or decorating of a house, everything depended on the dynamics of the marriage: whether he or she controlled the purse strings, who was the stronger character, who had the better eye, who was the more interested. Sometimes, as in the case of the 1st Duke and Duchess of Northumberland at Syon, husband and wife did the improvements together. There the Duke, the very able Sir Hugh Smithson, was much involved; the Duchess was likewise a strong character. The result is that although Alnwick Castle was more the creation of the Duchess, all the works at Alnwick, Northumberland House and Syon Park are to this day principally ascribed to the Duke. Because society accepted the husband as the dominant partner,[5] documentation inevitably credited the patronage of architects and the commissioning of furniture and paintings to men. In practice Georgiana Poyntz, Countess Spencer, had excellent taste and was a willing aide to her husband in the decisions for Spencer House, on Green Park in London. At Holkham Hall in Norfolk, Margaret Tufton spent seven years completing the building works after the death in 1759 of her husband Thomas Coke, Earl of Leicester, and gave detailed descriptions of her rearrangements.[6] Arthur Young, visiting in 1768, commented that 'Holkam [sic], the celebrated house of the Countess of Leicester, built by the late Earl, cannot be viewed with too much attention.'[7]

In the eighteenth century a number of redoubtable women were active in spheres largely male-dominated. As patrons, it was normal for women to participate in the commissioning of works of art, a model for which was set by George II's consort, Queen Caroline, and her daughters. There were female career artists: in 1768 Angelica Kauffmann and Mary Moser were founder members of the Royal Academy. Working in a studio partnership with her husband, Maria Cosway was in her own right a successful painter of miniatures. Mrs Eleanor Coade began to produce her fabricated stone at Lambeth in 1769: it was widely used for capitals, coats of arms and other ornamental devices.

The lady of the house may well have selected the porcelain and decided the curtain fabrics, but her particular ongoing task was that of making the house come alive. As an art gallery alone it achieved nothing: she had to create an atmosphere of warmth and hospitality, providing entertainment and making life enjoyable for family and guests. There are many accounts of legendary eighteenth-century entertainments that show how certain great houses came to life, even before the days of the house party. Queen Caroline animated life at Court in a way that her parsimonious husband abandoned after her death in 1737, when he closed up half of both Kensington and St James's Palaces.[8] Mrs Montagu likewise assured her husband that she was making their London home into a fine backdrop for 'Beaux and Belles'.[9] One of the purposes of the grandly decorated house was to support and promote the social fabric. This comfortable milieu was ideally adapted to the making of introductions that led to suitable marriages, as well as to sorting out local issues and political alliances.

When the decorating was complete, the 'Mistress of the House' also had to turn her attention to maintenance. Behind the elegant façade there had to run a serious organisation. This often involved a large number of servants, and it was the mistress who had a duty of care towards them, informing herself about their families and illnesses, their weaknesses and strengths. Mary, Duchess of Beaufort ran a household at Badminton of about two hundred: she reigned over it like a court. In the eighteenth century the staff were often known as 'the family'. Despite the ready availability of labour, it was often the lady of the house who had to be sure that the interiors, and the collections so carefully amassed, were cared for in the right way. This was something at which the Georgians and indeed the Victorians excelled. It was only with the decline of domestic service at the end of the Great War, or in particularly well-staffed houses[10] at the outbreak of the Second World War, that these skills of conservation were finally lost.

Once the whole dance of birth, education, marriage and house had been performed, it began again with finding suitable alliances for the children. Dame Alice Brownlow, as the mistress of Belton was known when a dowager, took seriously the question of five daughters, securing for them as husbands a duke and two earls. Jane, Duchess of Gordon did even better. She not only gained three dukes, a marquess and a baronet as her sons-in-law: she even had their titles engraved on her tombstone. An unhappy marriage to Alexander, 4th Duke of Gordon had not deflected her: like so many other women before and after her, at Kinrara in the Highlands of Scotland she created a beautiful house and through it reinforced tradition, culture and family.

Chapter 2

LOVE AND STRATEGY

'I never saw my lady...till an hour before our marriage. I made my addresses to her father, her father to his lawyer, the lawyer to my estate...the bargain was struck...What need have young people of addressing, or anything, till they come to undressing?'

Sir Positive Trap, in Henry Fielding's *Love in Several Masques*, 1728[1]

Before arriving at their position as mistress of a great house, the chatelaines of the period 1670–1830 were first subject to the marriage market. In the early eighteenth century arranged marriages were the norm, a principal aim being to secure or better the status quo, in the form of house, land and wealth. The higher the social status of the family, the more likely it was that the marriage would be seen as a financial deal.[2] When this worked, it worked well: couples such as the 2nd Duke and Duchess of Richmond, who had a very successful arranged marriage themselves, continued to believe in its virtues for their progeny. When Lady Mary Pierrepont, later Wortley Montagu, resisted her father's choice, he told her that 'he was very much surpriz'd that I did not depend on his Judgment for my future happiness.'[3] It was certainly hoped that there would also be affection: at Belton Sir John Brownlow declared in his will his 'earnest desire that a marriage should be effected between my kinsman Sir John Brownlow and my kinswoman Alice Sherard (if) the said (persons) may affect one another'.[4] The preference for marriage within one's social class and with mutual property advantages was reinforced by Hardwicke's Marriage Act of 1753, which said that banns had to be called and parental permission given if either party was under the age of twenty-one.[5] One result of this legislation was that young bloods seeking a fortune could no longer elope with susceptible heiresses of tender years.

A choice made solely out of passion was not expected to be the right one. However rebellious she was on her own account, eloping in 1712 rather than marrying her father's proposed suitor, once she was older Lady Mary Wortley Montagu reverted to the caution typical of her class. She came to disapprove of marriages for passion, suggesting in 1739 that arsenic should be put in the tea of one acquaintance rather than that she marry a mere singer.[6] Lady Mary may well have deserved the charge of hypocrisy; in 1736 she and her husband opposed their daughter Mary marrying the Earl of Bute, on the grounds that he had no money. When her father threatened to withdraw her dowry of £20,000, Mary married the Earl regardless. Another generation on, Mary's daughter Lady Louisa Stuart was not allowed to marry her beloved second cousin, Colonel William Meadows: she remained single.[7] Own-choice marriages left the parents furious, often out of sheer snobbery. When in 1766 the Duke of Beaufort married the second daughter of Admiral Boscawen, the Duchess of Northumberland reported: 'The Dutchess of Beaufort kept house & saw nobody on account of her Sons Marriage with Miss Betty Boscawen.' Friends and family felt obliged to follow her lead, except for one kind relative: 'The young Dutchess had no Jewells but a Pair of Diamond Ear Rings, presented to her by the Duke's uncle...'[8]

Conversely, where the only motivation was greed and social ambition, arranged marriages could engender unhappiness. In 1706 Mary Astell commented drily on the usual arrangements: 'What will she bring is the first enquiry. How many acres? Or how much ready coin?'[9] Similarly Elizabeth Montagu, as a young woman, asked: 'What is a woman without gold or fee simple?'[10] A possible love match between Lady Diana Spencer and William Hamilton, the grandson of the 3rd Duke of Hamilton, was avoided simply because neither had any means.[11] When in 1774 Thomas Noel, 2nd Viscount Wentworth, was short of money with which to maintain his mistress and his two much loved illegitimate children, it was natural, if distasteful, to him and to his sister Judith that he should try to find a wealthy wife to get him out of his difficulty. A suitable candidate was approached, but she politely turned him down.[12] As late as 1796 the Earl Bishop of Bristol was desperate for his son to marry the Comtesse de la Marche, daughter of the King of Prussia, who had £5000 a year and a principality: 'the beautiful, elegant, important and interesting object I have proposed to him.'

The Earl Bishop insisted: 'the example he has before his eyes in and within his own family ought fully to determine him against a love match; 'tis so ominous a lottery, so pregnant with blanks, so improbable a success.' Crudely he sought to tempt the young man with wealth rather than love: 'let him weigh all we offer to his ambition, his ease, his comfort, his taste and his pocket.'[13]

Nevertheless, any negotiations for a propertied union had to be carried out with discretion. In 1762 London society was somewhat irritated when the Duchess of Bedford not only blatantly pursued George, 4th Duke of Marlborough for her daughter, Lady Caroline Russell, but actually succeeded: the couple were married 'eight and forty hours after his grace declared himself a lover. The Duke of Bedford was always known to be a man of business, but he never despatched a matter quicker than this.'[14] The way in which Jane, Duchess of Gordon, attained grand matches for her five daughters was both frowned upon and secretly envied. Jane's eldest daughter Charlotte, Duchess of Richmond, followed her example. 'I hear the Duchess of Richmond's flight to Dublin is for the purpose of catching him for one of her daughters,' wrote Frederick Calthorpe from Hampshire, referring to Frederick Lord Hervey, son of the future 1st Marquess of Bristol: 'She had been endeavouring to entrap him during the last season, & though Hervey showed no penchant for the daughter, the Duchess the true daughter of her mother continues to persevere. I hope she will not succeed.'[15] As Charlotte had seven daughters she had much work to do. Her sister Louisa, wife of the 2nd Marquess Cornwallis, did the same. When in 1819 Louisa's daughter Jane married the 2nd Baron Braybrooke, rejecting a devoted suitor, Lady Williams Wynn wrote that 'the old Duchess must be proud to look down (if she can) on a daughter treading so worthily in her shoes.'[16] Georgina Gordon, as Duchess of Bedford, was happy to let her daughters marry for love, but even happier when her Louisa chose the future Duke of Abercorn.

Kind parents simply wanted the best for their children. Charlotte Grenville, the widowed Lady Williams Wynn, was very vexed in 1795 that her favourite, second son, Charles, was not marrying Elizabeth Acland, a considerable heiress for whom, however, he had little inclination. She told the nineteen-year-old boy that he had not tried hard enough to gain the girl's hand: 'the valour of a mouse is much too flattering a comparison to apply to yours.'[17] Later, disliking his own candidate, Louisa, who as the 13th daughter of Lord Courtenay was unlikely to have any fortune, she tried another suggestion: 'What do you say to the pretty Sophia Grimston, with a fortune of at least £30,000?'[18] Material comfort was an all-important goal, and Charlotte was in fact a caring and good-humoured mother, whose widowed status may have made her over-conscientious about her responsibilities. When her youngest son, Henry, turned twenty-five, she suggested that he think about marriage: 'You are a very rich single man, & might, with what you have & a very tolerably portioned wife, be a very comfortable double one, which, after all I am quite sure is the state from which you would derive most happiness.' Indeed, Henry made his own very good choice in Hester Smith, daughter of the 1st Lord Carrington. Money, love and class had combined and his mother was delighted.[19]

Sensible families thus had a balance of values, perceiving that the ideal marriage was probably a mixture of love and strategy.[20] As early as 1668, just before his own death, Sir Lionel Tollemache wrote a charming letter to his son, telling him: 'the action of your life upon which will depend your future happynesse is your marriage, and choise of a wife. Chouse a person of a good family, a comely person rather than a beauty, and of your own religion and a portion proportionate to your present and future estates.' When Lady Betty Seymour married Sir Hugh Smithson in 1740 her mother's friend, Henrietta Louisa, Countess of Pomfret, commented that she was very happy to hear of the 'Nuptials of our young Princess, who I am very sincerely rejoyced to hear is disposed of...(as every Body says) to a very Deserving Agreable Man which in my Sense, are better Epithets, than Powerful, Great & Rich.'[21] Although the Earl and Countess of Hertford had theoretically agreed to inclination over arrangement in their daughter's case, they had in fact stalled the process for six months, to be sure that her choice really was right. While love apparently triumphed over parental selection, the candidate was relatively wealthy and aristocratic, as well as tall, handsome and intelligent. As a match for their rather plump daughter, the Earl and Countess were doing well.

Throughout the century the recognition of the importance of 'inclination' grew, promoted in the literature of the period, such as Fielding's *Tom Jones* (1749), as well as lighter romantic novels.[22] In an increasingly free-thinking century, young people were beginning to question parental authority, as did Fielding's beautiful heroine Sophia, who refused to marry the odious Blifil; this tendency later reversed under stricter Victorian family regimes. Certainly contemporary observers felt that the growth of marriage for love was largely caused by the increasing readership of novels.[23] Another influence came via the Church: since the seventeenth century preachers had recommended the ideal of a companionate marriage. As the upper classes became more susceptible to the idea of emotional satisfaction within marriage, undoubtedly more complaints were voiced about the miseries of marriage for money. Looking back, both Lady Mary Wortley Montagu and Mrs Delany, mistress of Roscrow Castle, in Cornwall, and later Delville, in Ireland, felt that it was the insistence on 'riches and great alliance' that had caused their own first unhappy unions:[24] ironically, in order to avoid her own arranged marriage, Lady Mary Pierrepont had made the supposedly romantic, but actually disastrous elopement, while Mrs Delany, as Mary Granville, had married the repulsive elderly Mr Pendarves to please her uncle, Lord Lansdowne. Similarly, years later Hester Monro married Mr Thrale to oblige an uncle who would disinherit her if she did not: in the event he himself married, and disinherited her anyway.

With the new ideal of romantic love and a history of disastrous arranged marriages more openly recognised, an increasing number of young people accordingly made their own choices, especially once they were of age. It was not until about 1780, however, that most of the propertied classes in any way thought of accepting romance rather than land as the basis for marriage. The consequent success or failure ratings seem nonetheless to have altered little. Indeed, many late eighteenth-century commentators, not least the Earl Bishop of Bristol, saw the problems of romantic marriages as more numerous than those of arranged ones, and not without reason.[25] As early as 1732 Charles, 5th Earl of Sunderland, subsequently 3rd Duke of Marlborough, had himself made a successful own-choice marriage to Mary Trevor, the daughter of the 2nd Baron Trevor of Bromham, though much against the wishes of his dominating grandmother, Sarah, Duchess of Marlborough. However, when his daughter Lady Diana Spencer did the same, her choice of the dissolute and spendthrift Viscount Bolingbroke was a mistake. In 1779 the young and newly successful novelist Fanny Burney spoke disapprovingly of one Hon. Mrs W., a 'miserable runaway' bride, who had thereby disgraced her family and enraged her friends.[26] Later she chided her own great friend, the newly widowed Hester Thrale, for giving in to 'ungovernable passions' in the case of her second marriage, to Gabriel Piozzi, an Italian music master. Certainly he was considered beneath her in rank,[27] but after her first experience of marriage, Mrs Thrale could hardly be blamed. Throughout the period, elopement continued to mean social ostracism, unless the couple were exceptionally wealthy, attractive or important. However, at the turn of the century, the young Elizabeth Vassall, Lady Webster, was accepted back into society after leaving her ageing husband for the younger Henry, 3rd Baron Holland, whose child she was carrying, and whom she married immediately after her divorce; in the more louche and dissolute days of the Regency such behaviour was more likely to be condoned.

Whatever the options, the romantic ideal did not recommend poverty. The young Elizabeth Robinson, later the noted 'bluestocking' Mrs Montagu, denounced the idea of 'living in a cottage on love', which she said was 'certainly the worst diet and the worst habitation one can find out'.[28] When her nephew married the orphaned Miss Charlton in 1785, there was a great deal of mutual attraction: 'The Lovers sigh'd and look'd, sigh'd and look'd, & sigh'd again.' Nevertheless Mrs Montagu was also happy to report the girl's considerable fortune of £45,000 with an annuity of £3000. Whenever information was available, and sometimes when it was not, the Gentleman's Magazine gave added spice in announcing a marriage by reporting what it believed to be the fortune of the bride.[29]

The greatest literature of the time was equally circumspect. In Goldsmith's play She Stoops to Conquer (1773), as in Sheridan's The Rivals (1775), both performed at the fashionable, recently rebuilt Covent Garden, the respective hero and heroine, Marlow and Lydia, romantically fall in love with someone supposedly penniless: to their great good fortune and everyone's content, their beloveds turned out to be wealthy. Although the apparently current snobbish and materialistic approach to marriage[30] was attacked in novels, through the characters of Squire Western in Fielding's Tom Jones, of Mrs Bennet in Jane Austen's Pride and Prejudice and of Anthony Trollope's Lady Arabella Gresham in Dr Thorne, comfort remained an important goal. Even when Jane Austen's heroines did marry their man, he was lucky enough to have house, wealth and position. As late as the mid-Victorian novels of Trollope, the romantic marriages between Mr Gresham and Mary Thorne, Lord Lufton and Lucy Robartes and even Dr Thorne and Miss Dunstable were supported by wealth: in one partner only could virtue or beauty compensate for lack of high social position or an absence of fortune.

Radically, it was suggested in the literature of the eighteenth century that an illegitimate child from a good family, such as the eponymous hero of *Tom Jones*, could marry perfectly well, so gaining house, estate and position. Even the morally correct Jane Austen included naturally-born Harriet Smith in the social circle in *Emma*. Forgiveness for a mistake was an important Christian virtue, and it was held that the sins of the parents were not always to be visited on the child. Reinstatement into society through marriage was the fortune of many upmarket natural children, such as Henrietta le Clerc, daughter of the 3rd Duke of Richmond. As a young woman she was rather anonymously described as 'the poor orphan' whom his Duchess had turned into 'a lady of fashion'; she lived in the house of the Duke and Duchess and married General John Dorrien.[31] Alexander, 4th Duke of Gordon, and John, 3rd Duke of Rutland, likewise kept favoured natural children close to their own family.

Similarly, very grand and wealthy men often had the freedom as well as the character to marry whomsoever they chose, selecting beauty above fortune, spirit above social position.[32] This tended to happen either when they were young and passionate, like the Duke of Beaufort, or old and benign, like Charles Powlett, 3rd Duke of Bolton.[33] After the death of his first wife, the Duke of Bolton gladly married his actress mistress Lavinia Fenton, despite the drawback that their existing much-loved children remained illegitimate and she was beyond an age to produce his heir. Of the famously beautiful Gunning sisters from Ireland, Elizabeth married the young and besotted James, 6th Duke of Hamilton: he was so deeply in love that after a 'violent' courtship he insisted on marrying her immediately and without prior notice, on the evening of St Valentine's Day, 1752, using a curtain ring to swear his devotion. Elizabeth's sister Maria married George, 6th Earl of Coventry, who commissioned Capability Brown to rebuild his home at Croome Court, in Worcestershire, especially for his lovely bride. The celebrity culture of the eighteenth century ensured that wherever they went the Gunning sisters were watched and idolised, their public exposure the embodiment of what the poet Alexander Pope had grumbled against in the early 1730s: 'What's Fame? a fancy'd life in others breath.'[34]

An important ideal in eighteenth-century marriage was that the bride should be 'amiable'. Because they had themselves eloped with a very happy result, the 1st Baron and Baroness Holland were perfectly pleased when their eldest son, Stephen, chose his own bride. Like his father, Stephen did marry well, selecting Lady Mary Fitzpatrick, the daughter of an Earl. Lord Holland expressed his satisfaction rather stuffily, writing that 'he has chose well, for she seems to me, very good humour'd, & perfectly well bred',[35] whereas Stephen's mother was rapturous: 'She is a most amiable Girl, has a universal good character & superior understanding and sweet temper...My dear Boy doats on her...'[36] Of her nephew's bride, the intellectual Mrs Montagu similarly commented on her 'excellent understanding, & her gentle and unaffected manner'.[37] The 'understanding' that both these well-read women applauded in the bride was not so much book-learning as what might now be called common sense or emotional intelligence.

The marriage possibilities for the circle of people who might own great houses were therefore tight but not impenetrable. On the one hand duchesses often came from grand families themselves, and might well bring a fortune with them. The country squire with the large chequebook, meanwhile, might be attracted by class and title, as with John Parker and the Hon. Theresa Robinson; or the baronet might add to his bank book through acquisition of the merchant's daughter, as with Sir Matthew Fetherstonhaugh and Sarah Lethieullier. With parental connivance, many a well-bred gentleman set out upon an extremely happy life dependent on the fortune of his trade-descended wife. In their portraits by Thomas Gainsborough, Colonel John Bullock and Philip Delany Esq. can each be seen beaming with satisfaction, as a result of fortunes gained respectively from the Colonel's wife and the Squire's mother. For the woman, the basic source of her all-empowering position was a husband: an unmarried daughter never had quite the cachet of a wife and might at any moment find herself upstaged by an infiltrating stepmother. Owing to early death, at a time when women rarely lived beyond the menopause, second marriages for men were common;[38] it was not unusual for the mistress of a great house to have stepchildren as well as offspring of her own.

One of the principal requirements for an aristocratic bride was to provide a male heir, since most titles could not descend through the female line. The personal letters of many a landed couple show how much they felt this pressure. This also meant that chastity and fidelity were considered essential in a young bride, for reasons additional to the Christian moral ones: no landowner wanted someone else's child as his heir. Nevertheless couples were not as chauvinist about the births of daughters as some modern commentators might imagine: the Earl and Countess of Hertford were devoted to their daughter Lady Betty, both before and after the demise of her younger brother, and to her interests once she became the heiress designate of the Percy lands and titles. While the 2nd Duke and Duchess of Richmond spent twelve years waiting for a surviving son, they mourned the passing of a second daughter with no little distress and welcomed the arrival of a third. The 5th Duke and Duchess of Rutland were similarly distraught at the death of their eldest daughter, aged four.[39] Although they had to wait sixteen years for a little Marquess of Granby to survive infancy, there was never any suggestion even in their most intimate letters that they were anything other than pleased with their four surviving daughters. The frequency with which children died did not mean that their mothers were unmoved. At the death of her eldest son, George, Lord Ophaly, at the age of seventeen, Emily, Countess of Kildare, was completely stricken.

Once the heir had been born, and preferably the spare as well, aristocratic wives sometimes had extra-marital love affairs. Often these have been justified on the grounds of a marriage choice constrained by the requirements of fortunes and land. Not everyone had this excuse. In their forties Emily Lennox, Duchess of Leinster, Jane Maxwell, Duchess of Gordon, and Elizabeth Howard, Duchess of Rutland, were all unfaithful. However, these three women cannot be said to have suffered from arranged marriages: all had enjoyed many years of happy and intimate association with their husbands, who by all accounts had a strong interest in sex. However, in Emily and Jane's cases at the least, they may have been spurred to seek diversion and solace from the serial infidelity of their men.

Women who could not have children were usually stoical, and barely, if ever, referred to it in their letters. Mary Blount, Duchess of

Norfolk turned all her energies to her homes, at both Norfolk House and Worksop. So too did Sarah, Duchess of Richmond's younger daughter, Lady Louisa Connolly, at Castletown, where she found herself with a blank canvas of a house, an open bank book, many hours in the day, and a compliant husband who was said to be the richest man in Ireland. Diligent by nature, and with an informed understanding of art drawn from the great interiors of her London home, Richmond House in Whitehall, designed by Lord Burlington, Louisa turned her great fortune and her great sorrow into a magnificent creation, today the headquarters of the Irish Georgian Society.

Childlessness often brought out an especially practical aspect: once Louisa Connolly had finished the interiors at Castletown, she started a school and did a large amount of charity work. She was also very involved with the estate and supervised the making of cheeses in the dairy, and of bacon and sausages in the piggeries. After her separation from her husband, Mary Shireburn, Duchess of Norfolk immersed herself at Stonyhurst in rents and other estate matters. The young Mrs Pendarves threw herself into doing up Roscrow Castle in order to distract herself from her loathsome elderly husband; later, in a happy second marriage to Dr Delany, she decorated their Irish home, producing famous shell work and embroidery. After the loss of her young son, Mrs Montagu immersed herself in building works, social life and literature.

Although widows had for centuries been the only women with any rights before the law,[40] force of custom dictated that if they created grand homes, these were often town houses. While the country seat might be handed over to the heir, London would give a lady on her own a social life on the edges of Court. In the country many widows did move to the dower house, but this arrangement would be deliberately lower key, intended not to upstage the daughter-in-law, with the dower house not such a centre of fashion or design. Although they might be wealthy in their own right, which meant from their father, widows often received only a 'portion' from their departed spouse. However, those who did inherit in full, perhaps because there were no children, might draw on their existing skills to create yet another stylish home. Notable examples were the houses in Portman Square of the elderly, rich and solitary Elizabeth, Countess of Home, and of the more gregarious Mrs Montagu, who also masterminded the interiors of her country home while nonetheless encouraging her nephew to feel that he was the master there.

A married lady often had a great deal of domestic power. As early as 1682, in Ravenscroft's play *The London Cuckolds*, City wives were perceived as getting the better of their husbands, while letting them think they were the ones in control.[41] In politics this was a talent also exercised by Queen Caroline with her husband King George II.[42] Both Hester Thrale and Elizabeth Montagu made considerable play of acceding to their husbands' wishes: in fact they were brilliant domestic strategists who could more or less do what they wanted.[43] Despite incidents of violent abuse in some families at all levels of society, and a biased legal situation in which men could make off with their wives' inheritances, many men made very kind husbands. Chivalry, especially towards women, was after all the basis of the word 'gentleman'. Edward Chamberlayne in his *Angliae Notitia* said that Englishwomen had an excellent situation due to the 'good nature of Englishmen towards their wives'. He asserted: 'They are, generally speaking, the most happy women in the world'.[44]

Given a husband eminent enough to supply a large flow of money, it might be expected that some wives would overspend on the house beyond the borders of good taste. Vast extravagance did exist, but tempered with good judgement. The Duchess of Lauderdale, heiress to Ham House in Surrey, was for a time supremely acquisitive, but showed excellent taste in her choice of furniture and textiles. During an age when gentlemen often ruined themselves creating wonderful country houses, wives rarely seem to have got access to large sums, even if derived from their own fortune. In her travel diary of 1771, the Duchess of Northumberland, herself a great heiress, several times reported that she did not buy a painting because she 'could not afford it'.[45] If a wife did hold the purse strings, as with Lady Louisa Connolly, it was because her husband felt he could rely on her financial discretion. Certainly refurbishment by women was often tempered by that all-prevailing virtue of 'prudence', even in houses whose luxury cannot be doubted. Restraint was in any case an important element of classical architecture: by the 1770s 'elegant simplicity' was increasingly in vogue. The work of Robert Adam appealed to many patronesses, notably Mrs Boscawen, the Countess of Home, Mrs Montagu, Theresa Parker and the Duchess of Northumberland. Certainly Adam's style,

both in its earlier slightly rococo phase, and in its developed neoclassical mode, is often said to have a slightly feminine touch. He also tended
to be more concerned with interiors than with whole houses, just as a
woman was often the decorator rather than the builder.

Frequently in the eighteenth century, the fortune spent on a house
was newly acquired. Joseph Wright of Derby shows Mr & Mrs Thomas
Coltman setting out for a ride with their newly built Palladian mansion
beyond.[46] In his *Mariage à la Mode* series William Hogarth lampooned
the young Viscount who had to marry new merchant money in order
to pay his debts on the fine classical house that he was building, seen
through the window. The manner in which a house was decorated was
due to the knowledge and education on the part of at least one spouse,
or failing that to a developed eye. Many aristocratic and upper middle-
class women of the time were well educated. As early as 1655,
Margaret, Duchess of Newcastle declared: 'In Nature we have as clear
as understanding as Men, if we was bred in schools to mature our
brains.'[47] Much depended on the attitude of the father[48] or another
male mentor. Sir John Guise made sure that his daughter Annabella, a
'surprising genius', was taught 'the Latin, Spanish, Italian, and French
languages, all of which she is perfect mistress of, as well as all the best
books in them'.[49] Charles, 2nd Duke of Richmond saw to it that his
daughters studied classics and mathematics as well as French and
music. The Cambridge academic Dr Conyers Middleton was thrilled
by the precocious intelligence of his step-granddaughter Elizabeth
Robinson, the future Mrs Montagu, and took every effort to develop
her reading and interests. Lady Elizabeth Hervey, daughter of the Earl
Bishop of Bristol, was a great reader and interested in the arts. After a
long affair and two children by the Duke of Devonshire, she eventually
became his second Duchess. As successor to Georgiana, her talents
were well used at Chatsworth.[50]

From the initial springboard of male support, many women went on
to spread a love of learning to others of their sex. The emerging intellectual women writers who came to be known as the Bluestocking
Circle were perhaps a special case. Not all of them were interested in
visual things, but some were important figures on the London social
scene. Elizabeth Carter was expert in Greek and had studied nine languages, while Catherine Talbot was well educated in the classics, in
history, and in both English and French literature. Hester Thrale had

been taught Latin, logic and rhetoric, as well as languages. Dr Johnson and Mrs Thrale discussed 'the amazing progress made of late years in literature by the women', recalling the time when it was considered accomplished if they could even spell. Nowadays, Dr Johnson conceded, 'they vie with men in everything'.[51]

More commonly, an aristocratic woman's education focused on what was considered useful for her way of life. At Belton, where Alice Sherard was adopted by her great uncle Sir John Brownlow and reared with the aim of making her both the wife of her second cousin, his great nephew, and the mistress of Belton itself, she was suitably educated 'to his own liking'.[52] Lady Mary Wortley Montagu felt that women were not taught enough, admitting to her daughter that: 'The ultimate aim of your education was to make you a good wife'.[53] Even a 'relatively well-educated' girl such as Mary Dewes, the niece of Mrs Delany, felt that: 'In our childhood, writing, dancing and music is what is most attended to'.[54] Most well-bred young women could play a musical instrument: being able to give shining performances would impress a possible husband and subsequent visitors through a lifetime of social entertaining and long evenings. Modern languages such as French and Italian were also seen as being suitable for girls, more so indeed than for boys.

Elizabeth Montagu thought such virtues were not enough: '...in a woman's education little but outward accomplishment is regarded.'[55] When her niece went to boarding school, Elizabeth remarked that what she would learn was 'trifling', even as she admitted that dancing and deportment and a good atmosphere could be of no harm.[56] Similarly, Hannah More, at the end of the eighteenth century, attacked the idea of mere accomplishments: 'The life of a young lady now too much resembles that of an actress...the morning is all rehearsal and the evening is all performance.'[57] Perhaps it was because Sarah Lethieullier came from a respectable and cautious merchant background, possibly concentrating on mere 'accomplishments', that as Lady Fetherstonhaugh she did not have the confidence while on the grand tour to make any choice of pictures for herself. When her son, the young Sir Harry, succeeded his father at Uppark, she got into a terrible muddle with the accounts, something at which better schooled women such as Jane, Duchess of Gordon were apt to be very skilled.[58] Nevertheless, Sarah Fetherstonhaugh played an important part in the creation of Uppark, by the devoted support that she gave both to husband and son. It was by no means essential that the mistress of a great house be educated in anything more than so-called accomplishments. Where more was achieved, through building and decorating, a higher level of education was often the reason.

As wives and daughters were increasingly able to travel, so they could gain some aspect of their later education in Europe. In a touching gesture, a husband would often accompany his wife, or a son his parents, to Dover, to see them on their way. They would also meet them on their return. Crossing the channel was an ordeal: often the traveller had to wait a couple of days at the embarkation point in hope of a wind for sailing. She might then have to be rowed out to the boat in a dinghy. Once, on the 'packet', Caroline Holland had her chair strapped to the deck, in vain hope of avoiding sea-sickness, as did the Duke of Rutland on the boat to Ireland. To journey at all, travellers had to be intrepid: in September 1718 Lady Mary Wortley Montagu was one of the first women to cross the Alps, a feat which she repeated in 1739, carried in her sedan chair; the more nervous traveller would sail round to Leghorn. From the mid eighteenth century it was sometimes the custom for couples to go on a grand tour for their honeymoon; among the brides who did so were Sarah Letheuillier, Lady Fetherstonhaugh; and Arabella Swimmer, later Lady Vincent, who was painted in Rome by Mengs.[59]

Some highly educated women found it necessary to hide their learning. Lord Chesterfield said of Molly Lepel that 'she has all the reading that a woman should have, and more than any woman need have: for she understands Latin perfectly well, though she wisely conceals it'.[60] The elderly and 'proud' 6th Duke of Somerset took an unreasonable dislike to his daughter-in-law, Frances Thynne, because he considered her unbecomingly learned.[61] In 1753 Lady Mary Wortley Montagu told her daughter, Mary, Countess of Bute, that while learning should be encouraged in her reclusive eldest granddaughter, for whom they were not expecting good offers of marriage, the girl should be advised to conceal her knowledge 'with as much solicitude as she would hide crookedness or lameness'.[62] The girl's youngest sister later perpetuated this advice: Lady Louisa Stuart believed that 'the Classics are the foundation of all good sense and good taste', but while advising a friend to cultivate her Latin and Greek studies, she cautioned her: 'Nobody need know anything of the matter.'[63] Jemima Campbell, later

Marchioness Grey, was so afraid of being thought pedantic that when a new translation of Horace that she had ordered was delivered in error to her husband, she was genuinely worried about what he might think. Elizabeth Robinson said herself that she suffered from 'the female frailty of displaying more learning than is necessary or graceful'.[64] As a young woman she had taken care not to let anyone know that she had read anything other than 'my Grandmother's receipts for Puddings & Cerecloths for Sprains' until she knew them very well.[65] During a visit at Streatham Park, the home of Mrs Thrale, Fanny Burney hid the copy of Cicero that she wanted to read, 'because I dreaded being thought studious and affected.'[66] Later there was much laughter when she admitted to Dr Johnson that she had concealed a book she was reading under her gloves.[67] While making the clever Elizabeth Bennet one of her heroines, Jane Austen conceded that most people felt uncomfortable with well-read women, perceiving a danger that they might be argumentative. Such attitudes did not mean women could not be learned, but that they must be careful how they presented themselves.

There was also a view that women needed a certain level of education simply in order to know how to behave: it helped 'morals and conduct'.[68] Mrs Montagu commented drily that men knew 'fools make the best slaves', but that they also believed in a true level of education. She held that trying to keep a wife back could have its disadvantages: 'Sure the men are very imprudent to endeavour to make fools of those to whom they so much trust their honour and happiness and fortune.'[69] By the late eighteenth century it was often said that if a man wanted the new ideal of a 'companionate' marriage, he needed a well-read wife. Hannah More felt that 'When a man of sense comes to marry, it is a companion whom he wants and not an artist.'[70] Lady Louisa Stuart felt that attitudes had changed: 'Besides, it [education] is not run down now as it was in my time. Women are now permitted, if not encouraged to know something.'[71]

In the arts, throughout the eighteenth century women became increasingly prominent, not just as audience members or consumers of literature but also as writers or artists in their own right. They went to concerts, operas and plays, and periodicals such as the *Athenian Mercury*, the *Ladies Mercury*, the *Visitor* and the *Town and Country Magazine* were aimed especially at them. They were avid readers of novels,

The Nine Living Muses, by Richard Samuel, 1779.

of which over a quarter of the most popular writers were women. In 1766 a *Biographical Dictionary of Women* was published. 'Adult education' was already the pursuit of many city ladies: among the merchant classes, women were more likely than men of the same social standing to own both books and pictures.[72] Mary Blount, Duchess of Norfolk, Margaret Cavendish Harley, Duchess of Portland and Elizabeth Seymour, Countess and later Duchess of Northumberland were all sufficiently interested in the categorisation of the natural world, mainly birds, to be subscribers to George Edwards' *Gleanings of Natural History*, Vol. II (1760). In 1777 Richard Samuel engraved a group portrait of women in the arts, whose finished version was exhibited in the Royal Academy of 1779. Its nine contemporary subjects, arrayed in classical garb, included Elizabeth Montagu; Hannah More; Elizabeth Carter, the classicist; Angelica Kauffmann, the painter and a Royal Academy founder member; the singer Elizabeth Linley, wife of the playwright Richard Brinsley Sheridan; and the historian Catharine Macaulay.

Certainly the expression of learning and taste through the decoration of a house was seen in women as both acceptable and desirable. It became increasingly fashionable for the well to do to go on a tour of grand houses, whether or not they knew the owners. Through such visits married women informed themselves; young women too were semi-schooled in what would be appropriate to their own homes. In September 1732 Edward Harley, 2nd Earl of Oxford, set off to visit Houghton, Narford and other properties in East Anglia, with both his wife and his daughter, Lady Margaret, who later became the Duchess of Portland.[73] During the 1740s, before she was too busy at Court, Lady Elizabeth Smythson, later the Duchess of Northumberland, made an effort to visit as many finely built houses as possible, which she was especially able to do on the long journeys she made to and from Northumberland. When Lady Beauchamp Proctor made her second tour of Norfolk, in September 1772, she took with her the three young ladies of the Gore family.[74] Judith Noel, Lady Milbanke, dashed round the country visiting and socialising with her husband: in a few weeks in the summer of 1781 they went to the Duke of Manchester's seat at Kimbolton, to Oxford where various academics were invited in to entertain them, to the Dashwoods nearby at Kirtlington Park, to the Knightleys at Fawsley and to Sir Robert Gunning at Horton. That August they also stole two short breaks at their rented home at Aycliffe Heads near Durham before visiting the Lakes and Scotland for a couple of weeks in September.[75]

Given a privileged upbringing, an open-handed husband and a solid bank account, it might be thought automatic that a wife should make her mark in some way. However, the most pampered of young people are often low achievers. Disappointment in marriage, too, might dissipate a wife's energies rather than focus them more intensely on refurbishment or patronage of the arts. An eighteenth-century Sloane Ranger might well have a spoilt and difficult husband: the classic Tory squire, who preferred his horse and his bottle to all else, was affectionately lampooned in *Tom Jones*, in the figure of Squire Western. Invariably, the husband would be unfaithful. Although the Lennox sisters desperately hoped that their devoted husbands would seek them alone for passion and consolation, Caroline, Emily and even Louisa had to accept serial infidelity. Their sister-in-law the Duchess of Richmond turned a blind eye to her husband's amusements: 'As to my brother's flirting, she don't mind it one bit, provided 'tis with what she reckons creditable and genteel. She is vastly comical upon that subject...'[76] Among the distractions of a hectic and glamorous social life such as Georgiana, Duchess of Devonshire, famously enjoyed, there also lurked addictions such as gambling. It took particular qualities of drive, endurance and ambition to produce those women who became celebrated for the brilliance of their houses' interiors and art collections. Of necessity they were all hard workers, as well as practical, and interested in people. Only in this way could they fulfil what was expected of them, let alone surpass it.

Chapter 3

RITUAL, ROUTINE
AND OBLIGATION

The role performed by an aristocratic woman was essentially that which her husband proposed. He expected her to accompany him when required, and to be otherwise content with her own company. This would be for most of her time: in London he might be at Court at St James's Palace, or in the House of Lords; at his gentlemen's club in St James's, or gambling or drinking wherever he chose. In the country he might be hunting or shooting, at the races or riding out to inspect his estates. Many a gentleman, bookish or not, liked the solace of his own library: the number of both town and country houses that had a library was greatly on the increase, often combining it as a study. A wife was therefore expected to be independent but adaptable. In particular she was expected to run her husband's households in both town and country, to keep a watchful eye over domestic and possibly estate budgets, and to provide him with children. Often it was only as she got older that she would be able to develop her own interests.

London

The aristocratic year had its particular timetable. In London the political season ran from November to June. In her journal Caroline Holland, the wife of the energetic politician Henry Fox, Lord Holland, described in detail the time spent at their country home in Kent: usually this was only for a few weeks between June and September. For those with positions at Court, the London season was even longer. Under the first three Kings George Court life was tiresome and dull, as was shown in the diaries of Henrietta Howard, Countess of Suffolk, at the Court of George I (she became the mistress of his son, George Prince of Wales), and of Fanny Burney at the Court of George III. In the 1750s and 60s the Earl and Countess, later Duke and Duchess, of Northumberland, found it very difficult to get away at all to their home at Alnwick Castle, visiting just for a few weeks in summer. Both the Hollands and the Northumberlands had homes nearer to London, at Holland House and Syon Park respectively, which in summer they visited almost weekly. Court life was too demanding, however, for the Earl and Countess to spend a whole weekend at Syon: on Sunday mornings they had to attend on the King and Queen at Chapel, and afterwards they were obliged to be present in the Drawing Room. George III held levées, which were attended only by men, on Mondays, Wednesdays and Fridays, and a second Drawing Room, with Queen Charlotte, on Thursdays. These were opportunities for visiting foreign nobility and ambassadors to be presented, as well as recently married couples of noble rank. Court *habitués* simply hung around on such occasions in the hope that the King and Queen would talk to those of them whom they recognised. Most of the aristocracy also made sure that they were available for the King's formal birthday celebration. At the Court of George II this was in January; from the time of his grandson George III it was held each year on 4 June.

In London, especially in the second half of the eighteenth century, aristocratic men and women spent a great deal of time making social calls. This they frequently did, not in couples, but individually, both on account of independent preferences for personal friends and as a way of spreading the social obligations required by their station in life. Good manners required that very high-ranking people were formally called on as soon as they returned to town from any extended visit. Calls were made between about 12 and 3 p.m., and could also be made again after dinner, from about 7 in the evening. Etiquette required that if a caller came while one was out, and left a card, that visit must be returned the next day, if only by means of another calling card: not to do so was a rebuff. This meant that social London was galloping round in sedan chairs and carriages from late morning until night, catching up with their obligations as well as making voluntary calls. The arrangement was ideal for a woman on her own, such as the confident and gregarious Lady Mary Coke, who was widowed at the age of twenty-seven, having separated from her husband Edward, Viscount Coke, the only son of the 1st Earl and Countess of Leicester, after only two years of marriage. She need never be lonely, and could drop in on her neighbours Lord and Lady Holland for a drink after church on Sunday. It also suited socially discriminating wits and gossips like Horace Walpole and Dr. Johnson. Equally it could be tiresome, which is why bluestockings such as Mrs Montagu preferred a more organised evening salon, where topics such as literature, art and philosophy could be discussed. Much socialising also took place within the family, particularly at the dinner table, rather in the manner of French families nowadays.

There were many places in London for social activities both at grand private homes and elsewhere. Among public venues, balls took place from mid century at Almack's Assembly Rooms in King Street and, from 1771, at the newly opened Pantheon on Oxford Street. At Almack's, which was especially exclusive, admittance was controlled by seven formidable ladies known as 'patronesses'. Unlike the men who ran London's clubs, they allowed in no-one but people of rank, excluding those whose only claim was wealth or intellect. A weekly ball with a supper was held there on twelve occasions during the intense social season from early March to early June. This was where girls were launched on society by their ambitious mothers: it was often known as 'the Marriage Mart'.[1]

Charlotte Grenville, Lady Williams Wynn, relished this part of the social merry-go-round, not least in order to secure good marriages for her six children. Her description of tea-drinking highlights another fashionable activity: 'I have lately passed my Hours of Society entirely at Assemblies where the remarks of "how hot! how full!" & now "how black" washed down with the rinsing of a tea-pot & the squeezing of a musty lemon, is all the food to be had for body or mind.'[2] Tea, coffee and chocolate, all known in England since the Restoration, were served from purpose-made elegant silver pots. Silver bowls however would be too hot to handle, and it was with the import of attractive little porcelain bowls and saucers from China that tea-drinking became a social art. This was something that the mistress of the house could offer after dinner in the late afternoon, sometimes while her husband remained in the dining room, pouring claret for his male friends. She both brewed and served the tea: at first it was usually green tea, served without milk, but later black tea became popular. The lack of handles on the porcelain bowls meant that this expensive little non-alcoholic tipple had to be very delicately, not to say elegantly, handled. At a time when great emphasis was placed on manners, conversation and etiquette, the very expense of the tea made its consumption exclusively an upper-class activity. By 1710 the factory at Meissen had discovered the Chinese secret of hard-paste porcelain: in due course, much European and eventually English porcelain was produced, with teacups as one of the main wares. Tea-drinking thus introduced many women to the delights of collecting porcelain, not least the attractive little *déjeuner* sets for either tea or coffee created at Sèvres in the mid century. The expense of such vessels meant that special tea tables were created with a lip at the edge, so that the china did not fall off; sometimes the surface was also divided into round lipped compartments, so that one piece could not slide into another. In 1784 the tax on tea was removed, after which there was a massive increase in tea-drinking at all social levels.[3]

During the London season being in town gave access to a number of entertainments which in the mid and late eighteenth century were very much on the increase. This was an era that witnessed a great cross-over between fashionable social life and the arts, both pursued partly in public and partly in private homes. In the late morning the leisured rich could walk in St James's Park: Gainsborough delightfully shows fashionable young women eyeing up each other's costumes. In summer they could visit Vauxhall Gardens, either taking a barge across the river or, from 1750, crossing by Westminster Bridge. The 12-acre site, set amidst fields, was run from 1732 by the entrepreneur Jonathan Tyers: with its paved paths, music room, Chinese pavilions, bandstand and fifty supper boxes adorned with paintings by artists including Hogarth, it had a lively, popular atmosphere. From April to July people of fashion could take tea and promenade at the more exclusive Ranelagh Gardens in Chelsea, which opened in 1742. The entertainment here was at its peak in the evening, where groups settled to listen to music in the large Rotunda's delightfully painted little rococo boxes. Music was ever important, stimulated early in the century by royal patronage of the Italian opera and of works by Handel. Public subscription concerts were performed from the beginning of the century in York Buildings off the Strand and Hickford's Rooms in Panton Street, and subsequently in the newly formed Academy of Ancient Music and in churches such as St George's, Hanover Square. From the 1760s professional concert series drew well-known musicians to London from all over Europe, including Haydn and Mozart. Much larger concert halls began to open: from early 1772 musical performances took place at the elegant new Pantheon, and in 1775 the Hanover Square Rooms were opened. From 1784 a great and nostalgic public Handel festival took place annually. Music was also a popular form of entertainment at home. Elizabeth Noel described going to a 'charming concert at Lady Archer's' and planned to give a 'squeeze' of fifty people for a concert herself, the only way that she could give some kind of return entertainment for all the huge soirées that she attended.[4]

The theatre was also popular. In 1772 Elizabeth's brother Thomas Noel, Lord Wentworth, wrote to his other sister Judith: 'Plays and Operas are as yet the [season's] only diversion', and added, 'it is quite *the ton* to go to the former.'[5] In the late seventeenth century only two royal patent theatres had been open, but by the 1730s two more were available: the King's in the Haymarket and the Covent Garden Theatre, both much enlarged. By the end of the century the huge New Covent Garden had been built, as well as the Drury Lane Theatre. Despite the low social status of actors and actresses in earlier times, famous performers such as David Garrick and Mrs Siddons were lionised throughout London. Under the control of Garrick the theatre at Drury Lane was the meeting place of the rich, the grand, the beautiful and the clever. David and Eva Garrick had their own handsome villa beside the Thames, and were entertained by one and all. When Sheridan took over from Garrick at Drury Lane in 1776, he introduced the young actress Dora Jordan, who became extremely successful. She went on to have a long love affair with the Duke of Clarence, with whom she lived effectively as a wife, bearing him ten children, until he became King William IV and ruthlessly dumped her. Her life as an actress is a remarkable story both of her own hard work and of the extreme popularity enjoyed by good theatrical performances.[6]

In the early years of the eighteenth century it was difficult to see works of art outside a private collection. Hogarth and other artists subsequently began to use the Foundling Hospital in Bloomsbury, both as an ideal exhibition space and in order to raise funds for the hospital's orphans. Going to look at paintings became very fashionable and is an important indicator of how women became increasingly involved in the arts. In 1760 paintings could be viewed at the first public art exhibition, run by the Society of Arts, which later appended the Royal prefix; they could also be viewed from 1769 at the newly founded

Royal Academy rooms first in Pall Mall and from 1780 at Somerset House. Sotheby's opened in 1744 and James Christie held his first sale in Pall Mall in 1766. Sales were social occasions: the Duchess of Northumberland gave Christie's sales in her 1773 *List of Amusements* together with Royal Academy and Arts and Science Exhibitions.[7] There was also John Boydell's Shakespeare Gallery in Pall Mall. Although at first they were considered rather risqué, it eventually became acceptable for women to visit artists' studios, to view the paintings generally or to see how portraits of their own family were coming along.

One major result of the London season was that the aristocracy made friends with whom they might stay in the country. This was especially important for women, who could not readily share a life of hunting and shooting, had probably been educated at home, and were more dependent on relationships created through society contacts. Friendships between women were cherished accordingly: after she was widowed, Mrs Delany would spend half the year at Bulstrode in Buckinghamshire with the Duchess of Portland. When in 1761 the Countess of Yarmouth's new house was not yet ready, she went to stay for some weeks with the Duchess of Newcastle.[8] Through the London season, fashions in art and architecture were quickly taken up in the distant counties. Homes such as Chesterfield House and Norfolk House in London which were redecorated in the late 1740s and early 50s were a prime inspiration for the spread to the country of whole rococo interiors. By 1759 the highly cultivated Lord Lyttelton had a number of rococo rooms at Hagley, which were much enjoyed by Mrs Montagu and others of his friends from town. Throughout the century and beyond, town and country shared a reciprocal social relationship. Broadly speaking the country offered tradition; what London contributed was fashion.

Country Lives

Life in the country had a routine of its own, dictated both by the agricultural year and by the social demands of sports such as hunting and racing. The running of a country house obliged its mistress in particular to spend a great deal of time making and receiving calls, notwithstanding the rigours of travel. Often too the religious year included a journey into the country for Christmas.

A surprising number of upper-class women involved themselves in farming. Some, as widows, had no option but to run their own estates; others did so on behalf of a husband who lacked interest in matters agricultural. As a young widow Sarah Osborn, the daughter of Admiral Sir George Byng, took over the entire management of her son's estate at Chicksands Priory in Bedfordshire during his minority, leaving it to him in a much improved state.[9] In the mid 1750s the Countess of Pomfret reported from Hertfordshire: 'Russell Farm is a purchase of my Lady Essex's since the Death of her Husband on which she has built a cheerful convenient House from where she has a View & amuses herself with managing the Farm, which she does to perfection.'[10] Mary Shireburn, Duchess of Norfolk, concerned herself with the running of tenancies at her family estate at Stonyhurst in Lancashire, while at Worksop Manor the next Duchess, her sister-in-law Mary Blount, took a scientific interest in nature and agriculture. Both Lady Luxborough and Elizabeth Montagu described themselves as 'farmeresses': the latter gained an especial rustic pleasure from haymaking and harvest suppers.[11] Elizabeth, Duchess of Rutland, was a serious and economical farmer, who decided when to harvest the oats and won prizes and medals at agricultural shows.

The sporting year was more especially for the men, though many women also rode and shot. Stag hunting had taken place for centuries; from the late seventeenth century foxhunting became fashionable, influenced by hunts such as the Charlton in West Sussex. Various dukes had their own pack of hounds, such as the Belvoir, Beaufort, and Percy. Hunts began at 8 a.m. and often went on all day; indeed they might take place almost daily. Charles, 1st Duke of Richmond, Charles, 3rd Duke of Bolton, and John, 5th Duke of Rutland, to name but three, thought of little else. Hunting took place from November to April; thereafter a husband might be free to devote a little time to his wife and his social life before, in the north, grouse shooting began, on 12 August. Elsewhere, early shooting began with partridges in late September, followed by pheasant shooting to the end of January. Although this was a life of leisure, it was also one of physical endurance, courage and exertion, all qualities that were useful when men from noble families left home to fight with their regiment.

The racing year was important for many landowners and their

wives, partly as a series of social events: race meetings were often accompanied by an evening party in the local Assembly Rooms. In the late seventeenth century Charles II had made Newmarket fashionable, and during the next hundred and fifty years racecourses sprang up throughout England, even at small towns such as Basingstoke in Hampshire. On their return to Devon from London each June, Theresa Parker and her husband would take in meetings at Blandford and Exeter. Many a nobleman helped his nearby town to build their own public rooms, and attendance with his wife would from time to time be deemed necessary: in 1730 Charles, 2nd Duke of Richmond was the main subscriber for the Council Chamber in Chichester, while in 1776 Hugh, 1st Duke of Northumberland endowed the Assembly Rooms in Newcastle. Similarly Jane, Duchess of Gordon developed the Northern Meeting in Inverness, with balls and dances in the existing town hall. Another newly fashionable sport was cricket, first played regularly at Goodwood in West Sussex in the 1720s, where the Duchess of Richmond would allocate cash from her housekeeping for her husband's team.

Calling in the country was expected in a way similar to that in London, though in the late seventeenth and early eighteenth centuries calls usually took place a little earlier, perhaps by noon, and between 12 and 2 p.m. as the time of dinner gradually got later. Often, however, it was regarded as tiresome: those who were used to the wit and gossip of the London drawing room tended to be bored by their less intellectual country visitors. Addison commented: 'Giving and receiving visitors in the country from a circle of neighbours who...can be neither entertaining nor serviceable to us is a vile loss of time and a slavery from which a man should deliver himself if possible.' From her home in Ireland Mrs Delany wrote: 'This morning I have been busied with idle visitors...dull as cats and mute as fish...'[12] It is noticeable too that in the country many sporting men seem not to have bothered with the process of giving or receiving calls. Back in London, Theresa Parker singled out the country types as boorish: 'The worst of Spring in London is that the whole County of Devonshire come to town. Sir John Chichester just arrived – such a log of wood...Don't betray me about the County, but really they are for bad, though to anyone else I must only speak of them as worthy, respectable Country Gentlemen.'[13] Even in the wilds of Scotland at Gordon Castle, Jane, Duchess of

Gordon complained of too many droppers in: 'I almost wish we were in some silent Glen, far from the vagrant foot of wanderers.'[14] These were people who had come to stay: based only on an introduction it was perfectly acceptable for the upper classes to accept hospitality from whom they wished as they progressed round the country. As a result, many women in the country longed simply to get a day to themselves.

Even abroad, calling arrangements continued to strengthen and extend the social network. Visiting the Hague in October 1766, the Duchess of Northumberland described how 'The Ambassador carried me to pay a Visit to the French Ambassadress who was not at home, & afterwards to return those I had receiv'd the Night before'.[15] This convention had the advantage of giving visitors an instant social life among people of the same level in any foreign city. In particular it was an advantage shared on the grand tour by aristocratic travellers in Paris, Florence and Rome.

It was around this panoply of political, sporting and social engagements that aristocratic women had to organise the lives of their families. They also had to take account of the religious year. Piety was regarded as an important virtue in a woman, although a number of diaries suggest that many grand ladies were quite relaxed about their church-going, attending only on the majority of Sundays. For Catholics the act of worship was bound to be more private. After the disruptions of the late seventeenth century and the dangerous Jacobite risings in 1715 and 1745, Catholics continued to be barred from holding positions at Court. They were also not allowed to build a separate chapel onto their home, but only one that was incorporated as part of a wing and therefore unlikely to attract attention. One fascinating document details the various altar vestments required in the chapel at the Petre family's home at Thorndon Hall in Essex,[16] showing that they were able to worship in private, on all days of obligation, and to use varying forms of liturgy.

Christmas, in the eighteenth century, was quite a modest affair. Although the whole Lennox family used to assemble each year at Goodwood for the festivities,[17] and servants in very large houses were often given a dance, it was only later in the century that the fashion began for families to leave London for several days of celebration in the country. Many diaries show it to have been an ordinary day: in London in 1762 the Countess of Northumberland simply records that some of the royal family took the sacrament. In that same year James Boswell enjoyed the day in a largely secular manner: 'This day I was in a better frame, being Christmas Day, which has always inspired me with most agreeable feelings. Goes to St Paul's – sermon by Bishop of Oxford: then to Child's, where little was passing; then to Coutt's, then at Macfarlane's, and then went to Davies's.'[18] As late as 1799 the Duke of Rutland apologised to his wife for the fact that he did not get to church at all.[19] The recently established habit of going to the country for Christmas was deplored by Mrs Montagu, who in the 1780s preferred to stay at her new house in Portman Square. However, in the shires old English pursuits did take place, for although Christmas was not fashionable, it was squirearchical, and mummers, handbell ringers and singers would visit farms and country houses to entertain. Some families would travel long distances to spend Christmas in their ancestral home, which was decorated with holly and other greenery. The visit was long: they might stay until Twelfth Night, when there would be a party, with a large celebratory cake. Although traditions such as the Christmas tree and the turkey had not yet emerged,[20] the Christmas pudding was already customary.

The upper classes habitually undertook the most extraordinary amount of travel. As early as the late 1720s the Duke of Bolton would journey regularly from his home at Hackwood Park in Hampshire to hunt with the Charlton in West Sussex, over a distance that still takes an hour by car. Despite the hazards of wheels stuck in muddy tracks, a swaying and jolting ride, overturning carriages and drunken postilions, the aristocracy was not deterred. Much time was spent on organisation, wives often selecting new pack horses to add to their stables, or writing letters from town to tell staff approximately when they might arrive at the country seat. Inevitably travel increased in the second half of the eighteenth century as turnpike roads underwent improvement. In his diary for 1761–2, a visiting German Count, Frederick Kielmansegge, commented, '...no country is so well arranged for comfort and rapid travelling as this',[21] having found it easy on any journey to get fresh horses.

The Count also describes the different types of carriage. In London, vehicles known as hackneys were for hire, though they were not available beyond Leadenhall. The 3rd Duke of Richmond's elder sister, Baroness Holland, considered it beneath the dignity of her brother and his wife to use hackney carriages as much as they did. Grand families usually had splendid carriages painted with their coat of arms. Sir Joshua Reynolds had an especially smart vehicle, in which he used to send his sister Frances driving round London so that people could see his arms on the door. A post chaise could also be used: this was a much lighter carriage, not suitable for long journeys but very fast. At Saltram in Devon a ladylike phaeton was used by Theresa Parker to drive around the estate. Within London itself people often travelled by sedan chair, and as late as 1808–9, Jane Maxwell, Duchess of Gordon and her granddaughter Lady Jane Montagu were using 'chairmen' extensively to get round Edinburgh. Jams were by no means unknown in London. Mrs Delany, Horace Walpole and Count Kielmansegge all commented on the traffic at George III's coronation, in 1761: even though the Count had sensibly been on the street by 4 a.m., by sedan chair it took him one and a half hours to get the few hundred yards from Pall Mall to Charing Cross.

Whatever the personal rigours of travel, the reliability of the post was crucial for families with lives complicated by running more than one household. The idea of the post taking priority over all other travellers was long established, with postboys galloping into posting inns, and out again on a different horse, signalled by a bugle that was blown to make way for them. Until the early eighteenth century all posts went through London, but from 1720 a system of cross posts was established by Ralph Allen of Bath. Each town had a post office where the mail arrived and was sorted, but it was not until 1774 that post was delivered directly to individual houses. In the second half of the century the post was more often carried in stagecoaches. These provided a more rapid means of travel: in the 1760s there were eight a day from London to Portsmouth. Count Kielmansegge describes how the passengers would all start in silence, then begin by discussing the road, the weather, and the timing of the journey, eventually moving onto politics. In 1784 the first specifically designed mail coach, a fast-moving diligence, travelled from Bristol to London. These coaches usually carried four passengers as well as the coachmen, with a postilion if there were more than four horses, and a guard, handsomely liveried in scarlet with blue facings and white ruffles.

Correspondents who needed to take full advantage of the mail often had to check the time it would leave, and whether or not there was a

Sunday post. They also spent much time calculating when it might arrive. From Alnwick in 1768 the Duchess of Northumberland listed the five days each week that the post left for the South, and the five that it arrived. A particular footman was assigned to go to the post each day. The 5th Duke and Duchess of Rutland rightly assumed that their daily letters to each other between London and Lincolnshire would arrive the next day. In the early 1800s the Duke, in London, even complained that his wife's letter of Saturday evening had not arrived on Monday. For shorter distances, such as across London, a note might be sent by a running footman, or an express letter could be sent any distance by personal courier. In London the Penny Post had existed since the time of Charles II, with a uniform charge rate and delivery and collection every hour in daylight; towards the end of the eighteenth century a similar system grew up in other large cities.

Letter writing was an important part of daily life in aristocratic society. By this means husbands and wives professed their affection for each other when apart, friendships were maintained, political alliances reinforced, arrangements for travel and for all social intercourse were made, and visits and journeys were recorded. Writing letters was very much an acceptable occupation for the lady of the house who had no menial tasks to perform: as a result, in the course of a lifetime women such as Mrs Montagu wrote literally thousands. Letters were commonly four pages long, comprising the four sides of a sheet of paper folded into two. They were often expected to be read aloud to guests or shown to other members of the family; with famous people, publication was half expected. The development of a good epistolary style was therefore regarded as important and was carefully taught. Within the letter, there were important rules. It was polite to comment on the letter received: as a result a disproportionate amount of any letter might be the repeating back of news just given. To make the receiver feel loved, honoured and respected was seen as crucial, and displays of affection between friends could be delightfully unconstrained.

The writing of travel journals was also popular, and often aimed at a relatively wide readership. Many were written in draft, as was the Duchess of Rutland's scrappy journal of a visit to the Rhine in 1819, to be later tidied up, in the Duchess's case by a daughter who had accompanied her on the journey. Aristocratic travellers evidently felt it important to record their journeys for posterity. As a young wife Lady Elizabeth Smithson, later Duchess of Northumberland, kept a careful gazetteer of all country houses and attractive market towns she had visited and, like those of the Duke and Duchess of Rutland, the diaries of her foreign travels were later published. Caroline Holland's journal, listing exactly when the family stayed at their country home on the Isle of Thanet in Kent, also seems to have been intended for posterity.

The Daily Round

Most women whose lives are described in this book were early risers, in the country at least. Jane, Duchess of Gordon would walk and bathe before breakfast, while the Countess of Leicester at Holkham Hall was up at 6 a.m.[22] Breakfast was usually served between 9 and 10 a.m.; in the country it was a little earlier, whereas in London, owing to late-night partying, it might be as late as 10.30 a.m. Many women would then sit down to write letters, lists and diaries, and go through menus and arrangements with their staff, before having a walk or driving round their estate, as the Duchess of Northumberland did regularly in her post chaise at Alnwick. In London, Caroline Holland would often drive in the late morning out from Piccadilly to Holland House, and back again for dinner. Driving out was seen both as good for the constitution, fresh air being considered essential, and sociable, an opportunity for greeting one's acquaintances.

In the country, dinner was earlier than in London, usually by at least an hour. Dinner even at noon in the country is cited in the later seventeenth century, an unfashionable practice lampooned by Alexander Pope's *Epistle to Miss Blount* of 1714 in what he saw as the 'lone woods, or empty walls' of rural life. In the early eighteenth century 2 p.m. became the usual hour, and then by degrees 4 p.m,[23] which remained the average time in the metropolis for the thirty years or so that followed the mid century. At Goodwood in the 1740s one exceptional dinner began at 4 and lasted until midnight; normally the meal was shorter, comprising three courses. Four o'clock was a convenient hour, enabling morning activities for both men and women, after which they could dress for this, the main meal of the day. In 1761–2 Count Kielmansegge saw it as 'a very good thing for business men, who can thus have their long mornings to themselves'.

Towards the end of the century it became smart to dine even later, especially in London. Horace Walpole complained when the meal came to six o'clock, saying that he was 'so antiquated as still to dine at four'. At one famously late dinner, Walpole arrived at Northumberland House for 4, not to be served until 8.30, by which time, not having eaten anything since breakfast, visitors were virtually falling off their chairs with hunger. At the turn of the century some, such as the young Duchess of Rutland, still dined at 4 p.m. in London, but others aimed to eat late. When the Duchess of Gordon invited William Pitt to dine at 8 p.m. he responded that he was at that time going out to supper.

The habit of dining in the early evening likewise spread out of town: in Sussex, at Uppark, in 1795 the hour was fashionably late, between 5 and 6 p.m.[24] Country guests were often invited for dinner; Caroline Lybbe-Powys, the travel diarist, commented that in Worcestershire people would travel a long way just for this social event, despite the difficulties of travel: 'They make nothing of going a dozen miles to dinner, though they own to being bruised to death and quite *deshabillered* by the jolts.' Because of the problem of travelling home after dark, this kind of party was given at the time of the full moon.[25]

After dinner another opportunity existed for making social calls. As tea drinking became more and more fashionable, a late afternoon visit was possible. In the country this might often take place in a summerhouse, as for example at the Duchess of Norfolk's Gothick Farm at Worksop or Jane, Duchess of Gordon's folly at Cotton Hill on the Gordon Castle estate. Such gatherings occurred about three hours after the beginning of dinner, either as a finale to the meal itself or, in London, as a separate social occasion. Following an enormous midafternoon dinner, there was no principal evening meal, just a light and often very simple private supper at about 10 p.m. In London, however, this could become an elaborate social affair, after the theatre or opera. From 1810 to 1820 dinner became a little earlier again, before gradually taking place later, until tea had to be taken before and not after dinner. Thus by the mid nineteenth century the famous English midafternoon tea with bread and cakes had emerged, as a quite different occasion from the elegant aristocratic tea-drinking of the eighteenth century.

The Household

In the late seventeenth century, Badminton in Gloucestershire was one of the largest aristocratic households, where the Duchess of Beaufort managed a staff of about 200. In a small household of 1727, the widowed Lady Mary Howard had a staff of cook, under cook, maid, laundrymaid and housemaid in the apartments that she rented from her son, Thomas, 8th Duke of Norfolk, at Worksop Manor in Nottinghamshire.[26] During the mid eighteenth century a grand London household such as Northumberland House would have a complement of about forty, run by six senior and experienced staff. At their country seat at Alnwick Castle, the moment the 1st Duke and Duchess of Northumberland appeared, Mr Widdrington the gentleman agent would be there to greet them, ready to go through every detail of the estate. Working with the agent there might be a steward, who in a London house would be the senior member. Equal in hierarchy with the steward might be the antiquated post of groom of the chambers, as well as a chaplain and tutor: all of these could be posts for impoverished gentry or even descendants of illegitimate family members. Below this were the butler, housekeeper, clerk of the kitchen and head chef.

With so many reliable senior staff, the mistress of the house could delegate a great deal to steward and housekeeper. Duchesses often had a gentlewoman attendant, rather like a royal lady of the bedchamber, who helped with details of clothes and travel. Further down the scale were a panoply of kitchenmaids and chambermaids, footmen and scullions, all carefully trained by their seniors. In contrast, aristocratic women who lived entirely in the country and were therefore at home more of the time were likely to have a more hands-on approach to household management.

The late seventeenth century saw much promotion of domesticity as a virtue to be espoused by all women: even Louise de Keroualle, who one might think would not be very interested in the kitchen, was famous for the cuisine in her apartments, ensuring that her chef produced only the greatest subtleties for the King and his Court. However, by the 1740s it was seen as *infra dig* for a lady to know too much about what went on in the kitchen.[27] The master of the house might himself have engaged a French chef, who would have an agenda all of his own.

Mr Thrale considered that his wife's place was 'either in the drawing room or the bedchamber' and that 'his wife was not to think of the kitchen'. In his case this was largely an excuse to keep her out, because he himself was interested. Generally there is little evidence of aristocratic women being especially concerned with the routine workings of the kitchen, though they did often order up the most splendid feasts and also noted the amounts that were spent.

Wives were automatically expected to oversee domestic economy: many of their double entry account books survive. Sarah, Duchess of Richmond, an heiress in her own right, reminded herself: 'I must keep my housekeeping money and my pin money separate.' Money was usually drawn quarterly from a banker and either transferred into the account in advance or paid off in arrears. Sometimes Sarah would give her husband money for something he required, or pay for his boat along the Thames from Richmond House into the City. The Duchess of Northumberland made lists in her diary of meals respectively costing below 1s, 2s, 3s, 4s, up to 10s. Early in her marriage Elizabeth Howard, Duchess of Rutland, seems to have been reticent about spending her husband's cash, on which he kept a firm grip, though she subsequently had little cause for complaint. Domestic economy was an integral part of female aristocratic life: where husbands might spend fortunes on hunting, gambling or art, their wives were expected to exercise close control over household disbursements.

Occasionally women showed themselves very good at financial management on a larger scale. When Sir Watkin Williams Wynn died in 1789, he left his widow Charlotte to administer all his estates in Wales during the minority of their eldest son. He had enough confidence in her not to appoint anyone else to the task, whether as administrator, executor, guardian or trustee.[28] His trust was well placed: when, in 1819, Charlotte handed over the finances of her youngest son Henry, not only were they intact, but she was able to tell him from memory and with great precision what he would have, namely 'somewhat over £5,700 stock in your 3 per cents, which at £70 per cent (the price they bore the day it was settled) is worth £3,900, & I have a further sum of £71 to be placed to your Account with Coutts.' She also discussed whether he should have the money in exchange bills or stocks.

All the women mentioned at length in this book appear to have been good with staff, though elsewhere there were of course exceptions.

This was a skill, later honed to an instinct, which they learnt from their mothers. Following on from medieval tradition, there was still some tendency for staff to be seen as members of the family, with the owners of the household *in loco parentis*. Indeed, the household was often referred to as the family, though in a very large establishment responsibility for the servants would devolve more on the house-keeper. The making of wills reveals how much some women cared for their servants. In 1749 Mary Shireburn, Dowager Duchess of Norfolk, generously insisted that her servants be given two years' wages after her death. Later she revised the figure upwards for some of them, cre-ating annuities for life. Similarly, in 1817 Elizabeth Howard, Duchess of Rutland made a hurried will when fearing an early death after child-birth: despite her feverish state she especially remembered her servants and their wellbeing. When Mary Blount, the next Duchess of Norfolk, wrote from Bath in 1761 to give instructions following the dreadful fire at Worksop, she was concerned about the effect on some of the more vulnerable members of staff. She knew all their names, as well as what should be delegated to whom. In their instruction manual *The Compleat Servant* (1806), the authors Samuel and Sarah Adams, who themselves had been servants, recommended that lady employers be firm but not severe, kind but not familiar. There was an assumption that servants accepted their place, that they were 'in that state of life unto which it has pleased God to call them'.[29] Employers had to look to the whole life pattern of their staff: 'Next to the care and attention due to your husband and children, your servaint claims, as your nearest depen-dants; and to promote their good, both spiritual and temporal, is your indispensable duty. Let them join in your family devotions, and endeav-our to make them spend their Sabbath properly.' To most of the women in question, certainly there was little that the Adamses could teach about the care of staff.

The mistress of the house thus tended to have charge of two or three establishments. Each household had to meet enormous demands, and so did she. Constantly on the move, extraordinarily accessible to callers and to people who wanted to stay, she had to be punctually dressed and powdered, with her short-term arrangements made possible only by perfect planning for the long term. Expected to be amiable and elegant, amusing and organised, she had a life of purpose and duty far removed from anyone deserving the description of idle rich. If she were abandoned alone in the country, she must amuse herself rather than complain; if in London she showed fatigue, her husband would simply go out without her. All the women in this book developed prodigious powers of resilience, even in the face of a life frequently struck by the complications of pregnancy and miscarriage as well as by the tragedy of infant death, or indeed of having no children at all. Each of them embodied qualities that were later to be characterised as the British stiff upper lip.

Chapter 4

HOUSE BEAUTIFUL

More than a generation before the Palladian Revival of the early eighteenth century, Elizabeth Mytton, Lady Wilbraham, owned a 1662 translated copy of the first of Andrea Palladio's four books of Architecture. Elizabeth's family held land at Weston on the Shropshire-Staffordshire borders: she was the last of the line and in 1651 had married Sir Thomas Wilbraham. It was her ambition to build a new house at Weston, to which end she used her copy of Palladio as a building notebook. In 1671, the year in which she began to rebuild Weston Park, on four pages at the front and back of the book she noted the prices of materials, calculating the price of bricks from their beginnings in the kiln. Lady Wilbraham wanted to know how much 18,000 of them would cost and how many a man could lay in a day; she also recorded what it had cost a female friend to build her house. With meticulous curiosity, she jotted down the recipe for making mortar for pointing, and the costs of laying lead, of oak panelling and of sash windows. In the period after the Restoration of Charles II in 1660, many handsome, classically proportioned houses were built. Elizabeth's interiors at Weston Park are now much changed, but the exterior is a magnificent monument to a serious woman builder.[1]

A grand house could have one of many functions. Blenheim Palace was intended as a gift from Queen Anne on behalf of a grateful nation, to mark the Duke of Marlborough's great military victory at Blenheim in 1704 in the War of the Spanish Succession. From the beginning of this project, Marlborough's wife, Sarah Jennings, had wanted to be in control. Sarah was a close friend and confidante of Queen Anne, and the project was indeed as much for her as for him. She soon quarrelled with the architect, Sir John Vanbrugh: where he wanted to create a national monument, she wanted a grand but comfortable home. Very sensibly, she felt that the projected palace was too big, too dark and too martial. She insisted that a newly built great bow was taken down on the west front, so that more windows could be included for added light. She also insisted on a novel dormitory arrangement for servants, in the attics at the heart of the house, rather than in little closets tucked away near the main bedchambers. Owing to Vanbrugh's flights of fancy and changes of plan, costs escalated ridiculously. He was irritated by Sarah's interference: she was furious when he made it clear that he would not listen to a woman. In 1708 Sarah also quarrelled with her husband's patroness, Queen Anne, unwisely telling her monarch to be quiet. After Marlborough too fell from power, in 1712, building stopped for four years. It recommenced after the accession of George I, but so too did the quarrels with Vanbrugh, who eventually resigned. In 1719 the Duke and Duchess moved in, living mostly in a simply furnished room with a bow window in the east wing. Following the Duke's death two years later, the Duchess managed to adjust the aim of the whole scheme, so that instead of being representative of national pride, it became a monument to her late husband.

Sarah was more interested in the creation of Marlborough House in Pall Mall, where she lived throughout her long widowhood; she died there in 1744. This occupies a site adjacent to St James's Palace, looking both onto the Park and towards the fashionable buildings at the south of St James's Square. Having secured the lease of the site from the Queen, in 1708, she chose the eighty-year-old Sir Christopher Wren as her architect. The Duke left her to it, telling her: 'I have no great opinion of this project for I am very confident that in time you will be sensible that (it) will cost you double the money of the first estimate.' However, he wished her 'all happiness and speed' but hoped that it would not distract her from pushing on the works at Blenheim. Luckily for Sarah, the warrior was indulgent: 'I would have you follow your own inclinations in it.'[2] The Duchess laid the foundation stone herself in 1709 and employed over 100 bricklayers and masons on the site, as well as craftsmen from Blenheim and the gardener Henry Wise. The cost was indeed huge: at £50,000, it was £20,000 over budget. To meet it, Sarah simply borrowed £22,000 from the privy purse without telling the Queen. She swiftly fell out with Wren, and thereafter supervised the completion of the house personally: the shell was completed in 1711.

The design, in Dutch red brick, was simple and dignified: the Dining

Room alone now retains its ornamental plaster ceiling and its fine wall panelling, which is believed always to have been painted a simple white. The only ostentatious decorations were the magnificent historical paintings of the Duke's battles, lining the walls of the central saloon and the paired staircases: they were executed by Louis Laguerre in 1713–14. The elegantly built and magnificently situated house had one problem: Sarah was furious when her enemy Sir Robert Walpole deliberately acquired the land to the front of her site, even building on it so as to prevent her from constructing her own grand archway onto Pall Mall. She made the best of a bad situation by creating an entrance to the northwest, adjacent to the Queen's Chapel, a delightful little classical building by Inigo Jones. Confirming her love of a more restrained classical style, in 1732–3 she also had a villa built just outside London, known as Wimbledon House: this was designed by Roger Morris and Henry Herbert, 9th Earl of Pembroke.[3] Although the Duchess's personality was unattractively aggressive, she had a good sense of architecture and practical domestic planning, and she can rightly be seen as the most famous woman builder of her age.

Marble Hill, on the bank of the Thames at Twickenham, expresses another form of royal patronage. It was a discreet gift, for a lady in waiting to whom the Prince of Wales, later George II, was not a little attentive. Henrietta Howard is invariably described as a royal mistress; this she was, but the description belittles one of the wittiest and most attractive Court ladies of the day. Among her friends she numbered Alexander Pope, John Gay, Jonathan Swift and, later in life, Horace Walpole. All of these were men intolerant of difficult, stupid or ugly women, and loved Henrietta for her brightness and her calm, fair-haired beauty.

As the daughter of Sir Henry Hobart, Henrietta grew up at Blickling Hall in Norfolk. Orphaned at the age of thirteen, she lived as the ward of Henry Howard, 5th Earl of Suffolk, either at Audley End in Essex or at Gunnersbury in Middlesex. It was difficult to avoid marriage to the Earl's son, Charles Howard; unfortunately, Charles was a wastrel, a gambler and a drunk. As the couple tumbled towards separation and poverty, Henrietta showed a successful initiative by moving in 1714 to Hanover, in the hope of gaining favour at the Court of the Electress Sophia, mother of the future King George I. When George came to England later that year to succeed to the throne, his daughter-in-law

Caroline, Princess of Wales, appointed Henrietta as a Woman of the Bedchamber. Even the impossible Charles Howard was made Groom of the Bedchamber to the new King. For a few years the couple were secure in their employment at St James's Palace, even though life at Court involved long and dreary hours, as described in Henrietta's letters.[4] When the Prince and Princess of Wales were ordered by the King to leave St James's Palace, she went with them to Leicester House, her husband remaining with the King. By this time she was tired of Charles Howard's violence and tyranny; the marriage was effectively at an end. In the summer the young royals lived at Richmond Lodge, and it was probably here that her relationship with the Prince began, in about 1718, as she turned thirty. It was, however, an unusual and apparently not very passionate affair, one to which she had to submit in order to remain at Court, and of which the Princess Caroline more or less approved.

Henrietta's marriage to Charles had produced one child; as was usual for separated women, she was not allowed to see him. Partly as consolation, she began to make herself an extremely beautiful home. In 1723 Colen Campbell drew her a plan for the perfect little classical villa, whose design he published in 1725 in the third volume of his *Vitruvicus Britannicus*, referring to it only as 'A house in Twittenham'. The design was influenced and probably commissioned by Henry, Lord Herbert, later the 9th Earl of Pembroke, who was also in the royal service; building was enabled by a gift of £11,500 from the Prince. After the playwright John Gay saw the plan in the early stages of construction, Henrietta, at this time always referred to as Mrs Howard, wrote to him, imploring him to keep it secret.

From June 1724 Roger Morris set about executing the design on the superb riverside site: when Alexander Pope visited in September he noted that 'Marblehill waits only for its roof...' It was Pope who designed the gardens, with the help of Charles Bridgeman, who had worked nearby on Lord Burlington's new villa at Chiswick. There was, however, a three-year hiatus in the building scheme while Henrietta was apparently without funds. Work only resumed after the death of George I in 1727 when, to everyone's surprise, Henrietta was by no means banished from Court on the accession of her lover as King. Indeed it was the new Queen, Caroline, who insisted on her having an increased allowance, enabling Henrietta to pay off her impossible husband in a legal separation.

Within the house, a fine mahogany staircase was inserted, and fabulous ornamentation was carried out in the Great Room by the royal carver, James Richards. Although the plan of this room was based on the Single Cube Room at Wilton, the home of Henrietta's architectural advisor Lord Pembroke, its symbolic details were unique. In a scheme freighted with literary references reminiscent of the great Augustan era of ancient Rome, its decorations featured the sun-burst head of Apollo, the god of poetry; the panthers drawing the carriage of Bacchus, the god of wine; the amorini and shells of Venus, the goddess of love; and the owls of Minerva, the goddess of wisdom, as well as fruit and flowers to indicate harvest and plenty.

Despite her failed marriage, Henrietta did not lack for supporters. When in 1731 her brother-in-law the 8th Earl of Suffolk died, he left his personal possessions, including nearly sixty paintings, not to his younger brother Charles, but in trust to his 'wel-beloved sister in law Henrietta Howard'. These would eventually go to her son, Henry. Once her husband had succeeded as the Earl, Henrietta found herself Countess of Suffolk. In her elevated status having to perform menial Court duties was even more frustrating, but she managed to be promoted to Mistress of the Robes, with increased income and far less work. She wrote to Gay that 'every thing as yet promises more happiness for the latter part of my life than I have yet had a prospect of...I shall now often visit Marble Hill...and I shall see it without the dread of being obliged to sell it to answer the engagements I had put myself under to avoid a greater evil.'[5] In 1733 Charles died, and Henrietta made a happy marriage, in 1735, with George Berkeley, brother of her close friend Lady Betty Germaine. He was lame and she was deaf, but Marble Hill now became a delightful family home where they brought up her niece and nephew, the children of her brother John Hobart, their mother having died. Later her great niece Henrietta Hotham lived at Marble Hill with Henrietta in her widowhood, and eventually became her heir.

Pope's poem 'Cloë', written in 1738, portrayed Henrietta as concerning herself with furniture and furnishings. At Marble Hill she had four superb carved tables in the Great Room by William Kent. Unusually, the main supporter was not a Kentian eagle or Apollo, but a peacock, symbolising Juno. Henrietta also collected porcelain, creating

a china room in a cottage built to the northeast of the house. Much of
her furniture was japanned; this lacquered eastern style had become
popular from the late seventeenth century. As early as the 1670s the
Duchess of Lauderdale had a large collection of 'japanned' items
across the river at Ham House, as did Louise de Keroualle, Duchess of
Portsmouth, in her sumptuous apartments at Whitehall. In the early
1760s Mary Blount, Duchess of Norfolk was to acquire a prodigious
number of japanned oriental cabinets for her mansion at Worksop.

In the early eighteenth century there was a comparative lacuna in
royal patronage. The rambling Whitehall Palace had been destroyed by
fire in 1698, and subsequent monarchs did little more than bridge and
patch their other residences. However, while George II was something
of a philistine, Queen Caroline was interested in books and gardening,
and became a considerable patron of the arts. As Princess of Wales she
had been the first lady in the land in the absence of a Queen, her
father-in-law George I having locked his wife up in Germany on
account of her supposed infidelity. In her exalted position, Caroline
learnt how to influence the men around her without appearing to do
so: the ubiquitous courtier Lord Hervey said that 'her will was the sole
spring on which every movement in the Court turned...'[6] While the
King was away in Hanover, she rearranged a number of rooms at Kensington Palace with the help of Lord Hervey, who later reported the
King's snide comment to him: 'I suppose you assisted the Queen with
your fine advice when she was pulling my house to pieces.'[7] Queen
Caroline loved classical architecture and had a feeling for how a house
should look: the elegant White Lodge in the New Park at Richmond,
on the other side of the town from Kew, which had been built for
George I by Roger Morris, again with the advice of the 9th 'architect'
Earl of Pembroke, was completed for her on the instructions of the
new King. Caroline used White Lodge frequently and considered it her
future dower house.[8]

As a patron of architects and designers Queen Caroline was certainly
more active than either of the first two Hanoverian kings. After
George II also inherited the larger, red-brick Richmond Lodge adjacent
to Kew, by the Thames on the site of the earlier royal palace in the Old
Deer Park, he and the Queen made this their home. Here in the 1730s
the Queen spent large sums on landscaping the extensive gardens.
These were dotted with ornamental buildings, among which a rusti-

cated 'Merlin's Cave' and a Hermitage were by William Kent. For the Hermitage the sculptors Michael Rysbrack and Giovanni Battista Guelfi carved marble busts of scientists and philosophers such as Isaac Newton and John Locke.[9] At St James's Palace, William Kent built Queen Caroline a 'New Library', completed in October 1737. Terracotta busts of the King and Queen were made for it by Michael Rysbrack. It was in this room on the morning of 9th November that year that the Queen was seized with her final illness: within a fortnight she was dead.[10] A memorial painting attributed to Charles Philips shows the forlorn King George II standing in front of Queen Caroline's library, with her bust over the door.[11]

Royal patronage continued to focus on Kew, where both before and after the untimely death in 1751 of Frederick, Prince of Wales, his wife Augusta lived in William Kent's White House. Princess Augusta had the gardens further enlarged and improved, with exotic planting and numerous elaborate buildings, for which her architect Sir William Chambers was mostly responsible. The appearance of the garden is recorded in his *Plans, Elevations, Sections and Perspective Views of the Gardens and Buildings at Kew*, published in 1763. Princess Augusta's garden follies show an interest in every architectural possibility. The overall design was within a belt of trees, looking inwards, creating a sophisticated private world of the latest natural discoveries enhanced by architecture from all over the world. As well as an orangery and various temples, the Wilderness contained exotic follies such as the Alhambra, Mosque and Pagoda, of which the latter survives. In the flower garden the passion for chinoiserie was further reflected in a fretted aviary and an octagonal menagerie. At her death in 1772 her son, now George III, took over the house, combining Princess Augusta's gardens with those of his grandmother, the late Queen Caroline. Although the tradition of exotic planting continues at Kew, little remains of the two adventurous architectural ensembles commissioned by these royal ladies.

While Queen Charlotte cannot be called a great patron of the arts, her taste was less abstemious than that of her husband, George III, who insisted on having no carpets because he thought them unhealthy. It was the King who supervised the reconstruction of the newly acquired Buckingham House between 1762 and 1764, but it was on Queen Charlotte's initiative that her rooms were more elaborately furnished than

nknown Lady Seated in front of a House, by Thomas Gainsborough, *c.* 1750.

Mariage à la Mode: The Marriage Contract, by William Hogarth, 1743. While the old Earl and the rich merchant arrange the contract, the young Viscount and his bride look away from each other in mutual distaste. The chained dogs are an image of their future together.

Thomas Gainsborough: The Mall in St James's Park, *c.* 1783.

Opposite: A Tea Party at Lord Harrington's House, by Charles Philips, 1730. Henrietta Howard sits in the centre of the three groups. George Berkeley, who was to become her second husband, stands just to the left of the fireplace, near to his sister, Lady Betty Germaine, who is in the left-hand group, wearing a patterned dress.

Weston Park, Shropshire.

Lady Wilbraham, by
Sir Peter Lely, *c.* 1662.

Marble Hill, Twickenham.

Henrietta Howard,
later Countess of
Suffolk, by Charles
Jervas, *c.* 1724.

Marble Hill, engraved after Augustin Heckell, 1749.

Marble Hill: the Great Room.

Marble Hill: table by William Kent.

Firle Place, West Sussex: fox table. The chairs are later.

The Earl & Countess of Upper Ossory at Ampthill Park, Bedfordshire, by Benjamin Killingbeck, 1777.

View of Arlington Street from Green Park, watercolour by J. Whittock, 1848. Pomfret Castle is just to the right of centre, with No. 16 second from right.

those of the King, with personal collections of china, ivories, snuff-boxes, jade, lacquer and *objets de vertu*. When Caroline Lybbe Powys visited the house in 1767 she found the Queen's apartments filled with 'curiosities from every nation...The most capital pictures, the finest Dresden and other china, cabinets of more minute curiosities.'[12] The saloon, two storeys high, was decorated in an elegant grey neoclassical scheme: later in the reign, when the Queen started to give her 'drawing rooms' there rather than at St James's Palace, it served as the Throne Room. Entire rooms in three different houses were painted in the oriental style for Queen Charlotte, by her talented third daughter, Princess Elizabeth, including one in the Queen's House (as Buckingham House was now called).[13] In the 1790s a conventional Georgian house at Frogmore was remodelled for the Queen as a retreat from London, with the interior arranged to show her collections. It included a room decorated in about 1795 by Mary Moser with large flower paintings on black grounds,[14] and various Japan Rooms with red and black wall panels, some genuine, others the work of Princess Elizabeth; another painted room by the Princess is extant in Queen Charlotte's Cottage, Kew, created *c*. 1805.[15] The Queen loved flowers: at the Queen's House, even in March (1767), 'every room was full of roses, carnations, hyacinths, &c., dispersed in the prettiest manner imaginable, in jars and different flower-pots on stands.'[16]

Far removed, as a Catholic, from the world of a Court protégée, Mary Shireburn was nonetheless distinguished in her taste for classical architecture and furnishings. Mary was the daughter and sole heiress of Sir Nicholas Shireburn, the squire of the remote Stonyhurst estate in Lancashire. When she was only fifteen her ambitious and wealthy father had secured her marriage to Thomas, 8th Duke of Norfolk. The relationship deteriorated into an amicable separation, prompting Mary to become increasingly independent. After the Duke's death, in December 1732, the Duchess may have married Peregrine Widdrington, a member of another old Catholic family. Although there was never a civil marriage, as would have been necessary under the law, it is probable that the couple were married in a religious ceremony; this would mean that Mary could keep her property intact on behalf of her Shireburn heirs.[17] However, the situation caused some consternation among the priesthood: Catholic historians make references to the effect of 'whether or not she was married, she should have been'.[18]

James Gibbs: Design for 16, Arlington Street, London.

Mary ran Stonyhurst carefully, both when she was there and when she was away. In London meanwhile she built a remarkable house, at 16, Arlington Street. Its site had a 30-foot frontage, and was 238 feet deep, looking onto St James's Park.[19] The architect was James Gibbs, who as a Catholic was popular among his co-religionists. On 9 May 1734 Mary signed a document in her bold hand: 'Whereas I have appointed James Gibbs esq. to inspect a building in Arlington Street erecting by my order according to plans designed by him, & approv'd on by me I do here by agree to give him three hundred pounds for his said plans, and for surveying ye said buildings till they shall be completed.'[20] Gibbs and Widdrington were also the witnesses to a formal document between Mary and one Thomas Michener, to 'erect & Build a Messuage or Tenemon together with Several Outhouses and Offices thereunto...'[21] One of the outhouses was the rusticated entrance gateway, still seen in Arlington Street, through which visitors entered a courtyard and thence into the house. The building nowadays accommodates half a club, Over-Seas House, entered through its neighbouring half, Vernon House in Park Place, St James's. Mary was clearly well in control of the building details, receiving proposals from the carpenter for oak and fir flooring, and for masons' work, including Portland stone as well as moulded and plaster work.[22]

Through her will, made in 1749, and as a practising Catholic, both of whose husbands had fought in the rebellion of 1715 and had suffered as a result of their religion, Mary may have deliberately been trying to reignite the fortunes of another devotedly Catholic family. Originally she left everything to Edward Gascoigne, the husband of her cousin Mary.[23] However, following his death that year, instead of leaving it to the Gascoignes' son, she made a codicil,[24] willing 16 Arlington Street to William Hall Gage, subsequently the 2nd Viscount Gage, as well as 'all goods and furniture' except plate. The plate, described in detail, was left to Thomas Gage, William's younger brother. In further codicils[25] she left £7000 to Theresa Gage, as well as some diamond earrings, and £500 each to William and to Thomas Gage, who was setting off for America. Probably she was being generous to a Catholic family who had lost everything through their devotion to the Jacobite cause, giving Theresa what might be a dowry, the eldest son a house, and the younger one financial support.

The only surviving legacy of that relationship is the appearance of five very handsome side tables, now at the Gage ancestral home at Firle Place in Sussex, which are believed to have come from Mary's house in Arlington Street.[26] A particularly resplendent and unusual pair has marble tops over fox centre pedestals, and one side table is a classic of the period. All appear in a collection which otherwise includes no furniture of this date and standard. There is also a painting at Firle said to be of the Norfolk family.

When building on a relatively small site, grandeur often remained an option, as shown by several London homes. Of these a number were built by women who were widowed or single. One such was Lady Isabella Finch, the unmarried daughter of the Earl of Winchilsea. As First Lady of the Bedchamber to Princess Amelia, Isabella was close to life at Court. However, surprisingly in the light of the house created for her, she appears to have had rather a staid personality. In 1742 she commissioned William Kent to build her a three-storey, three-bay house at No. 44, Berkeley Square. This is another formal, classical house, but it is especially imaginative and theatrical, being centred on a superb divided staircase with an ornate ironwork balustrade. Walpole expressed his admiration, saying, 'The staircase at Lady Isabella Finch's, in Berkeley Square, is as beautiful a piece of scenery, and, considering the space, of art, as can be imagined.'[27] At the top a screen of Ionic columns and a barrel-vaulted ceiling ending in half-domes conspire to make the most of the space by ingenious perspective effects. The design was to be influential on Robert Adam's staircase built for the Countess of Home at 20, Portman Square.[28] Classical decoration was seen to be totally appropriate to the home of a lady, the rich carvings almost approaching the elaboration subsequently seen in the Rococo. This is apparent in the addition of little leaf twirls to a Vitruvian running wave below the twin half-domes of the ceiling. On the *piano nobile* Isabella had her drawing room at the front, looking onto the square, with a grand bedchamber and closet at the rear.

By later standards, owners of large houses were often remarkably unconcerned about demolishing or altering them in the name of fashion or personal convenience. Between 1769 and '72 the architect Sir William Chambers extended Ampthill Park, in Bedfordshire, for the newly married 2nd Earl and Countess of Upper Ossory. This perfectly proportioned double pile house had been built eighty years before, by Diana Grey, Countess of Ailesbury. At her husband's death in 1685, after nearly forty years of marriage, Diana needed to vacate their adjacent family home at Houghton in favour of her eldest son. She had borne no less than eight sons and nine daughters, of which she still had six to bring up. The Countess accordingly acquired a nearby sixteenth-century royal hunting lodge situated on a dramatic hillside, and demolished it. Influenced by classical architecture at nearby Cambridge, the new house on the site had two principal storeys, plus an attic floor tucked into the hipped roof and a basement half below ground. The internal arrangement was traditional for the period, with a central great hall leading to a spacious parlour and staircases at each end of the plan. Fine doorcases were carved with stylised acanthus leaves or naturalistic foliage.[29] Some generations later a pretty powder cabinet was among the refurbishments carried out for the hot-blooded Anne Liddell, Countess of Upper Ossory. The Countess had previously been married to the Duke of Grafton, from whom she was divorced by an Act of Parliament in 1769. By the time she married the Earl, she had already borne his daughter. She was a great favourite with Horace Walpole, with whom she maintained a lengthy correspondence, and who called her 'one of the finest women you ever saw…one of our first great ladies'.[30]

In the mid eighteenth century the new fashion for medieval Gothic was quickly taken up by several patronesses who had hitherto admired the Palladian style. At the family home at Welbeck Abbey in Nottinghamshire, Henrietta Cavendish Holles, Countess of Oxford and Mortimer, was a fanatical builder who between 1741–55 created new wings both to the south and north. She adapted the main hall into a great Gothick scheme with fan vaulting, based on the Henry VII chapel in Westminster Abbey. Her object was to create a suitable family seat for her descendants, and to give a sense of English history to her ancestral collection of 'All the family paintings of the Cavendishes, Holles, Pierponts, Harleys, etc. Noblemen, Ladys and gentlemen in any way related'.[31] In an outstanding example of the woman as guardian of the family history, she spent her widowhood 'in collecting and monumenting [inscribing] the portraits and reliques of all the great families from which she descended, and which centred in her'.[32] She commissioned both Jacobean Revival and Palladian chimneypieces and overmantels, as well as rococo decoration and chinoiserie, but utilised Gothick both in her private apartments including her library, and in public areas such as the staircase hall, and the chapel.[33]

One amusing if incongruous silhouette on the handsome Green Park skyline was that of Pomfret Castle.[34] This eccentric Gothick house was commissioned by Henrietta Louisa Jeffreys, granddaughter of the famous 'Hanging Judge' Jeffreys. Her mother was Lady Charlotte Herbert, the only daughter of the eccentric and drunken 7th Earl of Pembroke and his wife Henrietta de Keroualle, sister of Charles II's

French mistress, Louise, Duchess of Portsmouth. It was at the instruction of Henrietta Jeffrey's cousin Henry Herbert, 9th Earl of Pembroke, that the works at Marble Hill and at the royal White Lodge at Richmond were built, by Roger Morris, a pupil of Lord Burlington. So greatly did Henrietta admire Burlington that she referred to him as the 'the reviver of Taste in Building'.

In 1720 she married Thomas Fermor, who the following year was created Earl of Pomfret. His family home, at Easton Neston in Northamptonshire, was within striking distance of Sir Roger Newdegate's house at Arbury. Sir Roger, who was to marry Henrietta's niece, had a crucial influence on her preference for the Gothick. After the death of her second husband, and despite a court battle over the inheritance, Henrietta Louisa became very wealthy. In the words of Walpole: 'Five hundred as lady of the bedchamber to the late Queen, and fourteen thousand pounds in money in her own power…what a fund for follies!'[35] She had hoped to build a little country house on a farm in Bedfordshire, and asked Sir Roger for another design that 'wou'd suit my Gothick imagination'.[36] Subsequently she planned instead to build a London house. This was to be on a site adjacent to the home of her daughter, Lady Granville, in the fashionable Arlington Street, near to the Duchess of Norfolk's house at No. 16. The plot, looking out onto Green Park, became vacant in February 1757, and work began the following month.

Pomfret Castle, at 18, Arlington Street, was designed by Sanderson Miller, who lived quite near Easton Neston and had worked for Sir Roger Newdegate. Extraordinarily, it was to lie between classical houses, both adjacent and opposite. The incongruity of Pomfret Castle in this particular street is clearly shown in a watercolour by J. Buckler dating from 1831.[37] The three-bay house, with flanking turrets, lay across a court and was approached through a single-storey gatehouse. Its church-like interiors with their ornate stucco work in the Perpendicular style were much influenced by Newdegate. Some ceilings were panelled: others were delicately fan vaulted. Among its furnishings the Countess commissioned a very fine partners desk[38] whose design had appeared in Chippendale's *Director* of 1754; she also ordered a strange castellated cabinet with towers, painted with heraldry, in which to keep precious items collected on her travels. In the windows she hoped to use stained glass. However, the Countess did not live to enjoy her house: she died in 1761. Walpole had said that she had a 'paltry air of significant learning and absurdity',[39] but from her own letters a much more sympathetic picture emerges, of someone who was serious rather than humorous, intense and innocent rather than sophisticated.

In the decoration of existing houses, paints, wallpapers and hangings became increasingly sought after, often as an adjunct to panelling. Earlier builders and decorators such as Bess of Hardwick had mainly used tapestries, in harmony with panelling. From the mid 1720s tapestry was for a while less fashionable, and painted wood panelling became prevalent, before ceding in turn to stucco work. However, the use of tapestries had not disappeared altogether. By the 1730s some tapestries were being made in England, at the Soho factory, where the styles, much influenced by France, were lighter than before. After the end of the Seven Years' War (1756–63) a new type of tapestry began to be imported from the Gobelins factory in Paris. Often these were in the fashionably illusionistic French style, with the centre of the tapestry woven like a painting of a real scene, and with the whole item secured by a frame.[40] However, those commissioned from the Gobelins specifically for English houses might imitate the old English style, as with those made for the Earl of Coventry, adorning his house at Croome Court for his beautiful Irish bride, Maria Gunning.[41]

In the 1730s and 40s many more fabrics, especially damasks, became available for use as wall hangings and curtains, often imported from abroad. Silks had been available in London since the advent of Huguenot weavers at Bishopsgate in the early eighteenth century, but initially these were mostly for costumes. Now London silk damasks began to imitate those of foreign competitors. From 1766 trade laws protected the English industry, and silks could no longer be imported from France.[42] From the 1730s, wallpaper became increasingly popular. English wallpapers had been made as early as the sixteenth century; in the seventeenth century, flock papers were introduced. For these the designs were drawn or stencilled on sticky paper, which was then thickly covered with clippings of wool. Later these designs were printed from wood blocks.[43]

In 1741 Frances, Countess of Hertford, improving her newly acquired home at Richings near Iver in Buckinghamshire, wrote: 'Yesterday I was busy in buying paper, to furnish a little closet...The perfection which the manufacture of that commodity is arrived at, in the last few years, is surprising.'[44] She described how Isabella, the widowed Duchess of Manchester, had taken a tiny house on Englefield Green in Berkshire, added a porch bigger than the house, and 'furnished all her rooms with paper'.[45] The location of the home of such a highly connected lady between a chandler's shop on the one side and an inn on the other was obviously of surprise to her smart friends. Walpole also received a letter admiring this 'trinket', from his friend George Montagu. However, 'she has so begilt it and bepapered and ornamented it with her Grace's own hands that it would please you to see it'.[46] Walpole confirmed the temporary, but not total, eclipse of tapestries until the mid 1760s, in the country: 'People all disdain tapestry, because, they hear, that paper is all the fashion.'[47] In the last quarter of the eighteenth century further choices emerged with the use of borders both in paper and fabric. From the 1790s elaborate *passementerie* regained the level of importance it had reached in the late seventeenth century, reaching its apotheosis in the 1820s.

The fashion for oriental porcelain and furniture generated in turn a desire for the new Chinese wallpapers and silks. Some little oriental rooms or cabinets had been created as early as the 1690s: the Earl of Peterborough had one at Drayton, with garden scenes in lacquer, as did the Duchess of Lauderdale in her private closet at Ham. However, the new materials made the oriental vision both lighter and much more available. Before the 1740s they were only directly available from the east. The term 'India' paper, which was the name given to the Chinese wallpaper on the market thereafter, is not so much a geographical confusion as a reference to the East India Company, which imported it; in due course British manufacturers began to supply imitations. The earliest comprised different pictures, each on an individual piece of paper: in 1742 Lady Cardigan bought '88 Indian pictures at 4/6' in order to decorate a room.[48] All hand-painted, the most expensive of these had figures on them; the next price range depicted birds and flowers. There was a shop, or 'Chinese paper warehouse' selling such goods in at least three locations, including Newgate Street.[49] At Blickling Hall in Norfolk in the early 1760s a rococo Chinese Bedroom and Dressing Room were created for Mary Anne Drury, the first wife of John Hobart, 2nd Earl of Buckinghamshire. John, who had grown up at Marble Hill with his aunt, Henrietta Howard, deferred to her in matters of interior decoration until her death in 1767.

One expert decorator was Mary Granville, later Mrs Delany. She was very practical in her approach, advising friends to discard the older mode of backing wallpaper with canvas in favour of pasting it to the bare wall. She pointed out: 'when lined with canvas [it] always shrinks from the edges.' When Elizabeth Howard, Duchess of Rutland reported from Cheveley Park near Newmarket in 1801 that there was a mouse running under the wallpaper in her bedroom, she too must have had the old-fashioned type, stuck to battens on canvas. Mrs Delany was very proud of her own house at Delville in Ireland, in 1746 describing it thus: 'The front room is hung with a flowered paper of grotesque pattern, the colours lively and the pattern bold, the next room is hung with finest India paper of flowers and all sorts of birds...My dining room (vulgarly so called) is hung with mohair caffoy paper (a good blue).' 'Mohair' was woollen, sometimes partly silk, and sometimes watered. 'Caffoy' was a stamped woollen velvet used in the first half of the eighteenth century.[50] Mrs Delany's dining room was more correctly called the eating room at this date. Her account also showed that by the 1740s tapestries were sometimes used: 'Yesterday my upholsterer came and my new apartment will be very handsome. The drawing room hung with tapestry, on each side of the door a Japan chest, the curtains and the chairs crimson mohair, between the windows large glasses with gilt frames and marble tables underneath them with gilt stands.'[51]

By the mid eighteenth century London was the largest city in Europe. It was new to be able to go out and shop: fabrics and papers continued to be bought directly from merchants, but also began to appear in delightful window displays. Huge numbers of businesses were springing up. 'The finest shops are scattered up and down the courts and passages...The shops in the Strand, Fleet Street, Cheapside etc. are the most striking objects that London can offer to the eye of a stranger,' wrote a visiting French lawyer, M. Grosley.[52] Silversmiths piled up wares in their windows, as did vendors of china, the latter at shops such as Coopers in Jermyn Street. 'Every article that is elegant and fashionable may be seen, arranged with the utmost taste and symmetry,' commented a German visitor in 1785.[53] Wives who could not get to London to purchase such delights commissioned husbands, brothers or sisters. With items bursting onto the London market in this way, house decorating became increasingly competitive.

Fashions changed quickly with the availability of new styles. By the late seventeenth century a new aspect of house decoration had emerged as many women collectors began to acquire oriental porcelain. At Kensington Palace Queen Mary, the Stuart wife of King William III, began the craze of collecting what was generically known as 'China', comprising many types of porcelain from the east and the blue and white variety from Delft in Holland. 'The Queen brought in the Custom, or Humour, as I may call it, of furnishing houses with China-ware, which increased to a strange degree afterwards, piling their China upon the Tops of Cabinets, Scrutons, and every chymney-piece', wrote Daniel Defoe.[54] She massed the pieces on overdoors, often on brackets right up to the cornice, and similarly above chimneypieces, on specially made overmantels. On the tops of cabinets items were similarly crowded together, with some placed higher on purpose-made plinths.

Lady Betty Berkeley, daughter of the 2nd Earl of Berkeley, was also a passionate collector of china. She married Sir John Germaine in 1706, a year after the death of his first wife Mary Mordaunt, Duchess of Norfolk. He was nearly sixty; she was twenty-six. At his death, in 1718, Sir John left her their home at Drayton House, in Northamptonshire; she was to own it for more than fifty years of widowhood. Together Sir John and the Duchess had employed the celebrated William Talman to alter part of the house, whose original medieval form had already been much modified. Talman had designed an ornate Italianate south façade, with tall windows topped alternately by scrolls and pediments, a main doorway flanked by fluted columns, and busts on stone brackets.

During Lady Betty's time at Drayton the alterations continued. A courtyard colonnaded with Roman Doric columns bears her arms along with those of her husband.[55] Like many Catholics, Lady Betty had an especial taste for heraldry, and for the chapel gallery she had armorial tapestries woven at the new Soho workshops in London. These had a yellow ground and a light and lively design of French influence. The chapel had a secular feel, these being sensitive times, but at Lady Betty's instruction a reredos was made, with its pediment decorated by a crown of thorns.

At Drayton Lady Betty evidently had china on every ledge, overdoor and cabinet. Two paintings, now lost, depicted some of her favourite pieces, mostly Chinese and Japanese. Horace Walpole described the house: 'it is covered with portraits, crammed with old china, furnished richly, and not a rag in it under forty, fifty or a thousand years old.' He also commented on Lady Betty's care of the house and its treasures: 'not a bed nor a chair that has lost a tooth or got a grey hair, so well are they preserved.'[56]

Like her friend Queen Mary, the great heiress Elizabeth Percy, Duchess of Somerset, wife of the difficult 'Proud Duke', also fell prey to 'china-mania'. A pair of 'India Cabinets' in the King of Spain's Drawing Room at Petworth were each surmounted by no less than '22 pieces of China'. In her closet, glass panels over the door and chimneypiece carried '45 pieces of China'. A set of large covered jars of Chinese blue and white porcelain had carved walnut pedestals designed for them.[57] Both in this use of pedestals and with massed displays reflected in mirrors,[58] the Duchess again followed the example of the Queen.

With the manufacture of hard-paste porcelain at Meissen by 1710, it became fashionable to collect European as well as oriental 'china'. Caroline Holland loved Sèvres porcelain, which she bought in Paris, while the Duchess of Northumberland was a great patron of the English Chelsea factory. As it became an intrinsic part of domestic tableware, china was increasingly considered as much a necessity as a luxury. In his showroom in Grosvenor Square Josiah Wedgwood displayed whole dinner services laid out as for a meal. He knew where his market lay: 'It will be our interest to amuse and divert and please and astonish, nay, even, to ravish the ladies.'[59] Judith Milbanke, Lady Noel, begged her aunt Mary Noel to purchase her some china in both 1780 and 1783, firstly 'a complete table set of Wedgewood's things with any colour border you think proper' and secondly 'a set of Breakfast China with Coffee Cups, Chocolate Cups and two handsome Edgewood Tea Pots, one large the other middle sized'.[60] When they were first married, the young Duke of Rutland thought it appropriate to tell his Duchess, Elizabeth Howard, that she could find a china shop in Henrietta Street, near Covent Garden.

The Countess of Oxford's daughter, Lady Margaret Cavendish Harley, followed in her mother's footsteps, taking an interest both in interiors and in historical objects, if not specifically in the Gothick that the Countess had made such a feature at Welbeck Abbey. Margaret, Duchess of Portland as she became, was celebrated as a collector of curiosities. Horace Walpole wrote that: 'At first her Taste was chiefly confined to Shells, Japan & Old China, particularly of the blue & white with a brown Edge, of which last sort she formed a large Closet…but contenting herself with one specimen of every pattern She could get, it was a collection of odd pieces.'[61] When in 1778 King George III and Queen Charlotte visited the Duke and Duchess, at Bulstrode Park, in Buckinghamshire, they viewed her 'fine old china'.[62] Margaret Portland liked items with a specific historical context, keeping some of her collection in the 'Portland Museum' in her London house. Her taste was eclectic rather than artistic: Walpole observed that, of the thirty-eight-day sale of her collection, only eight days were spent on items other than shells, ores, fossils, birds' eggs and other items of natural history, and many of those were given to ugly snuff-boxes that had belonged to her mother.[63] The Duchess loved vases, and eventually surpassed herself by acquiring from Sir William Hamilton the great ancient Roman glass vessel now known as the Portland vase.[64] Through her correspondences with Mary Delany and Elizabeth Montagu, she also revealed her enjoyment of an intellectual, industrious life spent within a circle of close women friends.

Many women created some kind of decorative interior scheme themselves. From the late seventeenth century the tradition of painted panelling had developed into a fashion for painted rooms; initially these were often the work of foreign artists. At Castle Bromwich near Birmingham, Lady Bridgeman directed operations when Louis Laguerre painted her closet. Subsequently a number of women decorated whole rooms. Elizabeth Creed, the daughter of Sir Gilbert Pickering, painted commemorative wall monuments to her family in various churches, and was probably the artist of the Painted Parlour at Canons Ashby, Northamptonshire, of c. 1717. Her daughter Elizabeth Steward painted the entrance hall at her home at Cottestock Hall in Northamptonshire.[65] The accomplished Lady Diana Beauclerk, daughter of the 3rd Duke of Marlborough, painted the walls of her houses, Devonshire Cottage, Richmond, in 1782 and Little Marble Hill at Twickenham between 1785–6, as well as renovating her home at Lydiard Manor in Wiltshire.

Owing to its classical overtones, shell work also became a fashionable occupation. Mrs Delany created a grotto for her uncle, Sir John Stanley, for the Bishop of Clogher, and for herself, at Delville in Ireland.

Henrietta Howard had a grotto at Marble Hill, writing in July 1729 to Lord Herbert: 'I am at this time over head and ears in shell work.' Around 1763, aged eleven, her great-niece, Henrietta Hotham, told her parents: 'I have worked so hard in the Grotto and Rock that it is fear'd I shall damage my fingers.'[66] Itinerant paid shell-workers were available as teachers and assistants, as were embroiderers. Feather work was also an option, as taken up by the Duchess of Portland, who had a four-leaved screen in feathers in her Bedchamber at Bulstrode; in her house at Portman Square the Duchess's friend Mrs Montagu extended the idea to feathered tapestries.

On a larger scale, in the second half of the eighteenth century many grand houses also had a print room. As seen nowadays, engravings from this period have often been cut down; formerly they were shown complete, with an attractive border, above an italic inscription. It was customary for them to be pasted onto wallpaper, a task that women frequently carried out for themselves, as did Sarah Fetherstonhaugh at Uppark, and Louisa Connolly at Castletown. Both cut and pasted all the prints, creating a completely personal ensemble. In Louisa's every print depicted a painting from her family home at Goodwood, or a portrait of a family member, or had been sent to her by her nephew on the grand tour. Topographical or old master mezzotints could be bought by the set from a printmaker such as Mr Fry in Hatton Garden, especially 'calculated to be complete and elegant furniture for one room'.[67]

Among the Lennox sisters, a talent for decorating houses was innate: all his life their father, the 2nd Duke of Richmond, had involved himself in building schemes. Caroline, Baroness Holland made the dilapidated Holland House into a charming home, Emily, Duchess of Leinster decorated the empty interior of her husband's new family home at Carton in Ireland, and Louisa Connolly fitted out the newly built Castletown. A remarkable letter from Lady Sarah Bunbury to her sister Emily, written in September 1775, shows how much she too was ready to concern herself with the practicalities of creating a home for a large family.[68]

In idyllic surroundings at Black Rock, south of Dublin, Emily's numerous children had been educated by a Scottish tutor, William Ogilvy; he subsequently became the widowed Duchess's second husband. To allow a cooling off period from the scandal of duchess marries tutor, the couple lived for a time in France; meanwhile Emily wanted to alter and enlarge Frescati, as the house was known, ready for their eventual return.[69] To this end Sarah enclosed various designs for the drawing room, dining room and library, including two of her own for 'fitting up the drawing room ceiling in stucco' with paintings on paper or canvas to be incorporated into the seven moulded compartments; these were to be filled with 'light Herculean figures', in neoclassical mode. She begged Emily to secure John Ryley well in advance, who had already painted decorative panels at both Goodwood and Castletown. While the architect's drawings for the room were, she said, 'common, handsome, plain Italian finishing', her own were 'more uncommon, more showy'.

Though imaginative in her designs, Sarah was economical towards their expense: her sister did not have the resources of earlier years. For the walls, instead of expensive damask Emily could use one of a range of French fabrics in grey, green or white, from Bordeaux. If she selected white, she would need to animate the walls with her 'pretty blue and green Sèvres china vases, on pretty brackets', and the overmantel must be green. Curtains and chairs could be ordered in France, where gilding and upholstery was less expensive. The *trumeau* over the chimneypiece was to be 'covered with small pictures, china [and] Wedgwood's imitations of antiques' in the manner of their sister Caroline's dressing room at Holland House. Sarah also had ideas for the painted dining room, for which she tried to pilfer a ceiling design by the painter Daniel Gardner, who had just received it from a friend in Rome.

Sarah showed good sense, too, in wanting to organise the building of a new kitchen for Emily, and bullied the architect/builder into providing a new drawing that reflected her own ideas. Completely practical about heat and cold, dark and light, noise and food smells, she altered the proposals for other offices on the ground floor, and corrected Emily's placing of closets on the first. The year after this letter, Sarah commented to Emily on the part played by their sister-in-law, Mary, Duchess of Richmond in improvements at Goodwood: 'she enters into them a great deal for *her*, though not in the Lennox way yet.'[70]

Because the mistress of the house was the person in charge of social arrangements, it was often she who was responsible for the way in which the furniture was laid out. In the late seventeenth and early eighteenth centuries, from day to day this was still fairly adaptable, maybe with just some grand items of 'mobilier' left in place. Chairs and tables could be moved by servants as required, whether for music, for cards or for dinner. In a large saloon it would be traditional to have a large suite of chairs formally placed round the edge. By the second half of the eighteenth century an interesting temporary arrangement had emerged, for use in the evening. Fanny Burney's descriptions of evenings at home with Mrs Thrale at Streatham Park show that visitors often sat in a formal circle, or semicircle.[71] Horace Walpole complained of suffering 'four hours and a half in a circle of mixed company' when waiting for dinner at Northumberland House: 'We wore out the Wind and the Weather, the Opera and the Play, Mrs Cornelys's and Almanacks, and every topic that would do in a formal circle.' [72] In Mrs Montagu's house, whether larger or small circles were used, Lady Louisa Stuart found her hostess's salons too formal, and felt that people were left feeling single and isolated, 'partly owing to the awkward position of the furniture, the mal-arrangement of tables and chairs. Everything in that house, as if under a spell, was sure to form itself into a circle or semicircle.' She described one gathering that featured twenty to twenty-five women in a 'vast half-moon'. Certainly a big circle would expose people: Lady Louisa called it 'the worst shape imaginable for easy familiar conversation', and felt it only worked for 'snip-snap repartee'.[73]

Later this custom changed: Fanny Burney was amazed when Mrs Vesey for one soirée created an informal arrangement of threes, 'in a confused manner all over the room', so that some people had their backs to each other. This was copied by Mrs Cholmondeley, but whatever the drawbacks of a large circle the new layout was not always popular: 'You may imagine there was a general roar at the breaking of the circle.'[74] Due to the large number of visitors at a soirée five years later, in 1784, also given by Mrs Vesey, informality was instead created by the use of an inner boudoir, although circles still seem to have been customary.[75] As in Paris, for a specifically intellectual gathering the preference seems to have been for smaller rooms. This is borne out by Hannah More's description of a visit to Mrs Montagu, who evidently changed her arrangements to suit the evening: 'There were nineteen persons assembled at dinner, but after the repast, she has a method of dividing her guests, or rather letting them assort themselves into little groups of five or six each.'[76] At this date a separate dining room or 'eating room' had become essential, and was often one of the grandest rooms in the house.

That it was acceptable for women to commission building works was well established by the time of the Restoration. The eighteenth century brought expanding opportunities for them to make choices within their homes. As wallpapers and silks, porcelain and furniture became increasingly sophisticated, it was seen as natural for women not only to express opinions on what they would like to own, but to gratify a correspondingly wide range of appetites. By the early nine-teenth century, the immense influence of the Prince Regent in matters of taste meant that impatient changes of design were not associated merely with whimsicality. For those who could afford it, extravagance had become the norm.

Chapter 5

COLLECTOR AND PROTECTOR
LOUISE DE KEROUALLE,
DUCHESS OF PORTSMOUTH
1649–1734

Louise de Keroualle was the ultimate material girl. During her fifteen years at the Court of Charles II, the spacious apartments she occupied in the royal palace at Whitehall were famous for the magnificence of their furnishings. Later she made alterations to her château in the town of Aubigny in France and, at her death, her home in Paris was embellished from floor to ceiling with the finest tapestries. Paintings that once adorned her walls today form the foundation of the collection of the Dukes of Richmond at Goodwood House in West Sussex. Although in England Louise never had the refurbishment of one particular house associated with her, she was certainly one of the first great women collectors.

Childhood poverty and teenage insecurity, combined with a dazzling education in Court life and knowledge of her own real worth, were influences that combined to make Louise ambitious both for titles and for possessions. She came from a grand background, for which she was to be perversely mocked at the English Court. Her parents were the Comte Guillaume de Penancoët de Keroualle and his wife Marie Anne, who was herself the daughter of a marquis. The family was poor, however, so that Louise's difficulty was lack of dowry: with her background she would otherwise have been expected to make a fine marriage. Effectively she had to find a job, to which end two well-positioned family friends recommended her to the French Court.[1] Late in 1668, when she was nineteen, Louise became a maid of honour to Princess Henrietta of England, Duchesse d'Orléans in France, with a modest but useful salary.

Princess Henrietta was herself a delightful character, who 'danced with grace, sang like an angel and played the spinet divinely'.[2] The youngest and favourite sister of King Charles II of England, she had been made to marry her effete first cousin, Philippe d'Orléans, the younger brother of the great French King Louis XIV. However, Duke Philippe really preferred gentlemen and made no secret of his predilections; so Louise, as a maid-of-honour, found herself cast into a household where foppery was the norm and Henrietta was constantly humiliated, in an atmosphere of scheming and intrigue. The Orléans family normally resided at St Cloud, but Louise also attended the Duchess at the Palais Royal in Paris and at Versailles, where the King was making improvements to the pretty little red-brick château constructed for his father, Louis XIII. The gardens were developed first: by 1668 the great formal park had been laid out by Le Nôtre in its earliest stages, together with gilded fountains and ironwork emblazoned with the Apollo mask of the Sun King. There the courtiers used to walk and picnic, as well as attending the theatre, musical entertainments and soirées in the château, which, though beautifully furnished and ornamented, was not yet extended to the vast palace that it would become.[3] In January 1669 Louise attended a reception given by the Duke and Duchess for the Venetian ambassador. The poet Charles Robinet wrote to Princess Henrietta of the beauty of her new companion: 'My eyes were delighted with her / Your new maid-of-honour is as sweet as she is beautiful.' He also described her as 'a girl of great intelligence'.[4] Even at the French Court, however, Louise did not receive any serious suitors. It was tragically evident that her lack of appeal was simply due to shortage of cash.[5] Men of title looked for girls of fortune.

The most important man in Princess Henrietta's life was her beloved brother Charles. At Court she gained self-respect and a political role by helping her cousin Louis XIV to negotiate with him. The French King wanted to fight the Dutch in order to gain territory. He also sought to make England part of a great Roman Catholic alliance. The English King was simply in need of money. It was to further their mutual needs that Louis XIV asked Henrietta to make the journey to England to negotiate with her brother. Despite tantrums and jealous threats from Philippe, Henrietta was eventually allowed to depart; among her attendants was Louise de Keroualle. On the English coast, at Dover Castle, the entire royal family came to meet Henrietta, including Charles'

Queen, Catherine of Braganza. The reunion of the two long-lost royal siblings was so joyous, and the negotiations so successful, that the time allowed for celebration of the treaty was extended to two weeks. It was here that Louise caught the eye of the King: when the moment came to leave, Henrietta offered the King her jewel box, asking what he would like as a gift. King Charles II turned to Louise de Keroualle, saying, 'This is the jewel that I covet.'[6]

Three weeks after their subsequent return to France, Princess Henrietta tragically died, probably of peritonitis.[7] Although it would have benefited the French King too if Louise returned to England, this idea actually came from Charles. A message was carried to France by the Duke of Buckingham, and received by the King of France with a mixture of enthusiasm and calculation. At the time Louise was fraught with worry at the loss of her mistress and her job, and had even considered becoming a nun.[8] Now, in October 1670, she found herself at the English Court, in a role insisted on by the King himself: that of maid-of-honour to Queen Catherine.

It is often assumed that Louise de Keroualle became the King's mistress soon after arriving in England, but she was made of sterner stuff. Although lodged in the vast and rambling royal palace at Whitehall, and visited by Charles for about an hour every morning after his game of tennis, as well as later in the day,[9] she resisted his advances for a whole year. As a devout Roman Catholic, she had been brought up with the strictest morals; she could also see that the King was a womaniser and would never be faithful to anyone. His principal mistress was currently Barbara Villiers, who had otherwise been known as Mrs Roger Palmer, then as the Countess of Castlemaine (Mr Palmer became the Earl); around this time she was created Duchess of Cleveland (her husband even became the Duke). Barbara was sharp, promiscuous, possessive and out to get what she could. Never one to hold back, before being taken up by the King she had been found in bed with the rakish Lord Chesterfield, cuckolding his charming wife. Later, Charles forgave her when he found her in the arms of John Churchill, who subsequently became the 1st Duke of Marlborough.[10] She claimed six children by the King: he admitted only five. By 1671, the King was losing interest in her, being much taken with the East End actress Nell Gwyn, famous for her quick humour and superb legs.

Already, late in 1670, the French ambassador Colbert de Croissy was writing to Louis XIV: 'I believe it might be a good thing to make use of this girl.'[11] Throughout that winter and into 1671 Louise was encouraged both by him and by the French philosopher St Evremond to submit to the King. 'Let yourself go into the delights of temptation instead of listening to your pride,'[12] St Evremond told her, and, 'I fear you want to accomplish two things which are incompatible, love and reserved conduct.'[13] Louise, though, was watching and waiting. The Duke of Buckingham may have suggested to her that the Queen was often ill, and that she could herself become the King's second wife.[14] Certainly she enquired after the Queen's health with unnatural frequency.[15] Louise must also have been aware that when Frances Teresa Stuart, Duchess of Richmond, had resisted the King only some five years earlier, he had become increasingly passionate. Eventually Charles, the courtiers and her own feelings conspired, and Louise yielded to the King, at Euston Hall, near Newmarket, the home of Lord and Lady Arlington. A play created by Lady Arlington took place, involving a mock-rustic marriage with the King and Louise as lead players.[16] Bedded as part of the drama by the conniving courtiers, with a stocking being thrown out of the window to symbolise loss of virtue, even Louise could not hold back. The puritanical diarist John Evelyn was also present at Euston Hall and reported the day in his diary, writing however that although Louise 'was for the most part in her undresse all day, and that there was fondnesse, & toying', he himself was not present at any kind of ceremony.[17] This does not mean that no such thing happened. Certainly Evelyn was aware of the concurrent view in the house that she 'was first made a Misse' at this time. King Louis XIV subsequently presented the worldly Lady Arlington with a diamond necklace for her part in the long process of persuasion and seduction.[18]

For the rest of her time in England, Louise was to continue living at Whitehall Palace. Much loved by the King, she bore him a son in July 1672, nine months after their first union. The boy, who had therefore been conceived between two days' racing at Newmarket, was given the name Charles Lennox.[19] At the age of three he was created Duke of Richmond and Lennox: Louise cleverly rushed the letters patent to Lord Danby late at night before he was going away, so that her son could become senior to Barbara's boy, who was to be created Duke of Grafton. Louise chose to see herself as a sort of morganatic wife, putting up with other mistresses but insisting on her seniority. Despite royal favour, she was unpopular with the people, being both French and Catholic. At the time Catholicism was seen as representing authoritarianism, and the English people naturally feared the idea of any foreign dominance, mainly from memories of papal influence. It was thought that the King would be too greatly swayed by Louise, as indeed Louis XIV hoped. Effectively the French King was to set her up as a spy, paying for regular reports to the French ambassador. Initially Louise did try to persuade the King to convert, with a view to leading the country with him. Soon, however, both she and the French ambassador saw that for England to become openly Roman Catholic would be impossible, and that the monarchy would not survive such a change. Louise's help to Louis XIV was limited to reporting on the King's state of mind in matters of religion, while encouraging him to convert privately to Catholicism, a cause dear to her heart.

Despite political friendships, mostly short-lived, with the Lords Danby, Arlington, Sunderland and later Rochester, among the ladies at Court Louise remained unpopular.[20] Controversially, given that she was genuinely aristocratic, she was mocked by Nell Gwyn for giving herself airs. When Louise wore black in mourning for the death of the Chevalier de Rohan, she was indeed lamenting the head of a family from which she was descended. Other courtiers felt he was not a near relation,[21] and Madame de Sévigné, herself no admirer of Louise, wrote: 'The Duchess pretends that every great person in France is her relative.'[22] After Louise had been in mourning for the King of Denmark, whom she claimed as a cousin, Nell Gwyn appeared in deepest black, averring that if Louise was a cousin of the Kings of the North, she was related to the Kings of the South. In Oxford for the special summoning of Parliament in 1680, when the crowd jeered at the closed royal carriage, believing it to contain Louise, Nell stuck her head out of the window, and cheerfully announced: 'I am the *Protestant* whore.'

If Louise de Keroualle were truly aristocratic, so Nell constantly implied, she would not need to be anyone's mistress. When Louise tried to pull rank on the Marchioness of Worcester, who had taken possession in Tunbridge Wells of a house that she herself wanted to occupy, the lady told her that 'titles gained through prostitution' were never recognised by 'people of rank and breeding'.[23] Louise's own parents also disapproved deeply of her liaison: Louis XIV went as far as to write to them with a request for family reconciliation.[24] Concerned about the prospects of their younger daughter, Henrietta, they did unbend to the extent of sending the girl to the English Court in order for Louise to find her a husband. The Earl of Pembroke was chosen: he was a drunkard and the marriage was extremely unhappy. When they came to England in 1675 the Comte and Comtesse de Keroualle did not stay with Louise, nor did they ask to see their illegitimate grandson, Charles Lennox. She must have felt very much on her own. It is against this background of family isolation, Court suspicion and unpopularity with ordinary people that Louise's building and collecting must be considered. It was a quest for comfort, both physical and mental.

So too was her ambition for titles, both in England and France. As early as 1673 Lord Arlington helped her receive the titles of Duchess of Portsmouth, Countess of Fareham and Baroness Petersfield. Louise also wanted land, negotiating first for estates in Ireland, from which from December 1672 she was given £10,000 a year, and subsequently for ancient Stuart lands in France. Late in 1673 Louis XIV agreed to grant her the estates at Aubigny, which had been given in 1422 to the Scottish John Stuart of Darnley. With the death of John Stuart's descendant, Charles Stuart, 3rd Duke of Richmond, 12th Seigneur of Aubigny, in 1672, ownership of the estates was pending, the technical heir being King Charles II. However, no French king would allow an English monarch to hold land in France: nor would any English king be prepared to pay the necessary homage. To grant the land to Louise, who was in the service of both monarchs, was a satisfactory compromise.[25] Nine years later, between March and July 1682, Louise made a star-studded visit to the French Court, where, as requested in advance on her behalf, she was granted the honour of the stool or 'tabouret', making her equivalent to a French Duchess.[26] This was not enough: wishing to be a real one, in January 1684 she prompted her compliant royal lover to ask the Ambassador Barrillon to write to the French King.[27] Louis acceded to this request by return of post and Louise was granted the title of Duchess of Aubigny.[28] In practice she continued all her life to be known, even in France, and usually to sign herself, as the Duchess of Portsmouth, this being the title by which she was already famous.[29]

To keep the King's love, so Lord Arlington had advised her, what she should give him was peace and contentment.[30] Certainly her behaviour appeared gentle, compared with that of the demanding Duchess of Cleveland. As the French ambassador, Colbert de Croissy, wrote: 'She was no termagant or scold, but she did not hesitate to use tears.'[31] Louise was also adroit, discussing politics with the King, but never appearing to take her influence too far. He responded freely with gifts including jewellery: in 1674 she had wanted a pearl necklace costing £8000 and earrings, for which the Lord Treasurer had to provide 3000 guineas.[32] She also received a diamond necklace worth £12,000, and in 1675 Louis XIV rewarded her services with a present of diamond pendant earrings worth £18,000.[33] A jewel worth £13,000 had been made for the Earl of Ossory as a reward for a diplomatic mission: when he did not make the journey, this gem was presented to Louise. From the time that she arrived in England, her tastes in general were extravagant. She had a sedan chair that was far more splendid than that of either the King or Queen:[34] in its magnificence it was reminiscent of the beautiful barge lined with blue velvet that the King had once given Princess Henrietta. Her clothes were also luxurious: a bill describes a flirtatious male party costume ordered by her, comprising a 'coloured and figured brocade coat, Ringraw breeches' and a 'black Beaver Hatt', the latter with a scarlet and silver edging.[35] The costume was enhanced by 'scarlet and silver'd lace' detail, with the 'cannour' or knee frills similarly laced in scarlet and silver. Including real silver thread for buttonholes, and 'Rich Brocade at 28 sh[illin]gs ye yard', the whole came to an exorbitant £59.15s.9d.

Louise did not only seek to please the King in herself, but also took pains to provide him with the best food and entertainment, in a setting where he was surrounded by beautiful objects. Her apartments at Whitehall were in one of the most prestigious parts of the Royal Palace, at the south-west end of the celebrated Tudor Stone Gallery and below the fretted and gilded first-floor Matted Gallery, so called because of the rush matting on its floor. They were thus on the south-west corner of the Privy Garden, possibly overlooking the sundial lawn. In modern terms they lay between the street of Whitehall and the river. Only a garden's length towards Westminster, her descendants were to own Richmond House, at that time newly built for Charles Stuart, 3rd Duke of Richmond, but later remodelled for Charles

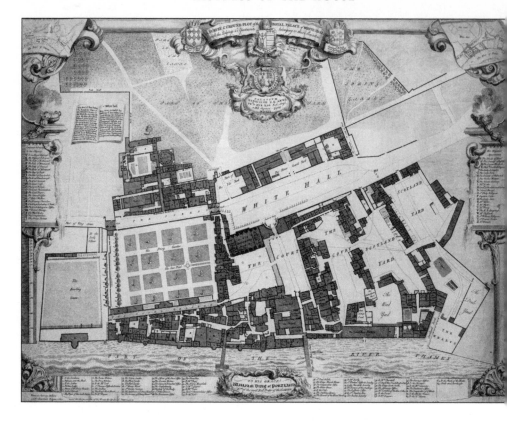

Plan of Whitehall Palace, engraved in 1747 by George Vertu from an original survey of *c*. 1680. Louise de Keroualle's rooms were in the low left-hand corner.

Lennox, 2nd Duke of the new creation.[36] In 1671 Louise's corner was one of the oldest parts of the palace, and the most confused in terms of building layout, but like his father, Charles I, the King used it for important courtiers, with the Matted Gallery acting as a spine linking his own apartment to those of the Duke and Duchess of York and Prince Rupert. In the autumn of that year a set of rooms intended for the new Lord Chancellor had been squeezed in between the royal apartments, but it is unlikely that he used it, and this may have been the space reassigned to Louise.[37] Colbert de Croissy commented: '...you may have heard from other sources, what a finely furnished set of lodgings have been given to her at Whitehall'. There she soon created a distinctive setting: in the same letter of October 1671 Colbert commented that 'when the King was with her, persons of breeding could, without loss of dignity, go to her rooms and pay him and her their court'.[38] These were extended for her in April 1672,[39] and again altered after she became Duchess of Portsmouth in 1673.[40] The King and Queen each had separate apartments overlooking the Thames, around three sides of a small courtyard: these were said to be cramped by comparison.[41] Louise certainly had a remarkable number of rooms, including fourteen garrets for staff. French visitors to Court were especially amazed to find the style in which she lived: the Comte de Limoges was awestruck that 'Mademoiselle de Keroualle alone occupies forty rooms in Whitehall, without taking the galleries into account',[42] meaning the Stone and Matted Galleries which provided a grand entrance to her apartments. With an impeccable sense of design and detail, Louise spared nothing to make her apartments distinctive so that important people would wish to visit. The King always received the French ambassadors there, as well as certain ministers. In 1675 Evelyn wrote: 'I was Casualy shewed the Dutchesse of Portsmouths splendid Appartment at Whitehall, luxuriously furnished, & with ten times the richnesse & glory beyond the Queenes, such massy pieces of Plate, whole Tables, Stands etc.: of incredible value etc...'[43] One of the huge pieces of silver was a 'cistern' or great wine cooler that the King gave her in 1672. It weighed an incredible 1000 oz.[44]

Life at Court was difficult for Louise between 1675 and 1677: 'The Duchess of Portsmouth is melancholy...and with reason,' wrote Lady Vaughan in February 1675.[45] Firstly she caught a venereal disease from the King and had to stay away from him. Not long after this, the King took up with the notorious Hortense Mancini, Duchess Mazarin. Louise ceased to take pride of place and later suffered a miscarriage. Although the King still visited her rooms, 'which are the place where he's seen most publicly', he spent many nights with Nell Gwyn.[46] A year later, in 1677, Louise still had poor health. Thereafter, she was restored to the King's favour, and in this respect never looked back, almost being treated as Queen: the complete rebuilding of her apartment at this particular moment, in 1678–9, is significant.[47] However, when a national panic set in at the time of the Popish Plot, Louise again faced universal animosity. The years 1678–81 were a period of great peril for her, and she feared she might have to return to France.[48]

Even in the face of political danger, Louise continued to redecorate her apartments. These rooms were hung with tapestries from the new factory of the Gobelins in Paris, representing the twelve palaces of King Louis. French craftsmen in particular tried to imitate paintings, in the manner of Roman Renaissance hangings rather than in the more northern lingering tradition of medieval tapestry. Evelyn was deeply impressed by these works: '...the new fabrique of French Tapissry, for designe, tendernesse of work, & incomparable imitation of the best paintings; beyond anything I had ever beheld; some pieces had Versailles, St Germans & other palaces of the French King with Huntings, figures, & landskips, Exotique fowle & all to the life rarely done...'[49] The rooms were also furnished with the newly fashionable inlaid cabinets,[50] and with tables, stands, screens, desks and buffets, Japanese lacquered cabinets and 'pendule clocks'.[51] Details extended to fine chimney furniture, and Evelyn specifically commented on the countless and massive items of silver in the form of huge embossed vases, sconces and 'branches', presumably candelabra. A reference to 'whole tables' indicated that even some of the tables were silver: certainly as a precedent Louis XIV had furniture at Versailles in solid silver.[52] Ormolu mounts for the furniture were designed by Louis XIV's great decorator Charles le Brun.[53] The windows were of crystal.[54] Evelyn also reported that Louise had a selection of 'His Majestie's best paintings'.[55]

Such was the fame of these apartments that they were visited by crowds of people. They were also much coveted, which did not add to Louise's popularity.[56] The King, who had spent much of his exile at the French Court, clearly felt at home in this little island of Frenchness. In 1683 Evelyn described a visit, following the King into her 'dressing roome, within her bedchamber, where she was in her morning loose garment, her maides Combing her, newly out of her bed: his Majestie & the Gallants standing about her: but that which ingag'd my curiositie, was the rich & splendid furrniture of this woman's Appartment, now twice or thrice puld downe, & rebuilt, to satisfie her prodigal & expensive pleasures...'[57] The King encouraged her collecting, in 1684 making her a gift of gold plate so magnificent that it was exhibited in the shop of the goldsmith who had made it.[58] This caused further outcry. Louise brought many French workmen to England, including a painter called Rambour who worked at Windsor,[59] and established royal workshops to help them.[60]

In her glorious apartments, Louise loved to entertain.[61] Necessarily, the French ambassador was often her guest. Four were present during the time she spent at Whitehall Palace: Colbert, Marquis de Croissy from 1669 to 1674, the Marquis de Ruvigny from 1674 to 1676, followed for barely two years by Honoré de Courtin, who was invalided out by the English climate, and finally Barrillon d'Amoncourt, the Marquis de Branges. In September 1676 Courtin reported: 'She has just given our Embassy a splendid dinner, to which Mrs Middleton, the Prince of Monaco, Sunderland, Sessac, and our people were all invited.'[62] Early the next year, she gave a dinner for the new ambassador, at which Louis XIV's chamber musicians, on tour in England, played for the King during his brief visit to the soirée.[63] Louise continually used the congenial atmosphere in her rooms to reinforce her influence; they were especially visited by members of the Court on Sundays.[64] In January 1682 she gave a banquet for the Moroccan ambassador and his suite. Evelyn was impressed by the foreigners, finding them 'of an extraordinary moderation and modesty, tho' placed about a long table, a lady between two Moores'. As well as some of the King's natural children, Louise was also generous in entertaining her rival Nell Gwyn and other 'concubines'.[65] The King clung to an innocent ignorance of the jealousies of his mistresses, being genuinely affectionate towards all of them.

The next year Louise made her triumphant visit to France, after which she was virtually invincible, even wielding considerable political power: the King 'happily let her transact much wearysome diplomacy for him'.[66] She survived a rather unwise flirtation with Philippe de Vendôme, the Grand Prior of France, who was banished for being 'a little too free' with her.[67] Given that the King had no legitimate children, Louise's relationship with his brother, James, Duke of York, the rightful heir to the throne, was obviously important. While daring to encourage the King to debar the converted and fanatical Catholic Duke from the succession, she also tried to be friendly with James, endeavouring to keep her options open. She had first met the alternative candidate, the young William of Orange, in 1670. Colbert de Croissy reported: 'Mlle de Keroualle was led out by the Prince of Orange, who seemed in her company to lose the indifference he has always shown to other ladies.'[68] When the young man came to Court in 1677 to ask for the hand of the King's niece, Princess Mary, who was next in line after her father, Louise did not oppose the match, even though it was so strongly against the French influence that she was paid to promote. The Prince visited her every day[69] and she appeared at the festivities to celebrate the marriage.[70] She even encouraged the friendship of the illegitimate Duke of Monmouth, and at one stage was deceived by courtiers into believing that her own son, the Duke of Richmond, had a chance of being chosen as heir. After all, the illegitimate daughter of King Henry VIII had ascended to the throne only 120 years earlier as Queen Elizabeth I:[71] indeed, the young Duke of Richmond was always called a 'Prince'. Monmouth himself was popular with the people but treacherous in the cause of gaining the throne: when he raised troops in 1685, it resulted in his execution. His full-length portrait still hangs at Goodwood, and is said to have been a personal gift from him to Louise.

Following her early insecurities about money, Louise never ceased to feel that she had to look both to her present situation and to the future. The King had always accepted that she was far more expensive to keep than Nell Gwyn. One extraordinary and amusingly blatant table of expenses is written with amounts in two columns,[72] showing the relative sums paid to her and to Nell. Between 3 June and 30 December 1676, Louise received £8773 to Nell's £2682. The following year Louise was given £27,300 and Nell only £5250. After a time the amounts settle into a pattern: whenever the Duchess of Portsmouth received £2150, Nell would be given £1250. No doubt the King was sweet-talking them both. Louise also received regular amounts from King Louis. Never one to miss an opportunity, when the 1683 Rye House Plot failed, Louise managed to be granted £2000 per annum from the confiscated estate of Lord Grey, due to go to her son when he came of age.

Image was ever important, and Louise was an active patron of portrait painters. It is not thought that she herself commissioned Sir Peter Lely, but she may well have ordered two important copies. One is after that commissioned by Robert Spencer, 2nd Earl of Sunderland, for his gallery of beauties at Althorp, of the young Louise as an Arcadian shepherdess, holding a crook and feeding a lamb. Louise's version was a gift to her sister, Henrietta, Countess of Pembroke, and still hangs at Wilton House in Wiltshire. A couple of years later Lely painted her in a similar three-quarter pose in 'undress', the celebrity fashion of the day, holding up a lock of her hair: Louise also owned a copy of this.[73] During the 1670s she commissioned Henri Gascars to paint her at least four times, twice with her son.[74] Gascars, who had painted Princess Henrietta at St Cloud, came to England at Louise's bidding in about 1672.[75] In one painting by him, now known only from an engraving, she is semi-reclining on a cushion, fondling a King Charles spaniel, which may be a slightly ribald reference to her royal lover.[76] Two further 'family' portraits by Gascars must also have been commissioned by Louise, one depicting the King in a rare Court view, with ladies beyond. Another shows the little Duke of Richmond as a child, dressed in Roman armour;[77] Louise was evidently interested in the fashion for classical references. During her successful visit to France in 1682 she was painted by Pierre Mignard, who shows her seated with her arm affectionately resting on the shoulder of her richly dressed black maid: Louise proudly twirls her skirt to show that she is sitting on the prized tabouret reserved only for duchesses.[78] Among her other commissions[79] she was also painted twice by Sir Godfrey Kneller[80] and by Verelst, as was her son.[81]

Tragedy came for Louise earlier than might have been anticipated. In 1685 the fifty-two-year-old King suddenly became ill. He had spent Sunday night, 1st February, in her apartments, but on Monday his speech became slurred and he had a fit. Louise quickly realised that the situation was serious and that it was not suitable for her to go to him in the royal apartment, where the Queen would visit. All five of his natural sons were summoned to the royal deathbed. Her first thoughts were not for herself, but for the King. Concerned above all about the safety of his soul, Louise summoned the French ambassador to bid him to beg James, Duke of York to send for a Catholic priest. This the Duke did. Upon the King's quiet assent, Father John Huddleston, who had helped him in 1651, was smuggled into his apartments with the help of a page. The last rites were received on Thursday. The King lapsed into unconsciousness and died, as a Catholic, at noon on Friday 6 February 1685.

Louise, now in her own eyes a widow, prepared to leave Court for France with her son. It was reported that she 'hath sent her goods and is retired to the French ambassador's':[82] however, there was a rumour, possibly malicious, that she was not allowed to depart until she had paid her debts and yielded up some of the crown jewels that were said to be in her possession. Louise persisted nonetheless in requesting that she be pensioned by the new King James II: she wished to be given the £19,000 that Charles II had allocated her in recent years.[83] Although he disliked her, James remembered his brother's dying wish for him to care for her, and indeed for Nell, and allocated Louise the relatively small amount of 3000 guineas per annum, with 2000 for her son. Though he assured her of his friendship, the whole transaction was really to ensure that the French king would continue to support him.[84] He also told her that she could keep her rooms at Whitehall.[85]

Louise retreated to France in August 1685, and made her way to Versailles. She returned to England for a time in 1686, and again in 1688 for the marriage of her niece Charlotte, daughter of the 7th Earl and Countess of Pembroke. When in that year the Protestant Prince William of Orange was invited with his English wife the Princess Mary to take the English throne, Louise returned yet again, briefly hoping that the dancing partner of her youth would favour her.[86] She soon realised that, on the contrary, she would be unable to stay at the English Court, given that courtiers and populace alike wished to support the Dutch against Louis XIV.

It has always been said that Louise left her celebrated apartments at Whitehall furnished. In leaving belongings there at all, she may have been trying to qualify for the hoped-for English pension: believing that William III would help her out, she wanted to keep open some possibility of return. However, the furnishing must only have been partial. It is invariably stated[87] that all her possessions were burnt in a fire in 1691 (some seven years before fire destroyed the rest of the palace) and that Louise was deeply distressed at their loss.[88] Evelyn, the only contemporary commentator, does not commit himself as to what happened to her belongings, preferring to voice his disgust with the Court of Charles II. On 10 April 1691 he records that: 'This night, a suddaine and terrible Fire burnt downe all the buildings over the Stone Gallery at W-hall, to the waterside, beginning at the Appartments of the late Dutchesse of Portsmouth (which had been pulled done & rebuilt to please her (no less than) 3 times & Consuming the lodgings of such lewd Creatures, who debauched both K. Char;2nd & others & were his destruction.'[89]

It would have been uncharacteristic for the materialistic and cautious Louise to have left her entire collection behind. One commentator mentions that when Louise finally left for France in August 1685, carrying her jewels together with 200,000 francs in gold that she had received on the death of the King, in addition 'several ships carried away her furniture and valuable oddments'.[90] A separate report stated that by the time of the fire, Louise's apartments had been taken over by the Duke of Gloucester, suggesting that they had been entirely evacuated.[91] A suite of marquetry furniture now at Goodwood has always been said to have been given to Louise by the King: it is likely that having furnished the Whitehall rooms it then travelled to France. Recently attributed to the English furniture maker Gerrit Jensen, it is in the Dutch manner, with marquetry in an ebony base. Little flowers of ivory and green stained leaves are inset. A North Italian cabinet of exotic marbles at Goodwood also belonged to Louise. Many portraits of himself and of other Stuart royals that are now at Goodwood are likely to have been given to Louise by the King. These too must have travelled to France: as well as being recorded in Paris, some are mentioned in an inventory of 1765 at Aubigny. As Louise loved tapestries, and at least one of her Parisian homes was full of them, it is probable that she also took these with her.

From 1688 the Duchess of Portsmouth was supported by an increased pension of 12,000 livres per annum from Louis XIV, with 20,000 livres for the Duke of Richmond: when the young man returned to England in 1692 she also received some of his pension. In France Louise lived for the next fifteen years at four different addresses in Paris. In 1714, living in the Rue des Saintes Pères, she paid huge sums for a chandelier and for looking glasses, and for gold goods 1520 crowns to the King's goldsmith Claude Ballin II.[92] An inventory made after her death in 1734[93] lists the contents of this, her last domicile in Paris. The house, in the fashionable quarter of St Germain des Près, was a traditionally large Parisian *hôtel* with two courtyards. It is astonishing to read from the inventory just how many staff lived there. Both the maître d'hôtel, M. de St Martin, and Louise's secretary, M. de la Tour, had rooms on the ground floor. The concierge had a room looking onto the courtyard, as did another two male members of staff, while a valet de chambre was tucked into the entresol. Various female domestics slept in two rooms on the third floor of the house: M. Baudouin the concierge also had his bedchamber up there, as did the main chef and the roasting chef. More senior members of staff had bedchambers on the second floor, where, just like the suite of a queen, Louise's three separate ladies of the bedchamber had their rooms, as well as her second valet de chambre, a page and her 'ecuier'. Louise's personal reception room was the 'third chamber' on the first floor, on the garden side. Possibly visitors went through an enfilade to reach this inner sanctum, in the accepted French courtly tradition.

As was normal in certain grand houses at the time, Louise had tapestries in virtually every room, and in the corridors. They even adorned the rooms of senior members of her staff: M. de St Martin had fourteen antique tapestries from Bergamo all around his room, while the concierge had five, and the antechamber on the ground floor contained nine. These were no ordinary works. In the second antechamber, on the first floor or *piano nobile*, three sets from Flanders recounted the history of Pyrrhus. In the room in which Louise died, overlooking the Rue de Verneuil, there hung part of a set depicting Cephalus and Procris. One of these, presumably too big for the space, was in the garde-meuble on the second floor. This room was a store, with the tapestries either rolled up or laid in a pile like carpets. These included more tapestries from Flanders: three panels of the story of Moses and three with a scene of children playing. From Beauvais, a set of eight recorded the history of the Muses; from Brussels another six represented the twelve months of the year, while a further set also from Brussels, of five pieces, showed the battles of Caesar. The fine set of eight panels from Gobelins, also in the garde-meuble, may have been the remainder of the famous palace series that Louise had put on show at Whitehall. Her zeal as a collector is shown by the very number of tapestries in this store high up in the house.

Against the background of tapestries of religious and classical subjects, Louise placed her fine walnut furniture, as part of a number of furnishings that included splendid looking glasses, clocks, china and carpets. Her picture collection was typical of the period: family portraits abounded, as did paintings of religious subjects. One interesting feature was her 'armoire de bibliothèque' which was perhaps a miniature book room rather than a full library: in it were listed 220 books, a very large number for the period. These include sixteen folio volumes on the history of the church, and twelve comprising Cervantes' popular novel, *Don Quixote*. A Bible now in the Goodwood library, dated Paris, 1667, with the text in French, is not specifically listed, but probably also belonged to Louise. It has a fine red morocco binding, tooled in gold.

Louise never ceased to feel that money was tight. From 1689 she relied on her estates at Aubigny for revenue,[94] and in 1698–9 she also visited England for six months, petitioning the King for the reinstatement of her pension, although she was not allowed to attend Court entertainments. She was moderately successful, eventually gaining 1000 livres a year, payable in France, as against the 8000 requested. During this trip[95] she also visited her son's newly purchased hunting lodge at Goodwood.[96] Louis XIV was always grateful meanwhile for her indirect help at the English Court, which had enabled him to make a number of territorial gains, notably Flanders, Alsace and Franche Comté. Every year from 1699, he stopped her creditors' many lawsuits against her, often bankrupting them. Even before the ageing French King's demise, Louise's solicitous daughter-in-law, Anne, Duchess of Richmond, also tried to act on her behalf, seeking unsuccessfully to get a larger English pension reinstated for her. Incredibly, Louise still seemed to think too that she was due something from the disposal of her Whitehall lodgings.[97] After the death of Queen Anne in 1714, George I agreed that she could come to Court. A yacht was prepared and sent by her son and Louise was received by the King.[98] When Louis XIV finally died in 1715, however, her revenues were cut, and, unable to maintain her lavish lifestyle, she had to leave Paris permanently for the country.

There she mostly lived in Aubigny itself, managing her estates in a way that tried to make a profit. She extended the château in town to link the main block with the chapel and furnished a few rooms for her own use in the romantic fifteenth-century Stuart château of La Verrerie, set beyond a shimmering lake in deep forests some fifteen miles out of town. Despite her hard head, she became increasingly pious, founding a convent[99] and using her own funds to decorate various churches. She was visited at Aubigny by her son the 1st Duke, and, after his death, by her beloved grandson the 2nd Duke. Louise was careful to the last: at her death in 1734, having returned to Paris to arrange her affairs, she left her fortune to her grandson, now not only Duke of Richmond and Lennox, but also of Aubigny. Sadly Louise never knew of the birth of her longed for great-grandson, Charles, the future 3rd Duke of Richmond, who was born the next year.

An inventory of items at the Château of Aubigny dated 1765, at the time of a visit by the 3rd Duke, suggests that Louise's collections were indeed a combination of pictures and furniture brought from England in 1688 and items acquired in France. Although this inventory was taken long after her death, it is highly unlikely that her grandson the 2nd Duke would have been shipping items over to her, apart from new commissions such as the double portrait of himself and his Duchess (now at Goodwood), painted at her request. We may therefore assume that she had acquired the English paintings, such as the ravishing portrait by Lely of Princess Henrietta, during her time with Charles II.

Despite the bad press that Louise received in her own day, and the taunts of subsequent commentators, she was sufficiently important to have her every move reported. Her fame was entirely due to her personal style and to the fact that she was much loved by the King. He wrote to her: ''Tis impossible to express the true passion & kindness I have for my dearest, dearest Fubs.'[100] In 1684 when requesting the Duchy of Aubigny for her, he wrote: 'The Duchess of Portsmouth and her son the Duke of Richmond are the persons above all in the world whom I love the most.'[101] She was also very popular among her own family and followers. Her granddaughter Caroline, Lady Holland, wrote to her sister Emily, Duchess of Leinster: 'The servants (and children of consequence)...were violently fond of the Duchess of Portsmouth.'[102] Louise should be regarded with admiration for her tenacity in making the best of a difficult situation, and with compassion: single motherhood was never easy, especially in a foreign country. Despite the taunts of Nell Gwyn she was not promiscuous. She may have been unnaturally acquisitive, but this is a characteristic that meets with praise in a male collector. It can truly be said that Louise made something of her life, creating a world of fine costumes and entertainments, of dazzling interiors and beautiful objects. For the King it was his relationship with Louise that brought him the greatest happiness. As well as her personal charms, her courtly sophistication and innately French understanding of men must have played a large part in retaining his attention for fifteen years. She also founded a dynasty, of which she was for many years the concerned matriarch. Through her actions she firmly established not only the titles of the Dukes of Richmond, Lennox and Aubigny, but also the foundation of their lands in France and of their art collection in England.

Chapter 6

RESTORATION DRAMA
ELIZABETH MURRAY,
COUNTESS OF DYSART AND
DUCHESS OF LAUDERDALE
1626–98

Returning from a walk to the nearby River Thames with her nurse, little Elizabeth Murray would run through the front porch into the marble flagged hall of her home at Ham House. She could dash straight out again onto the terrace that overlooked the formal garden spreading beyond. If her mother called her, Elizabeth would rush back through the length of the hall into the little parlour at the east end, richly decorated with leather wall hangings in red and gold. Perhaps her parents awaited her in their bedchambers, her father's up the stairs on the river side, or her mother's overlooking the garden opposite. Wherever she went, the flame-haired child, her parents' pride and joy and eldest of four daughters, was loved and welcomed.

Elizabeth's father, William Murray, had literally been the whipping boy to the future King Charles I. As a child, if the Prince was naughty, it was his friend and schoolmate who was beaten. The friendship endured: Murray became a Gentleman of the Bedchamber to the new King and was given a knighthood. Having acquired the lease of Ham House from the Crown, Murray had to give up most of the accompanying land when Charles I insisted on enclosing it inside the newly designated Richmond deer park in 1637: in recompense Murray was given the Lordship of the Manors of Petersham and Ham. Soaring to three tall storeys in a rich dark brick, Ham House had only been completed in 1610: a plan of it drawn by Robert Smythson dates from the previous year. Externally the house was symmetrical, but its interior had a traditional medieval arrangement. Along the narrow spine of the ground floor ran the Great Hall, with the staircase at the east end, leading on the first floor to the State Apartments and the Great Dining Room and Drawing Room. The State Apartments culminated across the western end in the transverse Long Gallery, its exterior projections matching those of the parlours on the east. Between these projecting wings and the narrow central section, dramatic turrets on each side of the roof were surmounted by ogee caps with gilded weather vanes, giving the house a romantic appearance.

Already by the late 1630s Murray had wished to update the interior of Ham House, in order to bring it up to the level of the latest fashions admired by the exclusive circle of royal courtiers around Charles I. This included the great designer Inigo Jones, for whom classical details, often sculptural, were all-important, and who drew his inspiration for interiors from Paris and the Court fashions of Queen Henrietta Maria's brother, King Louis XIII. In the Hall at Ham House, Murray enhanced the Jacobean chimneypiece with figures that may be Mars and Minerva, possibly taken from another chimneypiece above, and created a great arched entrance to his magnificent new staircase at the east end of the room, which swept important guests up to the State Apartments. Some of his white and gold sculptural decorations survive on the first floor, especially in the North Drawing Room,[1] and it is fascinating to imagine the original Carolean interiors, the overall design of which was directed by Franz Cleyn, the artistic director of the Mortlake Tapestries, who also worked at Holland House. The small Green Closet off the Long Gallery was decorated for Murray by Cleyn, who may have been responsible too for the Gallery's new staircase and panelling. In response to the same sophisticated Court influences, rich textiles were used throughout Ham, as curtains, hangings and upholstery. The schemes were colour coordinated, which was still relatively unusual at the time, as earlier hangings had more often been embroidered and therefore multicoloured. Expensive stamped and gilt leather was also used, notably in the parlour with its matching walls, curtains and seat covers. Curtains were hung on a rod and divided, rather than as a single panel. These fabrics, the very latest in design, were to inspire Elizabeth in her own later choices.

Elizabeth's parents were charming, educated people. Her mother, Catherine Bruce, came from a prominent Scottish family, of which the

Earl of Elgin was the head: her uncle was the Laird of Clackmannan. Catherine was described as a 'fine, discreet lady' while Elizabeth herself was remarked upon at an early age by Sir Thomas Knyvett, a Royalist who was staying nearby: 'Her eldest daughter is the jewel and indeed a pretty one, but for her deep colored hair. I know not how such a notion would relish, but she is said to have a very great fortune. The other sisters [Elizabeth's three younger siblings were all slightly hunch-backed] are pitiful, crooked things...I could find it in my heart to woo her for my son, for I am much in her favour. She seems to be a very good, harmless, vertuous, witty little bable.'[2] Like so many educated women at this period, one of Elizabeth's prime influences was her father, and his interest in the interiors at Ham is likely to have had a great effect on her. Notwithstanding the handsome set of state apart-ments on the first floor, the house was essentially family orientated, with a table for shovel board in the main hall, and a big nursery in a prime position on the southern garden front of the house, at the west end, behind which the service rooms were located. Elizabeth's happy childhood and a lively Richmond social life were clouded however by the outbreak of civil war. From 1645 William Murray, who had been created Earl of Dysart by the King,[3] had to go into exile in Paris for the part he had played in the Royalist cause, by carrying letters between Charles I and his escaped Queen, Henrietta Maria. Henceforth Cather-ine had to contend with the threat that the Parliamentarians might sequester her house. Elizabeth was also very much influenced by her mother's strength in these conflicts: Ham was a house for which it was worth fighting.

In 1648 Elizabeth married Sir Lionel Tollemache, 3rd Bt. He was a wealthy landowner with seats at Helmingham Hall and Fakenham Magna in Suffolk and at Harrington Hall in Northamptonshire. The couple had an affectionate relationship and children arrived in quick succession, with Lionel in 1649 and Thomas about two years later. For much of the year the couple lived at Helmingham or in London, first at the home of Sir Lionel's grandfather, Lord Stanhope, at the White House in Charing Cross, or from 1654 in fashionable Covent Garden. An 'annus horribilis' came in 1649, with the tragic execution of the King in January, and the death in July of Elizabeth's mother. Elizabeth now became the mistress of Ham, a job made more demanding by the fact that her three younger sisters were still living there. A painting by their neighbour Joan Carlile shows the youngest sister, Margaret, seated because of her infirmity, with Elizabeth and Sir Lionel standing beside her.[4]

Elizabeth was admired both for her looks and her learning. In 1650 Dorothy Long, a family friend from Richmond, remarked: 'Our Lady has grown a great student. She reads Dr Donne and Sir W. Rawley; works exquisitely in gum worke; hath entered herself Head of the 2nd Form in our Academy...' In quiet and uncertain times, Elizabeth was possibly part of some sort of learning circle: with other neighbours such as Lodowyck and Joan Carlile living in Richmond Park, the family were not short of intelligent company. Dorothy Long added that 'she knocks me down with my own weapon', meaning that she was a sharp conversationalist.[5] The following section of Bishop Burnet's description, the only part to be complimentary about her, fits in with the other reports:

'She was a woman of great beauty, but of far greater parts. She had a wonderful quickness of apprehension, and an amazing vivacity in conversation. She had studied not only divinity and history, but mathematics and philosophy.'[6]

Throughout this time the politically neutral Sir Lionel was a great help to the whole family, staving off threats of the sequestration of Ham. Through him, Elizabeth managed to get on well with Cromwell, though not, as the inimical Burnet mischievously implied, as his mistress. Burnet had his own reasons for wishing to smear Elizabeth: before his own marriage his wife had had an affair with the Earl of Lauderdale, Elizabeth's second husband.[7] A portrait of Cromwell in the Tollemache collection is testimony to some kind of friendship. In secret, however, the young Elizabeth Tollemache was pursuing her father's devotion to the Crown, as a member of the Sealed Knot, a society that worked for the Restoration of Charles II. In coded letters through which she communicated with the exiled royal Court, the King was 'Mr Sloane', her husband's brother-in-law Sir William Compton was 'Lawton' and she was 'Mrs Legge.' She also dabbled with invisible ink. Elizabeth was able to travel abroad without hindrance during the 1650s, and was not lacking in pretexts for getting near to the royal Court in exile:[8] it is possible that she visited Holland, where the family had property, and Paris, in 1654, 1656 and 1658, where one of her daughters was being educated.

In 1654 Elizabeth compiled an inventory, apparently written in her own hand, which gives an interesting picture of how Ham was used at this time. It was not a large house and in many ways the layout still yielded a rather medieval routine. At first Elizabeth was unsure how to name certain rooms which yielded a variety of purposes, the furniture simply being moved by servants as required. At this stage she used as 'my owne bedchamber' a principal ground-floor room on the south-east corner of the house, which looked out to the south onto the formal garden. There was an adjacent closet at ground-floor level in the turret; its equivalent differed, on the north side, in being an open arcade. On the first floor, in the same turret, her gentlewoman, a sort of lady-in-waiting, had a 'roome above'. In Elizabeth's bedroom there was also a second, pallet, bed for her maid. The room was hung with six pieces of tapestry, and contained a fashionable black ebony and red tortoiseshell cabinet from Antwerp. A Turkey carpet on the floor par-ticularly indicated a luxurious standard of living.

The most important area of the house was still this eastern end: for this reason Sir Lionel probably took over his father-in-law Sir William's room just up the grand staircase to the left, again in a presiding posi-tion. Proceeding back over the Great Hall into the Great Dining Room on the first floor, there were at this time windows looking over the gardens to the left, or south, as well as in the oriel over the porch on the north side. As the visitor entered the room, it was therefore T-shaped, and Elizabeth may have placed a long dining table across the far end in the medieval manner. In the 1650s both the Great Dining Room and the White Drawing Room beyond were hung with tapes-tries from the 'storie of Phaeton' series. The White Drawing Room had a state bed in the manner of a traditional Great Chamber, which was hung with 'white satine richly embroidered with needle work'. Beyond, the Long Gallery was called the Matted Gallery, like that at Whitehall. With the charming little Green Closet in the adjacent turret, this room was the climax of the sequence. On its far side a con-cealed door led to a secondary staircase down to the service rooms below, at the west end of the house. The parlour for senior staff was in a key position to the right of the front door.

Following her father's death in December 1655, Elizabeth took up the use of her hereditary title of Countess of Dysart, a Scottish title which could descend in the female line and which was senior to her husband's Baronetcy. Despite potential difficulties, she cleverly continued to maintain her position throughout the years of Commonwealth rule. There were apparently, however, few building alterations to Ham in the 1650s, a time when owners of estates needed to keep their heads down. The Countess was in any case often in Suffolk and busy with her young family: when her daughter Elizabeth was born at Fakenham in 1659 she was so happy there that she wrote: 'I desire to settel in Suffolk perhaps for my life.' She bore eleven children, of whom five survived to maturity.

At the Restoration Sir Lionel was made a Ranger of Richmond Park, and Elizabeth's support of Charles II during his exile was acknowledged by the grant of an annuity of £800 per annum. At about this time her sister Margaret was married and with her husband, Lord Maynard, became close at Court to Queen Catherine of Braganza. In these more favourable times the family was granted by the King the longed-for freehold of Ham, together with 75 acres, and a lease of the remaining 289 acres, all in trust for Elizabeth and her three sisters. The grant was dated 24 March 1665/66, and was specifically in recognition 'of the service done by the late Earl of Dysart and his daughter' to the Crown: their earlier loss of land in the New Park was also recognised.[9] After years of caution, abstention and diplomacy, Elizabeth now gradually embarked on acquiring items for Ham House.[10]

Elizabeth loved glamorous furniture, and she began to assemble a remarkable collection. She fitted out Cleyn's Green Closet with items suitable to its small scale,[11] and to link the Closet and the Drawing Room, a door was created, of which the doorcase, on the Drawing Room side, is in the style of the 1660s. Elizabeth retained her father's choice of green hangings for the Closet, as well as the rich decoration and the use of the room for various small but perfect works of art acquired by Murray, notably Royalist miniatures of Queen Elizabeth, Henrietta Maria and Charles II as a boy. Perhaps because of difficult circumstances around the time of the Restoration, Elizabeth began by adapting existing items rather than ordering anew. Two Japanese lacquer cabinets of c. 1630 were placed on stands with portly, pouting putti as caryatids; these were matched by a pair of long stools with similar androgynous caryatids, also on lions' paws. A small ebony table

was altered with the addition of silver mounts and was given sophisticated female caryatids, the bare bellies of the classical but flirtatious
nudes draped with descending bows. Each figure holds up a piece of
cloth in antique manner. The centre of the table top bears the mono-
gram of Elizabeth Dysart, and the Countess's coronet. The final
adaptation may date from as late as 1670, the year in which Elizabeth
was confirmed in her hitherto rather uncertain title.[12] A pair of sideboards have similar but remarkably lifelike female caryatid supports,
extraordinarily oversexed as they toy with their hair, with bows tidily
tied at their naked waists. Their centrally parted hair is drawn back
over ringlets in the fashion of the 1650s and 60s, though the caryatids
are, along with the other items, unlikely to have been made during
the puritanical Commonwealth but rather in the post-Restoration
period.[13]

In a different mode, an ivory cabinet, at the time usually protected
by a light worsted case, was a stunning addition in white. The inside
was completely fitted out in ivory: given the rarity of anyone ever
seeing an elephant and the extreme difficulty of obtaining any tusks,
this must have been a remarkable sight. Like the cabinet in Elizabeth's
own room, it was probably made in Antwerp. Presumably this was
specifically for the White Drawing Room, where it was first recorded,
but it was important enough later to be moved to the new State Bedchamber. From the late 1660s Elizabeth began to acquire further
carved, baroque furniture. She added a fireback to the White Drawing
Room, with a central shell and dolphins, and her set of Parisian
'Dolphin' chairs, six with arms and six without, may have arrived
before or after a visit she made to Paris in 1670. They were originally
gilded, silvered and painted in marine colours to suggest dolphins in
their natural element. This was the period when the Court of King
Louis XIV was not yet established at Versailles, and large chairs were
still a relatively rare commodity, stools and cushions still being much in
use.

In January 1669 Sir Lionel died. He and Elizabeth had remained
apparently happily married, although as an invalid he had spent much
time abroad. He clearly trusted Elizabeth's judgement: in a charming
letter to his eldest son, Sir Lionel begged him not to marry without his
mother's consent. He also made Elizabeth his executor and stipulated
that the two other executors were to make no decisions without her

agreement.[14] At 42, his widow was generally considered too old for remarriage. However, Elizabeth Dysart was lively and alluring. Not long afterwards, the Earl of Lauderdale wrote to a friend that he had been down to Ham 'to comfort the widow'. He stayed there for part of the summer, while visiting Epsom Wells for his kidney stone. Rumours, never substantiated, even suggested that this affair may have started while Sir Lionel was still alive. John Maitland, 2nd Earl of Lauderdale, was the unattractive but assertive Secretary of State and High Commissioner for Scotland. Like Elizabeth, he had a mane of flaming red hair. As a Scotsman, it was not surprising that he had known the Murrays and their daughter in the 1640s. He had gone into the Civil War as a Scottish Commissioner, but by the end was a Royalist, and was imprisoned during the Battle of Worcester at the time of the uncrowned young King Charles's escape. Lauderdale had eventually joined Charles II in Holland, returning with him at the Restoration and becoming a member of the Cabal, the King's close circle of political advisors, the name created from their initials. With all his worries over wars with the Dutch and his dependence on Louis XIV, the King looked less to the north, so that Lauderdale was given a virtually free hand to govern Scotland. At this time he was still married, but, like Sir Lionel, his wife was an invalid: a year later she took herself off to Paris, partly perhaps because of gossip about him and the Countess, leaving him virtually free.

Suddenly in 1670 Lauderdale's Scottish residences began to go through a metamorphosis, very possibly at the encouragement of Elizabeth Dysart. For his architectural adviser, Lauderdale turned to Sir William Bruce of Balcaskie, a cousin on Elizabeth's mother's side. Work began at Thirlestane Castle, his seat in Berwickshire, with the addition of two pavilions to the west, setting off a grander approach. On the ground floor, family living rooms were created, with a handsome stairway leading to refurbished state apartments on the first. Throughout the following few years Lauderdale was very involved in the details of this work, purchasing marble chimneypieces and deciding on plasterwork. From April to June 1671 he wrote letters from Ham, showing that he was now an established regular visitor to Elizabeth's home. His decision to add a further pair of pavilions, to the east, at Thirlestane was evidently stimulated by her: these were eventually linked to provide a pair of matching apartments. At this time Lauderdale managed to get Bruce appointed as Surveyor-General of the Royal Works in Scotland with the specific task of rebuilding Holy-roodhouse: there the Earl set himself up in great splendour.

In December 1671 the Countess of Lauderdale died. Seven weeks later, in February 1672, Elizabeth Dysart and John Maitland, Earl of Lauderdale were married; later that year he was created Duke of Lauderdale. The couple travelled to Scotland to visit the estates, taking with them Elizabeth's daughters Catherine and Elizabeth. William Bruce now provided Lauderdale with drawings for improvements to Brunstane Castle, on the edge of Edinburgh: as at Thirlestane, the aim was again to give an axial arrangement to a medieval, asymmetrical building. Work was completed in two years, followed by the laying out of the gardens. At Thirlestane Elizabeth herself made proposals for the setting out of the gardens to the south. In 1676–7[15] a wing was added at Lethington, later called Lennoxlove, near to Haddington, the best appointed of Lauderdale's three castles.

The Duke and Duchess each fuelled the other's habit of spending and building. For Elizabeth there was no more mere adaptation of furniture. In the words of Burnet: 'they lived at a vast rate, but she set everything to sale to raise money, carrying herself with a haughtiness that would have been shocking in a queen.' In 1671 she was in correspondence with Bruce about a new gateway to the north forecourt at Ham. The same year Lauderdale managed to acquire both the Manorial Rights of Ham and Petersham and the freehold of the remaining land at Ham.[16] From 1672 the Duke and Duchess made considerable building changes to the house, transforming it into a centrally arranged scheme with an emphasis on the southern side. Ambitiously, they built a whole infill section between the projecting wings on the south front, losing the little corner turret blocks and creating apartments both on the ground and first floors. They also made the further addition of small closets tacked on to the corners. The three-storey projections on the crossings were retained, mirroring those on the north front and elegantly breaking up the line of the façade and of the roof. (In the eighteenth century these window bays were rebuilt, and the top-storey bays were later flattened.) The new façade was raised very rapidly, with the walls completed by January 1673. While the alterations continued to work well internally, from the outside Ham became almost like two houses, with the rigorously symmetrical southern façade clamped to the more intriguing Jacobean northern one. The house now revolved round a central axis, so that on walking through the Great Hall to be greeted in the new Marble Dining Room (whose gateleg dining tables would have been folded up when not in use), the visitor either turned left to the apartments of the Duchess, or right to those of the Duke.

The arrangement of entering through a vestibule and saloon to paired apartments had become the fashion in French houses only since the construction of Vaux-le-Vicomte, near Paris, in the late 1650s. It was based on the traditional French courtly arrangement by which the visitor went through an antechamber to a chamber and then entered a private cabinet. As at Vaux, the Duchess's own little private cabinets were on the far corner of the house. Indeed, the chubby putti on the stands in the Green Closet may reflect those on a table from Vaux, dating from about 1660.[17] The arrangement of paired apartments on the ground floor also echoed that being created at Thirlestane; another new feature was marble chimneypieces, sent from Scotland. From the central Marble Dining Room, the visitor could walk out onto the terrace, newly laid with Portland stone.

The gentleman-architect in charge of the renovations at Ham was William Samwell; Elizabeth also consulted her cousin Sir William Bruce. In its new form Ham was completed in the winter of 1674–5, with the interiors fitted out by 1677. The particular aim of this scheme was to provide an apartment such that Queen Catherine could come to stay. It was envisaged that the Queen would sweep through the Great Hall and up the stairs, now slightly remodelled and redecorated, across the Great Dining Room into the North Drawing Room, and through a far door to the Antechamber that led to her own apartment.

Ham presents a remarkable example of the crucial importance of hangings and textiles in interiors at this time, and it requires some imagination to work out how dazzling and expensive they would have been. In Elizabeth's day the upstairs rooms alone were said to contain 148 tassels. Happily, the hangings survive in the Queen's Antechamber, which is still 'hunge with foure pieces of blewe Damusk, impaned and bordered wth. Blew velvet embroidered wth. Gould and fringed'. The blue damask has now faded to brown. The window curtains were 'white Indian Damusk fringed wth. Silke', hung from gilt curtain rods. Only in a very few refurbished houses are copies of such textiles ever as exotic as the originals, so that the full effect is no longer given.[18] This room had an earlier scheme at the time of the preparation for Queen Catherine's anticipated visit in 1673, when it was called the Green Drawing Room: Elizabeth may simply have felt that she had got the Antechamber wrong. The mixed silk and velvet hangings are certainly luxurious, and presumably an improvement on the previous ones: they would also have coordinated better with the blue scheme created in the Queen's Bedchamber. The hangings in the Queen's Closet beyond also show that Elizabeth loved this kind of 'impaned' look, with different fabrics combined together. In 1673 she ordered a set of twenty-four 'Cane bottome back stools'; these were lacquer chairs of which twelve were recorded in the Antechamber in 1679. They are English, of beechwood japanned in imitation of Japanese lacquer, with the initials ED in the back beneath a duchess's strawberry-leaf coronet. This indicates that even after she became a duchess, Elizabeth sometimes retained her title as a countess in her own right, perhaps when the item in question pertained especially to her family home at Ham.

In the exact centre of the south front, the Queen's Bedchamber was known by this same name in 1673, suggesting that a visit from Her Majesty was imminent. In her honour, gilded crowns top the overmantel and the piers. A gilded bed 'made in Portugall', either to honour Catherine of Braganza, or as a gift from her, was set on a dais behind a balustrade, in the manner fashionable in France. The elaborate parquetry floor of cedar inlaid with walnut from the dais survives, now set at a lower level, as does the plasterwork ceiling with the great oval of leaves that is so typical of the period. The room had two sets of furniture, each with its accompanying wall hangings, bed hangings and covers for seat furniture, one set for summer and one for winter. One set of bed hangings was blue and gold, lined with sky-blue satin.[19] Beyond the Bedchamber, the Queen's Closet, her tiny private cabinet, still retains almost all its original décor. Inset over the door and the fireplace are views by Thomas Wyck of various seaports, including Naples, at the time one of the most beautiful cities in Europe: all these were in place by 1677. In the ceiling a painting by Verrio depicts Ganymede and the Eagle. The room is elaborately carved, with another parquet floor featuring the ducal Lauderdale cipher and coronet. These details are repeated on the scagliola chimneypiece and windowsill, which are both by the Roman craftsman Baldassare

Artima. The marbling on the walls has been restored and the original window curtain of 'white Indian Damask' copied. The winter hangings are original: they are of 'Crimson and gould stuff bordered wth. Green, gould and silver stuff'. Another inventory description shows them as 'crimsosn & gould satten impaned and bordered with Cloath of Tissue green & gold, with a gold fringe'.[20] The juxtaposition of red and green, of gold and possibly silver produced a rich and warm effect. These hangings were originally protected by case curtains in crimson, which also hung from gilt rods. Two fine gilded chairs of state had adjustable backs for comfort.

Although it feels as if the Queen's cabinet is, like the Duchess's, on the corner of the house and so the finale in a procession of rooms, there are in fact others beyond: one closet for a lady's maid, then another pertaining to Lady Maynard's room on the corner.[21] The alterations at Ham were very well organised, with little corridors and staircases running behind the larger rooms, for use by the servants: Elizabeth had not stinted in the preparations for her Queen. It is possible though that Catherine of Braganza never came: she is only known for certain to have visited Ham once, in 1671, before Elizabeth's great alterations.[22]

The Great Hall was marbled in white at this time, making it very showy and much lighter. This effect was quite rare, possibly suggested to Elizabeth by some of the light interiors she had seen in Paris: it was also much used in the Duke and Duchess's apartments. Three inventories, dating from 1677, 1679 and 1683 and set in a leather-bound book, give indications of how the house was used.[23] The Hall itself, despite its grand new aspect, always had a family feel, with a billiard table in position, and an 'oyster' table for the provision of refreshments. This piece of furniture is circular, with a central hole with a basket for either uneaten oysters or their shells. Beyond the Hall, in the centre of the ground floor, the newly named Marble Dining Room was really a Saloon, in the latest French manner, so that the visitor walked through the Great Hall as the main vestibule, to arrive on the garden front in the centre of the suite. The black and white marble floor was laid in 1672. The walls had ornate gilt leather hangings (a section survives in the Museum Room), which were suitable for a dining room as, unlike tapestries, they did not absorb cooking smells. Many of the mouldings were enriched with carving, in typical Restoration style with leaves round the door cases and swags of fruit and foliage flanking the over-mantel painting. The room had two and later three oval cedar tables. Engravings of early layouts often show dishes arranged in concentric manner, for which these tables would be suitable, but this was still the family rather than the formal dining room. Two Dutch cedar side-boards with white marble slabs are still in the niches for which they were designed. There were silk lined leather covers to protect the tables and sideboards and to provide decoration for certain occasions.

Elizabeth was extraordinarily indecisive about where on this floor to locate her own bedchamber. At first the large chamber in the centre of the left-hand apartment (from the Hall), just beyond the new infill, continued to be her room. It had already been magnificently furnished, with curtains, and bed hangings all in matching crimson damask bor-dered with heavy fringe and gold drops. But a change was due. The room had the two added closets beyond and was now no longer on the corner of the house. In 1672 a new black and yellow veined chimney-piece was installed. The pine panelling was 'white & veined 4 times', and new sash windows were fitted, as well as shutters and silk sun blinds that slotted in to the frame at need. Overdoor paintings of birds dated 1673 were inserted, relating to the elaborate tall rectangular bird cages which were at the time constructed outside, on the wall of the house, to flank the bay window: a pair was also built next to the same chamber in the corresponding set of rooms. From the inventories it is possible to deduce that this room had three different schemes in the next ten years.[24] For Elizabeth, the walls were hung with yellow silk, to complement the yellow hangings on the bed: the room was referred to either as 'my Lady's Chamber' or as the Yellow Bedchamber. Ten chairs, four with arms, were upholstered to match, in yellow fringed damask, with additional yellow silk case covers. Beyond, the White Closet was her private cabinet, with painted marbling and hangings of 'white tabby with silver fring'. Two years later the colour was changed for grey. To the left of that closet, the Duchess had another, even more private, where she kept a number of precious personal possessions. Two bookcases were japanned, as well as a box for 'sweetmeats and tea'. Much of the furniture was lacquered, a style which she continued to enjoy: a little portable reading stand is set with mother of pearl and crowned with her cypher.

Despite these luxurious alterations, once the old nursery on the garden front in the matching apartment had been remodelled with an alcove for the bed, Elizabeth decided instead to take that for her chamber. The overdoors had already been fitted with seascapes, all dated 1673, for the purpose of the Duke's occupation, but by 1677 the couple had exchanged bedrooms. This was probably because the little turret room for the Duchess's gentlewoman had been lost in the remodelling on the south front, whereas in the Duke's apartment a room could be tucked behind the bedchamber, to the west. Elizabeth also particularly wanted to have a bathroom, and this could only be contrived close to the kitchen, in the basement at the west end, where it can still be seen. She retained her two newly decorated closets on the east end of the house, where she was accustomed to spend her time, and her husband retained his closet to the west. Her casual switching of rooms within the apartment rather nicely suggests that she and her husband were happy to wander in and out of each other's rooms, without too great a level of formality. This was, after all, not an arranged marriage, but one made by both parties out of mutual inclination in their maturity. It says a great deal about Lauderdale, that he swapped rooms at his wife's request, and did not complain that she had to pass through his dressing room to get to her bedchamber.

The Duke's new room was now amended by the addition of green and white damask hangings with a gold, scarlet, black and silver fringe, with further matching case covers for the chairs. The green was used with some of the existing yellow hangings. Elizabeth seems to have raised the standard of the actual chairs for her husband, moving out her own set of combined armchairs and 'backstools' (chairs without arms) covered in yellow, in favour of ten handsome new black and gold armchairs. These had case covers to match the green and white hangings. In 1683, after the Duke's death, a third scheme was to replace the green. The yellow hangings were either adapted to, or substituted by, yellow 'impaned' with blue,[25] with the ten black and gold chairs again upholstered to match.

Elizabeth continued to acquire furniture of a high standard. This included, in about 1675, an ebony cabinet inlaid with floral marquetry featuring little ivory flowers and leaves, the latter stained green. Dutch or Franco-Flemish marquetry cabinets, part of the new, baroque, nonportable furniture known in France as 'immobilier', were the fashion: some were made in England by the King's furniture maker Gerrit

Jensen. Elizabeth also had a cabinet in plainer kingwood. Two walnut side tables were likewise inlaid with coloured floral marquetry; with their barley sugar legs these are very similar to one that was owned as part of a set by Louise de Keroualle, Duchess of Portsmouth. Louise knew Elizabeth Dysart at Whitehall, where the Lauderdales also had rooms.

The Duke and Duchess also made considerable improvements in the gardens. It is not certain how much William Murray had done here, but a plan of 1671–2 attributed to John Slezer and Jan Wyck suggests eight grass plats below the house, with a wilderness beyond, a long orchard to the east and a long vegetable garden to the west, with an orangery at its northern end. This arrangement is confirmed in a bird's eye view in the 1739 edition of *Vitruvicus Britannicus*. There was also an important formal section of the garden at the east end of the house. In 1678 John Evelyn admired Elizabeth's improvements at Ham:

> 'After dinner I walked to Ham to see the House and Garden of the Duke of Laderdaile, which is indeede inferior to few of the best Villas in Italy itselfe; The House furnishd like a greate Princes; The Parterrs, flo:(wer) Gardens, Orangeries, Groves, Avenues, Courts, Statues, Perspectives, fountaines, Aviaries, and all this at the banks of the Sweetest River in the World, must needs be surprising.'[26]

In commenting that the house was 'furnishd like a great Prince's', Evelyn reflected the fact that by 1680 the Duke and Duchess were at the centre of society. However, the following year the Duke had a stroke and resigned from politics. He died in 1682, leaving what he could of his Scottish properties and all his movables to Elizabeth. This was challenged by his brother, who felt these should descend to Maitland rather than Tollemache heirs: Elizabeth responded by embarking on a long legal battle. She still also had the building bit between her teeth, and continued to spend money and make alterations at Ham until her death. The Duke's bedchamber, that had once been her own, was from 1679 named the Volury, after *volière*, the French for aviary; after the bed was taken out, this room, with its blue and yellow hangings in situ by 1683, was effectively a Bird Room. In about 1690 she altered the Great Dining Room, piercing the ceiling to create a great gallery and the resulting two-storeyed Great Hall. As a result of her extravagance, she began to have considerable financial problems: her daughter, Elizabeth, by then the Duchess of Argyll, told her that she had 'too many chamber lords', the rather senior gentlemen members of the household who oversaw the public apartments for visitors. Eventually she secured a mortgage of £7000 from Lord North.

In his long comment on Elizabeth, Bishop Burnet was often unfair: in view of his wife's affair with Lauderdale he was undoubtedly a biased critic with a grudge. However, some of what he says rings true. The following continues immediately from the earlier, more flattering piece quoted:

> 'She was violent in everything she set about, a violent friend, but a much more violent enemy. She had a restless ambition, lived at a vast expense, and was ravenously covetous; and would have stuck at nothing by which she might compass her ends.'

After his unsubstantiated account of her morals, Burnet went on to suggest Elizabeth's level of control: 'All applications were made to her: she took upon her to determine everything.' Perhaps there was nothing wrong with that: it was what her first husband had wanted. However, she does seem to have become sadly money-minded in advancing age: 'She sold all places, and was wanting in no methods that could bring her money, which she lavished out in a most profuse vanity.' She was certainly a very astute businesswoman, protecting her estate and her family, and her extravagance was nothing unusual at the Court of Charles II. Finally, an unkind cut which may or may not be true: 'As the conceit took her, she made him (Lauderdale) fall out with all his friends, one after another.'

Like many other matriarchs, Elizabeth secured considerable properties for her family. Initially her son, as Lord Huntingtower, inherited Lethington from Lauderdale; later, her daughter Betty (Elizabeth), whose marriage was in difficulties, lived in this property. At her death in 1698 Elizabeth's son, now the Earl of Dysart, inherited Ham. By the time Elizabeth died, she had not left her beloved home for eight years, living on the ground floor because of her crippling gout. Her two younger sons had predeceased her, leaving just her heir and her two daughters in Scotland: Catherine had married the Earl of Moray.

Soon afterwards the house was praised by the Hon. Roger North:

'This house is, in its time, esteemed one of the most beautifull and compleat seats in the kingdome. And all ariseth out of the skill and dexterity in managing the alterations, which in my opinion are the best I have seen. For I doe not perceiv any part of the old fabrick is taken downe, but the wings stand as they were first sett, onely behind, next the garden, they are joyned with a strait rang entirely new. And there are all the rooms of parade, exquistely plact...So the visto is compleat from end to end, with a noble roome of entry in the midle, which is used as a dining room.'[27]

In the twenty-first century, a visit to Ham provides an unexpected oasis of rural tranquillity close to London. Ideally one should arrive through the still surviving royal Richmond Park, enclosed and complete with deer, then skirt the attractive village green, turning right down the pretty Ham Lane on the west side of the estate to arrive beside the river. With gardens obscuring the later grand houses of the Orléans family and of Marble Hill to the north over the water, and a walk back through the park to Ham House, the visitor is already in an idyll. As well as the house at Ham, there are the attractive formal gardens and the very private walled enclosure in which to pass a perfect summer's afternoon.

Chapter 7

THE POLITICAL HOSTESS
CAROLINE LENNOX,
BARONESS HOLLAND
1723–74

On 2 May 1744 Lady Caroline Lennox slipped quietly out of her family home at Richmond House on the banks of the Thames at Whitehall, to elope with the politician Henry Fox. The marriage took place in secret, at the home in Conduit Street of their friend Charles Hanbury Williams. Immediately afterwards Caroline returned to her own home, staying there for five days before telling her parents, the 2nd Duke and Duchess of Richmond. Having previously dismissed Fox's suit on more than one occasion, the Duke and his wife were horrified. Caroline was banished from the house, and a ball proposed for the next evening, at which Frederick, Prince of Wales was to have been the guest of honour, was cancelled. The Duke and Duchess fled to their country retreat at Goodwood, near the Sussex coast, where they received many letters of condolence. Caroline had caused agony to her parents, shame to her family and loneliness to her twelve-year-old sister Emily, who was not allowed to contact her. As the marriage witnesses, the Duke of Marlborough and Charles Hanbury Williams were both temporarily cold-shouldered by London society. Hanbury Williams wrote to Fox: 'The Rage of His and Her Graces is very high and I hear intend making a point that nobody that visits them should visit you.'[1]

It was not surprising that Charles, Duke of Richmond, had banned Fox's proposal. Horace Walpole wrote that: 'His father was a footman; her great-grandfather was a King.'[2] Although he was the younger son of the self-made Sir Stephen Fox, and had often stayed at Goodwood, at thirty-nine Henry Fox was only four years younger than the Duke himself. Swarthy and a womaniser, he had neither fortune nor family seat, and was something of a rough diamond. He had become MP for Hendon in 1735, upgrading his constituency six years later when he became Member for the more fashionable town of Windsor. Caroline Lennox, nearly twenty years younger than her husband, was a nervy, anxious young woman. Her childhood had been warmed by tender and loving parents but clouded by her mother's many miscarriages and by several tragic sibling deaths. It was not until 1735 that a son and heir was born, twelve years after Caroline's own birth. Caroline was well educated by governesses at home and was a serious reader. She especially loved Roman history,[3] and when she finally visited Rome in her forties proclaimed it 'the heart of the Empire, muse of heroes and delight of gods'.[4] She had always been intrigued by Voltaire's *Candide*, and it was on the same trip that she visited him at Ferney in Switzerland.[5] It was largely for intellectual companionship that she had turned to Henry Fox, a choice which she never doubted. Despite Caroline's disillusionment on discovering that, like most eighteenth-century gentlemen, her husband for a time kept a mistress, it was to be a very happy marriage, lasting thirty years.

As a partisan of Sir Robert Walpole, Fox had been appointed Surveyor General to the Board of Works and Commissioner of the Treasury, but his break came after his marriage to Lady Caroline, when, in 1746, he became Secretary at War. Little could now stop Henry Fox's political advancement. In the next few years the Duke, first to his horror and ultimately to his pleasure, saw his son-in-law become a political star. It became very difficult for the family to continue ignoring the couple. When Emily married the Earl of Kildare in 1747 and was thus freed of parental constraint, the very next day she rushed to visit her beloved sister. The following year, with the birth of a son to Caroline and Henry, the Duke and Duchess capitulated, sending a letter via an intermediary to say: '...the conflict between reason and nature is over, and the tenderness of parents has got the better, and your Dear Mother and I have determin'd to see and forgive both you and Mr Fox...We long to see your dear innocent Child, and that has not a little contributed to our present tenderness for you.'[6] To celebrate the reconciliation, Fox gave the Duchess a beautiful little Meissen snuff-box with a portrait of Lady Caroline in the lid.[7] Christmas 1749 was spent at Goodwood as a united family.[8]

Mr Henry and Lady Caroline Fox at first rented the Conduit Street lodgings of Charles Hanbury Williams, but with his new post Henry needed a much grander house. Although Caroline was rather reclusive, Henry was by nature very sociable. In 1746 he acquired the lease to Holland House, an imposing but unfashionable and antiquated property in the western reaches of Kensington, still at this time a village abutting London. The house was completely different from the mansions of other politicians, such as Sir Robert Walpole's new and superbly classicising Houghton Hall in Norfolk. It was also nothing like Caroline's fine Palladian London family home at Richmond House, newly built to the designs of Lord Burlington. Holland House was 150 years old and was in a 64-acre unenclosed park, bounded to the south and east by the gardens of Kensington Palace. To the west the land was open, with artisans' cottages.[9] The red-brick, romantically turreted house had been built by John Thorpe in 1607 for Sir Walter Cope, whom it was said to have bankrupted.[10] In 1624 two wings were added to the south front of Cope Castle, as it was then known, with a classical arcade running round the inner walls of the central block. The work was done by Cope's ambitious son-in-law, Sir Henry Rich, the younger brother of the Earl of Warwick. He was later created Earl of Holland. The Great Chamber, above the main Hall, was decorated by Franz Cleyn, the architect-designer to Charles I: it became known as the Gilt Room.[11] The house was then lived in by the 2nd Earl of Holland, who also inherited the title of 5th Earl of Warwick. He liked Holland House enough to keep it as his family seat. It later passed to a cousin, William Edwardes, Lord Kensington, who leased it to Fox. Possibly Caroline liked it because it had a slight resemblance to her country home at Goodwood, which at the time still retained its Jacobean gables. At Holland House she exclaimed: 'I love these old-fashioned, comfortable houses.'[12] What she was to achieve was not a complete rebranding, but rather the conversion and enhancement of an ancient house that had a story all of its own.

The history of Holland House was extraordinary, both before and after the time when Henry and Caroline lived there. James I had visited it, and was met there by his children Henry, Prince of Wales and Princess Elizabeth, the future Winter Queen, ancestress of the Hanoverian dynasty. The King found the house very cold: he grew 'quickly weary' of 'Kennington', because, he said, 'the wind blew through the walls that he could not be warm in his bed'.[13] In the Civil

War the Parliamentarian General Fairfax adopted it as his headquarters. William III visited in 1689 with a view to making it his palace, and stayed there with Queen Mary while work was instead carried out at nearby Kensington Palace. The famous writer Joseph Addison lived there after his marriage to the widowed Countess of Warwick. He died in the house in 1719.

At the time of its acquisition by the Foxes, Holland House had been converted into apartments and rented out.[14] These had become unfashionable as an arrangement, and owing to lack of use the building had decayed. However, the layout worked well for Henry and Caroline as it meant that various members of the family could each have their own single-level suite of rooms. Among other friends, Henry gladly let Charles Hanbury Williams have rooms there: his elder brother, Stephen Fox, later Lord Ilchester, was also resident during visits to town from his own home, first from Redlynch in Somerset and later from Melbury in Dorset.[15] The family mostly used the ground floor,[16] with Henry's sitting room to the west, giving easy access to the garden. Early on they started to use the library as a sitting room. Caroline's sister Emily, Countess of Kildare wrote to her husband in 1755: 'I have now got into the library, which is a mighty pleasant room, and you will find it is a great improvement to Holland House to have a room in common so.'[17] The library had three non-matching writing tables, together with a set of six Pembroke armchairs. These, like most of the sets of chairs in the house, had a set of case covers, designed to fit in with the decorative scheme, which preserved the chairs both when the owners were away or when the room was just used for family and close friends. There were tables and stools and seven 'antique shap'd' ornaments, probably urns. Books included the fairly conventional classical, historical and political works that interested Fox, but there were also many historical works in French, representing Caroline's choice. Caroline created a traditional library arrangement, and was interested as much in comfort as in formality, with a crimson festoon curtain,[18] and a splendid Turkey carpet adorning the floor.

In some of the finer rooms the décor was kept intact, notably the main entrance hall[19] and stairs. Above the hall, the great Gilt Room on the first floor had been untouched since it was decorated for a fête in honour of Charles I and Henrietta Maria, its walls being lined with panels painted alternately with the fleur-de-lis and the Rich crosslet, with matching pedestals.[20] Caroline obviously had a considerable problem in the simple upkeep of the house: the gallery at the west end of the house on the first floor had no floor when the family moved in, and at one point a painted ceiling in the Gilt Room fell down and was whitewashed over. Here she created hangings to suit the gilded scheme, with three large white festoon curtains 'fringed compleat'.[21] Six chairs had their seats stuffed with canvas: their alternative case covers were calico, but again fringed to suit the scheme. Ten stools with needlework seats also had plain canvas fringed case covers. The sophisticated classical painted oak panelling in the White Parlour on the north side of the ground floor was retained. This included some small decorative motifs like tabernacles or classical doorways. Bulbous carved pilasters abutted the chimneypiece, and a quantity of strapwork suggested that this was an original Jacobean scheme.[22] The large adjacent room at the centre of the house also kept its original features, including two chimneypieces, and was used as the dining room.[23] King James I's comment about the cold was echoed by Emily, in 1761: 'I can't venture to go to stay at Holland House yet a while. I shou'd be killed there, I know, for I cou'd not (even for my first visit which I thought a little unkind) get them to keep the doors and windows shut. I really found it very cold, but I saw it was thought affectation and fancy.'[24] Characteristically, Caroline and Henry continued to leave doors and windows open with impunity.

For herself Caroline created one light, sunny, cosy corner, which is probably what made the house habitable. Like many London ladies, one of Caroline's priorities was her dressing room, where she could entertain friends privately and show off some of her personal collection of china. As early as 1755 Emily wrote to her husband from Holland House about the newly fashionable habit of drinking tea: 'There is company to dine here almost every day, and I am now got into the dressing room and drink tea with them every day.'[25] Later Caroline described the room enthusiastically: 'My London dressing room is thought pretty; with Horner's paper and the carving, of which there is a good deal, painted two greens and varnished.'[26] From this room she made extensions, in the form of an aviary and a conservatory, along the balcony above the arcade on the south front.[27] The whole must have been a delightfully whimsical and feminine ensemble, with rural overtones. Whereas in Paris carved rococo decoration was often accompanied by painted walls depicting birds, flowers and unnaturally pretty farmyards, here at Holland House the rustic idyll was for real. On sunny days this part of the house was a delightful contrast to the rest of the dark, chilly building, preferable not least because of the intimate scale of the dressing room itself. There was also a White Damask Dressing Room on the first floor, in which the hangings had gilt borders. The Print Room had decorations in yellow, with a yellow check window curtain as well as a printed cotton one, and a set each of yellow check and printed cotton chair cases. Possibly the schemes were for winter and summer. In 1760 the chapel on the ground floor of the house was restored: 'The Chapel will be lovely, it's really done with great taste, not gothick, as we found a pretty ceiling of Inigo Jones ready in it, which is in Italian architecture. The apartment above will be for Charles when he is at home, and when he is not, a very pretty warm convenient one for anybody.'[28]

Describing her own taste in decoration, in 1764 Caroline told Emily that she was 'out of conceit with Indian paper', as oriental or Chinese wallpaper was often called; her comment suggests that she was simply rather tired of the fashion for it. She was 'all for the magnificent style – velvet, damask etc. I have three immense looking glasses to put in my drawing room, and propose hanging it with a damask or brocatelle of two or three colours.'[29] She felt that one should always return to the classic: '...tho' whims and fripperies may have a run, one always returns to what is really handsome and noble and plain.'[30] This was for the Great Drawing Room, opposite the Gilt Room at the centre of the house on the first floor.[31] However, she admitted that she could be changeable in matters of taste, and in 1768 indeed created a scheme in a lighter mode. She wrote to Emily: '...you have no idea what a beautiful blue and white Indian paper I have just put up in the *salon* here.'[32] The hangings included two large cotton festoon curtains in blue copper plate with fringes, two white cotton festoon curtains and two printed cotton window curtains, together with a large Saxon blue window curtain and two matching door curtains. A set of six mahogany French armchairs had two sets of blue copper plate cases, as did three sofas and a bergère. The room also contained a large Turkey carpet and a pair of 'large remarkable rich coloured jars and covers' from Japan, presumably Imari. There was also a fine eight-leaved oriental screen.[33] The scheme sounds surprisingly naturalistic and simple in comparison with her earlier views, showing indeed how quickly her taste could change: the printed cotton curtains may again have been for summer use, as was the custom at the French Court. The furniture that she bought was of high quality, much of it from Paris, including a commode and two 'quoins' purchased for this room in 1764.[34] The commode was 'composed of rosewood, and ornamented with ormoulu' and the two 'coigns' were 'neatly inlaid, and embellished with ormoulu'. Elsewhere, she also had a silver japanned cabinet.[35] After Caroline's death, Walpole, who had evidently admired her collecting, wrote in 1775 that 'the sale at Holland House will produce treasures'.[36]

Caroline loved china, especially Sèvres, from whose factory some of the items mentioned in a letter to Emily in 1759 are likely to have been acquired: 'I hope Lord Kildare has made a good report of my blue gallery and my dressing room fitted up with a great deal of pea-green china and painted pea-green. I have been extravagant enough to buy a good deal of china lately, but I am in tolerable circumstances...'[37] Her collecting continued through winters spent in Paris. There were five 'fish-shaped' Sèvres vases in 'sea-green', decorated with ormolu and beautifully painted, as well as four gold-spangled cups festooned with golden flowers. Other Sèvres items included some superb basins in mazarine blue, five ultramarine vases[38] and a dessert service, painted in flowers with gilt edges. This comprised bowls, dishes, large and small tureens, pails for ice cream, monteiths or wine glass holders, and six dozen plates.[39] In France dessert services were always used for the stated purpose, that of a sweetmeat course, mainly comprising fruits, but the English sometimes bought them to use as dinner services, which seems to be the case with Caroline's larger Tournai service in blue, described as for 'dessert and table'. This comprised twenty-one round dishes, nine oval dishes, three oval tureens, forty-five table plates, sauce boats and tureens, nineteen compotiers or open dishes for fruit, ice pails, a butter box, a stand for pepper and salt, and even 'covers' or cutlery in this china.[40] As well as items from Chantilly and two Japanese dessert services,[41] Caroline also had a Dresden and Chelsea dessert service, with leaf- and shell-shaped dishes,[42] and Dresden tea and coffee services, beautifully painted with figures. Despite the conservatism of her tastes, her collecting eventually extended to the quite different and newly fashionable neoclassical style, with three very smart large 'mazarine china bottles', two of which were blue and one pea-green, with chains on the handles and stoppers in the tops.[43] The later letter to Emily from her sister Sarah about decorating intimated that the display of small pictures and china on Caroline's dressing room mantelpiece had included some Wedgwood.[44]

Life at Holland House was less formal than in some other great houses. Visitors enjoyed the spaciousness of country life so near to town. They also found it a good place to discuss politics with Henry Fox. Caroline often complained that his political associates arrived too regularly: 'Indeed when he is in business this place is quite like a coffee house.'[45] In 1762 she wrote to Emily: 'June is the month of the whole year to enjoy Holland House, which is more beautiful than ever this year, and I should rejoice at returning to it, could I enjoy any peace or quiet in the first part of the summer.'[46] Her preferred routine was to go to bed at 10 p.m., rise at 6 a.m., receive 'morning' visits, often unfortunately in her view as late as 2 p.m., and dine as near to 2 p.m. as she could.[47] When the following year the couple acquired a town house in Piccadilly, 'a delightful house...with a court before it and a fine long garden behind...',[48] Caroline still drove in her carriage to Holland House most mornings. Her ideal was to be at this semi-rural retreat, but without company: 'Health, spirits, solitude, and regularity, are things I enjoy...the two first very much owing to the two last, which are not in my power to enjoy long together at Holland House; a sweet place to be sure, with pretty loitering and sauntering about, great pleasure in my plants and flowers, but even that I can seldom enjoy for a whole morning without interruption.'[49] From 1745, Caroline bore four children: Stephen (who was always called Ste); Henry Charles, who died as an infant, while she was away at Bath; Charles James, who became the famous Whig politician; and Henry Edward.[50] Visitors enjoyed seeing Henry Fox at Holland House amongst his family. Caroline, though, became quite jealous: 'Holland House is so convenient for his intimate friends to be constantly with him, that they take up all the time I could see him alone, and plague me ten times more than people who have real business with him.'[51]

In the spring of 1747 Horace Walpole attended the housewarming party at Holland House; he gives an account of how Fox had taken a lease for the long term and was making 'great improvements'.[52] The party was described by the *Daily Advertiser*: 'Last Friday night a most splendid and magnificent ball, with a grand supper, was given at Holland House...by Henry Fox...to the Earl and Countess of Kildare, and to above three score other persons of quality and distinction.' Entertainment at Holland House tended to consist of dinners, at which the unruly Fox children generally misbehaved before the adoring audience of their parents and the couple's political friends. Larger parties were somewhat exclusive, and not at all on the vast scale of those given by some contemporaries: guests again consisted of the extended family, political allies and close friends. The guest list for a ball on 1 May 1753 featured many Lennox cousins, including Mr George Brudenell; Lady Anne and Lady Caroline Keppel; Commodore Keppel; and Caroline's Aunt Ann, Countess of Albemarle. Friends included the Duke of Marlborough, on whose son and heir Caroline later had her eye for her sister Sarah; the Duke of Bedford; and the Countess of Pembroke, with whose family there was also a connection.[53] Walpole did not think it was especially glamorous: '...the dresses were not very fine, not much invention, nor any very absurd.'[54]

In 1762, after some wheeler-dealing by her husband, Caroline was elevated to the peerage in her own right. Taking her new title from the house that she loved, she became the Baroness Holland. Henry was created Baron Holland the following year. Among further changes to the house, from about 1760 the couple transformed the long first-floor chamber into a picture gallery, for portraits of members of both their families. This was to be Caroline's great project, and one for which she was supremely well suited. The chamber ran for 112 feet north to south through the west wing. Caroline may have been describing a first scheme for the south end of this gallery, when she wrote to Emily in 1759 that 'I have fitted up the gallery with blue paper, gilt borders, and a few good pictures; it's very pretty; we breakfast in it...'[55]

Not unusually, the credit for this was given to Henry: 'The 1st Lord Holland fitted up this room as a picture gallery for family portraits; he blocked up the greater number of windows, and opened, in lieu of them, the large bow window on the west side, and opposite to the two doors...'[56] The resulting layout was well balanced, with the two doors leading eastwards to the rest of the house. Of these the south one led towards Caroline's own dressing room near the portico: she reported in 1764 that the two rooms together 'make a very convenient agreeable apartment *de plein pied* (which I have learn'd to like in France) when I'm here alone.'[57] The gallery, which was light and warm, contained two sets of six French armchairs, each with accompanying pairs of long stools, making sixteen stools in all. All were covered with tapestry, that on one set being pea-green. One fringed curtain was also in matching pea-green tapestry, with a 'remarkable large drapery window curtain',[58] presumably for the great new bay window, made to resemble tapestry and richly fringed. A painted floorcloth resembled an oak floor, giving a neutral effect.

Over the north door were placed Henry's arms, with Caroline's above the south entrance: these were altered after she became a baroness. The family portraits were therefore allocated to one or the other end of the room, set in their frames into the painted panelling. To the north end the portraits of the Fox family were 'inlaid with very narrow gilt cornices on a blue wainscot': the Lennox ones to the south were 'in like manner'.[59] Those of the royal ancestor of Caroline's family, King Charles II, and of his mistress Louise de Keroualle were specially 'inlaid and surrounded with small mirrors'. These were presumably the ones respectively painted after Lely and by Gascars, Louise's favourite if rather primitive French portrait painter. Louise de Keroualle was represented again, in a picture by Verelst with a pendant of her son the 1st Duke of Richmond as a child holding a parrot. The 1st Duke also reappeared with his Duchess, in portraits by Kneller that were smaller versions of the three-quarter-length ones already in the Richmond family collection.

The gallery thus provided a fascinating instance of how and why sitters commissioned more than one version of a portrait, and of how older second versions could later be passed down to different family members. Caroline naturally had portraits of her parents: that of her father was by Van Loo, painted full length in the robes of a peer.[60] She also owned the prime version of Batoni's portrait depicting her brother the 3rd Duke of Richmond.[61] Other members of the family were mostly painted by Allan Ramsay (Caroline herself, Emily, Louisa and Cecilia)[62] or Sir Joshua Reynolds (Henry, Caroline, their son Ste; Mary, Duchess of Richmond; Caroline's brother Lord George Lennox, and brother-in-law Thomas Connolly). Sometimes, as in the case of both Emily and Louisa, Caroline would request an artist's copy of a portrait that had already been painted.[63] In one single group Reynolds painted the young people, Lady Sarah, Lady Susan Fox-Strangways and Charles

James Fox, together at Holland House, as the place where their lives and dramas were currently being played out. This triple portrait was deemed important enough to hang over one of the two chimneypieces opposite the entrance doors, as was the ravishing one by Ramsay of Louisa aged fifteen.[64] Caroline, so impressed by the younger sister whom she hardly knew,[65] and who was newly arrived in London from Ireland, chose to have this one full length.[66] This arrangement of recent paintings meant that it was the up-and-coming generations who dominated the scheme, rather than the old and dead.

Caroline made a point of seeking out the best artists: Henry was painted by Hogarth, as well as by Reynolds on about five occasions. Ste was portrayed in pastel as a young boy by the very able but slightly more provincial William Hoare of Bath: Charles James and Harry were also included. Caroline's daughter-in-law, Lady Mary Fox, was painted in Rome by Batoni when the family travelled there in 1767. The gallery also included earlier portraits of Henry's parents, Sir Stephen and Lady Fox, by Sir Godfrey Kneller, and those of his brother and sister-in-law, now the Earl and Countess of Ilchester, by Francis Cotes, as well as a very pretty one by Ramsay of Lady Susan in a dress with blue bows. Typically, Caroline was not unduly consistent in her scheme of display: above all, the gallery displayed those who were near to her, and dear. Emily's husband, by now the Marquess of Kildare, was included in a fine portrait by Ramsay,[67] as was Sarah's husband Sir Charles Bunbury.

More than anything, what mattered to Caroline was family. She had been deeply upset by her parents' initial reaction to her marriage, and was further wounded when, at their deaths, in 1750 and 1751, their wills had given care of the younger children, not to her but to her sister Emily, until the time came for them to be launched on the London social scene. This had meant that the Lennox sisters, Louisa, Sarah and Cecilia all moved to Ireland. Caroline was therefore delighted when Emily's two elder boys, George, Lord Ophaly, and William, came to Eton. Describing them as 'our Etonians',[68] she looked after them through their schooldays together with her own two elder sons, Ste and Charles James, receiving them at Holland House in the holidays,[69] returning them to school, visiting them there, and nursing them all through whooping cough.[70] From Holland House she wrote to Emily: 'I am sitting in the pretty porch by the hall door in one of the niches...seeing our four dear boys play at quoits upon the green before the house.'[71]

Lady Sarah Lennox, leaning from a window at Holland House, with her cousins Lady Susan Fox-Strangways and Charles James Fox, by Sir Joshua Reynolds, 1762–64. One of the principal portraits in the Holland House Gallery.

As the younger sisters grew up the old family hurt was further assuaged when they came to stay with their aunt at Holland House, where they were often joined by Henry's niece, Lady Susan Fox-Strangways. Continuing a tradition of her own childhood, Caroline encouraged them to put on a play every winter at Holland House. One of her own performances, in *The Conquest of Mexico*, had been painted by William Hogarth. The picture, including her as a young participant and her parents in the audience, hung at Holland House, though not in the Gallery.[72] Horace Walpole attended one of the younger children's performances in 1761 and wrote: 'I was excessively amused on Tuesday night: there was a play at Holland-house, acted by children: not all children, for Lady Sarah Lennox and Lady Susan Strangways played the women. It was *Jane Shore*.'[73] Similarly Lady Susan's mother, Lady Ilchester, wrote to her husband that year: 'Fryday I was at the play at Holland House, *The Distressed Mother*. It was perform'd surprisingly well, and a very pretty sight.'[74] The next year one of the plays was *Tom Thumb*.[75]

Caroline was delighted to be able to 'bring out' the two cousins in the London season. The atmosphere was quite restrained: in 1760 Lady Susan reported that balls were few in number, and cards indispensable.[76] Because of the parties held during the season, dinner at Holland House took place at a late 4 p.m., followed by theatre or cards into the early hours.[77] During the summer season Caroline's sister Emily, who in 1766 became Duchess of Leinster, would often reside in their home in Arlington Street, while Thomas and Louisa Connolly had a house in Whitehall. Caroline's care of the girls at this stage of their lives also meant that it was she who bore the brunt of her younger sisters' problems, as well as those of Susan, to whom she was devoted. Not surprisingly, after all the exposure to the theatre given to the young people, Susan fell in love with an actor. Her marriage to William O'Brien caused great distress to her parents, but her kind and sentimentally inclined uncle and aunt Holland gave her both moral and financial support in her early married days.

The *histoire* between Lady Sarah Lennox and the young King George III has many associations with Holland House. In 1760 the King appeared to be falling in love with Sarah, having made leading comments to this effect to Lady Susan, so that the family really believed a proposal was forthcoming. Henry Fox, longing for such a grand

Louise de Keroualle, by Sir Peter Lely, c. 1671.

Goodwood House, West Sussex: cabinet given to Louise de Keroualle by King Charles II, part of a suite attributed to the English royal cabinet maker, Gerrit Jensen.

he Château de la Verrerie, Aubigny.

Ham House, Middlesex: the
Jacobean north façade of 1610.

Elizabeth Murray, Lady Tollemache,
later Countess of Dysart and Duchess
of Lauderdale, by Sir Peter Lely;
painted *c.* 1648, the year of her
marriage to Sir Lionel Tollemache.

Ham House: the modified south front.

Ham House: ebony table with silver mounts and caryatids.

Ham House: original hanging in the Queen's Antechamber.

Lady Caroline Fox, later Lady Holland, in masquerade costume, by William Hoare of Bath, *c.* 1750.

Holland House, Kensington, *c.* 1850.

Lady Louisa Lennox, by Allan Ramsay, *c.* 1759. Chimneypiece portrait in the Holland House Gallery.

Mary Blount, Duchess of Norfolk, English School, 1730s.

St James's Square, engraving, *c.* 1752.

The Music Room, Norfolk House, now in the Victoria & Albert Museum.

Ugbrooke Park, Devon: the Norfolk
House bed hangings.

Ugbrooke Park: cockatoo from the Norfolk
House bed hangings.

Mary Blount, Duchess of Norfolk, holding an
embroidery bodkin, by John Vanderbank, 1730s.

Worksop: the Gothic Farm.

Pediment for Worksop Manor, designed by Mary, Duchess of Norfolk.

Worksop Manor, Nottinghamshire, by William Hodges, 1777. The painting represents the house as it was intended to be. The north wing, shown in full, was completed, but not the return elevation on the right.

alliance, encouraged Sarah to pass time in the gardens at Holland House, looking attractively décolletée and rustic, so that the King would see her on his morning ride. From March to July of 1761 speculation was running high. However, the King's mother, the widowed Princess Augusta, heard rumours of the romance. She was far from satisfied that the daughter of a Duke whose original illegitimate descent from Charles II was at the time still in the public memory was good enough for her son. The King was whisked off to marry the far less attractive Princess Charlotte of Mecklenburg-Strelitz, and Sarah, who had never been especially enthusiastic about the idea, was left feeling stranded, at the tender age of nineteen. A cartoon, showing the King as Palemon wooing Sarah as Lavinia in the grounds of Holland House, provoked much public amusement. Embarrassed by events, Caroline was reasonably satisfied when, two years later, in the Holland House Chapel on 7 June 1762, Sarah married Sir Charles Bunbury. For the bride, however, sadness and loneliness followed: although the couple had a country home in Suffolk and a London residence in Spring Gardens, Sarah was to spend much time back at Holland House.

Caroline also had the task of looking after other homes. In 1762 she was spending two or three days a week at Holland House[78] and the rest of the time in central London, apparently lodging at the Pay Office, where Henry was Minister. From 1764 they used their newly acquired town house in Piccadilly, in order to be near to Parliament during the winter.[79] From there they would return to Holland House for several weeks at a time.[80] The couple decided that they also wanted a real country home, one where they could find more peace and quiet. Henry wanted it to be by the sea, so Kingsgate, on the island of Thanet in Kent, became their home for the summer months. It was an eccentric house, probably chosen by Henry rather than Caroline,[81] where he enjoyed developing some extraordinary garden follies: 'building old ruins and gateways I can't care about,' reported his wife.[82] In her quick, diligent way, Caroline kept a brief journal of the dates that each member of the family arrived there and left every year from 1762.[83] In 1767 Caroline was apparently planning how Kingsgate should be improved, intending it ultimately for the second of her spoilt and ungrateful sons, Charles James: '[I] have almost fix'd upon a plan for a new house, where I hope you'll spend many happy days after I am dead and gone.'[84] Winterslow, near Salisbury, was also purchased and enlarged for their eldest son, Ste, and his wife Lady Mary. As well as hunting and shooting, the tradition of performing plays continued, in a little theatre there.[85]

In 1763 Henry became ill, and over the next seven years he and Caroline spent a good deal of time abroad, wintering in Paris in 1763–4 and returning there after his retirement from politics the following year. Meanwhile, Caroline continued to be concerned for her younger sisters. To her horror, during one of the winters that she and Henry spent in Paris, Sarah took up with a lover. Yearning for affection, five years after her marriage, she had secretly been conducting an affair with Lord William Gordon. In December 1768 he became the father of her child, Louisa Bunbury. Sarah's disgrace was complete when she left Bunbury and openly kept house with Lord William. A certain amount of benign hypocrisy kept many an unfaithful marriage going, but for a well-born young woman to live openly with a man was unthinkable. Divorce, requiring an Act of Parliament, ensued. Tragedy was also to befall Caroline's youngest sister Cecilia, who came to her from Emily in Ireland, in May 1769. Caroline met Cecilia at Bristol[86] and took her to Holland House, where she spent some months. Unfortunately, she developed a dangerous cough, and Caroline became very worried about her. With a 'dreadful fit of low spirits' and aiming to go south to Nice for the sake of a drier climate, Caroline took 'poor Ly Cecilia as ill as possible'[87] via Kingsgate to Paris early in October 1769. Lord Holland wrote to a friend: 'I am not going abroad on account of my own health. But I am going because Lady Holland's good nature will not let her amiable sister, who is dying, go only with a servant.[88] Six weeks later, Cecilia died in Paris.

While Caroline was in Nice with her husband in December 1769, Sarah's affair with Lord William Gordon failed. Shipwrecked from society, she was initially taken in by the 3rd Duke of Richmond at Goodwood, but by degrees Caroline and Henry also provided her with a London base at Holland House. At first it was considered unsuitable for any lady to be in her presence: Lady Mary Coke, a near neighbour, found visiting the house very awkward, but not wanting to be unkind, stayed for cards. A regular visitor, Lady Mary tried to call in July 1772, but, she says, '...[I] saw Ly Holland with a Child in the Balcony: upon my coming She rose up in a great hurry & went out of sight, & I heard her ring the bell'. Tactfully, Lady Mary rode away, and subsequently heard that Sarah was expected to go to Kingsgate with Caroline.[89] Social acceptance was gradual, and the family very cautious. Happily the Duke of Richmond built Sarah a house on the Goodwood estate, where she spent a few quiet years before marrying the Hon. George Napier at the age of 31, moving to Ireland and giving her husband eight children.

In 1767 Lord Holland finally purchased Holland House, by which time most of the changes there had already been made. Arguably these might have been greater if the house had been his own, though living in the vast and chilly Jacobean interiors without benefit of ownership does not appear to have bothered Caroline, who loved the house regardless. The following year Lord Holland wrote to his brother Lord Ilchester: 'I pay a great deal more for Holland House than anything but Lady Holland's extreme fondness for it could make it worth.'[90] Despite her attachment to the house and its contents, it is true to say that Caroline's mind was mostly on people rather than things: she liked to study 'human behaviour'.[91] She was deeply religious, professing: 'Without religion, the life of man is a wild, fluttering, inconsistent thing without any certain scope or design.'[92] However she did not make a great display of her faith, and her Paris diaries suggest that she did not go to church more than anyone else. In her dealings with staff Caroline had a very good record, since it was natural to her caring, religious nature that she would treat them properly, as people, with a genuine interest in their concerns. Her maid, Milward, lived with her all her life, first at Goodwood and later at Holland House. Caroline was also close to Mr and Mrs Fannen, the Steward and Housekeeper at Holland House, and missed them greatly when in 1766 they retired.

From 1767 Caroline and Henry seem to have retired to Holland House for most of the year, and it was there that in the last part of their lives they spent many happy evenings at home, playing cards with friends, or reading. Lady Mary Coke, who lived just to the west of Holland House, found them attentive neighbours. From his study on the west side of the house, Henry could still get into the garden whenever he wished, owing to a shallow flight of steps, each just one inch high, so he could go outside 'on a ramp, in his wheelchair'.[93] Caroline, who was apt to make Voltairean jokes on the lines of 'il faut cultiver son jardin', engaged in gardening enthusiastically as she and her husband grew older. Although Henry's health was failing, Caroline was still in her mid-forties and very active. In the late 1760s the Hon. Charles Hamilton, the owner and creator of Painshill, helped her with garden design. Elizabeth Montagu, another long time admirer of Hamilton's garden, wrote drily in 1769 of his schemes for Holland House: 'Wealth inexhaustible executed his plans with rapidity, and it is become within a short time the finest villa in England.'[94]

In 1774 Henry died: Caroline was to follow him only weeks later. By then both had been ill for a while and even Theresa Parker at Saltram commented that Caroline's death was a release. Lady Mary Coke reported that Caroline's two sisters, Louisa and Sarah 'have behaved with great affection', but '[as] for her sons, at least for Mr Charles Fox, nothing can be said.'[95] Henry and Caroline's indulgent parenting was not well rewarded. Ste, always sickly, only survived them by months despite the attentions of his loving wife. By December 1774 it was known that most of the contents of Holland House would have to be sold the following year in order to pay various debts. Ste and Charles James had always been great gamblers, and in their later years Henry and Caroline had found their two elder sons a cause of much financial anxiety. In its way, it was a suitable finale to the life of Caroline and Henry that their intellects and efforts were most rewarded not by riches and further honours, but by the enormous political fame of their son, Charles James Fox, whose numerous images are still to be seen adorning Brooks's, the gentleman's club in St James's.

Holland House itself went into a twenty-year decline, before being reinvigorated by Henry and Caroline's grandson, the 3rd Baron Holland, and his wife. Their scandal was even worse than that of Caroline or Sarah: while on his grand tour the young man met and took up with the formidable Elizabeth Vassall, Lady Webster, a newly married young woman who did not get on with her husband. She shortly became pregnant with the young Henry Holland's child. On their return to England the couple lived together openly, marrying two days after Elizabeth's divorce came through.[96] It is interesting to contrast the life of Holland House under Caroline with its years of greatest fame, presided over by this younger, very lively Lady Holland, who swiftly refurnished many of the rooms and became a great political hostess. The Picture Gallery, admittedly very personal to Henry and Caroline, was altered to make a new library, though the portraits themselves did remain in the house. Happily, Elizabeth Holland retained the fine staircase, the Gilt Room and the White Room. Among her celebrated guests over the next half century were Talleyrand, Madame de Staël, Metternich, Canova, Byron, Macaulay, and Lord Melbourne, as well as four Lord Chancellors and nearly all the Whig politicians of the day. It was now Lady Holland who made the guest lists, her husband often not knowing who was coming to dinner.[97] Elizabeth was famous for being rude and outspoken: she often asked guests to send gifts of venison, poultry and game to augment her table, and loved to argue and squabble, but always with 'talent and good humour'.[98] Macaulay wrote that 'The centurion does not keep his soldiers in better order than she keeps her guests'.[99]

The Regency Holland House was brash by comparison with its earlier self. Caroline, who actually selected the house with her husband, had been a fascinating example of a woman taking on the difficulties of an existing, old-fashioned house, and blending her personality to its style rather than overstamping her own mark. It was a task demanding as much taste and skill as a complete re-creation. Her choices set a fine example, demonstrating a love of tradition, with just an overlay of current fashion: but what Caroline Holland's house expressed above all was her love of family.

Chapter 8

THE HEIGHT OF FASHION
MARY BLOUNT,
DUCHESS OF NORFOLK
1701–73

The supremely energetic and capable Mary Blount, Duchess of Norfolk, was one of the most remarkable and forward-looking women builders and decorators of her day. At Norfolk House in London she introduced the radical new rococo style to her interiors, including sensational carved furniture, while at Worksop in Nottinghamshire she personally designed a vast classical house, intended, she hoped, to be the dynastic home of the Dukes of Norfolk. She decided colours and textiles for her rooms, creating harmonies of tone and design, while also building a charming Gothick model farmhouse from where she could pursue her agricultural interests. As a patron of the East India Company she gave impetus to the fashion for oriental wallpapers and japanned cabinets. After her death, an old man who had worked for the Norfolk family for half a century said that 'the three greatest women whom God Almighty had ever created were Catherine, Empress of Russia, Queen Elizabeth, and Mary, Duchess of Norfolk'.[1]

The history of Mary Blount's childhood and education is teasingly elusive. The family was Roman Catholic: her great-grandfather, Sir Walter Blount of Sodington in Worcestershire, had been an ardent Royalist, who was created a baronet by Charles I. Mary's father, Edward Blount, the fourth son of Sir George Blount, 2nd Baronet, was a highly educated man and a friend of Alexander Pope, whose correspondence with him was affectionate and humorous. When in 1717 the Blounts were abroad, 'in a religious country' as the Catholic poet quipped, Edward was much missed: 'We are really...in want of a Friend of such an humane Turn as yourself, to make anything desirable to us. I feel your Absence more than ever.'[2] One letter reminds Edward Blount of how his children taught their host to 'slide down, and trip up the steepest slopes of my Mount' in Pope's famous garden beside the Thames at Twickenham.[3] Despite his wit, the poet was apt to take himself somewhat seriously, so it is agreeable to read of his relish at the Blount children's antics in his immaculate surroundings. In a letter of 1725, which yields a fascinating account of the garden's features – its subterranean way and grotto, the rill, the arch, the wilderness and the temple – he declares: 'Let the young Ladies be assured I make nothing new in my Gardens without wishing to see the print of their Fairy steps in every part of 'em.'[4]

Pope also knew the family of Edward Blount's Catholic wife, Annabella. In 1721 he described her family home at Rendcomb in Gloucestershire, where he was staying with her brother, John Guise: 'I looked upon the mansion, walls and terraces; the plantations and slopes, which nature has made to command a variety of valleys and rising woods.'[5] Annabella's father was Sir John Guise, 2nd Baronet. The early married home of Edward and Annabella Blount was Blagdon Manor, near Paignton in South Devon, an old house, with a great hall and arches to the buttery and pantry, set low down in a remote valley. Above the fireplace a coat of arms depicting Blount impaled with Guise, together with the initials EB and the date 1708, commemorates the date when Edward inherited the manor from his mother. Though recusant families felt obliged to live quietly at such a politically sensitive time, Edward Blount was a considerable landowner, with properties in Marldon to the north and at Aishcombe to the west. Papists had to report their land ownings, and his property concorde of 1717 with lists of tenants and tenements, 'messuages' and meadows, runs to nearly four sides of large parchment.[6] Pleasing details of the Blounts' married life are suggested in Annabella Guise's recently discovered recipe book. Abstention was not the Blount style: her recommendations for lobster pie, fricasseed eggs on little 'cocktail' toasts, and recipes received from neighbours show that she was sociable and hospitable. Annabella also listed medicines, some of which, such as snailwater, are more doubtful for human consumption.[7] Although Edward Blount did not take part in the 1715 Jacobite uprising, the family sojourn abroad from 1716 was due to the general suspicion of Catholics at this time. The visit to the villa at Twickenham must have been after Pope acquired it in 1719, but the family did not return to England permanently until 1723.

In November 1727 Mary Blount married the Hon. Edward Howard, another member of the small and close community of leading Catholic families. Her husband had already narrowly escaped death or imprisonment following his part in the 1715 Jacobite uprising: he had been tried for high treason but escaped punishment.[8] Like his elder brother, Thomas Howard, 8th Duke of Norfolk, the young man was looking for a good but not high-profile marriage. A settlement dated 12 October 1727 shows that Mary Blount, the second of four daughters and a co-heiress with her sisters, had a good dowry, of £6000.[9] As a security for the marriage, the Duke offered leases of land and tenements at the family home that he had inherited from his father, Lord Thomas Howard, at Worksop near Nottingham. At the time of their marriage Edward Howard was living in the south of France,[10] where the couple were to stay during their early married life. They returned to England in 1732 on his brother's death, when Edward, 'a shy, quiet, intelligent man',[11] became 9th Duke of Norfolk. Compared with the dramas of the previous three centuries, a tranquil stretch was about to begin in the history of the Norfolk family.

When the newly elevated couple was received at Court by the King and Queen, it was Mary who took the opportunity to emphasise their loyalty to the Crown: 'The Duke and Duchess were at court on Friday, where they were received with great distinction. The Duchess who is a sensible woman, and must act the man where talking is necessary, behaved much to her credit; she assured the Queen, though she and the Duke were of different religion, they had as much duty and regard for the King as any of his subjects, and should be glad of every occasion that gave 'em opportunity to show it.'[12] Mary in any case did not support the idea of a close Catholic enclave: 'Her house was the centre of whatever was great and elegant, in either communion; and by familiarising them with one another, their prejudices were softened, and their mutual good will encreased.'[13] Despite their Catholic affiliation, both the Duke and his brother before him had eventually become quite low key in their devotions. Mary may also have had some influence in creating the open approach that the couple were to pursue, wisely making their Catholicism more acceptable to others. Eighteenth-century attitudes to religion give an interesting foretaste of modern times. There was increased social toleration of all movements, mirrored by a hazardous latitudinarianism in the Anglican Church, and a turning away by the 'enlightened' from religion to science. This was set, however, against the background of a fear of Roman Catholicism, with its political repercussions arising out of potential foreign intervention; the decline in religious fervour was also countered by such extreme charismatic movements as Methodism, predominantly followed by the lower orders. Despite their religion, Mary's own Catholic family was also loyal to George II: her uncle, General Guise, fought on behalf of the Hanoverian King in the Highlands against Bonny Prince Charlie in 1745.[14] To emphasise their loyalty to the Crown and show their independence of any northern affiliations, at the time of the '45 the Duke and Duchess saw fit to move south from Worksop, to London.

Mary, Duchess of Norfolk was by nature both sociable and courteous. However, while she made and received visits in the conventional manner, the fact that she does not appear in contemporary diaries with the regularity of other great names suggests that the Catholic circle still bore some social as well as political restrictions. After the family had showed their loyalty at the time of the 1745 Jacobite rebellion, they had the confidence to build in London on a grand scale. Mary was to be the dominant force in the reconstruction of the family's home in St James's Square.[15] In 1722 the 8th Duke had purchased a house on the southeast corner for £10,000; this had been the first house that was ever built in the square, when it was created by the Earl of St Albans in the 1660s. The house was probably three sided, around a courtyard.[16] In 1737 when, after a furious row, Frederick Prince of Wales was required by his father, George II, to depart St James's Palace, several grandees were prepared to let him use their London homes. He accepted the offer of the Duke of Norfolk, and it was here, at the back of the house from St James's Square, in the right-hand wing towards Pall Mall, that the future King George III was born, in 1738. The Prince of Wales lived at Norfolk House for three years, and the Duke and Duchess remained close to his circle. They also managed to stay on good terms with the King and Queen, who were in fact grateful for their attentions to the Prince: Queen Caroline often invited the Duchess to her private parties.[17] During this period the Duke and Duchess lived further north, in Poland Street.[18] As well as owning the partly ruined Arundel Castle, the couple also maintained the remaining wing of an incomplete ducal house in Norwich as a workhouse for poor people.[19]

In order to create his new palace in St James's Square, the Duke bought the adjacent Belasyse House to the north, and pulled down both houses. The architect for Norfolk House was Matthew Brettingham, who had recently become famous for his work at Holkham Hall in Norfolk. Work began in 1748 and the house was occupied in 1752. The plain façade, with alternating triangular and segmental window heads, was regarded in its day as correct rather than successful. Already the advantages of combining elaborate interiors behind a plain exterior were being utilised in fashionable Palladian houses in England. Brettingham's circuit of state rooms, laid out around the central staircase on the *piano nobile*, and modelled on his earlier innovation in the wings at Holkham, was clever in itself. He also created a simple classical frieze in the hall, modelled on that at the old Arundel House on the Strand.

Norfolk House was exceptional for the adoption of the rococo style in ornamentation. It was only at Chesterfield House, habitable early in 1749 and with a similar façade, that this was to be seen in England in any complete sequence of interiors, and in carved *boiseries* or panels, although it had been fashionable for about twenty years in Paris, where the Duke and Duchess had spent time, and been received at the Court of Louis XV. So far the Rococo in England had been popularised by Huguenot craftsmen in individual objects, such as chairs and tables, mirrors and fire tongs, picture frames and trade cards, in silver and silks and, as a larger scheme, in the attractive boxes at Vauxhall Gardens. A small number of immigrant Italian *stuccatori* were also moving increasingly towards the Rococo in individual plaster ceilings and wall decoration.[20] In the event the Duke and Duchess used as their designer the Italian Giovanni Battista Borra (1713–70), who had arrived in England in 1751 and who, through Earl Temple of Stowe, was also associated with the Prince of Wales' circle. The change in direction was dramatic, from rich classical interiors such as the fashionable ones created by Lord Burlington and William Kent at Chiswick House to a style mostly based on shell-like decoration, shaped from nature rather than from formalised antiquity.

The style within Norfolk House was almost ubiquitous: three rooms on the ground floor had rococo ceilings, while all the upstairs rooms became either fully or partially rococo. However, Brettingham's completed ceilings were retained in the Green Damask and Crimson Drawing Rooms as well as in the Great Room, leaving a less fantastic effect overall than elsewhere in the house. In the Music Room, Brettingham's outlying structure for a classical ceiling, copied from Inigo Jones' Banqueting House at Whitehall, and its ribs painted with guilloches, was also kept; so too were his dado, door surrounds and outline wall panels. The rococo decoration at Norfolk house was not always as extreme and asymmetrical as the manifestation of the style at Chesterfield House, albeit that even Lord Chesterfield had given himself only four completely rococo rooms, with a more soberly styled library and dining room. Although within classical constraints the Duchess imposed the rococo theme as far as she could, she was sensible enough to go along with what had already been put up.

The origins of the decorative work in Norfolk House can partly be traced to a group of engravings, belonging to the Duchess, by the two leading rococo designers Gilles-Marie Oppenord and Juste Aurele Meissonnier.[21] One has a note in Mary's scratchy handwriting: 'French Designs of Finishings of Rooms.'[22] A number of schemes are inscribed as being commissioned by women. As visual sources, these illustrations offered several forms of inspiration, not least in the use of huge looking glasses. Engraved drawings by Meissonnier show French rococo interiors, with motifs such as trailing vines on the sides of the mirrors; but the Duchess seems to have been even more influenced by those of Oppenord, who had studied the Baroque in Italy in the 1690s. His designs, in the slightly restrained *régence* phase of the Rococo rather than the later more outrageous *pittoresque*,[23] were perhaps more suited to the plain shell of this Palladian house. On the stairs the prodigious gilded trophies, in the Italian idiom, were reminiscent of an engraving by Oppenord for 'Un Sallon a la Italienne'. This displayed a large military trophy in the centre of a panel, made suitable to a rococo rather than a baroque scheme by the great empty spaces of wall that set it off so handsomely. The ceiling in the State Bedchamber was outstanding in its gloriously free flowing design of arabesques and abstracted *rocaille* ingredients. Throughout, the carving, to Borra's designs, was by Jean-François Cuenot.

The Music Room was designed in a particularly hybrid Franco-Italian manner. This was the Duchess's most personal commission, and her first drawing room. Mary knew early on in the planning that she wanted musical trophies in the room: it was always referred to as the 'Musick Room', while as late as 1755 the two other drawing rooms along the front of the house were sometimes rather anonymously called the 'Middle Front Room' and the 'Third Front Room'.[24] One of her engravings by Oppenord shows musical trophies hung high on bows; in another, trophies of the harvest are similarly displayed. Items within Oppenord's trophies of peace, such as sheaves of corn, a rake and a tall pitcher, were used in similar arrangements in the Music Room. Between the bare bones of the compartmented ceiling, ravishing gilded trophies of the arts were inserted. These represented Music, Painting, Literature, Sculpture, Geometry, Architecture, Astronomy and Surveying, as well as a traditional central trophy of Arms and Armour. On the walls the wider panelling enabled the six musical trophies to be fuller and more dazzling than those in a somewhat cramped design on the edges of the ceiling. The room had three looking glasses, two on the wall facing out onto St James's Square and one at the north end.[25] The musical theme was purely decorative: there was no record of any music ever being played in the room, but simply of card tables, chairs and stools being used. Small dining tables were often kept in the corridor outside, showing that dinners or suppers could be provided where appropriate.

A report of her great house warming entertainment in February 1756 emphasised the Duchess's role as hostess, and the Music Room as her favourite drawing room. William Farington, the elder brother of the diarist Joseph, described how on arrival at the top of the stairs, guests passed through the anteroom, entering the Music Room from the centre of its longer wall, opposite the windows onto St James's Square. They were greeted at this point by their hostess: '...here the Duchess sat, the whole night that she might speak to every one as they came in...'[26] Thus Mary took the prettiest room, allocating her husband the grandest, the Great Room, much further on, with her niece to give him support. The writer Horace Walpole reported a quip by Lord Rockingham: 'Oh! There was all the company afraid of the Duchess, and the Duke afraid of all the company.'[27] The ravishing white and gold Music Room was rare, new and dazzling. William Farington responded with a note of puzzlement: he described it as 'Wainscotted in a whimsical Taste, the Pannels fill'd with extreem fine Carvings, the Arts & Sciences all Gilt, as well as the Ceiling, which was the same design'.[28]

Farington described another relative innovation at Norfolk House attributed to the Duchess, that of the predominance in every room of one principal colour for the decorative scheme. This had only previously been applauded in the Duchess of Lauderdale's decorations at Ham House in the 1670s, though it probably existed in some other schemes. He wrote: 'The Dutchess having been so kind to send me a ticket, on opening the Grand Appartment, which as was expected prov'd the finest Assembly ever known in this Kingdom, there were in all eleven rooms Open, three below, the rest above, every room was furnished with a different colour, which used to be reckon'd absurd, but this I Suppose is to be the Standard...'[29] Farington's description includes a precise account of the first-floor layout. Passing through the Antechamber and the Music Room he came to a room 'Hung & Furnished with Blew-Damask' (both the accounts[30] and inventory[31] describe it as green, and it is usually called the Green Damask Drawing Room). He continued to the Crimson Damask Room, described in the inventory as the 'Flowered Velvet Room'.[32] The apotheosis was reached in the Great Room, running back at right angles at the end of the wing; here the furniture was covered in crimson velvet.[33] The visitor would then turn back to view the state bedroom, 'hung and Furnish'd with Blew-Velour except the Bed'.[34] The gilding here was pale, in order not to clash with the embroideries. He then continued to the Chinese dressing room and closet, all on the garden side. The closet had niches in the walls for the display of china. In 1778 the house was described as 'superb, consisting of 8 or 9 rooms en Filade; 6 of them are *immensely* large, there are some *very fine* Pictures, amazing large Glasses...'[35]

Before commissioning the important rococo pieces of furniture, the Duchess had other items made. Joseph Metcalf's walnut and mahogany furniture in a hybrid English rococo style was all for the ground floor, giving it a very different character from the giltwood ensembles on the first floor.[36] He made two large mahogany settees, a large sofa frame and ten mahogany elbow chairs for the green family drawing room, as well as supplying material and labour for its three pairs of green damask curtains. The Duchess always had check case covers made for her furniture, and, scrupulously, these were made to match the scheme: contemporary paintings show that in other houses they were often of a quite different colour. In an antechamber on the ground floor she was economical: she had three pairs of curtains altered, adding 57 yards of narrow green fringe. For the ground-floor Great Drawing Room she had sixteen 'Virginia waulnuttree Elbow chairs': these were formal carved armchairs of the French type, in which guests had to sit up elegantly. There were three large sofas, again with case covers. These were in 'blew and white check' to match the 'blew Imbost Paper'.[37]

Ornamental Chinese decoration was often part of a rococo scheme, not least because the carvers were expert in both intricate types of design. Among her engravings, the Duchess had Chinese schemes by Oppenord. For the room Metcalf supplied the Duchess with thirteen pieces of 'China Patern Paper' and, unusually for her, three pieces each of green and of crimson damask, suggesting a mix of colours, perhaps to go with the wallpaper. Six walnut elbow chairs were, at least initially, covered with crimson serge, with six check cases, and the two pairs of window curtains had narrow crimson fringe. An ornate Chinese looking glass from the room, carved by Cuenot, has exotic Chinese paintings on one glass.[38] Farington wrote: 'the next room is intirely Chinese, the Hangings Painted either upon Sattin or Taffity, in the most beautiful India Pattern you can imagine, Curtains and Chairs the same, – the Toilet was vastly Magnificent, but I think only Gilt Plate, – on a Chinese Table stood a Basket of French China Flowers...'[39] The toilette service was by Kändler, the famous German rococo designer.[40] Like the adjacent bedchamber, this room had a lavish coved ceiling with rococo decoration.

Between March 1753 and February 1756 the French carver Jean-François Cuenot created much of the furniture at Norfolk House. He had already lived in London for nine years, and had also worked for the Duke of Northumberland. All the rococo furniture at Norfolk House is believed to have been commissioned by Mary.[41] On the ground floor the rococo ceiling of the Dining Room was echoed in a pair of remarkable gilt bronze pier tables and serving table.[42] Matching giltwood looking glasses were carved by Cuenot from designs by Borra[43] with an overmantel ensuite.[44] Similar pairs of tables in carved wood stood in the first-floor Green Damask Room[45] and Crimson Drawing Room; these too were by Cuenot to designs by Borra.[46] The Frenchman also carved three picture frames for capricci by Canaletto[47] for the ground-floor family drawing room and for the other paintings hanging in these rooms. On the first floor Farington commented on the girandoles, or candle holders, 'fix'd in the Frames of the pictures' as well as the 'round Landskip let into the looking Glass' over the chimneypieces in both the adjacent Green Damask and Crimson Rooms. The arrangement of a painting inserted into a mirror had been seen in the seventeenth century and originated from a continental design. Cuenot's accounts at Arundel mention his carving these 'Branches with floroons to hang on the sides of the picture frames' as well as countless ornamental items, and vast frames for looking glasses.[48] Massive giltwood pier tables were made for the Great Room, with a suite of rococo furniture for this and the two adjacent drawing rooms, the design for the settees[49] also deriving from one of the Duchess's engravings.

The Duchess was a celebrated needlewoman: on a visit to Devon in October 1770 Mrs Boscawen admired 'The Duchess of Norfolk's famous embroidered Bed'.[50] The hangings from Norfolk House had by then been sent to Ugbrooke Park, the home of her eldest sister, Elizabeth, Lady Clifford of Chudleigh, presumably so that Mary could use them on her bed there, in her old age. Recently conserved and rehung at Ugbrooke after years in storage, they have hitherto not been recognised as coming from Norfolk House, but are certainly the same set. In the State Bedchamber in the London house, Farington had admired the bed, suggesting that the Duchess had embroidered the cover: 'wch is Embroidery upon a peach colour'd silk, I'm sure I remember it begun near twenty years since, & it is just now finish'd, neither Baptiste or Honduotre [Hondecoeter] could paint finer Birds of Flowers than you'll find in this work...'[51] The hangings were evidently designed to suit the blue velvet of the London room: against the pale peach silk, the blue, among many other colours, is quite predominant. The design speaks of Mary's interests, including her private menagerie at Worksop, with cockatoos in different postures depicted on the foot curtains, different coloured parrots on the side and doves on the valance. The very high standard of embroidery suggests that in working on the curtains she may have been supported by professionals. Allusions to Mary's skill as a needlewoman are made in two portraits by John Vanderbank, a double one with her husband in which she has her embroidery instruments beside her,[52] and one at Ugbrooke in which she holds a bodkin. A set of twelve chairs and two stools supplied by Joseph Metcalf in 1750, for the ground-floor Great Drawing Room at Norfolk House, were covered in needlework done by her, with helpers.[53] The subject, Aesop's Fables, was very popular for seat furniture at the time.

In keeping with her skill as a needlewoman, Mary especially loved textiles. A set of armchairs covered with Soho tapestry was provided by Metcalf in 1750 for other ground-floor rooms at Norfolk House. Four tapestries for the Great Room were ordered directly from the Gobelins in Paris, in sizes that would exactly fit, and showing composite subjects from the usual separate designs.[54] 'Les Nouvelles Indes' recorded flora and fauna in the Dutch colonies, a type of subject made popular at the time by a new scientific desire to catalogue the natural world. The tapestries were produced by Neilson at a cost of £9 a yard.[55] Two fine doorcases were designed by Borra for the same room at the Duchess's request, ornamented with carved monkeys that relate to the tapestries.[56]

It was not surprising that Walpole should have been among the onlookers dazzled by the newly built house. At the housewarming party, he wrote:

'All the earth was there. You would have thought there had been a comet, everybody was gazing in the air and treading on one another's toes. In short, you never saw such a scene of magnificence and taste. The tapestry, the embroidered bed, the illumination, the glasses, the lightness and novelty of the ornaments, and the ceilings are delightful.'[57]

Farington further describes the layout of the dessert table at a dinner with the Duke and Duchess. The feeling is extravagant and Continental, reminiscent of table arrangements for the French Court:

'The table was Prepar'd for Desert [sic], which was a Beautiful Park, round the edge was a Plantation of Flowering Shrubs, and in the middle a Fine piece of water, with Dolphins spouting out water, & Dear [sic] dispersd Irregularly over the Lawn, on the Edge of the Table was all the Iced Creams, & wet & dried Sweetmeats, it was such a piece of work it was all left on the Table till we went to coffee.'[58]

For the Confectioner's Room on the ground floor, Cuenot had made five lacquered tables and three glasses, further suggesting the elaborate desserts issuing from a room probably adjacent to the Dining Room.[59] Three sets of damask table linen made for the Duchess in Ireland in 1740 bore arms in the centre of each cloth and napkin, and a crest at each corner.[60] For her table Mary ordered two silver vegetable dishes from Matthew Boulton.[61] She also had a Meissen tea service as well as a Chinese export armorial one, with the arms of Howard impaling Blount: it was Qianlong, dating from *c.* 1750.[62] A comment by Lady Pomfret that at a supper the Duke's table was 'under a Canopy' shows that despite the new acquisitions, old traditions were maintained.[63] In April 1757 another ball was given, described by Mrs Delany: this was 'for the Duke of Cumberland's entertainment'. There was dancing until 4 a.m.: 'the suppers and the desserts were the prettiest that had ever been seen; the dessert, besides the candles on the table, was lighted by lamps in fine green cut glass.' The little lamps were an innovation made by Mary. Always thinking of her husband's needs, she had ordered him a special menu: 'The Duke's supper was hot, two courses and dessert...' Indeed, the normally shy Duke appeared particularly relaxed: he danced all evening (it was the custom not to change partners very often) with Lady Coventry, one of the beautiful Gunning sisters. Mrs Delany commented, '...there was at least one happy woman for three or four hours.'[64] The elderly Duke must have been happy too.

With Norfolk House the Duke and Duchess, like Lord Chesterfield, had helped to create a new standard of interior design. The political separation of England and France had slowed rather than impeded the spread of the rococo style, which now spread quickly among those of the fashionable elite who did not object to its foreign connotations. It was used at Hagley Hall in Worcestershire for Lord Lyttelton, Saltram in Devon for Lady Catherine Parker and at the nearby Powderham Castle for the Earl of Devon, Barlaston Hall in Staffordshire for Thomas Mills, even Fon Mon Castle in Wales for Sir Brooke Boothby, and, in eccentric form, at Claydon House in Oxfordshire for Lord Verney. However, with the outbreak of the Seven Years' War in 1756, many English patrons remained loyal to the more English Palladian style, now in its second generation.

The Duke and Duchess's principal country home was still the fine

Elizabethan house at Worksop. Originally part of the estate of his ancestress Alethea Talbot, it had been left to the Duke's father, Lord Thomas Howard, as a second son. It only became the seat of the Dukes of Norfolk when his older brother Thomas inherited the Dukedom before him. The first recorded work for the 9th Duke and Duchess was in the gardens, where in the late 1730s the expert young botanist Lord Petre designed a huge scheme, covering 1700 acres and incorporating serpentine paths and varying glades in the new natural manner.[65] The Duke had always particularly concerned himself with the park; the Duchess's interests also included farming and the running of the estate. Among her books are many on agriculture, gardening and botany,[66] and she subscribed to important new works on natural history, such as a sixteen-volume work on the history of insects, and bird books such as Catesby's *Natural History of Carolina*. Many of these have embossed matching bindings labelled 'Castle Farm, Worksop', which was the farm complex Mary was building in the late 1750s.

The Duchess of Northumberland described the farm as 'a Gothic building designed by the Dutchess'.[67] Mary may have been assisted in this project by the architect James Paine. The choice of style shows how up to date she always was, the Gothick with its medieval and his-torical overtones being only newly fashionable for romantic garden buildings within the context of a classical house and Claudean land-scape. Possibly she was influenced by Sanderson Miller, who was part of the circle of intelligentsia surrounding Earl Temple at Stowe. The new building was a mixture of a working farm, the Duchess's personal estate office and a garden folly to be viewed to the southeast of the main house, as a romantic eye-catcher. Crenellated on the exterior, it mainly contained a large sitting room, beautifully ornamented with Gothic tracery. The furnishings included a 'Japaned Tea Table' and china cups and saucers[68] for social tea-drinking and, in the Duchess's bedchamber, a walnut bureau bookcase[69] where she sat and worked. A dairy was attached to the north side of the house, with cold slate sur-faces for milk and butter. Behind the little house, on the south side, a high crenellated wall surrounded a farmyard, where there were barns, stables and an open shed for the cattle to run into in bad weather.[70] In 1758 Walpole described her attention to detail: 'I am glad I am not in favour enough to be consulted by *My Lord Duchess* on the Gothic farm; she would have given me so many fine and unintelligible reasons why it should not be as it should be, that I should have lost a little of my patience.'[71] Walpole was a man who would snipe at any kind of efficiency or authority in a woman: the evidence suggests that Mary was forceful but not lacking in tact. However, Henry Seymour Conway, Walpole's cousin, confirmed her sense of detail in his response: 'Twenty reasons why the farmer's kitchen was turned to the north and his passage was four feet and one half wide and his scullery had a window such a way...'[72]

In London, in 1753, William Edwards, who had done a variety of work on Norfolk House, made a 'Chinese Modell for a Hen & Pidgeon house sent to Worksop Manor':[73] two years later he made 'a house for a Monkey',[74] as part of the Duchess's menagerie. This was on the northern side of the main house, in the newly landscaped section now called Menagerie Wood. Mrs Delany visited in 1756: 'We went on Sunday evening to the Duchess of Norfolk's menagerie at Worksop Manor, but I only saw a crown bird and a most delightful cockatoo with yellow breast and topping.'[75] The Duchess was an investor in the Dutch East India Company, from whose missions she received exotic animals and birds. From the *Boscowan*, an East India Trade ship, she was sent a 'loory' or parrot by its commander, one Captain Brand, to whom she wrote in 1760 to give him 'a great many thanks', reporting: 'it came in very good health safe to Worksop Mannor and is a most beautiful and uncommon bird.'[76] The menagerie had a large room decorated with India paper, to enhance the theme of foreign lands and species.[77]

At the same time many improvements were made to the main house, to the tune of £12,000 per annum paid to the workmen.[78] The Duke was excluded by his religion from holding offices of state, the duties of the Earl Marshal being carried out by his Deputy; nonetheless his finances were booming. The couple lived in comparative seclusion but surrounded by a splendour that became legendary: 'The magnificence of his domestic establishment, and the hospitality of his house, are still referred to by a few surviving witnesses and participants of the same, as the golden era of their recollections.'[79] The original house had five hundred rooms with a handsome Long Gallery high on the second floor, in the manner of Hardwick Hall.[80] In 1758 Henry Seymour Conway reported that the Duke and Duchess were thinking of creating a lake: 'The Duke does not positively know whether he shall do it or not, but the Duchess does and says, "My Lord Duke intends to do it very soon." I fancy she is in the right.'[81] Building work mainly comprised the filling in of the Jacobean H on the northern side of the house, creating more rooms.

The improvements were completed by the summer of 1761 and were enthusiastically described later that year in the *Gentleman's Magazine*: 'The Hall and all the apartments were newly finish'd by the present Duke of Norfolk. The Hall was Ornamented with Dorick Pill[ars] and Entablature, and the ceiling was extremely rich; as were those of the Apartments on the two Principal floors; and all were design'd and finish'd under the direction of Mr Paine.'[82] It would be entirely usual for work that had been directed by the Duchess to be attributed to the Duke. On the ground floor of the south front Mary had completed a Drawing Room suite with traditionally located State Bedchamber beyond, as well as 'the great Eating Room'[83] and 'other Apartments, for various conveniences'.[84] Leading from the grand staircase on the south front were ten spacious bedchambers, each with their own servants' rooms and closets. The Master Apartment, for the Duke and Duchess's own use, consisted of five large rooms on the north and east fronts of the first floor and was 'very Commodious'. They also refurbished the long gallery at the top of the south front by making part of it into the Duke's library. Walpole reported that, apart from retaining the bare chambers in which Mary Queen of Scots had been lodged, 'nothing remained of ancient time'.[85] In August 1761 the Duke and Duchess gave a magnificent party, at which the guest of honour was the Duke of York.

On 20 October 1761, fire consumed Worksop Manor, destroying most of the contents. When they heard the news in London, the Duke philosophically replied 'God's will be done', while the Duchess immediately thought of others who had suffered the same blow: 'How many besides us are sufferers by the like calamity?'[86] On 24 October she wrote a detailed letter, sent by express from Bath to Mr Sympson, the steward at Worksop, telling him to watch that no remaining sparks ignited, to wipe, air and fold anything that had been saved, and to send her a sketch of the remaining buildings. Already she thought of the needs of her husband: part of the fine early eighteenth-century courtyard should be redecorated so that he could stay there. Her letter expressed concern for the staff, that 'utmost care' was taken of anyone injured, that the poor health of Sympson's wife had not been aggravated by the shock, and 'that I may at least find the People well whatever else is amiss'.[87] The Duchess then allocated tasks to individuals. She was also especially concerned that the Chapel had, as reported, been saved.

By the end of the year the Duke had contracted with James Paine to rebuild on an even grander scale.[88] The discussion went on for a while: 'many...designs were laid aside and new ones ordered.'[89] When the Duke's heir, his nephew Thomas, died in January 1763, their plan for Worksop accelerated. The next heir was Edward, Thomas's younger half brother by Philip Howard's second wife, who was Mary's sister, Henrietta Blount. The boy was thus the double nephew of the Duke and Duchess and, since they were childless, like a son to them. Once the Duchess's interests were engaged, she was unstoppable. Building immediately began, and at speed, ultimately on young Edward's behalf. If finished, this would be 'the largest house in England'.[90]

The Duchess drew her own plan for the new Worksop, the main source of which was probably a drawing by William Kent or Colen Campbell for a royal palace.[91] The plan by James Paine is a modulated version of hers,[92] for which he made a specific charge for his drawing 'from Her Graces',[93] explicitly endorsing his own version as 'Designed by Her Grace the Duchess of Norfolk'.[94] Where the Duchess had planned a main drawing room on the eastern side of the house, he moved it to the west, which would get the evening sun. The house was to be a huge square block, with two matching internal courtyards, between which would run a grand Egyptian Hall from north to south. The north wing was to contain the family apartments, the west the great drawing room, the south the main entrance with two state rooms, and the east would have a great library on the first floor. Except for the latter, the main apartments were at ground-floor level. This arrangement was newly fashionable at the time; it was also what the Duchess had just arranged in the old house. She also designed two chimneypieces and the sculpture in two pediments, of which only the northern one was completed. Thomas Sandby, who visited in 1774, said that the whole project for the house was ridiculously large in scale, and that the Duchess had begun to think so herself, annotating a plan to say that 'if the whole of that plan was finished, she would still add one more room to it, wherein she might be confined as a mad woman'.[95]

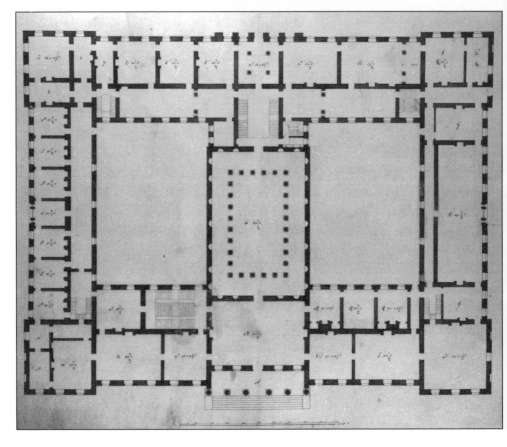

Plan for Worksop Manor, by Mary, Duchess of Norfolk. Only the north wing was completed.

In the event the north wing was built piecemeal, so that it existed as a complete house. The time scale of six years for this wing alone was that suggested in James Paine's contract of late 1761.[96] The Duke was then aged seventy-five and he and the Duchess must have realised that they might never build more than this: the present layout of the terracing suggests that the area was not fully landscaped to take the whole quadrangle. The foundation stone was laid on 25 March 1763 with the couple's nephew present; thereafter 'at least five hundred workmen were incessantly employed on the spot, chiefly under the superintendence of the duchess, who hardly ever quitted them'.[97] This was regarded as a glorious undertaking, as since the fire 'many families have been deprived of their support...But their Grace's [sic] benevolence has restored their hopes, by this most glorious undertaking; giving bread to and making thousands happy.'[98] The north wing was complete by July 1764.[99] As soon as the roof was on, there was a party, mainly for the 'workmen and labourers', numbered on the day at 350.[100] The Duchess had ovens put up in the courtyard and a country feast took place, 'with the most unbounded exultation'. There was music and country dancing, in which even the Duchess 'in the hilarity of the occasion' took part. In the afternoon her munificence was such that she sent for £30 in silver and scattered it all out of the window, causing a great scramble among the locals.[101]

Interior work began in 1765, enabling the Duchess to engage in her favourite pursuit of arranging the rooms. In her methods she showed herself very organised. A little book of sketches made by a surveyor of all the rooms was annotated in her hand.[102] This seems to have been her first attempt at laying out such a scheme; it must especially have helped in placing the furniture. As at Norfolk House, from the start she was interested in colour schemes. The First Drawing Room was to have crimson Lyons silk. It was eventually furnished with two large sofas, sixteen 'elbow' or elegant armchairs covered with crimson silk damask, two pier glasses and a large Turkey carpet.[103] In the Dining Room she planned for twenty-four chairs covered with red morocco leather and crimson damask window curtains. Here she wanted 'a compleat set of Dinning tables', suggesting that the layout for eating could be varied by joining up the tables. A 1777 inventory shows that twenty-five chairs were provided, with two large matching carvers for the Duke and herself, as well as one of her favourite black lacquer 'japanned' corner cupboards and a pair of large pier glasses with branches in the frames for lights.[104] The staircase led from the far side of the central vestibule and was painted by Theodore de Bruyn, a Flemish artist whom the Duchess had brought to England. It was in *trompe l'oeil* to represent sculptured panels of the arts, an echo of the Norfolk House Music Room.[105]

Further details come from a larger hard-backed book, evidence of an even more concerted attempt to get the furnishings and colours right.[106] In the Blue and Yellow Velvet Bedchamber a fringe in these colours ran round the top of the room. The white and gold framed furniture was covered in blue and yellow, lined with blue silk. Beyond was a 'Deckerwork' bedchamber, hung with white silk damask with yellow silk fringe round the top. The Deckerwork furniture was either some kind of canework or a straw-type fabric. It was lined with straw-coloured 'lutestrings', a light silk with curtains to match.[107] On the first floor the Duke's chamber and antechamber were both given blue paper, which was especially 'made to match ye Damask'[108] in the hangings and on the chairs. The Duchess took especial care over her husband's bedroom, having a bedstead made that was the same as in town.[109] She listed the exact pillows, bolster, mattresses, blankets and quilt required, and insisted that the carpet to go under the bed must extend several feet round the outside.[110] Clearly the Duke did not want to get cold feet when he got out of bed. Both rooms were initially to have night cupboards with folding doors for a chamber pot, though the Duchess seems in the end to have created a special private closet for the Duke, with 'A mahogany necessary stool with a Door to it to be kept in the water closet.'[111] The room for 'My Lord Duke's Gentleman' was to be reduced in size: the clerk added, 'for particular of Dimensions refer to my lady Duchess for orders.'[112] His Grace's books were in the way: in her own hand she writes 'NB the instant this room is finish'd, remove the Duke's Books…'[113]

The Duchess had a personal apartment of five rooms. It began with a little china cabinet, decorated with 'India' or oriental wallpaper. This was succeeded by her antechamber, in which she had two of her favourite oriental black and gold chests.[114] Her Dressing Room was hung with tapestry, while for her own bedchamber the Duchess specified 'olive & white on a muddy pink ground' as a temporary paper. In the event she seems to have retained it, covering her furniture with salmon-coloured silk to match. Even in rooms where furnishings were temporary, the colours and case covers matched each other. At this time she also moved all the ground-floor portraits from Norfolk House to Worksop, replacing the London ones with old masters. Portraits of the ancestors were perhaps more suitable for the country.

For the bedchamber of another complete 'South Apartment'[115] a green bed had to be 'mended and made as handsome as age will permitt/ because Call'd the King's bed'.[116] This may have been an item from old Norfolk House associated with the birth of the young George III some twenty-eight years earlier: its green silk damask was described as 'very old'.[117] As in so many houses, the naming of the room was optimistic: although the King never stayed at Worksop, one associated piece of furniture meant that the room came to be called The King's Bedchamber.

The attics were a source of some urgency: housing the servants was an essential priority before visitors could even be countenanced. The Duchess always thought of the occupants and their different levels in the hierarchy: one garret was to be hung with tapestries, and 'Her Grace's Woman's Room' was to have an 'english paper green and white mock flock' and to be 'same colour with the furniture'.[118] In the attics on the south side there were some especially pretty schemes, such as 'yellow Indian paper flower'd' matched by 'Yellow Damask bed window curtains and chairs'.[119]

The 'System Proposed' book also gave the Duchess's general instructions: all the beds were to be taken out of the stables, repaired and placed in a room where they would fit, and furniture for the attics was to be placed in each room, but not set up until the decorating was done. She would send designs for the window fastenings in the important rooms. The Duchess also thought about hiding what should not be seen: externally, in 1765 a screen wall to the service courtyard was begun, to the designs of James Paine.[120]

Regardless of so much planning and activity, Fate was to strike again. Not only had the Duchess suffered the agony of bearing no children and the destruction by fire of her country home, but also, in 1767, her beloved nephew Edward died of measles while the family was celebrating his twenty-second birthday. The Duchess, hitherto so resilient, never recovered: John Holland described in 1826 how 'the spirit of building was thenceforward paralysed, the undertaking neglected...'[121] James Paine commented that the tragedy 'could not fail to shock the usual and almost invincible fortitude of the good Duchess'.[122] Six years later the Duchess died. The Duke continued to use the house and to make developments in the park and grounds until his death in 1777.

The legacy of Mary, Duchess of Norfolk, is only tenuously available to us. There were no direct descendants to browse through her letters: indeed, there were no letters. At her death, the Duke burned all the Duchess's papers rather than have them inherited by his second cousin, Charles Howard, whom she had disliked. Worksop was sold to the Duke of Newcastle and was demolished in 1839, leaving only a fraction of the north façade and the stable screen, as well as the Gothic farm.

Norfolk House was taken down in 1938. At the Duchess's death, Horace Walpole told Madame du Deffand that: '*Le Pape vient de perdre une bien bonne amie, notre Duchesse de norfolk...femme fausse, intriguante, bigote, très suffisante et très absurde.*'[123] '*Bigote*' means devout rather than obsessive, but the two latter adjectives perhaps refer to her decorating extremes. In her personality there is still a trait that we cannot catch. Unusual terms were used by another contemporary, the Catholic writer Charles Butler: 'The duchess was gifted with great talents: was easy, dignified, and, when she pleased, singularly insinuating.'[124] The impression is that when she chose she could charm people completely: James Paine certainly did not find her difficult as a client. He also paid tribute to her many good works, commending 'a life constantly employed in promoting the good of mankind, in alleviating the miseries of the poor, and supporting the amiable dignity of this branch of the Howard family'.[125] Happily two fine monuments to a lady of fearless taste have recently been redisplayed to their best advantage. Her bed hangings are in the refurbished 'Norfolk Room' at Ugbrooke, and her Music Room from Norfolk House is in the British Galleries at the Victoria & Albert Museum.

Chapter 9

DYNASTIC DETERMINATION
ELIZABETH GRIFFIN,
COUNTESS OF PORTSMOUTH
1691–1762

It was Elizabeth Griffin's heroic destiny to save an ancestral home for her family. Her particular achievement was to stand her ground in a long legal battle to retain the handsome but ruined Audley End in Essex. Where building and restoration were needed, she also ensured that these were carefully carried out, to the highest standards. Against the odds, she also managed the feat of reconciling two entirely separate families of heirs in their potential claims: when her two immediate successors proved worthy recipients, Elizabeth's endeavours for Audley End were well rewarded.

It is hard to say who was the lesser catch when Elizabeth Griffin married her cousin, the elderly Henry Grey. She had a reasonable dowry but was not a particularly great heiress; he, as so often at this period, exemplified the ageing and respectable gentleman who was acquiring a young, attractive and competent wife to lighten his days and dutifully release him from some of his burdens. Although Henry's surname was Grey, he was the son of Richard Neville: in accordance with the terms of his parents' marriage settlement, he had at birth received the family name of his maternal grandfather, Lord Grey de Werke.

On her husband's death in 1740, Elizabeth inherited his attractive estate at Billingbear in Berkshire. Both the delights and the disappointments of nephews are a common feature in inheritances: this time it was a disappointment for Henry's nephew, Richard Aldworth. The solicitor, John Sanderson, wrote to him regretfully: 'I am sorry to tell you that you have no immediate provision made for you. The Lights [lighthouses in East Anglia] and his whole personal estate of every kind whatsoever is given absolutely to Mrs Grey and she is made sole executrix.'[1] This was in trust for life. After Elizabeth's death the inheritance would go back to Richard, providing he assumed the family name of Neville; but it would be a long wait. Sanderson clearly felt that Henry Grey had been manipulated by his wife: 'Tho' your uncle seldom spoke of you lately without tears in his eyes, yet he had not courage to add a codicil to it in your favour.' Sanderson had been longing for him to change the will back again: 'there was one ready in a friend's hand to have offered if he had shown the least inclination.'[2] Elizabeth cannot be entirely blamed: in his will,[3] Henry Grey mentions the fortune that she had brought to the marriage, discreetly emphasising that she must live according to her status both in her own right and as his widow. However, Richard's friends were dismayed on his account: William Sturrock wrote to him of his 'disappointment', suggesting that 'an artful woman hindered him in his last moments'.[4]

Elizabeth and Richard nevertheless maintained an affectionate relationship. In 1741 she wrote to him with great understatement, saying that she might be about to change her name to Lymington. She married forthwith John Wallop, Viscount Lymington, who in 1743 was created Earl of Portsmouth. In 1745 Elizabeth's life changed again when she unexpectedly became one of the heirs to Henrietta Howard's son, Henry Howard, 10th Earl of Suffolk, at Audley End.

The land at Audley End, the site of a Benedictine abbey, had been granted at the dissolution of the monasteries to Sir Thomas Audley, Henry VIII's shrewd and ruthless Lord Chancellor. His daughter Margaret became the wife of Thomas Howard, 4th Duke of Norfolk; it was their son, Lord Thomas Howard, who inherited the house and who, under James I, was created Earl of Suffolk. For his enhanced status the Earl built a palatial two-courtyard house in expensive dressed stone, entered from the west and designed with two royal suites to the north and south of the central courtyard. Below these he and his wife had their own suites. The cost was a phenomenal £200,000, far more than the contemporary Hatfield House with similar suites, which only cost £12,000. Audley End was completed in 1614, in which year the Earl became Lord Treasurer of England. Amid allegations of corruption he was relieved of the post in 1618, subsequently committed to the Tower, and made to pay a fine. Audley End survived, but ten Earls of Suffolk never recovered from the subsequent debts. The house was even sold to King Charles II, who used it only briefly. It was later bought back by the 7th Earl.

By the time that Elizabeth, the great-granddaughter of James, 3rd Earl of Suffolk, was a co-heir in 1745, much of Audley End had been pulled down or reduced. The outer, western courtyard had been removed in two waves. Bothered by debts, Henry, the 10th Earl, had already had estimates for pulling down a further section. A surveyor called James Scott had examined the house in February 1745 for him, and concluded the Long Gallery on the east side to be especially 'ruinous'. Scott opined that its towers were in a very bad state, especially the Clock Tower, and that the chimneys were dangerous. He had two proposals, both of which involved taking down the Gallery entirely, and suggested an arcaded way to cross the court from wing to wing. In this way the connection would be maintained, and the dilapidated section removed. The Hall section at the centre should be kept, 'especially as it affords your Lordship the two best rooms in your House, the large parlour and Fish room over it, and wants but little repairs in comparison with the Gallery part'.[5]

Another co-heir, George, Lord Hervey, wrote immediately to the Countess on hearing of his own claim: 'As soon as I heard Lord Suffolk was dead, I sent to your Ladyship's house...it was reported that we were the heirs at law.' He sent a solicitor to find out more, and wished that she were in town: 'Our interests are mutual, our claim is reciprocal, our affairs are blended together.'[6] On the death of the 10th Earl of Suffolk, aged 38, intestate and without children, Thomas, 2nd Earl of Effingham, from another branch of the Howard family, took possession of the house, believing the whole estate to be his. It was the clever James Sanderson, acting for the Countess, who, finding a paper by chance, worked out that the 1687 will of James, 3rd Earl of Suffolk meant that when the line of his brothers died out, as had happened with the death of the 10th Earl, the inheritance should revert to his direct heirs.[7] This would invalidate the settlement made by the 7th Earl to the Howards of Effingham. Together with her sister, Mrs Anne Whitwell, for one half share, and Lord Hervey for the other half, Elizabeth spent two years in a legal wrangle to establish their inheritance. Though the bequest to her had been a considerable surprise, she was a woman described as being 'proud as Lucifer',[8] and she was not going to give up. In October 1747 judgement was pronounced in favour of Elizabeth, together with her co-heirs.[9]

The sisters consequently inherited valuable agricultural land to the east of the house. However, the mansion, mill and park were excluded, because they had belonged to the Crown when the 1687 settlement was made, and justifiably belonged to Lord Effingham. It was four more years before the Countess, ever determined, was able to buy the house itself from the Earl. Colonel William Vachell was appointed receiver of the estate and worked extraordinarily hard on her behalf, establishing the inheritance, sorting out such details of the estate as the tenants' rents and beating down Lord Effingham on a price for the house. This was done by looking closely at valuations of the actual building materials.[10] Finally on 9 September 1751 the price was agreed at £10,000: of this, only about £3000 was for the dilapidated house, albeit that its construction, nearly 150 years earlier, had cost a prodigious sum totalling many times as much. Also vested in the property was the right, still held by the Barons Braybrooke, to appoint the Master of Magdalene College, Cambridge.

Throughout the protracted negotiations, the Countess and Hervey, who in 1751 became 2nd Earl of Bristol, corresponded pleasantly enough, each giving way on points to help the affair through. Hervey wrote, 'As we are both willing to come to a division I make no doubt we shall end it amicably',[11] to which she responded, 'I agree with you my Lord, that when people are of a peevish, litigeous [sic] disposition, they may always find Bones of contention.' Happily in her case this was not to be so: 'I hope all things will be settled in a ye most amicable and speedy way.'[12] The next year, 1752, Vachell congratulated her on her tenacity: 'I flatter myself that I shall now have the pleasure to congratulate your Ladyship on having got through a long Chancery writ, and on completing as good a purchase as has been made in Essex for many, many years.'[13] Lord Bristol was also impressed: 'I congratulate your ladyship on having completed the purchase of Audley-end, I hope you will live long to enjoy that, and every other share of good fortune which such a character, and so deserving a conduct entitles you to.'[14]

Nevertheless, delays continued. In June 1752 the Countess wrote: 'I grow horrid Cross with these dillitory proceeding about Audley-End…'[15] It is to the Earl of Bristol's great shame that at the end, once his inheritance was secure, he refused to pay Colonel Vachell any fees, saying that he thought an allowance from Chancery was enough, that Vachell was the Countess's man rather than his own, and that he should have been able to elect his own representative.[16] Elizabeth's letter to her co-heir was a masterpiece of frost, telling him that she did not like his letter, that he could have objected to the arrangements, and that they had to be represented by one person only. Without actually telling him to pay Vachell, she implied her bad opinion: 'When I think I've Acted Right, I never repent...We have my Lord Happily gon thro' a very long law sute of the division of a large Estate, with as few difficulties As the nature of the Case would Admit, Which I think I may justly say was in a great Measure owing, to a reciprocal Compliance between your Lordship and my Self.'[17] The Countess had every motive for being furious on behalf of Vachell, a family friend who had figured in Henry Grey's will, and who was also involved in running the Billingbear estate for her. It is not known if she made up the deficit, but she clearly treated Vachell well. In 1757 the Colonel thanked her for 'such punctual payments' of his annuity and mortgage interest, saying that he hoped indeed to accept her invitation to Billingbear, 'the Place of all other I ever preferr'd'.[18]

At Audley End, the Countess soon instigated the pulling down of the ruined Long Gallery.[19] In its place an open ground-level arcade was created behind the Great Hall to link the north and south ranges, as had first been suggested by James Scott. The work was supervised by the London architects Phillips and Shakespear, with John Phillips himself in charge. Economy was ever important: nearly seventy tons of lead were sold off locally, as well as timber, floorboards and panelling. Other materials from the Long Gallery were reused in the arcade, notably some of the arches with their curious multi-arch subdivisions. A huge programme of improvements was begun: guttering, glazing, roofing and plumbing were replaced, staircases repaired, and plasterwork restored. The room most often mentioned in the accounts is the 'Fish Room', in the location often given to a Jacobean Great Chamber on the first floor at the end of the Hall, and so called because of its ornamental plasterwork, depicting dolphins and sea-monsters. Its preservation as one of the glories of Audley End today is entirely due to the Countess, on whose initiative the plasterwork was thoroughly restored.

The degree of control exercised by Elizabeth over building works is exemplified by a letter of 1753 from John Phillips. He had written directly to her to report on a balustrade relating to the corridor or arcade behind the Hall: 'which Ballustrade is done exactly to the drawing your Ladyship has fixed on, and will range with the Arcade, and it could not be done other ways, than it is, to preserve the line of Building.'[20] In particular Phillips had made it appear 'as tho' this was part of the original Pile', and this because she had given him 'express command' to make it look original. Evidently he had already had one confrontation with the Countess when, unusually for a builder, he had had to apologise for letting the work get so far ahead. Since the Countess wanted to control and approve as building proceeded, Phillips had promised that 'nothing more shall be done concerning it till I have your Ladyship's further orders'.[21]

The Countess's aim was to make the house affordable and controllable. She also succeeded in retaining its attractions: Count Kielmansegge, who visited in September 1761, said that 'The house at Audley End was in former times the largest place in all England, and, although a great part of it has been pulled down, it remains one of the most perfect pieces of architecture in the Kingdom.'[22] Elizabeth seems to have instructed the builders mostly from afar, either when living at Billingbear, a 'dear and delightful place',[23] or while spending part of the winter season in London. She also had work done in the gardens: Count Kielmansegge commented that the grounds were not remarkable but 'will be improved by the changes...which the owner is now very busy making.'[24] Always her aim was to make the two estates secure and to provide for her nephews. Richard Neville Aldworth, the nephew of her first husband Henry Grey, was one; the other was John Griffin Whitwell, her own nephew. Henry and Elizabeth had no children and both young men were the sons of their sisters. It was on their behalf that the Countess sought to extend the honour and status of both the Neville and the Griffin families.

The Countess's will, dated 9 June 1759 and proved on her death in 1762,[25] shows how very carefully she had thought about posterity. In 1749 the two nephews complied with her wishes that in order eventually to inherit their separate estates, they should assume the appropriate names and arms, namely those of their mothers' forebears rather than of their fathers'. They both already had their mothers' family names as their middle name, so in changing their fathers' surnames, the maternal names were curiously doubled up. The heir to Audley End thus became John Griffin Griffin while the heir to Billingbear became Richard Neville Neville. In Elizabeth's will she clearly showed some preference for her own Griffin nephew, letting Richard retain the furniture and household goods at Billingbear, but leaving John all the plate and linen from that house, as well as the books and pictures, that were not actually marked with the name of Grey or Neville. This meant that Richard lost 'almost all the Good & valuable Pictures', suggesting that Elizabeth had either inherited these herself or collected them during the marriage. Perhaps they simply were not marked: certainly she regarded them as her own property to dispose of as she chose. The East Anglian lighthouses, which should really have gone to Richard, went to John, probably because Elizabeth felt that he needed more income for his larger estate. If John had no sons they were to revert to Richard. Magnanimously, Richard accepted that John came first: 'She loved no Soul but him, & after him I seem to have been as well with her, as any one not excepting her own dear Lord.' He felt that 'she has show'd me, not only Justice but Affection'. Where Richard admitted that 'thro' old Grey's folly I have been a sufferer', he never begrudged John, as 'so good a man is better'd by it'.[26] Indeed, when John inherited a piece of land that the Countess had bought adjacent to Billingbear, he immediately gave it to Richard's son. A few days after this, Richard revealed that more of the Billingbear rents were to come to him, as well as a Jamaican property, inherited from Lord Grey de Werke, who had been Governor of Barbados: this too had been done with Richard's son in mind. Thanks to the Countess's thoughtfulness, rather than disputing any part of her will, Richard Neville Neville was thus able to view his own inheritance with optimism.[27]

Elizabeth's husband, the Earl of Portsmouth, inherited the house in town. As a further exercise of control through her will, the Countess left her niece, Mary Whitwell, an annuity of £50 and £5000 of capital 'provided she marries with the consent and approbation of Lord Portsmouth and her brother Sir John Griffin'.[28] In bequeathing the house to John, Elizabeth had made sure that he received it in a reasonably sound condition. It was the first time Audley End had been left to an heir without carrying terrible debts or appalling building requirements, so giving him scope to make his own mark. The next decorations at Audley End were perhaps surprising: Sir John Griffin

Griffin, as he was now known, made an extraordinary decision to ask Robert Adam to renovate a number of poky, ground-floor rooms on the south front, a request which greatly displeased such a fashionable architect. The Gothick chapel was also created at this time, as was the picture collection, developed on the foundation of the works from Billingbear.

In the longer term, the separate inheritances of the two lines were not achieved. Sir John Griffin Griffin had many honours, being able at his own request to reinstate his great-grandfather's title of Lord Howard de Walden: he was also subsequently created Baron Braybrooke. However, he had no children. At his death the estate passed right back to Richard Aldworth Neville, the son of the Countess's other heir and a third cousin by marriage, one generation removed. By Elizabeth's will Richard was likewise required to take the Griffin name and arms, though in the end the arms sufficed. John Griffin Griffin had also ensured that the Braybrooke title would go with the inheritance. Richard Aldworth Neville, the 2nd Baron Braybrooke, was encouraged by Lord Howard de Walden's widow to live at Audley End, not waiting for her demise: 'the best return you can make me is living in this place with comfort to yourself and affectionate recollections of those who have inhabited it with so much delight for such a number of years.'[29] When, as the 2nd Baron Braybrooke, Richard Aldworth Neville came to live at Audley End, a new chapter commenced in the history of the house. It was his son, the 3rd Lord Braybrooke, who principally created the interiors seen today, including the dining room, now put back upstairs and a charming first-floor drawing room on the south front. Although she had not managed to preserve the family name, Elizabeth Griffin, Countess of Portsmouth, had linked house, land and family arms, to the honour of her successors.

Chapter 10

EQUAL EMINENCES
ELIZABETH SEYMOUR,
DUCHESS OF NORTHUMBERLAND
1716–76

Elizabeth, Duchess of Northumberland was a large, cheerful woman. Contrary to her rank and status, she could be quite unladylike. Brash, jovial and confident, she enjoyed shows of grandeur such as being escorted by a large retinue of footmen, but still took an interest in ordinary people. The Duchess was a great character who ran great houses: she also created one that particularly displayed her own taste and interests. At Alnwick Castle, her ancient family seat in Northumberland, her design decisions produced a remarkable suite of state rooms in her beloved 'Gothick' style. As a result of her travels throughout England, she also developed considerable knowledge of other grand houses and of the craftsmen of the time. She was thus qualified to help her extremely able husband, Sir Hugh Smithson, and their decorator Robert Adam in the superb refashionings of their homes at Northumberland House in the Strand and Syon Park on the edge of London.

While her husband provided the main impetus behind work on these two houses, Elizabeth played an important role in managing the refurbishments and the execution of designs, and in acquiring furniture. She also collected paintings, prints, ivories and objects of historical interest. An inexhaustible writer of lists, she managed each of her homes with infinite care, detailing the tasks of their servants and the costs of provisions and travel. Her marriage with Sir Hugh was a life-enhancing partnership; it was also one which demonstrated that when it was the man who had an eye for decorating, it was worth letting him have his way. However, as heiress to the great Percy estates, there was no question that Elizabeth would ever be put down.

Only two generations before the birth of Lady Elizabeth Seymour, the Percy family had almost seen their ancient titles extinguished. The death in 1670 of Jocelyn, 11th Earl of Northumberland, had meant that the greatest heiress in England was now a three-year-old girl. This red-headed child, teased in verse as 'Carrots',[1] was Elizabeth Seymour's grandmother. Lady Elizabeth Percy had two miserable childhood marriages before marrying Charles Seymour, 6th Duke of Somerset, who, because of his pomposity, snobbishness and egotism, became known in old age as 'the Proud Duke'. With his wife's much needed fortune, he rebuilt Petworth House in West Sussex, a Percy family seat since 1150, where at his insistence they lived in a state of extraordinary grandeur. The Duke and Duchess of Somerset's son, Algernon, Earl of Hertford, married Frances Thynne, daughter of Henry, 1st Viscount Weymouth; they made a charming, affectionate couple. Every summer for a few weeks they lived in part of the dilapidated Alnwick Castle. There the Countess pursued her literary studies, with a poet in residence each year to assist with her verse, including James Thomson (1700–48), author of *The Seasons*, who in 1728 insisted on dedicating *Spring* to her.[2] Their two children, Lady Elizabeth, who was always known as Lady Betty, and Lord Beauchamp, were born nine years apart, so that Elizabeth was always something of a little mother to her brother. On his mother's death in 1722, Lord Hertford made a successful claim for the dormant barony of Percy, in the belief that his mother would have been able to inherit the Percy barony in her own right.

The Proud Duke was a problem to the family. He hated his son, who wisely stood back from the stream of vitriol routinely addressed to him. He also thoroughly disliked the fact that his daughter-in-law was bookish. In his granddaughter Elizabeth this seems to have resulted in a mixed attitude to learning. She was well read in her own family history[3] but when she subsequently contributed to a volume of amateur poetry published by a group of ladies whom she had met during the season at Bath, her poem about a butter muffin was considered neither witty nor elegant. The Countess educated her children diligently, 'inspiring into their youthful minds the principles of virtue, and the love of religion'.[4] Though the Hertfords were devoted to their daughter, the Countess may have recognised that Elizabeth was not by nature intellectual.

When Elizabeth Seymour was courted by Sir Hugh Smithson, the

4th Baronet, there was no inkling that she would be a great heiress. This was the main reason why up until that time she had no suitors. Her only fortune was to be a not unreasonable £10,000 on her grandfather's death. The dashing Sir Hugh, from a family of Yorkshire squires, wooed Elizabeth in his own county, at the home at Swillington of Lady Lowther, who was something of a matchmaker. An intellectual woman, in London she was, like Lady Hertford, part of the Countess of Pomfret's circle. For Sir Hugh, marriage to the daughter of a future Duke was ambitious, but not impossible: his family, originally haberdashers in the City of London, had already intermarried with the northern aristocracy. The fact that Elizabeth was at least partially a northerner was important, as well as the contacts offered by marriage to such a high-ranking family. For her own part, ability certainly counted: Sir Hugh was one of the best-looking and most accomplished men of his day, with 'an advantageous figure, and much courtesy in his address'.[5]

When in October 1739 Sir Hugh told Lady Elizabeth that he intended to approach her father to ask for her hand in marriage, she was flabbergasted and gave him a half-hearted refusal. She wrote to tell her parents, 'awkwardly', as she put it: 'You will guess how much I was surprised and confounded at so extraordinary a compliment...I was astonished when he mentioned it to me.' She knew that any marriage would be seen as something to be decided for her, and promised that she had done nothing to encourage Sir Hugh. Confusingly, she said that even if her parents did approve, she would turn him down. A day or two later she wrote them a postscript, saying that her head was 'in such a puzzleation'. At the age of twenty-two Lady Betty had fallen deeply in love. Astutely, the Countess replied in a way that both gave an opinion and allowed herself a way out: Sir Hugh's birth and estate, she felt, were not quite good enough for her daughter, but what were her own feelings? Elizabeth wrote back, now openly admitting that if her parents had agreed, she would have accepted: 'Nay, I should not scruple to own that I have a partiality for him.'[6] However, as they had not agreed, she was prepared to refuse him. At this stage her parents made enquiries about Sir Hugh. Apart from his wide personal popularity, he had over £4000 a year, and was heir to another property worth £3000. Lord and Lady Hertford decided that the couple must not see each other for six months, after which, if their mutual affection continued, they themselves would reluctantly consider the match.

Anxious, pining and miserable, Elizabeth became so ill that her kindly intentioned parents suddenly consented. Sir Hugh was deeply grateful: 'As I was extremely sensible that I had neither fortune nor any other qualification sufficient in itself to procure me so great an honour, my hopes only depended upon Lady Betty being moved in my favour by the sincerity of my love.' In his courtship Sir Hugh had certainly made every effort, even agreeing to Lord and Lady Hertford's request to avoid speaking to Lady Betty 'in publick places', until everything was sorted out.[7] He also managed to mollify the Proud Duke, by persuading his prospective parents-in-law to let the grandfather Duke think he had been approached before anyone else in the family. The Duke of Leeds wrote on his behalf to the old man, asking permission from Sir Hugh to make an offer for her.[8] Although the Duke of Somerset felt that Sir Hugh's antecedents were not really good enough,[9] Elizabeth Seymour was not an heiress and he was not unduly concerned. Providing Sir Hugh's family was 'Gentlemanly and respectable'[10] he would agree, though he was not averse to seeking an additional early settlement from Sir Hugh's great uncle. After a year of high emotions and tactful negotiation, the wedding of Sir Hugh Smithson and Lady Elizabeth Seymour took place on 18 July 1740.

The couple were to spend a happy four years at Sir Hugh's family home at Stanwick, near Richmond in North Yorkshire. In 1744 Elizabeth's world completely changed, with the death of her younger brother while in Italy on his grand tour. Although her father was still alive, this meant that for the second time the Barony of Percy and the vast estates in Northumberland and Middlesex would eventually devolve on a woman. As the Seymour heiress, Elizabeth would also technically stand to inherit some of the estates of the Dukes of Somerset.[11] Her family did not know at first that there was a worrying alternative. If the Proud Duke had his own imperious way, almost all the estates might descend down his preferred line, to his younger daughter's son, Elizabeth's first cousin, Charles Wyndham. Unconcerned at the grief of the stricken parents, the Proud Duke flew into a rage at the death of his grandson, blaming the calamity on Lord Hertford. In an act of subversion, meanwhile, to keep the Percy estates[12] within his own chosen descent he secretly begged the King to create him Earl of Northumberland.

Despite his German origins the King was greatly impressed by details of ancient English lineage: now, fortunately, he sensed that something was wrong. As Elizabeth's immediate family rallied to the cause of her rightful inheritance, a worrying weekend ensued. The Countess described in dismay how the King had nearly signed the Proud Duke's proposal on Monday, but 'we did not hear of it until late on Friday night'.[13] On the Saturday morning the Earl wrote frantically to the Duke of Newcastle, whom he felt could intercede with the King; but the Duke was going out of town. Urgently, Lord Hertford wrote on Monday to the King, sending his son-in-law to deliver the letter. The King called in the eloquent Sir Hugh to see him. Always good in face-to-face contact, Sir Hugh succeeded in convincing the King of his wife's rightful inheritance. It was thus largely owing to Sir Hugh's confidence, easy assurance and determination that the Percy estates were saved for Lady Elizabeth. Lady Hertford also contributed by writing a charming letter to her father-in-law, pointing out that he could have the Earldom if he really wanted, but that her daughter was the rightful heir to the Percy estates and had never done anything to displease her grandfather. Together the family succeeded, and the old man retreated.

At the Proud Duke's death, in 1748, Lady Elizabeth's father not only became 7th Duke of Somerset but also was especially made 1st Earl of Northumberland in a new creation. This was a far-sighted arrangement. When a title is new it is possible, with the monarch's permission, to have it created on particular terms. With this patent an unusual stipulation was included, that the Northumberland Earldom should go at the new Duke's death to his son-in-law, Sir Hugh Smithson, and subsequently to his heirs by Lady Elizabeth. While this showed how much the family trusted Sir Hugh, it also established an insistence on the Percy blood line. In addition the Duke became 1st Earl of Egremont, with another unusual remainder, to his nephew, Charles Wyndham. This created a satisfactory arrangement all round. On her father's elevation as 7th Duke of Somerset, Elizabeth automatically gained the junior courtesy title of Baroness Percy: in that year she was also given Syon Park by her father.[14] At the death of Elizabeth's father only two years later, in 1750, the couple therefore became the 2nd Earl and Countess of Northumberland of the new creation. Sir Hugh also took the family name and arms of Percy.

This was the moment at which the magnificently rebuilt seat at Petworth was split away from the Percy inheritance. Not all the estates that had originally belonged to the old Northumberland Earldom went with it: the Proud Duke had managed to ensure that, together with other Seymour estates in Yorkshire and Cumberland which were in his absolute disposal, Petworth went to Charles Wyndham, now 2nd Earl of Egremont. Ultimately this was a fortunate gesture for posterity, ensuring that Petworth House developed a distinct lineage all of its own, rather than being subsumed under the aegis of Syon.

The Earl and his Countess, who was still often known as Lady Betty, soon started extensive building works. Horace Walpole reported on October 1752: 'They are building at Northumberland House, at Sion, at Stansted [Stanwick], at Alnwic and Warkworth Castles.'[15] He considered the couple extravagant and showy: 'They live by the etiquette of the old peerage, have Swiss porters, the Countess has her pipers – in short they will very soon have no estate.'[16] From the start Elizabeth seems to have been so dazzled by her husband that she acceded to his every whim. He certainly liked display. Her mother laughingly described their unsuitable clothes on a visit soon after their marriage to Sir Hugh's great uncle at Tottenham Cross: 'Though in the very midst of summer, they were both of them dressed as for a holiday; she in a silver stuff of four pounds a yard, and Sir Hugh in a lead colour and silver stuff coat embroidered with silver...'[17] Although Elizabeth seems to have caught her husband's love of finery, she retained a proper moral sense, writing occasionally in her diaries such strange little aphorisms as: 'A woman without modesty is like a ragout without salt.'[18]

The Countess also commenced on a great learning cycle of art and architecture. On the back of a letter written to her mother in August 1740, she mentioned studying the architecture of Vitruvius, Palladio and Inigo Jones, with Sir Hugh as her instructor.[19] Inevitably the couple were invited to visit many grand houses, but they also went out of their way to see others. In her diary Elizabeth sought to describe and catalogue more fine houses than she could ever possibly visit, as well as market towns and various colleges at Oxford and Cambridge. In the early 1750s alone she wrote about Ragley Hall, Stowe, Ickworth, Strawberry Hill, Castle Howard and Woburn Abbey, to name but a few. Her descriptions recorded interiors and items so diligently that sometimes they read as if taken from an early guidebook, but she also commented on whether she found the rooms attractive, if the situation was fine or ugly, and if the offices were sensibly disposed. She especially admired the Gothick, visiting Guy's Tower at Warwick Castle in 1752 and Horace Walpole's Strawberry Hill again in 1762, where, she believed, she 'never saw anything half so pretty'.[20]

In particular Elizabeth loved the derelict Alnwick Castle, which had been in the Percy family since 1309. Upon this new inheritance she brought her family back to the castle of her childhood, which, before the restricted summer occupancy of her parents, had not been inhabited for over a hundred years. The locals were delighted by the family's return, which brought excitement, employment and purpose to the area. On the first visit of the Earl and Countess, in 1751, there was nowhere suitable in the main part of the castle for the couple to sleep, and they had to stay in the old exchequer house, next to the gatehouse in the outer walls. The castle became Elizabeth's absorbing passion. She was fascinated by what she called her 'braw rough ancestors',[21] whose history she scrutinised under the enthusiastic tutelage of their chaplain, Thomas Percy. The Countess breathed new life into the traditions of her ancient family home, and made a point of entertaining the neighbourhood worthies and attending the local theatre. Encouraged by her husband to make her mark, she also reintroduced the ancient tradition of riding the bounds, and brought back the July fair. She loved the bleak Northumberland landscape, with its grey stone buildings, intimate green valleys, dark rivers and low trees, all swathed in a pale northern light. The wild sea was another attraction: 'I went (having a Passion for beholding the sea in a Storm & the Wind being very high) to Alnmouth, & so along the sands. The waves were seriously in a Passion & raged & dashed with their utmost violence.'[22]

Elizabeth's modifications to the Castle were in the Gothick style, which she felt was suitable to the ancient medieval building. She created a suite of rooms on the first floor of the old keep, some of which was rebuilt from the foundations. On the exterior a series of neat Gothic windows was inserted at the principal level, with little quatrefoil windows above. These were rather more regular than would be usual in a real medieval building, reflecting the more ordered planning inside. In particular Elizabeth turned the emphasis to the landscape beyond, creating window recesses for viewing. These were in each of the external towers, which were now opened out into the new rooms. At the same time the park beyond was replanted: the Earl was already

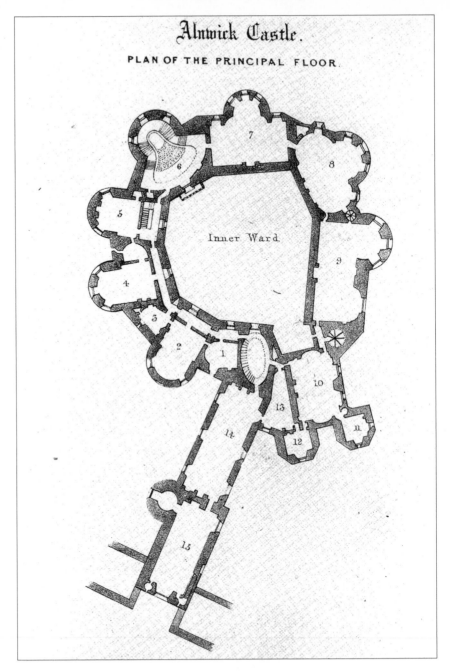

Plan of Alnwick Castle, after Elizabeth's remodelling. The Dining Room is at 9, with the first Drawing Room, later a Breakfast Room, at 10. The Saloon is at 7, with the new Drawing Room at 8, and State Bedchambers and Dressing Rooms from 1–5. Adam's Library was at 14, and his Chapel at 15.

celebrated for his knowledge of gardening and trees.[23] Outside the keep, but still inside the ramparts, the Gun Terrace was created for walking, and as a vantage point from which to admire the landscape. To commemorate the Countess's ancestor Harry 'Hotspur', the 1st Earl, crusader and warrior, who had died at the Battle of Shrewsbury and been immortalised by Shakespeare, a seat named after him was created in one of the wallheads.[24] Elizabeth also created a garden gate so that the grounds were more accessible from the main rooms. Ever keen on nobility and ancestry, in 1774 as an adornment to the park she was to erect a statue to Malcolm, King of the Scots and defeater of Macbeth. Malcolm was no Percy, but he had been killed just north of the castle, in 1093. Optimistically, Elizabeth claimed descent.

Internally the Dining Room was the first scheme to be executed. This was on the site of the medieval great hall on the first floor, adjacent to the gatehouse. Here the room was transformed, by a riot of Gothick tracery applied to the walls. The chimneypiece was flanked by a lion and a unicorn, the two supporters of the family arms, each holding a shield. Above this, Elizabeth's own portrait in coronation robes was placed in a fine white frame of which the uppermost part was a Gothic canopy, its sides emblazoned with various family coats of arms, including Percy, Lucy, Poynings and Fitzpaine. Elizabeth had the family arms placed wherever she could: the ornamental ceiling had a patchwork of such emblems, including the rather more ambitious ones of Charlemagne and the Dukes of Brabant, from whom she believed she was descended, as well as those of the old English families of Seymour, Latimer and Thynne. Amid such display, Elizabeth was also practical: a large window recess was used for a table when the family were dining alone, or as a second table for 'large public Dinners'.[25] Adjacent to this, and as the first point of entry, a drawing room was created, immediately above the gatehouse. Both were admired by the Edinburgh architect John Adam, who visited in 1759: 'The dining & drawing room…are all extremely noble & elegant in the Gothick taste but the drawing room pleased me most, at least it struck me with that idea. The ornaments of both these rooms on walls & ceiling are done in very good Gothic style, of stucco. My Lady's Bed Chamber, Dressing Room &c. are very suitably finished.'[26] All the early work was probably by Henry Keene who was employed from December 1750 to November 1759.[27]

In time, the entrance to the new rooms was moved from the main gatehouse to the far side of the courtyard, where James Paine created a grand new elliptical staircase, completed in 1764. The original medieval sequence was thus reversed, with Saloon, Drawing Room and State Dining Room running in that order clockwise. With the more private apartments situated on the opposite side, a whole circuit was created. Thus the antiquity of the castle was maintained while grander new rooms were introduced for formal entertaining.

An image of these breathtaking new decorations at Alnwick is seen in an 1823 drawing by the Duchess of one of the window recesses in the Saloon, now part of the Music Salon. Three architects were used by Elizabeth, though since her changes were later overworked by Salvin in the mid nineteenth century for the 4th Duke, an imaginative reconstruction has to be made as to how her castle appeared. It must have made her Northumbrian and Scottish neighbours gasp. Draughty old castles were quite normal, as were new classical interiors, but to find new Gothic interiors so completely trellised and perfected in an ancient castle was delightfully extravagant. All the changes at Alnwick were done as homage to Elizabeth's ancestors, but while the interior offered a comfortable and prettified version of the medieval style, the exterior presented a theatrical, chivalric silhouette. Visiting in 1772, Elizabeth Montagu reported: 'It is the most noble Gothick building imagineable. Its antique form is preserved on the outside. Within the apartments are also Gothick in their structure and ornaments, but convenient and noble; so that modern elegance arranges and conducts antique strength and grandeur, leaves its sublimity of character, but softens what was rude and polished.'[28]

In the 1750s Elizabeth had listed in her journal 'Works order'd at Alnwick'. She was as interested in the estate as in the house, mentioning roads, pheasant cages, a fish pond, a hot house, the planting of nearby Hulne Wood, the ice house and the coal vaults.[29] She often went out with her husband in the post chaise to view the estate: later she listed some ninety-eight rides and drives.[30] By the late 1750s in summer many passing visitors were received, as well as the local gentry: after church on Sundays there were usually eight or ten guests for 'dinner'. Time also had to be given to Elizabeth's desk: before leaving for London in October 1759 she described herself as 'Busy packing, settling Accounts' and writing letters.[31] In her absence, John

Drawn on stone by J.D.Harding. *Printed by C.Hullmandel.*

Recess in the Saloon,

Gothic interior at Alnwick Castle, from a sketch by Charlotte, Duchess of
Northumberland, 1823.

Bell of Durham was clerk of the works. He lived in the castle to oversee the restoration, maintaining some continuity in the scheme. A carver worked for twenty years on embellishing the towers with medieval style statues, including some original ones, to give it an heroic, antique effect. The internal modifications at Alnwick also continued over a period of many years, being for a time much slowed down by the Earl and Countess's London life.

Following the Earl's appointment as a lord of the bedchamber to George II in 1753, the couple's existence revolved around the Court. Their two large homes in the south, Northumberland House and Syon Park, respectively in central London and to the west in rural Middlesex, were both useful for a life in attendance on the ageing and widowed King George II. Syon, beloved by them for its gardens and pleasure park, was ideal as a nearby retreat from a busy city life, but was also close to the royal Richmond Lodge at Kew. The journey from Syon to Northumberland House was recorded on one occasion by Elizabeth as taking one hour ten minutes; often it was made by river.

Northumberland House was a large courtyard house between the end of the Strand and the Thames, where the top of the present Northumberland Avenue falls. The Earl now had the north front remodelled, and completed an ambitious plan for an additional south-west wing, including a room of new Soho tapestries in the outermost corner. He also extended the opposite wing as a ballroom and picture gallery, in which he had copies of paintings by the great masters. This meant that the south front of the courtyard house had two arms extending beyond it to the river, thus embracing the wonderful waterfront views on that stretch of the Thames and taking advantage of the great 4-acre garden. The new gallery was opened in May 1757. Walpole however was dismissive of its style: 'It is a sumptuous chamber, but might have been in better taste.'[32] Count Kielmansegge admired its setting as 'rightly considered one of the best houses in London, particularly on account of its large saloon and gallery'.[33] The Earl, for whose own servants he published 'Rules for a Family', believed in management and control: however, it was often the Countess who had to see his arrangements through, even if by nature she was not quite so exact. Indeed, Horace Walpole described one dinner that was delayed by several hours because the Countess kept delaying the meal for new arrivals – and then repeating courses when extra guests showed up.

In summer the Earl and Countess usually spent some weeks at Syon, as well as at Alnwick. Once Parliament was sitting in the autumn they did not return to Syon, but in 1761 they did commission an extensive remodelling of the house. The fact that the area was now so fashionable, with Princess Augusta, the Dowager Princess of Wales living over the river at Kew and the King and Queen regularly using their house at Richmond, was an added reason for creating something glorious. The refurbishments at Syon were therefore more obviously fashionable than those at Alnwick, but they still made concessions to the shell of the existing Tudor courtyard house, whose external brickwork and crenellations were retained.[34] The Earl and Countess first called in the young designer Robert Adam in 1760, soon after his return from Italy. Throughout the whole process it is clear from the Earl's Memorandum Books[35] that it was he who was calling the shots, issuing lists of items required for certain rooms. Adam was also allowed much intellectual freedom of expression, such as the use of rare Doric friezes. The new rooms for entertaining consisted of five large spaces. On the western entrance front an all-white Hall was recreated with the emphasis on sculpture, while the adjacent Ante-Room to the right brought a glorious vision of ancient Rome. On Elizabeth's account, Adam decided to combine the new Library, formerly the Jacobean Long Gallery, as the Ladies' Drawing Room. Female guests, he felt, should be more than one room away from the Dining Room in order not be disturbed by the sounds of male laughter. The ravishing result showed Adam at his most cohesive and creative. Portrait medallions around the gallery were painted to show the lineage of the Percy family. On entering the Gallery from the Red Drawing Room, a false bookcase on the right concealed a door, from where visitors could walk out onto the south lawn: as at Alnwick, care was taken to make the garden more accessible from the house.

The Countess was involved personally in the organisation of rebuilding, watching over the restoration work and reporting back by letter to her husband: on 9 August 1762 she recorded a visit to the house with her younger son: 'The Hall & Dining Room Ceilings finish'd Attic partly floor'd.'[36] The Dining Room was the first of the state rooms to be finished, in 1763. In the first three rooms of the suite, sculpture and fine marbles were especially in evidence: the Earl had gone to great pains to acquire marble copies of antique statues. Elizabeth listed the prices of some of these, including £300 for the Gladiator and £200 for copies of bas-reliefs, as well as for stucco, chimneypieces and furniture elsewhere, and a cost of £4000 for the whole apartment.[37] With the royal family so close at hand, the impressive collection throughout the house of earlier royal portraits, initiated by her ancestor, Algernon, the 10th Earl, was especially important. Later, Elizabeth was to embark on her own picture collection, which so animates Syon as it is today.

At all the family's homes, it was Elizabeth who was credited with the entertainment: she became especially famous for commissioning wonderful illuminations. With the huge riverside garden lit up, the scale at Northumberland House was overwhelming. Often entertainments were given to cement the Earl and Countess's relationship with the royal family. In 1758 a supper was given for George II's mistress, Lady Yarmouth, at which Walpole found the sugar dessert decoration excessive: 'The dessert was a *chasse* at Herenhausen, the rear of which was brought up by a chaise and six containing a MAN with a blue ribband and a lady sitting by him! Did you ever hear such a vulgarism.'[38] As part of a great and extravagant joke, the 'man' represented the King himself, wearing the Order of the Garter. In June 1762 the Countess gave a party for Queen Charlotte's brother, Prince Ernst of Mecklenberg-Strelitz. Horace Walpole was snide, but could not conceal how impressed he was by the attention to detail:

'Lady Northumberland made a pompous *festivo* for him the other night; not only the whole house, but the garden was illuminated, and was quite a fairy scene. Arches and pyramids of light alternately surrounded the enclosure; a diamond necklace of lamps edged the rails and descent, with a spiral obelisk of candles on each hand; and dispersed over the lawn were little bands of kettledrums, clarinets, fifes etc. and the lovely moon, who came without a card.'[39]

Elizabeth's guests mostly appreciated her hospitality and her kind nature, as well as the magnificence of the soirées. Affable and hospitable, she always invited far too many people. When Count Kielmansegge visited in November 1761, she had issued invitations to at least 600; luckily he felt that the house was 'well adapted for so large a party'.[40] When he was there the following January, she had sent out

636 invitations, and could not remember how many people she had also asked verbally.[41] In December 1762 James Boswell left his card there more than once and as a result gained an invitation to a rout: 'Three large rooms and the gallery (a prodigious one) were full of the best company, between three and four hundred of them. The gallery is like one of the rooms in Holyroodhouse for size and richly adorned on the walls and ceiling with landscapes and gilding. The King and Lady Northumberland are exhibited in full length portraits, in their robes...my Lady came up to me with the greatest complacency and kindness.'[42] The Countess even took him to meet her husband. Boswell was vastly impressed: 'This is indeed a noble family in every respect. They live in a most princely manner, perfectly suitable to their high rank. Yet they are easy and affable. They keep up the true figure of old English nobility.'[43] In his attempts to persuade her to recommend him for an army commission, Boswell came to be a great nuisance to Elizabeth, admitting that he would 'run about the house like a tame spaniel...full of joy at being reckoned the particular friend of the heir of that great house of Percy, and a woman of the first consequence on London.'[44]

In 1764 an especially grand evening was recorded by the *London Chronicle*. The coolness with which the Countess had postponed the festivities, reinstating them for the next day between two visits out of town, shows her remarkable authority:

'Lady Northumberland being under a necessity of leaving town on Monday...the grand illuminations designed as a compliment to his majesty's birthday, were postponed till her Ladyship's return, which was on Tuesday evening; when everything was conducted with a decorum and magnificence peculiar to the Countess of Northumberland: 1500 persons of distinction were invited and the garden was decorated with 10,000 lamps, 400 of which being fixed to the balustrades descending by the steps, had a most beautiful effect. Two bands of music were provided, one in the house (where the great gallery was illuminated to an astonishing degree of splendour) and the other in the garden...'[45]

Horace Walpole was amused by the grandeur: 'You would have been diverted at Northumberland House; besides the sumptuous liveries, the illuminations in the garden, the pages, the two chaplains in waiting in their gowns and scarves...'[46] However, there was traffic chaos at the end. Owing to the entrance into the courtyard being very narrow, a great *bouchon* of carriages and sedan chairs built up, so that guests could not depart until 2 or 3 a.m.

Walpole was always rather unkind about Elizabeth, poking fun at her for having 'a pyramid of baubles upon her head' at a subscription masquerade in 1749.[47] When her husband was Lord Lieutenant of Ireland in 1763 he grumbled: 'I do not think it necessary to scatter pearls and diamonds about the streets like their Vice-Majesties of Ireland...'[48] Certainly the couple lived in Dublin Castle at enormous expense. The next year Walpole denounced the Countess for having more footmen than the Queen to precede her sedan chair, ultimately acquiring a total of eight. Nevertheless, the Countess was proud of their popularity during their two years in Dublin. Walpole habitually felt that she was prone to vulgarities and lacked style. When the Earl and Countess were about to visit Paris in 1766, he wrote rather unpleasantly to Lady George Lennox, who was already there, warning her: 'Well there is my Lady Northumberland coming to you, with her belly all diamonds, and her hand in her breeches...'[49] Costume was not her forte: in September 1761 Mary, Duchess of Richmond had said to Lady George that Elizabeth's dress 'was made of silver ground with velvet flowers of all colours it look'd like an old Bed'.[50]

It would be satisfactory to think that Dukedoms were always created voluntarily by grateful monarchs, but the evidence is that they were often requested by the recipient, however discreetly. In 1766, Hugh Smithson managed to manoeuvre himself into a Dukedom, as a sop to his being turned down for Lord Chamberlain. Although he really wanted the glitzy title of Brabant, he was created 1st Duke of Northumberland and Earl Percy, with his heirs limited to any children by his present wife, Lady Betty. This was Elizabeth's third change of name and title: from Lady Elizabeth Seymour, to Lady Elizabeth Smithson; then to Countess, and ultimately Duchess, of Northumberland.[51] She took it all in her stride. Walpole continued to taunt, giving her the soubriquet of the Duchess of Charing Cross.[52] However, he admired the way that, by canvassing every day in the midst of Covent Garden, she helped to get her son re-elected as MP for Westminster. She was, he admitted, 'a true Joan in spirit, style and manner'.[53]

Elizabeth, Countess
and later Duchess of
Northumberland, by
Sir Joshua Reynolds,
1759.

In time Elizabeth began to collect items which she later described in
a catalogue of *Historical Curiosity's* of *c.* 1773. This was for her
'Musaeum' [sic] at Syon, first mentioned in her diary for 1762. In 1765
she purchased for £2.12s.6d from the sale of effects of the deceased
Ebenezer Mussell lot 77, described as: 'Queen Elizabeth's gloves, knife
and fork, work bag, pin-cushion and tooth-pick – Mary Queen of Scots
hair cap, Oliver Cromwell's night cap, camp pillow, silk sash, tobacco
stopper, and Charles IId. Night cap.' All these somewhat optimistically
accredited items survive at Alnwick, except for the toothpick and
tobacco stopper. She also acquired coins, medals, bronzes and

enamels.[54] Her collection of objects perhaps reflects the delightful cheerfulness but apparent lack of finesse in her nature. Walpole described her as a 'a jovial heap of contradictions...her person was more vulgar than anything but her conversation, which was larded indiscriminately with stories of her ancestors and her footmen...She was mischievous under the appearance of frankness: generous and friendly without delicacy or sentiment.' He said that 'Show, and crowds, and junketing, were her endless pursuits'.[55]

Collecting was natural to the Duchess, who eventually began to travel a good deal on the Continent. In buying paintings she was discerning, economical and disciplined: from a private collection in The Hague in 1769 she bought a Jacopo Bassano of *The Adoration of the Shepherds*, a 'Palamedes' of 'a conversation with a red Bed in one Corner' and 'a picture with a Church and steps and two fryars distributing alms'. She especially liked Dutch paintings: in 1771 she bought 'my best Teniers' at The Hague, as well as some others. In Antwerp on the same trip she wanted to buy seven paintings from one of the three Beschey brothers, but although she returned the next day, 'we did not deal.' At his brother's house she asked the price of a picture, called for her coach in disgust, and then acquired it for just over half the original amount: this was *Hermit in his Cell*, which still hangs at Syon.[56]

The Duchess also collected prints, usually in large sets or albums, and often by the finest Antwerp printmakers of around 1600.[57] Many of their subjects were biblical, or portraits and topography, perhaps hunting subjects, though not old masters; in addition she assembled a light-hearted album of mezzotints satirising *macaronis* (foppish young men) and the extreme fashions they affected. She also collected ivories in large numbers, noting their acquisition in her diaries, simply as 'I bought two charming ivories' (23 April 1771) or in 1772 at Ghieslinghen, a town of ivory turners, 'bought a great many of their Toys for a few shillings'.[58] The subjects are mostly classical, from the seventeenth and eighteenth centuries. Some have since been collated in a large nineteenth-century cabinet at Alnwick. All the Duchess's acquisitions were diligently recorded in her 'Musaeum Catalogue', which ran to nine small volumes and included pictures, a whole volume of prints, books and curiosities. She even took the trouble to make indexes.

Wined and dined by the European nobility, sought after for her opinions as well as her bank book, Elizabeth had begun to enjoy a new independence. In 1770 she wrote: 'Having long determin'd to quit the Court where I found I had no longer the Degree of favour I had before enjoy'd and my health being not so good as when I was younger and also the part my Lord had taken in politics making it much more eligible for me to be no longer a dependant [sic] a State I ever detested and longing to Enjoy my Liberty entire made me resolve to resign my post of Lady of the Bedchamber to the Queen.'[59] Resigning her position at Court, from 1769 to 1772 she made annual sojourns to Paris, where she bought furniture and Sèvres porcelain. On 16 May 1770 she attended the wedding ceremony of the Dauphin, later Louis XVI, and Marie Antoinette. She was undaunted about the difficulties of foreign travel, stoically putting up with wheels breaking off the coach, drunken postilions, sleeping in stables, damp beds, appalling food and bad weather. Her most constant companion was Tizzy, her dog.

During this time building increased again at Alnwick. After he had completed the work at Syon in 1768–9, Robert Adam went north to finish off the Duchess's suite of Gothick interiors. In the Saloon the background wall colour he chose behind the white trellising was blue, with straw-coloured compartments in which were helmets and trophies of war. Each door was surmounted by six Gothic brackets supporting a superb cornice, on which was placed a small Percy lion: above these were figures of St George slaying the Dragon, patriotic images of the family's history of conquering their evil foes. The Great Drawing Room, in the middle of the suite, was finished and first used on the Duke and Duchess's wedding anniversary in July 1770.[60] From its three window recesses was 'a beautiful and extensive View of the Country with the River Alne meandering in the Vale'.[61] Four Gothic pilasters supported arches that divided the ceiling, in the manner of fan vaulting. The ceiling was again richly ornamented, the colours of the background being Adam's very un-medieval green and pink.

Adam also created a library and chapel in a new wing adjoining the main circuit in the keep, which linked it to the middle gatehouse.[62] Some of the twenty-four stools for the chapel survive, light and pretty with their fretted Gothick tracery. A banqueting room was created by Adam inside the inner bailey, in the upper level of the rebuilt eastern tower. On her visits to Alnwick, Elizabeth had noted items of furniture, and their maker, and in a book of circa 1773 she made a list of fashionable cabinetmakers, including the names of Chippendale, who had dedicated his *Gentleman's and Cabinet-maker's Director* to the Duke, and of Cobb and Vile, Ince and Mayhew, and Linnell.[63] She also began to introduce French items, by then widely fashionable for drawing rooms, such as huge looking glasses: that in the Great Dining Room, supplied from Paris, cost £355.

In her methodical manner, much in keeping with her husband's efficiency, the Duchess also made many lists pertaining to household management at Alnwick. She described the numbers of rooms and the numbers of beds 'quartering the Family', which included servants: in July 1768 staff alone numbered fifty-two, of which about forty came from London, including the ubiquitous footmen. The numbers subsequently soared upon the arrival of family and guests with accompanying servants: by then the footmen numbered eleven, with six kitchen staff. Usually numbers for 'publick' dinners, which took place on Thursdays and Sundays, varied between fifteen and twenty-five. Silver for use at table was sent in chests from London. On a non-public day, the Duke and Duchess would dine at a table with their chaplain, the Revd. Mr Percy, while there would also be a Stewards' table for about twelve and a Pantry table for eleven. Care of each fire was again allocated to a particular individual, a very sensible precaution in the days when houses so often caught alight from a spark. Often the Duchess noted the contract made with a particular servant, perhaps locally hired, their duties, wages and where they were to live, and exactly what extras they were to receive. The housekeeper stayed at Alnwick all year and consequently had to make lists for the Duchess of all wines, distilled waters, medicines, sweetmeats and pickles made by her: all had to be clearly labelled, including her initials. Tea and chocolate for preparation in the Still Room had been brought from London. There were instructions for the Servants Hall, with 'swearing, cursing indecent or abusive language' banned at table. Confirming the daily schedule for the staff, the Hall was to be open between 9 and 10 (for their breakfast, after several hours of work) and to be opened again for two hours when their Dinner Bell rang, locked again until Supper, and left open until the Duke and Duchess rang to go to bed. The servants thus had a very long day, but it was punctuated by a proper time allocated for their meals.

While working at Alnwick, Robert Adam was also asked to remodel the great dining room and drawing room at Northumberland House.

These were on the first floor of the main south range, with views down to the Thames. Despite three ceiling drawings being made in 1770, work in the drawing room did not commence until 1773, possibly because the Duke was trying to find a way of manufacturing plate glass in England rather than sending for it to France. The Glass Drawing Room at Northumberland House was a brilliant, radical creation, being lined entirely with panels of plate glass in deep crimson.[64] Its furniture had two patterns of red fabric, one with gold vases and foliage, the other a crimson, green and white silk damask that was also used at Syon and at Alnwick. The room was not uniform: with its green-banded ceiling and green dado, entablature and doors, this extraordinarily sophisticated and brilliant scheme was described as a 'harmony of many contrasts'.[65] No evidence can be produced for the Duchess having a part in the design, but she made a partial list, with those for Syon and Alnwick, of the prices of paintings, chimneypieces, and furniture acquired at this time for Northumberland House. Had she entertained from the Glass Drawing Room it might well have set a fashion. Unfortunately the style never took off, probably because of her death, in early 1776. The glorious decoration was there: the mistress of the house was not.

After thirty years of marriage, and various infidelities on the Duke's part,[66] in her letters Elizabeth still addressed her husband very affectionately. She had once been told by a fortune-teller that she would not live beyond the age of sixty, as a result of which she believed that she would die on her sixtieth birthday. This she did. With unusual modesty she had requested that the number of people attending her funeral should be as restricted as possible; in the event this did not happen.[67] As befitted their liking for pomp and show, and their love of each other, the 1st Duke and Duchess of Northumberland lie buried together in St Nicholas' Chapel in Westminster Abbey. However, it is at Alnwick that the Duchess's memory has always been especially strong: on the estate a number of monuments were erected to her by her husband, notably a tower at Brizlee, designed in 1781 by Adam in her beloved Gothick style. The Duke also built an observatory at Ratcheugh and a garden house at Hulne Priory, where visitors could picnic in a room decorated by Adam, gazing at his wife's beloved view of the ruins of the ancient abbey. His adornments to the Chapel glorified her to the extent that Judith Milbanke, who visited in 1784, felt that it 'has much more the appearance of being dedicated to the late Dss than to the Almighty'. According to her description, 'Both sides are covered with her Pedigree derived from the Emperor Charlemagne, blazoned in a magnificent and gaudy style – in a large window at the upper end is an immense Sarcophagus of white marble sacred to her Memory, most beautifully carved and with her bust in front of it.'[68] At about the time of the Duchess's death the couple had commenced the building of a ballroom in Newcastle, for assemblies.[69] It was, of course, ascribed to the Duke. However, with her good nature, vast wealth and especial love of her own county, it would have been typical of the Duchess of Northumberland to wish to encourage the social life of her townspeople.

When some eighty years later the Gothick decoration at Alnwick was removed by Anthony Salvin in favour of Renaissance-style interiors, Salvin was himself reluctant to depart from the medieval character of the Castle. The great Victorian architect of the Palace of Westminster, Sir Giles Gilbert Scott, bemoaned the destruction of Elizabeth's schemes as 'one of the greatest and most lamentable mistakes which has been made in the present day'.[70] Her contributions to the collections at Syon House were considerable, but the Duchess's most individual monument was her fluttering, chivalric castle.

Chapter 11

BLUESTOCKING BRAVADO
ELIZABETH ROBINSON,
MRS MONTAGU
1720–1800

'In the winter of the year and the winter of our life, our principal enjoyments must be in our house.'[1]

Elizabeth Montagu is best known as a lady of letters. She was a leading member of what Admiral Boscawen called 'The Bluestocking Circle', a loosely constructed group of friends, mostly women, who enjoyed discussing literature and philosophy. It was Elizabeth who had devised the term 'bluestocking', but in jest and with reference to a man. In a letter of 1756 she used it to describe an eccentric scholar called Benjamin Stillingfleet, whose simple crime was sartorial, that of wearing blue worsted stockings to a gathering where smart white hose would have been more appropriate. Her description became synonymous with the image of an intellectual, in this case a slightly blundering botanist who cared little what he wore. In its subsequent early usage, the term applied both to men and to women: 'Mr. Montagu passd ye Xmass at Sandleford, I with the blue stocking philosophers. I had parties of them to dine with me continually...'[2] In addition to Elizabeth Carter and Catherine Talbot, the first generation of Elizabeth Montagu's London circle included Elizabeth Vesey, Hester Chapone and the newly widowed Mrs Boscawen. They were to be joined by the actor David Garrick and his wife Eva; Lord Lyttelton; Anne Donnellan, versed in music, the classics and religion; and for a brief but intensive four years, William Pulteney, Earl of Bath. By the 1770s the celebrated young novelist Fanny Burney and the intellectual Hannah More had joined their gatherings, though they never considered themselves part of the inner Bluestocking Circle. An important member of the group in its later form was the lively Hester Thrale, at whose elegant home at Streatham Park Dr Samuel Johnson was a semi-resident. Dr Johnson had some admiration for Mrs Montagu, but they quarrelled in print over Shakespeare and were never close friends. The portrait painter Sir Joshua Reynolds and his sister Frances were also regular visitors to Mrs Montagu's soirées, as was the political philosopher Edmund Burke. Elizabeth Montagu's principal literary ventures were three dialogues anonymously contributed to Lyttelton's *Dialogues of the Dead* (1760), her ambitious *Essay on the Writings and Genius of Shakespeare*, published in 1769, plus a lifetime of correspondence.

Elizabeth Montagu was remarkable not only for her literary pursuits and contacts, but also for her considerable building achievements. As a wife she commissioned a very fine London house and made some alterations to a home in the country, but it was as a widow that she reached her architectural apotheosis, building a sensational new town house and making equally impressive alterations to her country seat at Sandleford Priory in Berkshire. In an age when the preferred style was essentially classical, and an increasingly refined and defined classicism at that, in selecting schemes for building or decoration it was advantageous to have had some extra education, and in particular some understanding of the antique. Mrs Montagu is a particularly interesting example of a woman who was enabled to compete with men by her lively mind and by her essential fearlessness.

Elizabeth Robinson was the daughter of a reluctant country squire who preferred to be in London. Matthew Robinson had been educated at Trinity College, Cambridge and owned property in Yorkshire. His wife Elizabeth Drake, herself well educated, had inherited homes in Cambridge and in Kent, where young Elizabeth Robinson, the fourth child and eldest daughter, spent her early years from the age of seven at Mount Morris, near Hythe.[3] This was an elegant, newly built house, with fine walled gardens. Elizabeth learnt French and Italian and came to understand Latin, though later 'she sometimes denied it'.[4] Her three elder brothers, who inevitably were given more education, always encouraged her desire to learn; but the real catalyst in Elizabeth's education was the time spent at Cambridge with her grandmother and step-grandfather, Dr Conyers Middleton, who was the university librarian. The couple lived in what Walpole described as 'an excellent house adjoining Caius College and looking into Theatre Yard, and near St Mary's Church, in the most cheerful part of the town'.[5] There, encouraged especially by Dr Middleton, Elizabeth avidly discovered the classics. He persuaded her to pay attention to 'learned' conversation and to follow the strict mental discipline of summarising the talk.[6] This made her into an excellent listener. Later, Dr Middleton told her he had observed her 'amiable qualities from her tenderest years'[7] and reminded her 'that Cambridge had had a share in her education'.[8] With a further three younger brothers, who were born in the Middleton house, and a sister, Elizabeth was the strongest character in the family. The fact that the learned doctor should select a girl in whom to take a special interest, rather than the usually preferred boy, is an indicator of her intelligence and precocity.

It was due to Dr Conyers Middleton that Elizabeth made the most important friendship of her life. It is not exactly known when she met Lady Margaret Cavendish Harley, but it is certain that Dr Middleton went to the family home at Wimpole Hall, a few miles outside Cambridge, where he may have been librarian to Lady Margaret's father, Edward Harley, 2nd Earl of Oxford.[9] The Earl had a remarkable library and was an obsessive collector of manuscripts and coins. When Lady Margaret received her first letter from Elizabeth, dated 24 February 1732, Elizabeth had already been to stay. Lady Margaret was seventeen; Elizabeth was really still a child, having not yet turned twelve. It was the elder girl who had encouraged the younger to write. Over the following years the friendship developed, mirrored in their correspondence, which included serious discussion of literature and drama as well as mildly salacious gossip about engagements and married couples. Through this introduction to aristocratic life, as well as to art collections, fine houses and elegant parks, Elizabeth Robinson entered a new world.

In 1734 Lady Margaret married the Duke of Portland. This was an arranged match, which suited both families. He owned fine estates: she, as a great heiress, brought added revenue. Over a period of several years Elizabeth used to stay on with the Portlands in London at the end of the social season, after her own family had relinquished the house that they used to rent for a few months at a time in Jermyn Street. The first record of this arrangement was in 1738 when she was invited to help with the formal social ceremonies following the birth of the Duchess's child. Elizabeth wrote to her father that she would need a new 'Suit of Cloaths' in order to go about with the Duchess to meet 'all the people of quality of both Sexes'.[10] Mr Robinson sent £20, and Elizabeth displayed commendable economy in buying a 'second': 'I have obey'd your commands as to my cloaths & have bought a very handsom blue & silver Ducape within the twenty pound, a little accident which has happen'd to the silk in the Lomb made it a great deal cheaper...'[11]

Already Elizabeth could see the social advantages of the friendship, even though she loved high society not just for its cachet but also for the stimulus it gave to her energetic mind. The young Duke and Duchess made their country home at Bulstrode in Buckinghamshire, an august house with Dutch gables, built by Judge Jeffreys in 1686 and bought in 1706 by the 1st Earl of Portland. In 1740 Elizabeth stayed with them there for the first of many happy visits. She loved the beautiful park, with its great gardens, menagerie and aviary, and enjoyed the Bentinck family tradition of feeding the hares on the lawn.[12] In 1740 she wrote to her friend Mrs Donnellan: 'I am Happy in the Best Company, in the finest Place, the House is magnificent, the Gardens and Parks are Beautifull.'[13] The size of her own apartment struck her with awe: Elizabeth reported to her sister Sarah that if they were ever to be two elderly spinsters, it would be quite space enough for them both.

Inevitably Elizabeth had begun to think of her own future. It was obvious that possibilities on the scale of Bulstrode were only tenuously available. Although as a cousin of Sir Thomas Robinson of Rokeby she came from the edge of the aristocratic world, the barrier was money. Most gentlemen would seek to augment their own estates by marrying a girl with a good dowry. Mrs Robinson certainly viewed the lack of a fortune as an impediment; she also perceived that her daughter was exceptionally choosy. For her part Elizabeth did not believe that men could be so mercenary as they were represented: 'I am not at all of your opinion in two things. The first that I shall never marry, & the Second that the wisest & best Men marry for money, I think Sense & virtue in a Man will induce him to chuse prudence & virtue in a Woman, & surely Sense only teaches a person the true value of things...but till I can meet with a Deserving Man who rightly thinks the price of a Virtuous Woman above Rubbies I shall take no other obligation or name upon me but that of being...your most Dutifull Daughter...'[14]

Despite this apparently romantic response to her mother, Elizabeth was pragmatic: 'For my part, when I marry, I do not intend to enlist entirely under the banner of Cupid or Plutus, but take prudent consideration and decent inclination from my advisors.'[15] Given the impediments of high standards and a small dowry, Elizabeth's gentleman of fortune was not a bad match, although rather alarmingly he was, at fifty-one, nearly thirty years older than her, and a bachelor, when a widower might have been safer. Mr Edward Montagu seems to have courted Elizabeth in London, probably in the spring of 1742. Socially it was a reasonably good match: he was a grandson of the Earl of Sandwich. Attractions of her own included what her nephew later described as 'the peculiar animation and expression of her blue eyes...and...the contrast of her brilliant complexion with her dark brown hair'.[16]

The marriage was satisfactory financially as well as socially advantageous. In personal terms it appeared at the start to be slightly less than perfect. Elizabeth was not radiant in the weeks leading up to her wedding, and commented that marriages were created in an extraordinary way, 'unlike the matching of shells with their proper kind'.[17] She told the Duchess of Portland: 'I really behaved magnificently; not one cowardly tear, I assure you, did I shed at the solemn altar; my mind was in no mirthful mood indeed.'[18] Years later she remarked to the unmarried Elizabeth Carter: 'You and I, who have never been in love...'[19] Theoretically she was everything that one could wish for in a wife; dutiful, charitable, intelligent, good-natured. Her husband was antisocial, of a scientific bent and not necessarily very exciting. However, the early days of the marriage proceeded well: she found him easy to live with and referred to him as 'my friend'.[20] That autumn she wrote that 'Since I married...I have never heard him say an ill word to anyone; nor have I received one matrimonial frown'.[21] With the financial insecurity of her background making her take nothing for granted, she was deeply grateful both for the advantages brought by the marriage and for Edward Montagu's devotion. The marriage gave her a new outlet for her energies and talents, freeing her from the doubtful situation of being single and hard up; it was thus natural for her to be committed to him. The couple seem to have become reasonably fond of each other. Elizabeth wrote to her husband: 'I am thankful for the benefits of fortune, and pleased with them, but really attached only to the person who bestows them'[22] and 'While Heaven shall lend me life, I will dedicate it to your service...Your kind behaviour and conversation has made my Being of such value to me.'[23] In 1745, worried about her health, Mr Montagu wrote to her: 'The happiest days that ever I passed in my life have been with you, and I hope Heaven will give me the long enjoyment of your charming society, which I prefer above everything on Earth.'[24]

Early in her marriage Elizabeth Montagu made a series of visits to her husband's different properties, of which the first was to Dover Street, in London, on 10 August 1742: 'This morning I have been looking over the house, and seeing many things better than I deserve, in which I am to have a share...I find the house very good and convenient, and I hope I shall spend many happy days in it.'[25] In time Mrs Montagu was to live in three fine London houses; meanwhile there were the country properties to see. At the time of her marriage she had no idea what these houses were like, even though she would have to live in at least one of them. At Allerthorpe, her husband's estate in Yorkshire, initially she was not so charmed, but persuaded herself to look at the positive aspects: 'We have at present very fine weather, the sun gilds every object, and I assure you it is the only fine thing we have here, for the house is old and not handsome: it is very convenient, and the situation extremely pleasant.'[26] Four days later, she was more optimistic: 'I think it is the prettiest estate, and in the best order I ever saw; large and beautiful meadows for riding or walking in, with a pretty river winding about them, upon which we shall sometimes go out in boats.'[27] On this visit she had to stay in the north for six months, during which time she visited a secondary estate at Denton, and collieries near Newcastle. Dutifully she would continue to visit these every autumn throughout her married life and into her widowhood, entertaining the miners and their families to banquets, and providing them with meat, clothes and even education for the children. She never forgot that it was their hard work that provided the revenue for her great schemes.

A further addition to Mr Montagu's fortunes came through the death of his first cousin in 1758. More land at East Denton came his way, as well as cash and collieries, and Denton became the principal northern estate. On the couple's initial visit in that year, however,

Denton Hall was 'not fit for our reception'.[28] Eventually Mrs Montagu arranged the rooms, mostly from a distance, including three garrets for servants. Even for the rooms she and her husband were to inhabit, she aimed for simplicity and economy, buying second-hand items and 'the cheapest kind of carpet', and sending tables from London that she did not like so that she could have new ones in town.[29] The process of inheritance together with its responsibilities was described by her as 'the usual accompaniment of riches: a great deal of business, a great deal of hurry, and a great many ceremonious engagements'.[30] Taking over from her unworldly husband, she played her part, to the extent of arranging for fifty boys to be taught to read and write by a schoolmaster at Denton, and making plans for local girls to be taught knitting and spinning.[31]

The country house on which Mrs Montagu concentrated most of her energies was Sandleford Priory, just south of Newbury. When they married, her husband already owned a long lease on the house. On her first visit she reported: 'I think I may say you never saw anything so pretty as the view these gardens command, for my part I would not change the situation for anything I saw.'[32] The house itself was somewhat antiquated. The original Priory had been founded around 1200[33] by Geoffrey, 4th Earl of La Perche and his wife Matilda of Saxony. Forsaken in about 1480, the site was given to the Dean and Chapter of Windsor, and in the early eighteenth century the house there was being let out,[34] before Edward Montagu gained the leasehold in 1730. It therefore had no ancient family connections, and a more selfish wife might have requested a remove to something better than a modest manor house on medieval foundations. However, Elizabeth Montagu loved the location, eventually commissioning a painting of herself and her husband against the view from the house, rather than the building itself. To this day the prospects to both west and south remain unspoilt.

Mrs Montagu did not make major changes to Sandleford Priory for some time, perhaps because her husband liked it as it was, having already lived there for twelve years as a bachelor. Certainly he was reclusive: 'Mr Montagu is always so loth to change place.'[35] He preferred to be at his books, studying mathematics and astrology. Elizabeth stayed regularly at Sandleford, in the course of fluctuating between town and country, northern and southern estates, and visiting Bulstrode several times a year for conversation and company. Early in the 1740s the Duchess of Portland sent her a dozen orange trees for her conservatory,[36] and later Elizabeth asked the Duchess for two peacocks to console her white peahen at Sandleford. In 1743 a tree was planted to the south in joyful celebration of the birth on 11 May of their son John, who was always known as Punch. A letter describes the wearing domestic bustle of moving the ménage to the country: 'Bag and baggage we arrived here on Thursday night: first marched the child crying, nurse singing and the Abigails talking, Mr Montagu, my sister and myself brought up the rear.'[37] In 1744, when there was an epidemic of smallpox in London, Elizabeth kept her son in the country, but sadly Punch's Oak, still there today, was to survive much longer than its young owner. When he died in September 1744, the devastated couple consoled each other: she wrote that her husband 'loved his child as much as ever parent could do', but that he also showed her 'an example of patience and fortitude'.[38]

From Sandleford Elizabeth made many local visits. In Berkshire she went to the gardens of Stephen Poyntz at Midgham near Aldermaston, to West Woodhay Manor and Cranbury Park, and to Basildon Park with its famous grotto; she also visited Beaulieu, the Montagu family seat, in Hampshire. At West Woodhay, she was anxious that the owner should be out, suggesting genuine curiosity about the house rather than a desire to make social contact. That this was an established convention is illustrated half a century later in Austen's *Pride and Prejudice* (1813), when Elizabeth Bennet is persuaded by her uncle and aunt to visit Mr Darcy's magnificent home, but is horrified and embarrassed to find him returning unexpectedly. Mrs Montagu's expeditions also included Salisbury, Wilton House, where she admired the Double Cube Room, Stonehenge, Amesbury, Marlborough and Savernake, all in Wiltshire. Further travels subsequently took her to Thoresby in Nottinghamshire, Lord Burlington's Assembly Rooms at York, and for sociable weekends to her friend Lord Lyttelton's fashionable new house at Hagley in Worcestershire. Nearer to London she visited Pope's garden at Twickenham, the Hon. Charles Hamilton's gardens at Painshill and David Garrick's villa on the Thames at Hampton. She was becoming well equipped both to decorate her own houses and to plan their gardens.

It was in London that Mrs Montagu's first major building scheme took form, offering a good project in which to immerse herself after

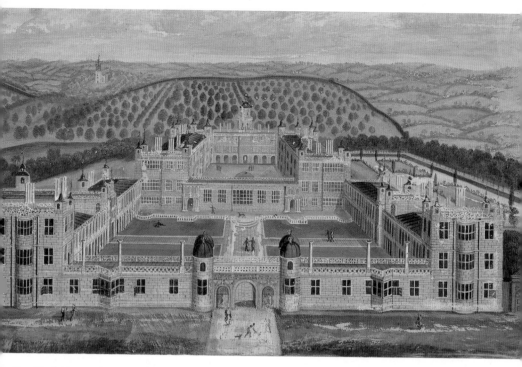

Audley End, Essex, showing the scale of the house before the near courtyard and the far gallery range were pulled down: late eighteenth-century watercolour based on earlier engravings by Henry Winstanley.

Audley End: the Countess of Portsmouth's rebuilt gallery, on the far side of the main range as seen above.

Audley End: the Fish Room, now called the Saloon.

Opposite: Audley End, Essex.

Alnwick Castle, Northumberland, by Canaletto, 1752.

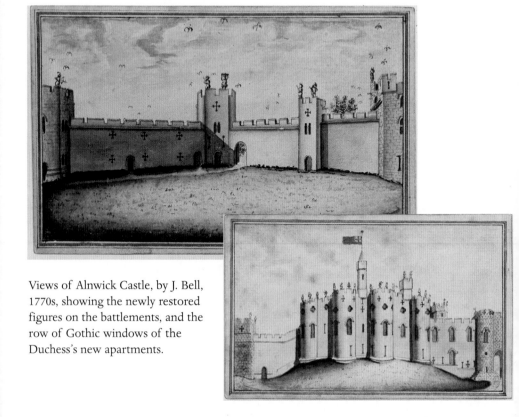

Views of Alnwick Castle, by J. Bell,
1770s, showing the newly restored
figures on the battlements, and the
row of Gothic windows of the
Duchess's new apartments.

Syon Park, Middlesex, by Canaletto, 1749.

Northumberland House, London, by Canaletto, 1752.

Sandleford Priory, Berkshire.

View from Sandleford Priory, looking towards the village of Newtown and the Hampshire Downs, with Edward Montagu seated, his wife Elizabeth beside him, and her sister Sarah Robinson to the left, by Edward Haytley, 1744. Elizabeth's beloved haymakers are shown beyond. The far pond may be that made the previous year from the three smaller ponds. The formal pools were subsequently subsumed into the landscape park.

Sandleford Priory: the ceiling of the Octagonal Drawing Room, by James Wyatt.

Hill Street, London: the Zephyr ceiling by James 'Athenian' Stuart, painted in 1767.

Joseph Bonomi: Design for the Great Room at Montagu House, 1790. Through the window at the end can be glimpsed the side of the Countess of Home's house at 20, Portman Square, revealing the angle at which Montagu House sat across the corner of the square.

Punch's death. From Dover Street she supervised the building of a handsome brick house not far away at 23 Hill Street (now number 31), starting in 1744: 'We shall stay in London about a week getting a plan for finishing a house which we are to have in a street near Berkeley Square, in a street not yet built...'[39] This was in a very fashionable part of London, and just round the corner from Lady Isabella Finch's recently built house by William Kent at 44 Berkeley Square. The house is similarly quite narrow, with rooms on three storeys. Mrs Montagu had three principal rooms for entertaining on the first floor, a long room along the front of the house with a newly fashionable rococo ceiling, and a 'dressing room' and formal bedchamber at the rear over-looking the garden. Elizabeth was one of the first hostesses to create a room in the Chinese style. This was the room to the left at the rear of the house.[40] She professed not to take the idea too seriously: 'Sick of Grecian elegance and symmetry, or Gothick grandeur and magnifi-cence, we must all seek the barbarious gaudy goût of the Chinese; and fat-headed pagods and shaking mandarins bear the prize from the finest works of antiquity.'[41] In fact her enthusiasm was whole-hearted: in January 1750 she told her sister that 'It is like the Temple of some Indian God', adding: 'The very curtains are Chinese pictures on gauze, and the chairs Indian fan-sticks with cushions of japan satin painted: as to the beauty of colouring, it is carried high as possible...'[42] The visit-ing salonnière Madame du Bocage was very impressed on her visit that year: 'We thus breakfasted to-day at my Lady Montaigu's in a closet lined with painted paper of Pekin and adorned with the prettiest Chinese furniture, a long table covered with pellucid linen, and a thou-sand glittering vases presented to the view coffee, chocolate, biscuits, cream...'[43] On Christmas Eve, 1752, Elizabeth Montagu described how the previous evening 'the Chinese-room was filled by a succession of people from eleven in the morning till eleven at night'.[44] The following spring she told her husband: 'I had rather more than an hundred visi-tants last night, but the apartment held them with ease, and the highest compliments were paid to the house and elegance of the apart-ments.'[45] The Chinese room was also used for her more private meetings with her bluestocking friend, the reclusive Elizabeth Carter.[46] A comment addressed to her friend in December 1765 suggests that she was moving towards having the room toned down: 'I rejoice that we may so soon meet in the Chinese room when the elements are much mitigated, as befits the winter season.'[47]

Never one to let fashion pass her by,[48] in order to have her dressing room altered Mrs Montagu turned to the young Robert Adam, whose first commission had been the home at Hatchlands near Guildford of her friend Mrs Boscawen. He was also said to be a relation.[49] Ladies' dressing rooms or boudoirs came to be one of Adam's specialities: they were like jewel cabinets, containing especially precious items for show.[50] Mrs Montagu's 'Silver Room', as it would always be called, was a rare exercise in his Chinese manner. In replacing the earlier Chinese decoration at Hill Street, Adam reduced the amount of chinoiserie: two drawings by him dated 1766 show a classical ceiling, with eight chinoiserie roundels inserted into the scheme, and a carpet in a related design.[51] While Mrs Montagu was out of town in June, her sister Sarah received 'Mr Adams': 'He brought the pattern of the ceiling...He has promised to get the people about preparing it directly.'[52] However, his proposed chimneypiece was described as an undue expense: 'Mr Adam is a traitor to betray me into the vanity of a marble chimneypiece.'[53] Nevertheless, she capitulated: the chimneypiece may be the surviving one now in the Great Room at the front. By October of that year, the works were well under way, Robert Adam writing to her: 'I hope this month we shall nearly finish your room in Hill Street. The gilders are at work and I am doing all I can to push them on. My long absence from town has made them more Dilatory than they otherwise [have been]. The Chimney piece is out up and I am convinced you will like it...the taste of it harmonizes with the other ornaments of the Room. The paintings [presumably the ceiling panels] are almost finished, of the moment the gilders have done...I shall put them up. I cutt [sic] away that disagreeable projection over the Chimney altogether, so that now the Cornice runs round the whole room...'[54] He was also hoping to get everything finished, with the workmen out of the house before her arrival.

In January 1767 Mrs Montagu wrote 'from our palace in Hillstreet' to her sister Sarah that: 'My Dressing Room is really wonderfully pretty. Mr Adam has done his best, he has exerted much genius on the doors in emulation of his Rival Stewart. I assure you the dressing room is now just the female of the great room, for sweet attractive grace, for winning softness, for le je ne sais quoi it is incomparable.'[55] She was so pleased with the doors, their panels painted by Cipriani,[56] that she declared them 'pretty enough to make me a thousand enemies. Envy turns livid at the first glimpse of them.'[57] The rivalry between Adam and James 'Athenian' Stuart was well known: indeed, it was to be displayed in adjacent rooms within the very house. Mrs Montagu had known of Stuart, who was primarily a decorative wall painter, both from her friend Lord Lyttelton, who had employed him on a temple in the gardens at Hagley Hall in 1758, and from the 1st Earl and Countess Spencer, for whom he designed dazzling interiors on the first floor at Spencer House on Green Park between 1759–65.[58] He was first commissioned to paint a room at Hill Street in 1759;[59] unfortunately, he was known for being lazy and disorganised,[60] and a letter from Sarah shows that by December 1765 he still had not begun work at Hill Street: 'I find Mr Stuart has had no pity on you or your third room.'[61] Sarah suggested to her sister creating a window, which in the event was done in the adjacent dressing room, in Adam's redecoration. In April 1766 Elizabeth told her husband: 'I have just now received the letter and having had Mr Stuart with me and had a great deal of useful talk with him about the agreement and if not such as it should be in every respect I certainly will not sign it.'[62] Eventually Stuart started painting her bedroom at Hill Street: she wrote in November 1767 that 'Mr Stewart has painted me some of the sweetest Zephirs and Zephirettes in my bedchamber that ever I beheld',[63] but the scheme was not completed until June 1772. In May 1773 Mrs Delany described 'Mrs M's (Hill Street) *room of Cupidons*', which had recently been opened 'with an assembly for all the foreigner, the literati, and the macaronis of the present age'. Painted 'with bowers of roses and jessamines entirely inhabited by little cupids in all their wanton ways', the choice was generally seen as rather a lapse of taste, the comments being 'many and sly'.[64] Nevertheless, Mrs Montagu was obviously proud of her scheme, of which the surviving ceiling is in the elegant neoclassical manner. It shows a zephyrette, or west wind, at the centre, surrounded by putti in eight terracotta roundels, the medallions therefore paired with the adjacent scheme by Adam. The putti are enacting the signs of the zodiac, with a further four medallions added to the rococo ceiling in the Great Room, which also survives. Stuart's chimneypiece, cornice and doorcases for the bedchamber are also extant.

At Hill Street Mrs Montagu entertained such leading figures in London society as David and Eva Garrick, along with those ladies, including his own wife, whom Admiral Boscawen had earlier derisively christened 'The Bluestocking Club'.[65] Among some intellectuals of the time there was a revulsion against card-playing, in favour of serious conversation: accordingly at these soirées not only was there no gaming, but little talk of politics.[66] Hannah More dined there regularly, recording in 1775 what must have been a fairly typical party, comprising 'Mrs Carter, Dr Johnson, Mrs Boscawen, Miss Reynolds and Sir Joshua, the idol of every company', as well as 'Some other persons of high rank and less wit'. She applauded her hostess: 'Mrs Montagu received me with the most encouraging kindness; she is not only the finest genius, but the finest lady I ever saw; she lives in the highest style of magnificence; her apartments and table are in the most splendid taste...Then her form...is delicate to fragility; her countenance the most animated in the world...'[67] The next year she described how she had just spent 'one of the most agreeable days of my life, with the female Maecenas of Hill Street'.[68] This was again a dinner invitation, from which she travelled home with Dr Johnson, her hostess teasing her that there might be a 'Scotch elopement'. Certainly conversation was seen as a new art, one cultivated both by the more fun-loving Mrs Thrale and by Mrs Montagu, who invariably dominated the talk. Despite their reservations about her as a friend, Fanny Burney describes the rapid, brilliant and 'flashing' manner of her speech,[69] while Mrs Thrale could not help admiring her intelligence, writing: 'Yesterday I had a conversazione. Mrs Montagu was brilliant in diamonds, solid in judgement, critical in talk.'[70] Dr Johnson grudgingly admitted 'That lady exerts more *mind* in conversation than any person I ever met with.'[71]

Given Mrs Montagu's eventual building achievements, it is surprising that throughout her letters she commented less on architecture than on the countryside, on the glories of nature and on vistas natural or man-made: 'The beauties of a palace are not so enchanting as those of a garden or park.'[72] At Stowe she loved the landscape, saying, 'it gives the best idea of paradise that can be',[73] but was not impressed by the follies: 'no-one durst say that they [the garden buildings] were absurd.'[74] On a Scottish tour in 1766 she wrote that she would rather dine in 'the rude magnificence of nature' than in 'the meanest of ye works of art',[75] thus anticipating the movement towards the Picturesque so recently begun by Edmund Burke.[76] In 1770 she admired

Kedleston Hall, in Derbyshire, 'where the arts of ancient Greece and the delicate pomp of modern ages unite to make a most magnificent habitation'. Yet despite thinking it 'the best worth seeing of any house I suppose in England', she qualified her approval: 'I know how it is that one receives but moderate pleasure in the works of art. There is a littleness in every work of man. The operations of nature are vast and noble...'[77]

Elizabeth Montagu certainly wanted her homes to be beautiful, but mainly as a backdrop for her social and intellectual life, which is where her real interests lay. It is not true to say that she was especially materialistic. From an early age she had no illusions that a woman's place in the world could be significant without a dowry, making her 'a toy while she is young and a trifle when she is old'. Money brought both pleasure and power: 'Gold is the chief ingredient in the composition of worldly happiness.'[78] However, character was more important than belongings: even before she was married she derided the 'mighty Possessions and vast Tenements' of some 'Dull mortals'.[79] She told Elizabeth Donnellan that she sometimes wished 'to snatch the Duchess of Portland from her great Possessions on earth'.[80] Despite Hannah More's description of her as a 'Maecenas', Mrs Montagu was a creator of settings rather than a collector *per se*. With her active brain and natural desire to control, she simply could not resist imagining aesthetic improvements: 'my mind...was incessantly forming landscapes.'[81]

It is hard therefore to reconcile the attitudes expressed in Mrs Montagu's writings with what some of her contemporaries saw as an excessive love of display. Fanny Burney quoted Mrs Thrale telling Dr Johnson that 'you who love magnificence, won't quarrel with her, as everybody else does, for her love of finery',[82] while Fanny herself in an equally veiled criticism said that one has to allow a little for 'parade and ostentation'.[83] Among other things, it was felt that Mrs Montagu wore too much jewellery,[84] especially in later life when she dripped with diamonds. Given the newness of her wealth, she simply could not resist playing with it. She was also censured, again by Hester Thrale, for 'only cultivating people of consequence'.[85] There may be an element of truth in this, but often her friends were intellectual or religious as much as aristocratic: it could be argued that she simply liked interesting people. She enjoyed the slight upward social movement provided by her marriage, but what she relished far more was having the means and the confidence to pursue her interests and her friendships, as in her long correspondence with the Scottish philosopher Dr James Beattie, a man of humble origin. This was confirmed by Lady Louisa Stuart, who said that Elizabeth Montagu knew everyone: 'authors, critics, artists, orators, lawyers and clergy of high reputation; she graciously received and protected all their minor brethren, who paid court to her; she attracted all tourists and travellers; she made entertainment for all ambassadors, especially if men of letters.'[86]

At Sandleford attention was anyway first focused outdoors, where Mr Montagu was making changes to the grounds, throwing three of the old ponds there into one,[87] and planting chestnuts and oaks.[88] In October 1765 Elizabeth told Mrs Carter of her plans for changes there by Robert Adam: 'Mr Adam, I assure you is an admirer of the Gothick, but he says it is too expensive for us, so my dear Athenian maid – you will be a la greque as you ought to be, & I assure you there is a stately owl who almost every night solemnly paces over the bowling green... Mr Adam will contrive us an admirable apartment below & two good apartments above the stairs.' The emphasis in her letter was nonetheless on the gardens: 'The kitchen garden is to be carried to the other side, the barns are to be removed, the granaries demolished...'[89] Elizabeth also planned to enlarge the stream, saying that she disliked 'large pieces of standing water' and loved a 'winding river'.[90] All this was in keeping with her feeling for nature.[91] She loved to place her desk under the elm trees in order to write her many, many letters[92] and told her sister: '[Sandleford] is a mere summer house, one would never be there but when one could live in an arbour.'[93] In 1773 she described her enjoyment of giving a harvest party: 'I assure you it was very splendid in its way. We had a large lamb roasted whole, and crowned with garlands of flowers, and much of other good cheers. I have a great pleasure in feasting those who are seldom feasted...'[94] To James Beattie she wrote: 'I had yesterday thirty-six haymakers, and their children, at dinner, in a grove in the garden. When they work in my sight, I love to see that they eat as well as labour, and often send a treat...'[95] In 1775 it was at Sandleford that she nursed her husband throughout his long, last illness. He was buried twenty miles away in the nave at Winchester Cathedral. Having been ever tactful, it was only after his death that she felt free to carry out some long-nurtured ideas of her own.

Plans for a new house in London were already afoot in the spring of 1775, in Portman Square, which was then beginning to be laid out. In April a site was leased, shortly before Mr Montagu's death in May. Getting wind of the project, James Stuart wrote in the spring of 1777, saying to Mrs Montagu that he wished 'to request the honour of seeing her...before any other artist is spoken to'.[96] Building commenced that year, with the walls above ground by June.[97] Elizabeth suggested playfully to Sarah that 'I believe by November...all the stars should be twinkling in the blue firmament I shall be wishing my great room was finished & the Lustres glittering in it & my self sitting in the Center, beaux spirits in one hand, some gentlemen & fine ladies (without any esprit at all) on the other, feathered nymphs & great – maccaronies circulating about.'[98] In August Sarah told her that: 'Mr Cutts & I walked on Thursday to visit your new house. It is – almost all round as high as

Montagu House, Portman Square, in the nineteenth century.

the top of the Hall Door.' The builders were still working at 8 p.m., often continuing until after dark, by candlelight.[99]

At No. 22, Montagu House sat across the northwest corner of the square. It comprised seven bays, with Venetian windows at each end of each side on the first floor. Mrs Montagu took pleasure in imagining the house as the fashionable social backdrop that it would become: 'It will serve as umbrellas and fans for Beaux and Belles.'[100] By December 1778 she was 'well pleased' with the compartmented ornamental ceiling of the 'Gallery', the room above the front door.[101] In April the next year she approved the shade of grey for the apartment in which Mr Leonard Smelt, the surveyor and a former tutor to the royal princes, was to lodge, with his wife, during the works; also the cotton fabric that she 'had destined' for Mrs Smelt's room, asking too what paper she would like best, 'one of the same pattern or a grey, or one with flowers on grey ground, some of that sort I have seen very pretty'.[102] Here too Mrs Montagu was showing an unaffected concern for people who worked for her.

In June 1779 Elizabeth began to lay out the garden. She had by then lived at Hill Street for thirty years and longed for the increased space: 'I am impatient to have my new house fit for habitation, as I think the large and high rooms and its airy situation will be of great service to my health; and I am sure such noble apartments will be a great addition to my pleasures.'[103] From October 1777 she had been trying to sell Hill Street. This took over four years. She kept muttering about lack of funds while it did not sell, but always with humour: 'While my new house is building till the other is sold I am in the condition of the poor people who say they have a wolf within them which wolf devoures what should nourish them & tho they eat a great deal they are still hungry & meager.'[104] Despite the high level of expenditure on her new house, financially she managed well. Her husband had left her a generous £7000 a year and she was determined to pay for the whole project out of income, over a period of five years: 'I shall have attain'd my object to change a small House for a large one without making any scar in my affairs, which I think will be a great achievement.'[105] Nearly four years later she declared that she had succeeded: 'My house never appeared to me so noble, so splendid, so pleasant, so convenient, as when I had paid off every shilling of debt it had incurred...'[106]

There were many practical problems with the Portman Square

house. She rejected one of the new type of printed 'mechanical paint-ings' executed by Francis Eginton for Boulton and Fothergill, on the grounds that it was ill drawn. In April 1780 some specially commissioned doors arrived prematurely for the Gallery, for which the supplier, the Birmingham entrepreneur and designer Matthew Boulton, a cousin by marriage, received a complaint.[107] Mostly items were arriving late because James Stuart had not given Boulton's firm the design. Two weeks later Mrs Montagu asked Leonard Smelt to sort things out with Stuart:

'I am so solicitous to have our House ready for us to inhabit, & I know, by experience, Mr. Stuart is apt to forget that his promises are not fulfil-l'd, & talks of designs for chimney pieces & Pillars, &e, &e which exist only in his brain, & when I write to the workmen who are to execute them to know why they are not finished they answer they will set about the moment Mr. Stuart gives them the designs. I wrote a most indignant letter to Mr. Eggerton at Birmingham to know why some order which architect had given them more than a twelve month before were unexe-cuted, he answered that he had not received these orders, & behold the designs were lying in the dust & confusion of Mr. Stuart's study in a very incomplete & unfinishd state...'[108]

She wrote again the next day, telling him that James Stuart was unreli-able, forgetful, dishonest, and had been 'for a fortnight together in the most drunken condition' with the workmen.[109]

Undismayed by the slow progress, Elizabeth wrote in October 1780 that 'I am more and more in love with my new house', optimistically proclaiming that 'When a fog obscures Hill Street there is a blue sky and a clean atmosphere in Portman Square...'[110] So proud was she of her venture that she allowed people to visit the house while it was being decorated, but only if they had previously applied for tickets. She went to the City to select lamps for the hall and had already taken delivery of a silver dinner service from Matthew Boulton. She stipu-lated that this be of 'elegant simplicity', for not more than twelve or thirteen guests, with her arms engraved on each piece.[111] Large numbers of plates were delivered, as well as a tureen, sauceboats and ladles, together with the advice that 'all silver exposed to the London air will grow black and Tarnish'd unless kept up in paper & bags'.[112] In

1780 Boulton also became involved in an arduous project to help her to obtain plate glass for specified windows: less brilliant crown glass was to be used in her own bedchamber which looked on to the next door house.[113] After many difficulties, she obtained the glass herself,[114] but the windows were still unready when she visited in October, making the mansion 'literally and metaphorically a Castle of the air'.[115] Her last payment to Stuart was made in March 1781, after which she still had problems in getting Boulton to deliver mirrors for the Gallery, for which she had enlisted the help of James Wyatt.[116]

While fitting the house out, Elizabeth wisely consulted the needs of her staff, writing in the early summer of 1781: 'I hope by the end of the week the wishes of my housekeeper, caprices of my laundrymaid, the fancies of my housemaids, the demands of my cook, and the accommodation of my Butler will be fulfilled, completed and answered, and I assure you they make a total of no small significance.'[117] In early November she wrote: 'I have been in a strange kind of bustle, giving directions for small but necessary articles which had been neglected but that must be completed before I can inhabit my new house.'[118] The furniture was moved shortly afterwards and a letter to her 'first correspondent' from there is dated 12 December, describing how despite the 'din of hammers' she had now dined in her new eating room, and how quietly she had slept in her new bedroom.[119]

Although the process of decoration continued over the next ten years, the house with its vast and lofty rooms was loved and appreciated by its owner from the start. It had 'ample rooms for company, its cheerful rooms for private enjoyment'.[120] She prepared for her first Christmas with happiness, enjoying the quietness of the season in town,[121] when others had left for the country as was the 'ton'. Elizabeth considered this a rather tedious habit: she herself usually spent the whole winter in London, returning, if she left at all, for the New Year.[122] The next summer, of 1782, she stayed in town because Sandleford smelt of new paint, and enthused about her London home: 'The moon shines with all her majesty into my eating room and at night I send away the candles to take a walk in it.'[123] She certainly enjoyed the spaciousness: 'I believe Portman Square is the Montpellier of England. I never enjoy'd such health as since I came to live in it.'[124]

Among the many people who came to view and marvel at the house,

James 'Hermes' Harris, the literary intellectual and philosopher, was particularly impressed by its fashionable Grecian style: 'I am to inform you I have see an Edifice which for the time made me imagine I was at Athens, in a House of Pericles, built by Phidias.' He especially admired Elizabeth's hand in it all: 'I felt a more solid satisfaction, the satisfaction of reflecting, that, in my own Country, the genius of Phidias could still produce an Architect, and the genius of Pericles still produce a Patroness.'[125] The greatest compliment of all came from the often critical Horace Walpole, who visited in February 1782: 'On Tuesday with the Harcourts at Mrs Montagu's new palace, and was much surprised. Instead of vagaries it is a noble, simple edifice. Magnificent, yet no gilding. It is grand, not tawdry, not larded and embroidered and pomponned...'[126] Current fashion, as much as individual taste, may partly have been responsible for the absence of gilding. On the ground floor the visitor entered through two halls punctuated by freestanding Ionic columns and adorned with sculpture by Bonomi.[127] The wrought-iron balustraded staircase was top lit. On the *piano nobile* there was a circuit of five rooms for entertaining.[128] Over the main entrance the Gallery had apses at the ends, and an Adamesque ceiling, with paintings possibly by Angelica Kauffman.[129]

The most famous part of Montagu House, at the front of the building, under a square coffered coving,[130] was the Feather Room.[131] Here were hung several extraordinary and original tapestries made of feathers. The scheme for these seems to have been Elizabeth's own idea, after she had learnt how to do feather work along with her friends the Duchess of Portland and Mrs Delany. As in the customary manner of shell collecting for the decoration of follies, family and friends would help supply the basic material. In February 1784 Mrs Montagu asked her sister-in-law: 'If you have an opportunity of getting me any feathers they will be very acceptable. The brown tails of partridges are very useful tho not so brilliant as some others.'[132] Later she especially wanted the neck and breast feathers of a stubble goose.[133] Mostly the feathers were from peacocks, pheasants' tails, or those of 'a handsome cockerel'. The tapestries were made at Sandleford, where the feathers were mounted on canvas by Mary Tull. It was not easy work: if it was being carried out in the body of the house, which was being re-roofed, the feathers were liable to 'mount on the wings of the wind', so Elizabeth had to move to the newly built octagon room.[134] Conservation

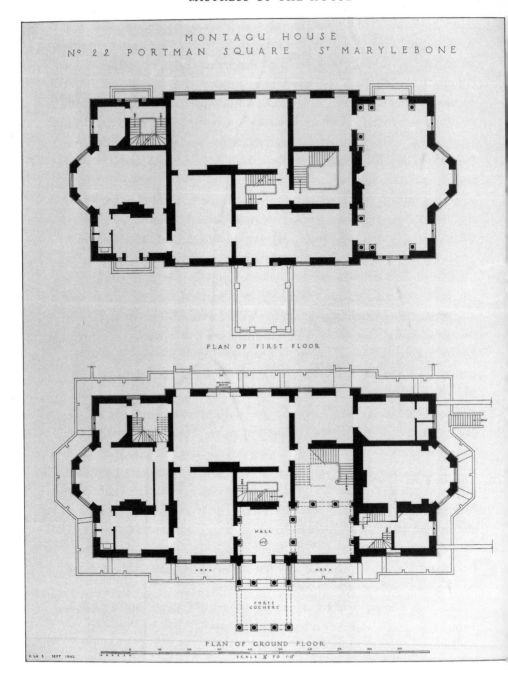

Montagu House, floor plan.

was also difficult: once the tapestries had been installed, the walls of the room 'had to be covered with a paper hanging lined with linen to preserve it from moth and summer dust'.[135]

The *St. James's Chronicle* described the room: 'wholly covered with feathers, artfully sewed together, and forming beautiful festoons of flowers and other fanciful decoration. The most brilliant colours, the produce of all climates, have wonderful effects on a feather ground of dazzling whiteness.'[136] The tapestries were 'executed by Mrs Montagu herself, assisted only by a few female attendants, instructed for that purpose'.[137] When the room was opened the poet William Cowper sang an ode to it: 'The birds put off their ev'ry hue/To dress a room for Montague.'[138] From the Feather Room, initially denoted as a Morning Room, the visitor could enter the private Dressing Room, whose commode had been painted with four muses by the decorative painter Giovanni Battista Cipriani. The other door from the Feather Room opened into the large dining room, for which James Wyatt had also advised, in collaboration with Cipriani and Biagio Rebecca.[139] On the garden side a grand coffered arch supported by Ionic columns led to an antechamber. This little room had a ceiling decorated in the Pompeian style, with paintings in the grotesque manner on the overdoors, recalling those in Spencer House. It gave access to the Great Room, which ran across the northern end of the house.

As early as 1781 Mrs Montagu commented that while she aimed to give the rest of the house 'a sort of splendid comfortableness', the Great Room would take time to complete, 'as it is rather popular & magnificent than dedicated to comfort and friendship'. Here she would pursue 'the modern folly of assembling great numbers together' rather than the 'modern sin of shifting the company assembled', presumably to smaller rooms.[140] By the late 1770s Stuart had become impossible to work with, mainly due to the influence of drink: the room was completed after his death in 1788. The first design for this huge space by Joseph Bonomi was made in 1782 and exhibited at the Royal Academy the following year.[141] He had worked as a draughtsman for the Adam brothers for eighteen years, and through his marriage was related to Angelica Kauffmann. By the time that he drew her a second design in 1790, there were a few amendments.[142]

Elizabeth had now moved from the relative lightness of her other schemes to the massiveness of the pure antique. In the executed scheme the Corinthian gilded capitals on green scagliola columns emphasised the status of the Great Room as quasi-palatial.[143] The fine barrel-vaulted ceiling was inset with paintings: the centrepiece was said by the *St. James's Chronicle* to be by Rigaud, while the other paintings were probably by Bonomi himself.[144] The walls were hung with pure white damask, while the white satin curtains were fringed with gold. The window frames were of solid white marble. Chiaroscuro panels painted by Biagio Rebecca for the doorways were so beautiful that Mrs Montagu called him back to quote for a design resembling white marble bas-reliefs as overdoors: the results were much admired.[145] Bonomi designed a special carpet, its architectural detail echoing the designs for marble or scagliola.[146] The *St. James's Chronicle* further reported: 'the chandeliers and looking-glasses are superb; and the whole is an assemblage of art and magnificence which we have never witnessed in a private room.'[147] Walpole attended the opening of 'her great room and the room with the hangings of feathers', on the morning of 6 June 1791.[148] Even Queen Charlotte visited, taking with her the six Princesses. For Elizabeth, this was the ultimate accolade: 'The honour and the delight I received by her Majesty and the princesses visit, no pen can describe, no paper contain.'[149]

Throughout the building of Montagu House, Mrs Montagu had seven or eight 'agreeable persons' to dinner two or three times a week, with individual friends on other days.[150] In 1787 she wrote that she had been there three weeks and had not had three hours of leisure.[151] Quite shamelessly, in her search for perfection, Elizabeth had consulted every available expert on what was seen as the truly antique style. Her new home was an intellectual response to the Countess of Home's ravishing house next door at No. 20, but Stuart's initial intransigence, and her own perfectionism, meant that the timing of the building programme could not match that of Wyatt and Adam. Great entertainments[152] continued to take place in what she termed her 'palais de la vieillesse'.[153] Montagu House, subsequently the home of the Portman family, was one of the period's last remaining private houses on this scale in central London, retaining its front drive with trees, railings and handsome gateposts until being bombed during the Blitz, in 1941.

Meanwhile, changes were made in the country, where Elizabeth always spent the summer, calling it 'the life of the golden age'.[154] In the

Montagu House: the Great Room, 1894.

creation of her principal ground-floor rooms at Sandleford Priory, she brought urban sophistication and dazzling design to provincial Newbury. The rooms were at the back or more private side of the house, where she transformed the defunct Canons' Chapel into a dining room. The chapel wall at the east end was moved out to gain the correct classical proportions, and in the huge space three separate tall windows were inserted, admitting a wash of morning light. Beyond lay magnificent views over the valley to the east. Mrs Montagu regarded the vista as a crucial part of the scheme, to be incorporated into the room's design: '...having, at my request, made a fanlight over the east window, so that, the arch formed by the trees is now visible, these rooms are the most beautiful imaginable.'[155] Three tall windows also punctuated the wall to the south. With dinner timed for mid afternoon, the light would by then stream in from the south. The scheme was powerfully elegant, with a strong acanthus decoration placed over the doors. When the room was first in use, in July 1781, Elizabeth wrote with her usual wit about the chapel having been 'taken from the owls the bats the rats & mice', all the while enjoying the anticipation of a visit from the Archbishop of Canterbury: 'This morning has been entirely wet & gloomy & yet my reform'd chapel...looks cheerful & pleasant from the windows & within very comfortable from a large fire.'[156] The converted chapel is still known by the girls at Sandleford, in modern times a school, as MMDR, or Mrs Montagu's Dining Room.

A marvellous octagonal drawing room joined the former chapel to the rest of the house. It shows Wyatt at his neoclassical best, in a mode reminiscent of Stuart rather than Adam. Below the dome-shaped ceiling, fine classical medallions were set within round arches. The chimneypiece also incorporated Wedgwood medallions, in slate-grey. Ever in control, Mrs Montagu still had to chivvy: 'Mr. Wyats room which he has built for me will be charming the walls have been hard many weeks & have waited for the blue tyles, & he is so idle as not to have given an order for them tho frequently solicited.'[157] She also became quite desperate for him to get the slates onto the roof.[158] A year later, she was thrilled with the results: 'My octagon drawing room far exceeds anything in my house in Portman Square as a Building and from its prospect derives still greater charms.'[159] At each end a link to the next room was provided by a square alcove with columns. The entrance to this new wing was a slightly raised-up, colonnaded antechamber, provincial in scale, and created out of the former drawing room, which led off the main hall. The sequence of rooms created a 100-foot indoor walk. A kitchen passage cunningly ran past the oval room to the north, to allow service to the dining room.

Meanwhile, the grounds were landscaped in order to maximise the views from the house. In 1781 Elizabeth brought Capability Brown to Sandleford, albeit that she was set on economy, feeling that she had gone rather too far in London: 'I told him I had sacrificed so largely to the City Demons, Pomp and Vanity, in Portman Square, I could offer but little to the Rural Deities.' She admitted a puritanical streak: 'I have some plebeian sentiments which forbid my incurring debt, so his improvements must not go beyond what my cash will immediately answer. I shall begin by embellishing what lies under the view of my new rooms.'[160] Brown cleared the earlier gardens on the site, except for the bowling green behind the house, and created a simple parkland. Elizabeth was delighted with her garden designer: 'He is an agreeable, pleasant companion, as well as a great genius in his profession. I consider him a great poet.' Vistas were ever important to her, combining a love of the natural with a feeling for the poetic: 'As fast as time wrinkles my forehead, I smooth the grounds about Sandleford...In a little while I shall not see anything belonging to me that is not pretty.'[161] Her dislike of follies remained: she wanted a 'beautiful pastoral scheme'.[162] She wrote firmly: 'We shall not erect temples to the gods, build proud bridges over humble rivulets, or do any of the marvellous things suggested by the caprice, and indulged by the wantoness of wealth.'[163]

Brown visited twice in the winter of 1781/2 and Elizabeth reported him as working 'his magick act on the groves woods etc.'[164] There was much progress: 'Mr Wyatt has nearly completed what belonged to the architect; and Mr Brown, by removing a good deal of ground and throwing it down below, to raise what was too low, while he sank what was too high, has much improved the view to the south.'[165] Her interest in the rustic, so fashionable at the time, and in ordinary people, also meant that she now enjoyed employing twenty unemployed weavers as her haymakers. The view from the eating room was superbly achieved: 'From the east window in the eating room we see them working in several places between the trees & it forms the prettiest perspective scene imaginable.'[166] Despite the death of Brown in 1783, the work continued as he had instructed, with the rivulet to the east of the house being widened,[167] to make 'a piece of Water at the side of a Wood, which will in time embellish the scene...'[168] She was pleased with the result.[169] Thirty men were still working on another river extension in 1787.[170] Looking at the slow progress of the newly planted trees, Mrs Montagu was philosophical that 'the hopes of their giving pleasure to those I love, when I am no more, will render them objects of pleasant contemplation'.[171]

In the summer of 1782 the work indoors at Sandleford was intensive:

'At my arrival I found my house in all the litter & racket various works & workmen could occasion. Stone masons were laying the floor in the hall, & carpenters at work on the stair case, & many artificers were busy at the Stucco on the outside of the new rooms. I gave these gentry a soft rebuke for not having perform'd their task in the time allotted...'[172] Undeterred, she proceeded with the next stage: 'This morning... Mr Wyatt arrived here & is now making a design for the improvement of my bedchamber & dressing room.' Noise and mess at the house were so considerable that summer that she decided to go north until October,[173] returning directly to London; likewise the following autumn, when the new work was again being rushed through before the winter.[174] The rooms were still drying out in the summer of 1784, at which stage the house was in 'a miserable condition'.[175] For the dressing room, built above the library, James Wyatt used buttresses to support a balcony with an iron balustrade round the great bow window. He decorated the room with his unusual anthemion and umbrella frieze. On the southwest corner he created for his patroness a huge bedroom in a simple antique style, with wonderful views of the Ridgeway to the south. The paired columns at each end of this magnificently proportioned space had unusual hybrid capitals, which Wyatt devised specially. The only decoration hinting at femininity was the neoclassical chimneypiece; with its elegant and restrained mouldings, the room's powerfully simple decoration reflected its owner's intellectual mind.

Guest bedrooms were also created, on the west and east sides of the narrow main body of the house. These still retain their long-leafed Wyatt friezes. A new drive was also being created: 'no longer shall you approach it by the way in which wagons travel to Winchester, but about a quarter of a mile from the House a pretty gate should admit you into the grounds, & bring you by a winding path to the door.' All the landscaping and office work was making the place appear 'with the bustling industry of the beehive': Elizabeth admitted that she was 'the Queen bee'.[176]

A setback occurred in October 1784, when a fire broke out in the house, beginning in Elizabeth's old dressing room: the incident was blamed on Wyatt's workmen, who had moved a beam. The blaze occurred at 4 a.m.: Elizabeth's nephew Matthew, who from early adulthood had also come to live in the house, heroically 'jumped out of bed, rush'd into my room, & begged that he might immediately conduct me downstairs with a tender zeal equal to that of the pious A[e]neas'. She was so glad that no lives were in danger that she did not worry about the property, saying that the damage was 'very trifling'. Others at the scene said that she was extremely brave.[177]

The principal ground-floor improvements continued up to 1786. Despite the accent on classicism, Mrs Montagu finally let Wyatt gothicise the exterior, creating an extraordinary hybrid.[178] As a young man Wyatt had been averse to the fashion for Gothick Revival, but in the 1780s he became its principal exponent: his first exposition of it, from 1779, was at Sheffield Place in Sussex. For him, Sandleford Priory was thus an early essay in this style. Whether or not Mrs Montagu saw the crenellations and tracery as a reminder of the original priory's ecclesiastical purpose, it was certainly a considered decision: 'Where a part is to be extended beyond the firsts intention, the additions should be Gothick; for symmetry not being the object of the Gothick architect, irregularity is not considered an imperfection in their designs...I am more a friend to the Gothick on the outside than within.'[179] The house was rendered, with extra tracery picked out at the back to suggest a Gothick window. Its colour was probably slightly more stonelike or sandy than the present grey. Wyatt also gothicised the front entrance hall, with fine tracery doors, fretwork and niches; likewise the inner hall, with beautifully executed fan vaulting. The combination of styles is neither unappealing nor overbearing, but shows that Mrs Montagu was prepared to enjoy some architectural fun.

Over the years many people of note came to visit at Sandleford, including Mrs Boscawen's daughter, the tall and elegant Duchess of Beaufort, with her Duke. Mrs Montagu was flattered that her cousin the Primate came to stay regularly, as well as a succession of deans and of earls, of Edinburgh intellectuals, including Dr James Beattie, and of bluestockings, a large proportion of whom were women on their own. She loved having young people to stay: Dorothea Gregory, the daughter of Dr John Gregory, a widowed Edinburgh friend, came to live with Elizabeth following her own father's death. Elizabeth's younger brothers came to dinner every Sunday and stayed in the holidays, and her nephew Matthew, son of her late brother Morris Robinson, lived at Sandleford from about the time that he left Harrow. When he became her heir, at Elizabeth's request he changed his surname to Montagu:[180]

this was the name by which she always addressed him. Matthew's elder brother inherited the Robinson title to become Lord Rokeby. In 1785 Matthew married Elizabeth Charlton, who brought with her a large fortune. He subsequently remained at Sandleford with his wife and expanding family, while Mrs Montagu considered herself grandmother to their ten children. The impression of Sandleford in the late 1780s and '90s is of a lively and happy family home: now that he had a 'fair Eve' as his wife, Matthew considered it 'a Paradise'.[181]

Of Mrs Montagu as a person there was some divergence in view. Although worshipped by her immediate bluestocking friends, both male and female, and admitted by Fanny Burney to be 'the first woman for literary knowledge in England',[182] the young novelist also described her as 'a character rather to respect than love'.[183] This was confirmed by Sir Nathaniel Wraxall, who, while admiring the intelligence in her countenance, said that her features had in them 'something satirical and severe, rather than amiable or inviting'.[184] It may have been that people misread Mrs Montagu's quick intelligence for sharpness: she liked to control the conversation, and even to control people, but she was certainly extremely thoughtful for others. She was very good with staff, and was kind to ordinary people: her staff at Sandleford in 1784, included a blind employee.[185] She was generous in giving annuities to people in need, often without knowing them. At her May Day party on the lawn at Montagu House between 1 and 4 p.m., any chimney sweep who cared to turn up was given roast beef and Yorkshire pudding.[186] Certainly Mrs Montagu had an iron hand, but she was too intelligent not to keep it constantly concealed in the velvet glove.[187] Lord Bath[188] said that he did not believe that a more perfect human being was ever created, a view with which Edmund Burke concurred. Edward Wortley Montagu said that she was the most accomplished woman he ever saw, while Lord Hardwicke placed her portrait at Wimpole Hall as a gesture of admiration.[189] Dr Johnson, who gave her the name of 'Queen of the Blues', admitted that she was 'a very extraordinary woman'.[190] Lady Louisa Stuart, perhaps snobbishly, sometimes wanted to laugh at her, but conceded that she had 'quick parts, great vivacity, no small share of wit, a competent portion of learning, considerable fame as a writer, a large fortune, a fine house, and an excellent cook'.[191]

Mrs Montagu was a talented natural organiser and leader. These abilities were supremely well channelled into her building schemes, and into shaping the adjacent landscape. Time that she would otherwise have devoted to child rearing was spent visiting other houses, gardens and towns, and creating the interiors of her own homes, the greatest of which began some twenty years after her marriage. The conventional in her behaviour hid the romantic in Elizabeth's soul, which was expressed more through strong colour and design in her building schemes and in her love of landscape than in any other aspect of her life.

Chapter 12

LANDED WITH THE PAST
THERESA ROBINSON,
MRS JOHN PARKER
1745–75

'...On Monday came through charming country to this delightful place. I could not help thinking how happy you would all have been to see the manner in which I was entertained, French horns playing all dinner time and again in the wood in the evening when the guns were fired...'[1]

When, in May 1769, Theresa Parker arrived as a new bride at her husband's family seat at Saltram in Devon, she was overjoyed with her surroundings. Standing high up to face south to the nearby estuary, and east and west to the small hills of rural Devon, the house was light and sunny. It no longer looked like the old-fashioned dwelling that it really was; instead it appeared classical and symmetrical, thanks to modernisation work undertaken by Theresa's mother-in-law, Lady Catherine Parker, who had died in 1758.

Lady Catherine Poulett married John Parker in 1723. For twenty years she and her husband lived in the old Tudor manor house at the family estate of Boringdon, adjacent to Saltram. Lady Catherine was not happy with either home as it was: what she wanted to build was a substantial classical house, as exemplified in a plan inscribed 'to Lady Katharine Parker at Saltram'. As the daughter of the 1st Earl Poulett, Secretary of State and Lord Steward to Queen Anne, she was both wealthy and forward-looking. After a number of suggestions,[2] a compromise was reached, in which the west, south and east façades were each wrapped in a newly classicising exterior, with the front entrance on the south, probably moved there from the east. It is believed to be on Lady Catherine's initiative that the rococo decoration was chosen in what is now called the Entrance Hall, said to date from *c.* 1750, as well as in the adjacent Morning Room and Staircase Hall.[3] The marvellous Chinese wallpapers at Saltram can also be ascribed to Lady Catherine. It was normal to confine this new style of papers to bedchambers and dressing rooms: the latter were semi-public in London, but in the country were more private, although still used for entertaining special guests. At Saltram, Chinese papers were used for two bedchambers and two dressing rooms, possibly with a third bed and dressing sequence.[4] Mr Parker and Lady Catherine also purchased a set of padouk Chinese Chippendale chairs, Chinese mirror paintings, Chinese porcelain and possibly the Chinese Chippendale mahogany bed. It is difficult to find concrete evidence that any of the work apart from the architectural drawing is of her personal commission, but there are many suggestive pointers. The decoration that is believed to be Lady Catherine's choice is exciting for its innovation, but less well informed than the later amendments.

Legend suggests that Lady Catherine had first wished to live at Saltram when her husband became ill, seeing it as her dower house: in the event they moved there together, so that it was ironic that she should in the end predecease her husband. Whatever the context of the move from Boringdon, it would be difficult for anyone who loved southern views and the play of light on water to ignore the delights of the location at Saltram. Certainly it was the situation that initially was so appealing to the daughter-in-law whom Lady Catherine never knew.

The daughter of the first Baron Grantham, the Hon. Theresa Robinson had been brought up at the Court of her godmother, the Empress Maria Theresa, in Vienna, where her father was the British Ambassador. Her family home was at Newby (now Baldersby) Park in Yorkshire, which was one of the earliest Palladian Revival houses, built by Colen Campbell for her grandfather, Sir William Robinson. Theresa met her country squire through her elder brother, the Hon. Thomas Robinson, who was Foreign Secretary to John Parker's close friend from Oxford days, the 2nd Earl of Shelburne. The latter must have been delighted with his part in providing a young and attractive second wife for his recently widowed friend;[5] John and Theresa Parker were extremely happy together. Of her early married life, Theresa's sister Anne wrote: 'Theresa is as well as possible in very good spirits, and both she and Mr Parker very happy as you may imagine.'[6] When he visited Saltram in September 1769, just five months after the marriage, their brother Thomas observed: 'I do not recollect anywhere to have seen any Gentleman live in better or more handsome style than our Brother-in-law. The Chere is delicious – the table plentiful, the wines good, and the servants attentive & numerous.'[7] To John Parker's respectable bank balance and healthy country living Theresa was to bring an intuitive understanding of classical design, of colour and of comfort.

Theresa Parker was gentle and dignified; pomposity was alien to her nature. In letters to her brothers her affectionate personality shines through. The elder, Thomas, who became the 2nd Baron Grantham on the demise of their father in 1770, was posted the following year as Ambassador to Spain; their younger brother Frederick accompanied him. Lord Grantham called her 'the best of Daughters, Sisters, and Wives';[8] her letters of reply show how much she missed both brothers in their absence abroad. They were a close family, their sister Anne, or Nanny, spending much time with Theresa at Saltram. Thomas, an amateur architect, enjoyed sharing an interest in design with his bright and enthusiastic sister. He was a member of the Society of Dilettanti from 1761, a Fellow of the Society of Antiquaries from 1763 and at the age of twenty-five was made a Fellow of the newly formed Society of Arts. Theresa's letters to Fritz, as she called her younger brother, reveal her playful sense of humour as a perceptive bystander, making fun of London life without being severely critical.

Theresa knew her own views on marriage, believing that one must marry the right person or not at all, as indeed was to be the case for her sister Anne. Theresa herself did not marry John Parker, who had been a widower for five years, until she was about twenty-four.[9] Her dowry was £12,000, which was not a particularly large sum. She thoroughly disliked the way that society mothers encouraged their daughters to marry for rank or money: 'I think nothing contributes more to the many unhappy Marriages one sees than want of nicety in the young Women at Present, who are much more to blame in that respect than the men. They set their caps at every man of fortune that comes out, are strongly seconded by their mothers and take the first that offers.'[10] When, five years after her own marriage, her elder brother asked her to think about trying to find a wife for Frederick, she said that one should not look for money: 'I should advise him not to think of so much as £60,000 and to study nothing but his happiness.'[11] She further believed that he would be happier if he had a pretty wife: 'He says nothing of beauty – which I don't understand; indeed I must talk to him fully upon the whole subject before I allow him to think of a wife.'[12] As a family they were not snobbish. Anne failed to be impressed when a dinner companion insisted on relating her entire (and undistinguished) pedigree: 'I found means to make my escape.'[13]

By the time that Theresa arrived at Saltram, John Parker had already called in Robert Adam, to request a Saloon and a Library, having inherited the house the previous year.[14] The basic shape of the so-called Great Room, comprising two smaller rooms combined into one vast double cube with a deeply coved raised ceiling, had already been created.[15] The Venetian window was also in place, and the chimneypiece by Thomas Carter the younger had been paid for by John Parker, Senior.[16] Probably through Theresa's intervention, Adam's ceiling design of 1768 for John Parker, Junior was much modified when the room was completed. The gryphons holding up medallions on the cornice were retained, but a lighter ceiling was created, still in three sections, each containing an oval surrounding a lozenge and a roundel instead of the initially proposed repetitive and rather heavy shell-based ovals.[17]

The Parkers did not just let Adam take over. Theresa and her husband decided to keep the new Carter chimneypiece in the Great Room: Adam's own design for a chimneypiece was therefore redundant. Although they had paintings by Zucchi on the ceiling,[18] as part of Adam's design, they did not agree to the inset overdoor and overmantel paintings that he proposed, leaving the spaces bare for old masters that they would themselves acquire. These paintings would give the room its own personality, not only with the inclusion of Theresa's full-length portrait at the far end to match that of Sir Thomas Parker on the opposite wall, but also by showing her own selection of paintings. The plasterwork in the two rooms was by Joseph Rose.[19] Following Adam's colour plan, Theresa wrote to Frederick in London in September 1769 asking him for 'some patterns of Blue Damask, as we shall soon write to Genoa and wish to fix upon the best Blue for setting off the pictures'.[20] Frederick obliged: a year later John Parker 'left with Mr Robinson to pay for ye Genoa Damask…£300'. Acquiring the damask directly from Genoa meant that it would be of the highest quality, rather than the generic alternatives available in London.

The carpet for the Great Room was designed by Robert Adam, and made by Thomas Whitty, at Axminster, not far away in west Dorset. Whitty was not yet famous, and the price was relatively modest.[21] As was typical of carpets both designed by Adam and made by Whitty, the Great Room design is loosely based on the ceiling.[22] While the central lozenge shape of the ceiling instructs the main central motif in the carpet, the latter diverges quite considerably in that it has no ovals, only one central roundel, and extra lozenges in the borders. It also has the additional chunky floral garlands so typical of Whitty: Adam's light harebell garlands in the ceiling are not echoed in the carpet. The quarter shell motifs are on a much larger scale in the carpet than the half shell motifs above. The strong pink in the division lines may derive from Adam's proposal for the curtain colour.[23] The Saloon carpet was delivered on the morning of 23 September 1770 and was 'spread upon the lawn' for admiration. It was deemed 'very beautiful indeed',[24] and its dazzling colours still give an extra depth and excitement to the Saloon.

In the Red Velvet Room on the southeast corner of the house, the young Parkers repainted the rococo decorations, changing their mind halfway through. Theresa's brother Frederick reported in September 1770 that they painted 'the ground of the Ceiling lightest of Greens and the Cornice Pink. They had painted the Shutters & doors &c pink but not liking that they turned it to white & Therese with her usual taste orderd all the mouldings, & parts of the Capitals of the Columns to be Gilt, which makes the Room much chearfuller and handsommer.'[25] From the Red Velvet Room an elegantly furnished entrance that may have been introduced by Lady Catherine framed the Great Room. For it Adam was asked two years later to provide a design for console tables and mirrors. Joseph Perfetti was paid £41 for 'Table Frames in the Velvet Room' in March 1772.[26] These related to gilt tables he had made for the Great Room, in 1771. An 'inlaid table' paid for in 1771[27] could be the fine scagliola one still present. It is also possible that the suite of gilded armchairs and window seats in the room, dating from the 1770s and retaining their original red velvet,[28] were made for Theresa. They were exactly the type of light and elegant gilded French furniture with cabriole legs that was so popular in English drawing rooms in the 1770s. A payment was made in 1771 'To

Reilly at Paris', which was followed up with a second one 'To Walle & Reilly for Cabinet work': it is possible that the firm could have been making this suite of furniture for the Parkers in Paris.[29]

It is difficult to understand the design of the Eating Room at Saltram until one pictures the bookcases that Adam created for it: originally the room was to have been the Library. The bookcases were shown in his immaculately drawn scheme,[30] which John Parker had commissioned in April 1768. The room would have retained its elegant neoclassical atmosphere, with painted bookshelves set in a classical frame, and enhanced by urns on the cornice, the shelves probably with fine gilded detail. The paintings by Zucchi for the Library were finished by September 1769, when Theresa, ever vigilant, asked Frederick to look at them in Zucchi's London studio and give his opinion.[31] This was a sensible precaution: his paintings for country houses have been described as 'ruins-by-yard'.[32] While creating the room as a library, Theresa always envisaged an eating room somewhere else, but it was not until 1778, three years after her death, that her husband made the alterations, largely because of a fire in the house late that summer. However, rather than carrying through Robert Adam's plan for a grand circular dining room on the west front, linked by a gallery to the Great Room, John Parker changed the function of Adam's library, which the architect himself had wished to retain.[33] Although the dining room suggests the work of Adam, the replacement of bookcases by a second series of Zucchi paintings creates false proportions in the wall arrangements, of a kind that the great architect could never have allowed;[34] in consequence the room is too stylised, and less seductive than the glorious Saloon. Moreover, the Eating Room carpet too closely imitates its ceiling, unlike that of the Saloon. It is believed therefore not to have been designed by Adam, but to be taken from a drawing of the finished ceiling.[35] The room as it is reflects neither Theresa's certain hand, nor her sensitive understanding of their decorator: indeed, Adam always placed the dining room well away from the drawing room.[36] Adam's bookcases were removed to the then eating room to the left of the main entrance, which became the new library.

Theresa was very involved in the picture collecting for Saltram.[37] The present collection was mostly accumulated by John Parker, Senior, possibly having been started by Lady Catherine, together with paintings commissioned by John Parker II from his friend Sir Joshua

Reynolds, and acquired by his son, the Earl of Morley. Other works, such as the Neapolitan scenes, may have been bought on the younger John Parker's honeymoon with his first wife, who had died in Naples. The collection does not, as one might expect, include paintings of his horses and dogs,[38] suggesting that he was not over involved in building it up: indeed, John Parker had not done a grand tour until his first honeymoon, and retained his strong Devonian accent throughout his life. When Georgiana, Duchess of Devonshire took Lady Elizabeth Foster to Saltram in 1781 she wrote that 'I had the pleasure of finding Parker as dirty, as comical and talking as bad English as ever'.[39]

While extending the existing old master collection, Theresa appealed for help to her elder brother, Lord Grantham. In 1771 she wrote to him: 'Remember that if you meet with anything abroad, of pictures bronzes etc. that is valuable in itself, beautiful and proper for any part of Saltram we depend so much upon your taste and judgement that you must not lose an opportunity of procuring it for us.'[40] Six months later she reminded him: 'Are you likely to pick up any very good Picture to match our Vandyke as to size and partly to subject.' She then qualified her request: the subject did not have to relate after all, as the two would hang over doors at opposite ends of the Great Room, and 'consequently cannot be seen at the same time'.[41] Theresa was also trying to find 'two very good landscapes' for the same room. Her husband had offered Sir Joshua 800 guineas for two Claudes in the summer, but the businesslike painter wanted 1000. However, the Parkers had just bought a landscape by de Loutherbourg, 'the finest landscape painter in France', at whose house they had called 'by mere chance'. Theresa described the painting as 'one of the most pleasing I ever saw'.[42] She was proud of having 'discovered' the artist, for two of whose works she was awaiting delivery on 1 September 1772: 'I expect home today, two very pretty Landscapes for the Great Room by Loutherbourg, much the best I have seen of his performance tho' he is in great repute in France.'[43] Two years later Theresa was still looking for a picture for one overdoor in the Great Room: 'We cannot find a companion to our Vandyke we went to see one today which there was no objection but that of not being pleasing Countenance, otherwise it was about the same shape, size, proportion & number of figures...'[44]

One of the glories of Saltram are the portraits by Sir Joshua Reynolds. The artist was brought up in nearby Plympton, where his father was the schoolmaster; Lady Catherine Parker is said to have presented him with his first drawing pencil. He trained locally in the studio of Thomas Hudson, whose elegant portraits of the local aristocracy still adorn adjacent family seats. Reynolds was fortunate enough to sail from Plymouth to the Mediterranean with one of his early clients, Captain the Hon. Augustus Keppel, and thus to visit Italy and learn all that was needed to complete the classical education of a gentleman painter. In London he set up a studio to rival that of current favourites Van Loo and Allan Ramsay, working in an organised fashion to ensure that he received a new sitter every hour, on the hour, rather in the manner of a dentist. It was natural that both John and Theresa should be portrayed by Reynolds, who had already painted other members of the family. In London the Parkers sometimes dined with Reynolds in his 'charming House upon Richmond Hill'[45] or he with them. Theresa read at least one of his Discourses or lectures on art.[46] Modestly, John Parker only commissioned a small full-length, which was exhibited at the Royal Academy in 1773. He is shown in full country mode, leaning on a gate. The unusual scale may be explained by the restrictions of its being painted on a visit to Saltram, perhaps in September 1770.[47] Theresa's portrait, painted in 1772, was a larger affair altogether. Anne wrote: 'I expect Theresa every minute to carry me to Sir Joshua's where she is sitting for her picture, a full length to answer Sir Thomas Parker in the great room at Saltram.'[48] As the mistress of the house, evidently it was Theresa rather than John whose picture was to be a pair to that of an earlier ancestor.

Contrary to custom, when she had her portrait painted, Theresa was expecting a baby, a fact that both she and Anne realised their brothers might find shocking. Anne took the view that the picture could be modified: 'Sir Joshua says it need not be done quite exact at now.'[49] Theresa herself remarked that 'Sir Thomas Parker wants a companion so much in the great Room at Saltram, that it could not be delayed another year'.[50] She had finished the sittings by April 1772 and reported that the picture 'is universally allow'd to be very like'.[51] An amusing dispute followed about the pose: 'Mr Parker says I am drawn feeling my Pulse. It may not be the less like for that, as I am apt to do so.'[52] This was confirmed by her brother: '...you are very apt to hold your arm.'[53] The discussion about likeness continued: 'I am sorry you have heard that Sir Joshua's picture of me is not like, most people think it is. Some abuse it, & some admire it.'[54]

Reynolds had already painted Theresa, in a half-length portrait, and in 1773 she was thinking of having a likeness of her little boy John inserted into this. On one detail at least, she sought to assert her taste over that of her husband: 'I have some thoughts (that is) Mr Parker talks of having the little Boy put into the half length at Sir Joshua's, which remains just as you left it, only in bright yellow, which he is very fond of at present, but I do not approve of...'[55] In the event, the boy kept pulling faces and it was some time before the double portrait was achieved.

Some of the large paintings by Angelica Kauffmann now hanging on the main staircase may also have been intended for the Great Room.[56] Kauffmann had painted John Parker on his tragic first honeymoon in Rome in 1764, and she continued to be a favourite at Saltram. In 1767 she painted Reynolds' portrait for John Parker. Following Reynolds' precepts, classical subjects were the height of fashion, and Angelica had exhibited three such subjects, from the *Iliad*, the *Odyssey* and the *Aeneid*, at the Society of Arts in 1768, the year before she became one of the first members of the Royal Academy. To these works she added one from the *Achilleid* of Statius for the first Royal Academy exhibition. All four scenes were snapped up by Theresa for Saltram. Two more, *Vortigern enamoured of Rowena* and *The Interview of Edgar and Edwina*, exhibited in 1770 and 1771, were subsequently acquired, each for £40.[57] These had apparently been painted for another client but left on the artist's hands.[58] As well as reflecting her genuine interest in classical subjects, Theresa's acquisitions showed a combination of determination, pragmatism and economy that was entirely usual in country house collecting.

Theresa was especially interested in obtaining smaller objects for the house. Four early Wedgwood engine-turned creamware vases, now adorning the chimneypiece in the Library, are believed to have been bought by her.[59] She had a taste for urns in the Etruscan style; in 1770 she and her husband acquired a large pair in plaster to stand in niches in the Library, for which Peter Vannini was paid £50. Wedgwood and Bentley's new black basalt Staffordshire ware therefore also had an appeal for her. In August 1771 she wrote: 'We have just bought a beautiful lamp of the Black Staffordshire ware and also four little figures painted upon black grounds, copies from the Herculaneum Boys which they now paint in perfection upon that ware.'[60] The latter may have been on vases, or little candlesticks. There are three pairs of black basalt vases still at the house, as well as at least two single vases, all adorned with putti and classical scenes, mostly painted in red and cream or brown and white, and all dating from 1770–5.[61] All of this interesting small collection was apparently acquired by Theresa.[62] She also bought three elegant greeny-blue 'pebble' vases by Wedgwood and Bentley, made in imitation of natural stone and originally gilded.

Adorning the Great Room today are four magnificent urns: these are blue john candle vases, mounted in ormolu and made by Matthew Boulton. They were based on vases made in 1770 for King George III: it was Boulton's practice to offer follow-on ornaments to other patrons. Lord Grantham had ordered a version for himself in 1771, as well as obtaining these items for Theresa at her request.[63] Theresa had certainly made the most of some time in London, writing to Frederick in April 1772: 'I was at the Exhibition of Ormolu this week, there are some new things, but nothing that I much wished to have, being satisfied with four of those Urns you bespoke for lighting the Great Room.'[64] Gilded tripod tables were designed for the vases by Adam, to whom Boulton sent a drawing of the plinths.[65] The same 1772 letter describes Theresa's love of Wedgwood, showing that the rivalry between the two makers was being fought out on her own mantlepieces: 'I think upon the whole Wedgwood beats them in taste but perhaps it may be owing to his material, admitting to be better executed, perhaps with respect to Figures.'[66]

Following her elder brother's lead, Theresa started to make her own designs: subsequently Frederick invited them both to design an inkstand for him. Theresa told him in September 1772: 'I am impatient to hear your view of the Inkstand...I think it could be made up very pretty in Boulton Ware. The boys Or Moulu & Pedestal of a white composition that he often makes use of, with the ornaments gilt.'[67] Meanwhile Lord Grantham wrote to Anne of Theresa's drawing: 'I am delighted with her Design, and am choaking with Jealousy and Admiration of it.'[68] Theresa was not yet entirely confident about her designs and, when she consulted a craftsman about having it made up, was not offended when that of Grantham was preferred. Both her brother's drawing and the inkstand made from it survive at Saltram. Theresa also consulted her brothers about her design for a silver bowl, to be made out of three racing prizes that she and John Parker had won at Bodmin: 'I shall soon submit to your judgement a design for a large piece of Plate to be made out of the three Cornish bowls.'[69] Lord Grantham responded: 'There is not a wave in the Form, or a Line in the Ornament which I would wish to see altered...Your Choice of the Medallion is very truly happy, and your Inscription Very plain.'[70] By early 1773 the work was being carried out: 'The Bodmyn Bowls are now making into a Cistern.'[71] The creative process involved in both these items shows not only attention to detail, but also an instinctive sense of form.

Once the decoration of the house was complete, Theresa began to spend more time on sketching: 'I have just finished the best Drawing I ever did in its way. It is a copy of the three...Figures in the Aldobrandini Marriage.'[72] It often happened at that date that paintings were studied through prints and sketches, passed on by travellers to their friends and acquaintances: this work was known to Theresa through a drawing of it that Lord Shelburne had brought from Rome.[73] In 1772 the Parkers also acquired Angelica Kauffmann's working library for her classical figures, comprising nine volumes of old master prints together with one of drawings.[74] Theresa later reported the purchase of two Bartolozzi drawings,[75] and of fifty first-state mezzotints by Watson.[76]

In fulfilling her social role, Theresa was at pains to do her duty. One is drawn to her straightforward personality, with her proper values, her dancing sense of humour, and her dislike of superficiality. Even her impatience with county society is endearing, showing that she had too lively a mind to want to waste time in conversation that was less than interesting. Talk of country sports did not appeal: her brother-in-law Mr Montagu Parker 'seldom shone in conversation, but in Woodcock season'.[77] In 1772 she wrote to Fritz: 'We must spend the next week in returning all our Dining visits which we do not enjoy the thought of much...But as we are at home mornings and evenings it is of no great concern.'[78] She loved just to be with her husband at Saltram: 'We are here at present quite alone, which we like very much.'[79] Theresa was not antisocial, but she liked to choose her friends carefully: she was quite happy to dine regularly with the Bastards from Kitley and the Edgecombes from Mount Edgecombe. However, 'We expect a good deal of Company this week, Sir Thomas Acland, Sir F Chichester, and half the County. You may guess how agreeable it will be; how far I shall think so, I may as well keep to myself.'[80] This was from the wife of the Member of Parliament for the whole of Devon: she was wise to keep quiet. Theresa had no malice: these were entirely private letters to her brothers and possibly she did not even complain to her husband. However, she was a discriminating judge of character. Although she did not admire William Pitt, Lord Chatham, she was prepared to receive 'so remarkable a man' just because she knew she would find him interesting.[81] Her letters from Saltram often said that there was 'no news': by contrast she clearly enjoyed the stimulus of visitors such as Georgiana, Duchess of Devonshire, Sir Joshua Reynolds and Dr Samuel Johnson.

Theresa was an indoor person. Her sister Anne wrote: 'Mr Parker and I have been often in the Phaeton, when it was too dirty for me to walk, Theresa is much too prudent to venture in it, she does not even go down to the stables, we take a sober quiet airing in the post Chaise step by step...'[82] This is not to deny that Theresa understood her husband's outdoor needs. He was constantly out shooting or riding, on his horse 'from Morning till Night' in the 'incessant violent rains'.[83] Despite her aversion to cold and dirt, she took a great interest in the garden and the park, choosing the ornamental buildings herself. As early as the summer of 1771 she asked Lord Grantham to send her a drawing for a garden folly, a design of his that she had seen briefly before: 'pray don't forget the Castle...something must be built upon that spot & I know no other plan will ever please me so much as yours did, as far as I ever saw of it.'[84] This glorious and romantic folly still stands today, in a prime position at the end of the garden, overlooking the estuary. It is octagonal and battlemented, with windows on each of four sides. Theresa also applied another design of her own selection to the Saltram landscape by seeking to copy a lodge from the Sussex home of Lady Pelham. She told Fritz, 'We have thought of building one of the Stanmer lodges by Mr Greenslade's gate at the entrance of the new road by the Embankment.'[85] Two months later the Stanmer lodge had been started. Theresa also described the progress in the gardens, which included moving the kitchen garden, and the plans for the future: 'The Hot Houses, Kitchens, Gardens etc. are just finished, the Castle, the other lodges, and a Green House employ the next year, and after that we turn Farmers, and make such improvements in Land, Estates, Ploughs etc. that Posterity shall bless the day...'[86] Building in the garden was completed the next year, 1773, when Theresa wrote:

'We arrived here last Monday...and found the place in the highest beauty. The new Lodges are prodigiously pretty, and by building them at the highest part of the lane, & taking in the Clump of Oaks you would be astonished to see what an improvement it makes.'[87]

In between her town and country houses, their contents and gardens, Theresa was busy with her family. Although her children did not arrive annually in the manner of some eighteenth-century families, and perhaps because of that, she loved motherhood. Her son John, born in 1772, was often mentioned in letters to her brothers, and Lord Grantham remarked upon her enjoyment of motherhood, perhaps considered unusual in upper-class women, who were not expected to care for their children hour upon hour, and upon her sense of duty: 'I can conceive that seeing your dear little boy so much and so often as you do, with so much feeling and task as you have, you must admire him more than you yourself ever thought you should.'[88] Theresa responded with a charming description of the toddler, aged nearly three:

'You would have been delighted just now to have seen a meeting between my little boy & one of the same age that was sent to see him. little John is always very happy on these occaasions, first creeps up & just touches the other, then kisses very gently, then comparess their Eyes Nose Mouth to his, & next their Shoes & Buckles, this kindness lasts generally till the other grows morre acquainted & I suppose always ends in a quarrell.'[89]

No-one knew that Theresa's short life was soon to draw to a tragic end. Looking back it is touching to read of the joy given to her in the summer of 1775 by the beautiful surroundings that she had created. In June she wrote to Lord Grantham from London that she was longing to get to Saltram, 'which I think I shall enjoy much more than ever this Summer...' Expecting her second child, she commented, '...it must of course be in a quiet way. I propose sitting much in the Green House & drawing a good deal & I think the place must be in the highest beauty. We have no visits to make...'[90] Everything one knows of Theresa is expressed during this, her last summer. To her great joy, a daughter was born: Lord Grantham wrote to John Parker to congratulate them both, sending 'the most anxious wish of my heart that you and Theresa may ever continue, the same affectionate, happy & united couple that you have ever hitherto been.'[91] When Theresa was taken ill after the birth of the little girl, also named Theresa, she was struck by her husband's devotion: 'had my Fever lasted a few days longer he could not have stood it, as I believe he neither Eat, Drank, Slept or even could compose his Spirits till many days after I was free from every complaint.'[92] She was overjoyed to receive four miniatures of her beloved brothers, still far away in Spain, and generously allowed Anne, as the elder, to choose first which to have.

Family devotion and love of home were never greater. Believing her to be recovered, Mr Parker left for town. One can only imagine the agony with which those at Saltram had to dispatch a messenger to London, bearing the news of Theresa's sudden death.

Her obituary was written by the great Sir Joshua Reynolds, who at this sad time generously cancelled the payments owed to him by John Parker.[93] In it, before finally making mention of Theresa's good natural taste,[94] he summarised her popularity, 'her amiable disposition, her softness, & gentleness of manners', and her sense of duty: 'Her whole pleasure and ambition were centered in a consciousness of properly discharging all the Duties of a Wife, a Mother, & sister, and she neither sought for, nor expected fame out of her own house – As she made no Ostentation of her Virtues, she excited no Envy…Her virtues were uniform, quiet and habitual…Her person was eminently beautifull, but the expression of her countenance was far above all beauty that proceeds from regularity of features only.' So impressed was Reynolds by her nature that he came back to it: 'The Gentleness & benevolence of her disposition were so naturally impressed on every book and motion, that…she was sure to make every one her friend, that had ever spoke to her, or even seen her.'[95]

Theresa's son, John, who inherited the title granted to his father in 1784 and became the 2nd Baron Boringdon, was also to become a widower. It was his second wife, Frances, who created another episode in the history of Saltram's interior decoration. She too loved the house, writing on her arrival as a bride in 1809:

'The place is a thousand times more delightful than all the possibility of my imagination had conceived it; it is so gay, so riant, so comfortable and so everything that it ought to be that it is impossible to love and admire it enough.'[96]

Her husband was created an Earl, so it was as the Countess of Morley that from 1815 Frances made changes to Saltram in tune with the fashionable Regency style of the day. Some of these survive, such as the mahogany library bookcases; others, including the red flock paper in the Morning Room, have been removed in favour of an early eighteenth-century appearance. What Frances did was entirely suitable for her day; mercifully she undid little of her predecessors' schemes.

At Saltram there is a feeling of decorative history established in layers. It was Catherine who created the present exterior appearance and arrangement of the house, but it was probably the gentle Theresa who, through her natural good taste and love of quality, through her letters and through her reputation, more than anyone left her elegant imprint upon Saltram. The closing words of Sir Joshua Reynolds' obituary represented his view that art should be used to uplift and instruct the human spirit. He felt that even Theresa's perfect artistic taste was secondary in importance to her wonderful personal qualities: 'In so exalted a character, it is scarce worth mentioning her skill & exact Judgement in the polite arts, she seemed to possess by a kind of intuition that propriety of taste & right thinking, which others but imperfectly acquire by long labour & application.'[97] From the Founder and First President of the Royal Academy, this was high praise indeed.

Chapter 13

SECLUSION IN SCOTLAND
JANE MAXWELL,
DUCHESS OF GORDON
1749–1812

Here lived the lovely Jane
Who best combined
A Beauteous form to a
Superior mind

Sir John Sinclair

A famous beauty, the young chestnut-haired Jane Maxwell was described as 'The Flower of Galloway' and celebrated in song as 'Jenny of Monreith'.[1] Such praise might be thought incongruous by anyone who had known her a few years before. Jane, or Jeany, as she was called in childhood, was the second of the three daughters of Sir William Maxwell, 3rd Baronet of Monreith; her mother Magdalene was the daughter of William Blair of Blair. While she was still young her parents separated, leaving Lady Maxwell to bring up her boisterous daughters alone, while Jane's elder brothers lived with their father. The all-female family lived in Edinburgh, not in the city's fashionable Georgian New Town, but in the old area of the Royal Mile, in a second-floor apartment in Hyndford's Close, where Jane had been born. Here the streets were still narrow and basic, and they lived without luxury. Jane and her younger sister Eglantine, or Betty, were wild children: they used to watch for a local herd of pigs to be driven out of the yard in the mornings, and would then leap on to their backs for a ride along the streets.[2] In a similar game, jumping from one travelling cart to another, Jane lost the forefinger of her right hand. Their language was rough, and the girls themselves were beyond control.

Despite an impoverished childhood, during her teens Jane became well educated in the true manner of the Scottish Enlightenment. Edinburgh in the latter part of the eighteenth century was a centre of intellectual activity, in which such thinkers as Adam Smith and David Hume were making their ideas widely known. The family were much influenced by the eminent Scottish judge Henry Home, Lord Kames, who took a great liking to the thirteen-year-old Jane, encouraging her to visit his home in order to develop her reading. He believed firmly in the education of women, and came to consider her as his adopted daughter. Jane also learnt feminine 'accomplishments': she took lessons in drawing and singing, and was always to love music. Throughout her life she kept up with all the latest books and sought ways to extend her education.

At the age of seventeen[3] Jane became engaged to a young army officer, said to be a member of the Fraser family, who was serving at the time in the Black Watch, the original Fraser Highlanders having been disbanded after the '45.[4] In 1766 he was sent away to fight in America: subsequently he was reported missing in battle, believed dead. A number of other suitors made approaches but were rebutted, though one of them, James Ferguson of Pitfour, for the rest of his life, at Pitfour House, would offer a toast to the Duchess of Gordon. Jane met Alexander, 4th Duke of Gordon, at a ball in April 1767, when he was travelling south for his sister's wedding. The dance had been specially put on for Alexander by Charles Gordon, his kinsman and man of business; however, the diffident young man was reluctant to attend, saying that he had nothing to wear and no-one with whom to dance. Both were already provided, his blind date being Jane Maxwell.[5] He was much smitten by her lively beauty, and when the handsome twenty-four-year-old offered for Jane's hand, her parents were delighted to accept. She was only eighteen.[6]

Jane married the Duke of Gordon in two ceremonies, on 23 October 1767 at Ayton in Berwickshire, the home of her elder sister, Catherine Fordyce, and on 28 October at the Fordyces' home in Argyll Street, Edinburgh. Probably they were married in the two locations because of their parents' separation: Sir William Maxwell's home was not far from Ayton. It is also likely that the first ceremony was Presbyterian, for the Maxwells, while the Edinburgh wedding was Anglican, for the Duke of Gordon. First the couple travelled north to Gordon Castle, arriving at the New Inn in Aberdeen on 29 October 1767. A dance was given for them at Tomintoul by fifty gentlemen, all with the name of Gordon. In December they went south on a countrywide tour culminating in their presentation at Court and the Duke taking his seat in the House of Lords as one of the sixteen peers for Scotland. There was one dismaying episode: when the couple stopped again at Ayton on the route north, Jane, to her shock, received a letter addressed to her in her maiden name from her former suitor, the young army officer, in which he said that he wanted to return to marry her. Incredulous at learning that he was still alive, she rushed outside weeping, and was found beside the River Eye, prostrate with grief.[7]

'The Duchess triumphs in a manly mien / Loud is her accent and her phrase obscene', wrote one wit. Aware of his daughter's wild ways and concerned about how she would perform in her new role, on her marriage Jane's father wrote her an endearing letter, full of sound advice. He emphasised the importance of good behaviour, telling her that her charms might fade and that 'commonplace small talk' must be dropped, as it could not be entertaining to 'people of good sense'. Above all, she must not let her new rank go to her head: 'the blazing star of grandeur' should not make her look down on people, as 'titles only ennoble when properly placed'. He warned that she would soon be called 'to a distracted gay hurry' where she would see 'pride, envy, rancour and falsehood reign without control' and that London was not 'the high road to heaven'.[8] Lord Kames similarly wrote proffering advice, in particular that when in London she should avoid 'play', by which he meant cards, and that she should never be separated from her husband in their 'amusements'.[9] Jane tried to follow this advice, assuring him that when in London she preferred to be at home with her Duke rather than out partying, and shuddered at the horrors of addictive gambling.[10]

Although she was always said to be beautiful, Jane undoubtedly differed in speech and behaviour from other women of her rank. She was not conventional, and behaved exactly as she saw fit. Her accent was always Scottish, her voice was usually loud, and she had a great sense of humour. Indeed, her rank meant that she did not have to conform: Sir Nathaniel Wraxall described how, 'Exempted by her sex, rank and beauty from those restraints imposed on women by the generally recognised usages of society, the Duchess of Gordon frequently dispensed with their observance.'[11] Her manners were said to be at least a little uncouth, and 'Neither in her person, manners, or mind was there any feminine expression'.[12] Elizabeth Grant of Rothiemurchus, in childhood a near neighbour, described her as being 'the life of all circles she entered'.[13] She was completely confident: 'Her features, however noble, pleasing, and regular, always animated, constantly in play, never deficient in vivacity or intelligence, yet displayed no timidity.'[14] Clearly her attraction was largely due to charisma: '[She was] above middle size, very finely shaped, she had dark expressive eyes, very regular features, fine complexion, and a most engaging expression. She was eminent for agility and grace in the performance of those exercises which display beauty and symmetry, and for the gaiety, spirit and brilliancy of humor and with which so agreeably set off her acute and vigorous understanding.' This accolade was from a young subaltern, Pryse Lockhart Gordon, who visited her at Gordon Castle and considered her 'unquestionably the most beautiful and fascinating woman in Great Britain'.[15]

Jane's early show of emotion for her former suitor would be seen as having a dampening effect on relations with her husband. The Gordon marriage[16] was always tempestuous, and neither partner was faithful to the other. The Duke was interested in his estates and tenants, in farming and sport, but only slightly in politics. He wanted to do his best for local people but was not personally ambitious, and it may be that his wife was too much for him. The Duchess centred her energies on her children, who arrived at more or less two yearly intervals: they were Charlotte (1768), George (1770), Madelina (1772), Susan (1774), Louisa (1776), Georgina (1781) and Alexander (1785). An illegitimate son of the Duke already lived at the Castle, where he was accepted by Jane with affection. His name was George: when the Duchess bore her own son, the heir, he too was deliberately given the name of the King, to whom, at such a politically sensitive time for the Scottish, the Duke always wanted to show his loyalty. Jane simply referred to them as 'The Duke's George' and 'My George'. Nearly all of the Duke's known natural children, of which there were nine,[17] were to be brought up at Gordon Castle. So good was Jane as their alternative mother that one son named his own daughter after the Duchess.[18]

When Jane arrived at Gordon Castle in 1767 it was a gaunt, old-fashioned house. The fortified castle with its six-storey tower and a cluster of outbuildings had been erected by George Gordon, 2nd Earl of Huntly in 1479. The wealthy Duke had already drained the surrounding Bog o'Gight (meaning windy bog), creating a flat grassy parkland; now he involved himself in a programme of rebuilding. The Edinburgh architect John Baxter was commissioned to build a castellated block around the tower, with two large outlying pavilions attached. The foundation stone for the two-storey east pavilion was laid on 20 July 1770, with the birthday of the Duke and Duchess's son, the little Marquis of Huntly, inscribed on it in Latin. The block contained the kitchen, brewhouse, bakehouse and dairy, together with servants' apartments, while the west block, for which the foundation stone was laid on 29 June 1773, was laid out in apartments and contained the stables and coach house. In 1776 the Duke and Duchess 'amus'd themselves' helping the masons build the stair.[19] The ensemble, almost complete by 1778, measured a vast 568 feet and was described as 'a noble pile fit for a prince'. It cost the Duke £9594.[20] There was elaborate plasterwork in the important rooms, such as the large dining room, drawing room, main library and at least one dressing room, and one rather striking Doric frieze was 'Enrichd with Deers heads, bells & Trigleaves'.[21] The deer's heads were the Gordon crest: to make a frieze based on the family arms in the main entrance hall was not unusual.

Under Jane's tenure, life at Gordon Castle began to smarten up. During the mid 1770s a footman called Alexander Milne left his employment with the Duke because he refused to wear livery, cut his hair and wear a powdered wig. In 1776 the Duke and Duchess decided that the village of Fochabers was too near to their grandiose new home, and arranged to have it moved further away. The Duke also set about creating ornamental lakes and gardens, followed in the 1770s by a kennel and two bridges.[22] His favourite tree was a willow that he had planted as a child, while Jane preferred a particular lime whose branches she had trained to form an arbour in which she could sit. She was an early riser and told Lord Kames in the spring of 1779: 'I go every Morning before Breakfast to visit the Shrubbery.'[23] This may have been her garden at Quarry Wood, a short ride along an avenue to the northeast of the house. It was planted with unusual trees and shrubs and was entered through a substantial arch. She also had her own summer house at Cotton Hill, in which the plasterers created a special decorative trophy of garden implements on the wall.[24]

Jane was an active chatelaine, supervising accounts for both house and farm and overseeing the dairies. She bought new table linen for the castle, changing to a damask inset with the 'Cumberland knot' and exhorting her housekeeper to make an inventory of the annual linen acquisition.[25] As well as overseeing the servants, including their moral and religious education, she especially looked after the tenants, finding young people jobs in which they could better themselves. Often the tenants were uneducated and extremely poor; the fact that a long-lived lease kept a roof over their heads did not necessarily mean they had employment. Jane was concerned to avoid idleness both for herself and for others, instructing families on the estate to be thrifty and industrious and wanting to teach both boys and girls how to knit.[26] In 1770 she had asked Lord Kames where she could find a 'broad Damask Loom' for her weaver: by then she had taken over the farm of Cuttlebrae near to the castle and was soon producing the best flax in Scotland.[27]

As a friend and neighbour the Duchess took an interest in other people's problems and worries. She was particularly kind to the philosopher-poet Dr James Beattie of Aberdeen, helping him through his wife's mental illness. After staying at the castle in 1780, escaping the torments of life at home, he wrote to her: 'I saw by many instances every day how solicitous you were to withdraw my view from everything that could create or revive painful thoughts.'[28] He later described her sympathetic nature, calling her 'the consoling friend of every scene of sorrow'. Jane never mocked people of any level of society,[29] always giving them her full attention and letting them talk about whatever most interested them.[30]

During the years when Jane was mistress of Gordon Castle, her home always had a reputation for fun and laughter. In 1774 she wrote that she had managed to ignore the bad weather because of the 'constant dancing & singing, which has made the longest day seem short – I still ride walk and bathe every morning.' Considering that the letter was written in November, it shows how tough she was if she really meant sea-bathing, which she often undertook in the summer, decamping for a few days to Peterhead. She often wrote her letters against a background of noise: 'There is much chattering in the Room – of men footmen Dogs Children.'[31] Her own 'State Room' was adjacent to the children's nursery, so a letter '...is wrote in a moment...& all the dear little things Prattering in the room'.[32] Her parents, separately, often came to stay, as well as her brothers and sisters, her aunt Mrs Blair with her daughter, and even her grandmother Magdalen Blair.[33] It also was perfectly acceptable for people of a certain status who had been given an introduction to the Duke and Duchess to deviate from their route in order to stay a few days. In 1779 they had so many travellers, or 'wanderers' as she called them, that the Duchess said they rarely had less than twenty people at table.[34] The piper would play at breakfast time, when the houseguests would all assemble. Scribbling a letter from her desk, the Duchess reported: 'The Duke is crying Jane come away to Breakfast.'[35] In December 1779 she commented, figuratively rather than literally, that she had 'a Hundred people in the house'.[36]

Despite his early admonitions against too much amusement, from nearby Aberdeen Lord Kames, by then an old man, missed the gaiety of the Castle. Life in town was grey by comparison: '…like the children of Israel in the wilderness we long for the flesh pots of Egypt, which with the addition of musick, dancing, and chearful company, are found no where in greater perfection than upon the banks of the Spey.'[37] From his great house at Stowe, Lord Temple also commented on 'All the Feasts, Balls & Delights of turning night into Day and Day into Night' at Gordon Castle.[38] Music was always available. Their butler, William Marshall, was a talented fiddler, and was encouraged to compose his own strathspeys. With Jane pressing the project into action, Marshall first published his 'Strathspeys and Reels with bass for the Violincello or Harpsichord' in 1781.[39] He also composed personal reels for main events in the life of all the family. Marshall's music was often pirated by the fiddler and composer Neil Gow, and especially by his son Nathaniel; in their Band of Music from Perth they played at many of the Scottish balls. Elizabeth Rose of Kilravock reported that: 'All is singing, violin playing and health at Gordon Castle.'[40]

Between May 1785 and November 1786 the family lived in Edinburgh, in their town house in St George's Square: during this time their eldest daughter Charlotte turned eighteen and some social life was considered necessary for her.[41] Jane was meanwhile developing her intellectual interests, partly with the help of her friend Dr James Beattie, whom she called her 'guardian angel'. He would advise her what to read; she would then discuss her new discoveries at dinner, in the manner of the French *salonnière*. Some contemporaries were a little cynical about her desire to be 'the arbitress of literary taste and the patroness of genius',[42] but no-one could deny her intellect; moreover she was fearless and unconstrained, not caring what anyone thought of her. In November 1786 Henry Erskine, Dean of the Faculty of Advocates, introduced the young poet Robert Burns to the Duke and Duchess. Jane subsequently invited Burns to intellectual supper parties at her home at St George's Square.[43] In September 1787 he visited Gordon Castle, describing Jane as 'charming, witty and sensible'. With the perception to see the talent behind his roughness, she gave a great fillip to the poet's career:

'The town is all agog with the ploughman poet who receives adulation with native dignity and is the very figure of his profession, strong and coarse, but has a most enthusiastick heart of love. He has seen the Duchess of Gordon and all the gay world.'[44]

London society was also greatly impressed by Jane, who from 1778 used to go 'to town' regularly for the season. At a ball in London in 1785 Lady Louisa Stuart described her lively Scottish dancing: 'Her Grace of Gordon bounced away according to custom.' She did not wait to be asked to dance, but insisted on a General dancing with her himself. Jane was considered, however, to be bossy and argumentative: 'She looks as fierce as a dragon, and contents herself with spending her breath upon politics, and ringing a daily peal in the ears of her poor husband, with whom, Lord William says, she squabbles more than ever.'[45] She was much admired in her thinking by William Pitt the Younger, for whom she canvassed strenuously in the 1784 elections: he called her 'The first whipper-in of the Tories'. In support of members of his government she gave sumptuous suppers and balls, for which William Marshall would travel south to provide the music, giving them a truly Scottish flavour. Jane's London home thus became the social centre of the Tory party in the same way that Devonshire House in the time of Georgiana, Duchess of Devonshire was the focus of the Whigs under Charles James Fox. Indeed, their rivalry was lampooned in a contemporary novel,[46] with Georgiana as the Duchess of Belgrave and Jane as the Duchess of Drinkwater. As someone said to need only five hours sleep, Jane was so energetic and intellectually alive that Horace Walpole wrote: 'Hercules could not have achieved a quarter of her labours in the same space of time.' He described how in one day she went to hear music by Handel played in Westminster Abbey, then to the trial of Warren Hastings in the Great Hall, followed by a soirée, from where she went to Ranelagh Gardens and then to another house to play cards. The next evening she gave a ball herself, leaving for Scotland the following day.

As a matchmaker the Duchess was unrivalled: 'For their [her daughters'] elevation no sacrifices appeared to her to be too great, no exertion too laborious, no renunciation too severe,' reminisced Sir Nathaniel Wraxall.[47] Three of Jane's daughters married Dukes, one a Marquess. What is particularly remarkable is that she managed this from the remoter parts of Scotland, whither grand English people did not yet travel and where there was very little social life. While she cannot be proved to have originated the match for every single daughter, she certainly tended to bring them to the clinch if the suitor was particularly acceptable. Jane was lewdly mocked in contemporary cartoons for exploits such as trying to get a particular young couple into bed.[48] Firstly Jane's second daughter Madelina married a cousin, Sir Robert Sinclair, Bart. As Lieutenant Governor of Fort George, the impressive army garrison built near Inverness, he was a well-respected figure. Jane tried hard to marry her eldest daughter Charlotte to the youthful Prime Minister, William Pitt, taking the girl with her in her carriage to Lord Dundas's house at Wimbledon, where Pitt often spent the evenings, and where she sometimes also gave parties for the politician. However Dundas cleverly forestalled any relationship by pretending to woo the girl himself. In 1789 Charlotte married Colonel Charles Lennox, the nephew and heir of Charles, 3rd Duke of Richmond. There is evidence that she rushed the couple to the altar: the marriage was celebrated in her dressing room at Gordon Castle with only herself and two serving women as witnesses.[49] For her third daughter, Susan, the Duchess determined on William, 5th Duke of Manchester. Having failed to meet up with him racing at Newmarket or at the family home at Kimbolton in Huntingdonshire,[50] she 'dropped in' en route for Scotland later in 1792. In the short term the introduction was a success. Susan married her duke within a year, in October 1793, but she left him for a footman, partly because of his infidelity, and thus acquired a notorious reputation. The fourth daughter, Louisa, married Charles Cornwallis, Viscount Brome, subsequently the 2nd and last Marquess Cornwallis.[51] In this case the couple had fallen in love, but again it was Jane who brought it to fruition.

For her youngest daughter, Georgina (also frequently called Georgiana),[52] Jane made an attempt at the widowed and wealthy William Beckford: he allowed her to visit his home at Fonthill for a week, for the whole of which he deliberately remained closeted in his study, commenting afterwards that, 'I never enjoyed a joke so much.'[53] Next she succeeded in almost engaging the girl to Francis, 5th Duke of Bedford. For this most eligible of bachelors, Jane was in competition with her greatest rival, Georgiana, Duchess of Devonshire. Awestruck onlookers called the competition the Clash of the Titans. However, Francis suddenly died in March 1802. Unbowed, the Duchess took Georgina to Paris, which was much visited by the British in that year, following the break in English-French hostilities marked by the Treaty of Amiens. At a dinner at the Palace of the Tuileries presided over by Napoleon, with Josephine, at the head of a dais, Jane flounced in late, seating herself on the Emperor's right above everyone else in the room.[54] She also invited him to her ball.[55] There was a purpose. Jane, greatly impressed by Napoleon, had now set her heart on Georgina marrying Eugène Beauharnais, the son of Josephine. Indeed the two young people were much attracted; Napoleon, however, was not interested, preferring to try for a royal match for his stepson. At this time John, 6th Duke of Bedford, the younger brother of Georgina's dead former suitor, came to Paris. A great affinity sprang up between the two bereaved young people, and in June 1803 Georgina married the new Duke. The wedding in Fife House, Whitehall, was quiet, but after the couple had departed Jane gave a triumphant late evening party for 500 guests: they danced until 7 a.m.[56] She had also performed other marital business in Paris, sweeping Ann Thomson, the mistress of her son, George, with her, supposedly for the visit, but marrying her off to a merchant in order to clear a marital path for the Gordon heir.[57] Jane excited much critical comment by her unashamed antics in marrying off her children. An early biographer commented that 'during her whole life [she] unscrupulously pursued a career which had one sole object in view – family aggrandizement'.[58]

Jane was also instrumental in creating the most fashionable event in the Highland social calendar. The Northern Meeting was begun by a group of thirteen gentlemen who met in Inverness on 11 June 1788 to discuss how social life in the Highlands could be improved. Elizabeth

Grant of Rothiemurchus credited its initiation, however, entirely to Duchess Jane: 'She persuaded all the northern counties to come together once a year about the middle of October and spend the better part of a week in Inverness.' For the Duchess, with her enthusiasm for dancing and cards, this was a project that came naturally. It was difficult in the Highlands for the many educated people from remote areas to meet like-minded souls with any frequency. Distances were long and roads were poor: from Inverness the routes to the north and west were both extremely hazardous. In addition to the aristocracy and gentry, many professionals such as doctors and lawyers took part, as well as the provosts, merchants and excise men of Inverness. With its big distances and harsh climate, Scotland was less snobbish and more community-minded than England, so that the social variation was accordingly wider.

The week of the Northern Meeting was very structured. Each day the members and their guests would assemble at a predetermined inn for dinner, which took until 6.30 p.m. Business or politics were not to be discussed, which must have meant that the men could only talk about hunting, shooting and stalking, a rather dubious advantage. The ladies would retire, toasts would be drunk and bills paid. From 8 p.m. a ball took place on the first floor of the town hall. It was especially the Duchess's idea that the main point of the meeting should be the dancing. Highland dancing was especially traditional in the northeast, its neat footwork deriving from sword dancing and from the need to dance within a fairly small space. Relatively early in the eighteenth century this tradition had already been influenced by English country dancing: for example the reel of the Duke of Perth, first recorded in 1734, is a reel of three from the Highlands combined with an English country dance. The ball ended at midnight, when tea and coffee were served. Next morning there would be a 'publick breakfast' at the inn of the previous evening, after which many of the men would go hunting with hounds brought over by the Duke of Gordon and Hector Monro of Novar. The ladies would make visits to their friends in the town. The Duchess always took a large party and encouraged her friends to do the same. She particularly liked to have 'stray English' in her group, both because they so admired the powerful Scottish scenery and because of her instinctive desire to make social connections for other people.

A TARTAN BELLE of 1792.

Jane, Duchess of Gordon as 'A Tartan Belle', engraving, 1792

At a ball in London in 1792, the Duchess further marked a turn in fashion towards Scotland, by dressing from head to foot in Black Watch tartan taffeta. Tartan had been proscribed for nearly forty years after the 1745 rebellion, its use only being permitted again from 1782 in order to help recruitment for the British Army, as Highland regiments were drawn in. Now the Highland Society in London was encouraging Scotsmen to wear full Highland dress whenever possible. The 4th Duke's first regiment of Fencibles wore a plaid, and when the Marquess of Huntly raised a company for the Black Watch in 1791, Jane was vastly impressed by the sight of her son being presented at Court wearing the kilt. The recruitment process involved appearing at markets and fairs, with pipers and drummers to attract attention. Recruiting for her son to raise the Gordon Highlanders, Duchess Jane showed a great sense of theatre: she would wear a special black feather bonnet and ride on a white horse.[59] She offered the men the King's Shilling (a golden guinea) from between her teeth, so that they could say they had kissed a duchess.[60] The Duchess had some Black Watch tartan woven, first in China and then at Spitalfields, and reintroduced it as a fashion, most notably with designs for the regiments. Tartan became the rage: her valet wrote that 'scarce a respectable female but wore a tartan waist to her gown at least, and there was hardly a waiter at any inn in London but appeared in his tartan waistcoat.'[61] Both tartan and Scottish dancing became so popular in London, promoted not least by the future King George IV, that by 1822 an English dancing master, watching a reel at Almacks, commented that 'The Scotch are ready to dance a reel morning, noon or night, and they never seem to know when to leave off.'[62]

In her forties and fifties the Duchess's liveliness, wit and open manner continued to make her popular: possessing 'an open ruddy countenance, quick in repartee, and no one excelling her in perform- ing the honours of her table, her society is generally courted.'[63] By the early 1790s, however, the Duke and Duchess began to live apart. From the late 1780s the Duke had taken up with Jean Christie, the daughter of his housekeeper, who was to bear him several children.[64] While the Duchess spent some of the winter in London, the Duke became increasingly antisocial. Jane first mentioned her plan for a separate home south of Aviemore, adjacent to the Rothiemurchus estate, in a letter to James Beattie of August 1792: 'I am going to build a shieling at Badenoch.'[65] In that year she was given a separate income of £4000, which she later insisted was part of a deal by which she would leave Gordon Castle. However she still continued to put on a good perform- ance: when Lord Montboddo and Lord Kames visited the castle in 1796, the former commented on her wit and brilliance, and on the Duke's sense of humour on this 'delightful day', concluding that 'Her Grace has a brilliancy and radiance about her like the rays round the head of an apostle'.[66] The birth of a son to Jean Christie in 1797 must have especially upset the Duchess, and although she had tolerated earlier affairs, she came to hate her husband's mistress. She lamented that she was criticised for not living at Gordon Castle, when a woman who was accused of trying to poison her 'lived as his Wife and had chil- dren every year'.[67]

The couple were almost completely estranged by the late 1790s. For the summers Jane stayed at her home at Badenoch, in a farmhouse at Kinrara.[68] This was not her first experience of living in rural simplicity. Like many lady owners of grand houses, she had earlier sought a retreat from the pressures of this type of lifestyle, in a simply furnished cottage at Glenfiddich, built in 1772–4.[69] She used to go there with the children, who, following the educational precepts of the French philosopher Jean-Jacques Rousseau, would play with animals, make gardens and swim in the sea; Jane believed in fresh air as an antidote to all ailments.

When Jane moved to Kinrara, Elizabeth Grant of Rothiemurchus was a child living on the neighbouring estate; she subsequently wrote a memoir that included her very earliest memories. In it she remarked, 'This beautiful and very cultivated woman had never, I fancy, lived happily with her Duke', and described how, among 'the peep of the towers of Gordon Castle' and 'the trees that concealed the rest of the building...the Duke lived very disreputably in this solitude, for he was very little noticed, and, I believe, preferred seclusion.'[70] She also gave the only contemporary record of Jane's early life at Kinrara, in the old farmhouse, which was so modest that the kitchen had to be converted to give her a drawing room. Jane and her youngest daughter, Lady Georgina, who was not yet married, lived together in the little house, which she decorated with whitewash and calico, filling it with flowers and making it into a rural idyll. She converted a barn into a 'barrack' for lady visitors to stay in, with a stable for the gentlemen. The barn was attached to the tiny house, which was on the top of a knoll, with the kitchen and stables in the stedding or farmyard below.[71] The food was all prepared by her French chef in a cauldron, 'which he had ingeniously divided into four compartments', the only disadvantage being that he had to make sauces of the same colour each day. Young people especially loved what Elizabeth Grant described as a 'backwoods life', so different from their own habitual upper-class surroundings: 'Half the London world of fashion, all the clever people that could be hunted out from all parts...flocked to this encampment in the wilderness during the fine autumns to enjoy the free life, the pure air, and the wit and fun the Duchess brought with her to the mountains.'[72] Jane's favourite footman, Long James, would play the violin for dancing, accompanied by other guests to create a little band.

The old farmhouse at Kinrara, engraving, 1801.

The invasions of visitors, not least English, were such that in about 1802 the Duchess began to build herself a new house, a mile upstream. Quite unlike the usual type of baronial house found in the Highlands, this was a supremely elegant home, with an enfilade of rooms for entertaining. Facing south onto the Spey, the paired dining and drawing rooms each had a bow window at the end, respectively to east and west, with a three-light window to the south, making them extremely light. The rooms were linked by an ante-room which had the Gordon deer's head and triglyph frieze above the drawing room door. Above the drawing room, the Duchess slept in the southwest bedchamber, looking over the Spey and along to Geal-charn Mor, on the Ardverikie estate. Even in the new house, with nine bedrooms, guests were often numerous enough to have to sleep in the main reception rooms. Elizabeth Grant looked back at the festivities of the summer of 1804: 'I joined in all the fun of this gay summer. We were often over at Kinrara, the Duchess having perpetual dances, either in the drawing-room or the servants' hall, and my father returning these entertainments in the same style.'[73] Jane's son showed her much loyalty during this period: 'Lord Huntly was the life of all these meetings; he was young, gay, handsome, fond of his mother, and often with her, and so general a favourite that all the people seemed to wake up when he came among them.'[74]

At this time the Duke and Duchess began to quarrel about money. She accused the Duke of being surrounded by extravagant, greedy and drunken 'Blood Suckers' at Gordon Castle, which she visited in 1804.[75] Although the evidence suggests that the factor, James Hoy, was a book-loving man, who may have drunk claret most evenings with the Duke but was otherwise abstemious, the Duke was certainly out of control. He had recently added £100,000 to his debts and now paid the Duchess a poor allowance. From Kinrara she wrote letters in 1804 to their accountant Francis Farquharson in Edinburgh to complain: 'why am I at the end of a life, spent for his credit – my own honour and his children's welfare, to be a prisoner, and really upon bread and water if the sum you mention was to be my allowance.'[76] Her request was for the reinstatement of her agreed £4000 a year[77] and to be able to go to London, for which the biting problem was the considerable expense of the journey. It was not until the summer of 1805 that Jane decamped to London, where she stayed in 'a small room twenty feet long in a Hotel in Albemarle St.'[78] She looked back on the two happy summers just gone by: 'I know there must be a large sum due for the two seasons I was at Kinrara.'[79] Finally, that autumn the couple made a settlement in a decree arbital, by which the Duke gave Jane an annuity of £4000, together with a sum of £2000 for furniture, plate, linen and other items needed for her own separate home.

Life got harder nonetheless for the Duchess. In 1808 Lord Alexander, her younger son, died at the age of twenty-three. Preparations for his funeral in Scotland were extensive.[80] The Duchess ordered quantities of black-edged writing paper for her letters,[81] as well as diamonds for her mourning ring.[82] After the separation of the Duke and Duchess of Manchester, their eldest daughter, Lady Jane Montagu, went to live with her grandmother permanently. Unable to make the required repairs on a house she had leased in Edinburgh,[83] from late 1808 until April 1809 the Duchess stayed for some months instead in Dumbucks

Hotel in the city.[84] This sojourn was partly for the benefit of young Lady Jane's education, which included regular lessons in mathematics. Items bought in the early spring of 1809 in Edinburgh were largely perquisites for Jane's, or Jeannie's, schooling and development, on account of which the Duchess hired a piano,[85] and bought fine drawing instruments.

Despite her financial worries, in early 1809 Jane was thinking about extending the house at Kinrara, and was paying for new plans and elevations.[86] She bought an exorbitant 445 shrubs, 100 large larches and 50 mountain ash, as well as 100 other trees.[87] Her tree planting is still very much in evidence, especially to the west of the house. Considerable building and plumbing work was carried out, and the north side of the house was extended, to include an arcaded entrance porch. Following a great shopping spree in Edinburgh in April, purchases sent to Kinrara[88] included furniture and upholstery, notably three chairs,[89] a mirror in an ebony frame,[90] a Wedgwood supper set with a tray and a large amount of china and glass.[91] Jane also bought music, including Thompson's songs[92] and Clementi's octave lesson.[93] There is always the sense that she knew how to use the long grey Scottish winter profitably, stretching her mind with occupations and distractions. A much-used little travelling desk is still in the house.[94]

In 1809 and again in 1811 Jane visited the Duke and Duchess of Richmond in Dublin. Despite complaining of 'great blindness', for which she had earlier bought a 'pr. concave eyes' (or spectacles), she continued to find balls and assemblies 'irresistible'.[95] She also spent time in London in her last years, usually in miserable lodgings or meagre hotels. At her deathbed in April 1812 her children flocked to her side, only Georgina being absent, and even the Duke travelled south to see her and show kindness at the end. Jane died aged 63, in Pulteney's Hotel, at 105 Piccadilly, in the arms of her eldest daughter Charlotte, Duchess of Richmond, and in a state of 'perfect resignation'.

As requested in her will, Jane was buried on the banks of the Spey at Kinrara near to the trees that she had planted out. Her tomb is on consecrated ground, on the site of the ancient St Eata's chapel.[96] As she wished, the Duke had the marriages of all their daughters engraved on her tombstone: it is believed that Jean Christie encouraged him to complete this project.[97] Knowing that her son would one day be the 5th Duke of Gordon, Jane was proud to consider herself as the mother of four dukes. In 1820 the Duke married his long-term mistress, Jean Christie, but she chose not to live at Gordon Castle, claiming that none of his friends would visit him there.[98] Jane had made it into a singing, dancing family home, and her full-length portrait in peeress's robes by Sir Joshua Reynolds was still hanging in the drawing room.[99] During the fifteen years of the Duke's sole residence the Castle had become drab and unappealing. Perhaps Jean Christie felt that the memory of Jane Maxwell was too strong.

The tombstone of Jane, Duchess of Gordon, at Kinrara.

John MacCulloch, a contemporary traveller, who recorded his annual journeys in the Highlands between 1811 and 1821 in six letters to Sir Walter Scott, described the spectacular, undiscovered landscape at Kinrara when he visited just before Jane's death in 1812. He tells how the continuous birch forests covering the rocky hills and lower grounds are mixed with open glades and irregular clumps, and with fir trees higher up, producing 'a scene at once alpine and dressed; combining the discordant characters of wild mountain landscape and of ornamental park scenery.' To this he felt was added 'an air of perpetual spring, and a feeling of comfort and seclusion'. He greatly enjoyed his stay: 'A week spent at Kinrara had not exhausted the half of its charms;

and when a second week had passed, all seemed still anew.' MacCulloch mourned especially for Kinrara, that 'the mind that inspired it was
fled, and the hand that had tended and decked it was cold'.[100] The combination of wildness and civilisation, of bright energy and comforting
warmth that was expressed in the Kinrara landscape exactly describes
its mistress, whose greatest art was always to make people feel at ease.

Chapter 14

REGENCY DISDAIN
ELIZABETH HOWARD,
DUCHESS OF RUTLAND
1780–1825

'The Castle has been built from the present fortifications by the present Dss
who has made the place, the Duke taking no part in the improvement.'
Diary of Harriet Arbuthnot, 1823

Elizabeth Howard, Duchess of Rutland, was a builder *extraordinaire*. Between 1801 and 1825 she rebuilt Belvoir Castle in Leicestershire, at her death bequeathing only its completion to her husband; and she was the driving force behind the construction of York House on the Mall in London for her lover, Frederick, Duke of York. Elizabeth was also the first person in England to introduce the French Revival style for an entire interior. She was a talented watercolourist and an enterprising landscape gardener and estate manager.

In every way Lady Elizabeth Howard was suitable to be the wife of a duke. The daughter of the 5th Earl and Countess of Carlisle, she grew up at the monumentally beautiful Castle Howard in Yorkshire. Some way south in Leicestershire, on the death of his father the young John Manners had inherited the title of 5th Duke of Rutland when he was only eight. Elizabeth later claimed that she had fallen in love with him when she was fifteen: he had been nearly three years older. For the Duke's coming of age in January 1799 a huge party was given at his family home of Haddon Hall, in Derbyshire; the next month he proposed to, and was accepted by Elizabeth. It was a love match from the start. Romantically, he wrote just after the betrothal: 'I have dwelt but upon <u>one</u> <u>dear</u> object since I left London; a thousand circumstances, which before appeared trivial and uninteresting, return now with double consequence to my recollection, and prove to me most forcibly, that my heart and soul are wrapt up in one object.'[1] Shortly afterwards, however, he had had to leave, firstly to go hunting in Leicestershire and then to visit his regiment in Dublin. Until his return to London on 31 March they wrote regularly, she anxiously tracking the progress of his journey. At first she was pleased for his sake that he was fulfilling his duty: '...believe my dearest Duke, that to do the thing you wish, or desire will ever be my constant duty, and my greatest pleasure...',[2] but impatience later broke through, and she longed for his return 'from that horrid, that hateful country'. In a pattern that appeared throughout her letters again and again, she expressed guilt for having complained, yet dreaded another parting: 'Oh, no my dearest my beloved Duke, that cannot, that is not I am sure your plan; it is; that when we meet, it will be, to never, never part.'[3]

Although the couple were soon to be married, no wedding date was fixed at the time of their betrothal. It was normal to give short notice, at a time when marriage ceremonies were very low key and took place simply when it was convenient for the couple and their parents. The Duke reappeared in London according to plan on 31 March, and sent Elizabeth a note by footman, asking if she would be at home later that evening. There could have been little doubt. Two weeks later, on 22 April 1799, the couple were married. The eighteen-year-old Elizabeth moved out of her parents' house in Grosvenor Place and into lodgings in Oxford Street with her young husband.

Within a month the Duke was back with his regiment, and, despite his bride's hopes of going with him, he travelled alone. Certainly he missed her: 'Indeed my dearest Elizabeth, I love you very dearly; solemnly will I ever fulfil the oath which I took this day month, to guard, protect, and love you with my heart and soul. My heart is torn by contending passions when I am absent from you; you may therefore guess how forced must have been my opinion, & how contrary to my own wishes, when I advised you to remain in London.'[4] Left alone for five weeks, the young Duchess wrote to him daily, as he had requested, and as did he to her. But Elizabeth was lonely.

What most upset the young Duchess in the course of that year was their first Christmas. On 24 December the Duke departed for London, apparently on 'business', which included buying wine, sorting out his finances and spending time with the Prince of Wales.[5] Elizabeth, who was now expecting a baby, was left at Belvoir Castle to look after her houseparty. She was not happy, writing on Boxing Day how she awaited anxiously the news that he had arrived safely, 'which will make me if not quite happy yet much more so than I am at present; if I should not hear from you today, I know not what I shall do.' She was to be alone for a whole week, 'yet I fear it will be a very very long one and not at all a merry Christmas'. The Duke's letters were loving and intimate: he assured her that '[I] shall be most delighted when I am again employed in keeping you warm.'[6] However, he was clearly pursuing his own interests, and had not thought too much about where his Duchess was going to live or, indeed, whether she would like his ancestral home at Belvoir Castle.

So far, it seemed, she did not. Apparently Elizabeth had not visited Belvoir before her marriage: in February the Duke had mentioned that he longed to introduce it to her, hoping that she would 'regard its old walls with the same veneration that I do myself'.[7] Although the Duke's ancestors had lived at Belvoir since the eleventh century, and some of the ancient castle walls were incorporated in the existing one,[8] the present castle was mainly a design by John Webb, carried out between 1662 and 1668. In fact it had been built for a woman, the Countess of Rutland, daughter of the 1st Lord Montagu of Boughton. She had first requested a plan as early as 1654: her husband the 8th Earl, who was a Parliamentarian, had retired to their other home at Haddon Hall after the earlier, Tudor house built for the 1st Earl had been demolished by order of Parliament in 1649 as a Royalist stronghold. The Webb house is known today only through a model made by the local vicar in 1799, and from a painting by Jan Griffier, both at Belvoir Castle. The Countess had also created fine terraced gardens, while a hundred years later the 4th Duke had the surrounding park landscaped by Capability Brown. Although the model now looks very fine, and commentators often lament the destruction of the Restoration house, it was rather square and squat, too low for the views to be fully appreciated, and probably with small, dark rooms. The fact that the Duke described it as 'old' suggests that it was rather tatty. Certainly Haddon Hall was for various generations the better loved family home.

Beneath the surface of an intense and happy marriage, little frictions were beginning to build. During their first winter the Duke spent all his time at Wilsford, his hunting box about ten miles to the northeast, where he rode to hounds virtually every day from early morning often until dusk. Having experienced the vicissitudes of life married to a man with commitments to the Army, Elizabeth now found herself a hunting widow. In November of the following year, the beginning of the next hunting season, when she wanted to come to Leicestershire from her home at Castle Howard, it even seemed hard to find her anywhere to stay en route for Belvoir Castle. 'I really scarcely know how to advise you on your destination,' her husband wrote, evasively: it was very uncomfortable at Wilsford unless she brought just one maid and very few things.[9] She responded: 'I only wish that it rained so hard, or else froze enough to hinder you going to hunt those nasty fens – I do not envy the way in which you pass your mornings, & I hope you are almost tired of living without me.' She was about to arrive at Belvoir and requested: 'You must give up hunting Tuesday or Wednesday and come over to see me, else I shall say that you like hunting better than me.'[10]

From January in the winter of 1801 Elizabeth again spent most of her time in London. The Duke thought that it was the best place for her to be: he noted soon after Christmas that as Elizabeth would not wish to come to Belvoir without their baby daughter, it might be better to stay in town.[11] In the summer she began the habit of going on a seaside holiday, which was considered to be good for her health, especially at this delicate time when an heir was so longed for. Devotion and tension threaded their correspondence. While she yearned to be in a perpetual passionate clinch, and the Duke was by no means averse to his marital rights ('You are very much missed in the large bed'),[12] it seemed his sporting programme could not be interrupted.

The Duke's priorities were hunting, shooting, an heir – and his Duchess. The heir was obviously crucial. Although the Duke's charming and devoted letters often made him sound quite modern and egalitarian, begging her to write every day with 'a constant account of all your feels',[13] he was, like most men, not very interested in moans and complaints. The true reason for the invitations for his wife to give full rein to her thoughts was his extra attentiveness when she was pregnant. They loved their little daughter deeply, but there was mounting pressure to produce an heir: 'I am not less anxious than you for a little boy...'[14] she wrote during her next pregnancy in 1801. Elizabeth had been taught by her mother that men only liked happy women and that whingeing was unattractive; and whenever she fell to complaining, she continued to apologise. The Duke automatically expected good behaviour from her, and that she would give him all the freedom he required, as well as tenderness and support when he was at home: 'Only continue as you have begun in your behaviour to me, and you will always preserve entire my sincerest love and attachment.'[15] This she tried hard to do, and was very successful at it, sometimes simply being playful about their separation: 'you are a dear wicked man not to come to town.'[16] There was just one area in which she could not compromise, and that was the state of Belvoir Castle.

To grow up at Castle Howard had been a joy and a privilege: Elizabeth felt that to live at the old Belvoir Castle was not. Certainly she was the moving spirit behind the transformation of the house.[17] The young 5th Duke's father had already asked Capability Brown to draw up plans for its 'castellation and modernisation',[18] so some idea of a replacement had already been afoot during his minority. Elizabeth's restlessness coincided with an idea that was already planted in the Duke's mind: it may have been as early as their second autumn there, in 1800, that he commissioned James Wyatt for the remodelling. A later memorial document by the Duke records that they started pulling down the southwest front on Good Friday 1801.[19] The aim was to create a feudal palace, high on the hilltop, perhaps as imposing and imaginative as Castle Howard, but in the fashionable new 'Gothick' style, which appealed to the Duchess and in which James Wyatt enjoyed working. Wyatt was in his picturesque phase, having just completed the eccentrically Gothick Fonthill Abbey in Wiltshire.

At Belvoir Wyatt aimed to create magnificent views both to the surrounding countryside, and from the country to the house itself. His version of the castle, in brilliant yellow ironstone with grey stone dressings, and the fourth on the site, was aptly described as 'a vision of golden spires and silvery towers'.[20] The surviving southwest and southeast fronts are in fact only muted Gothick, with short rows of symmetrical windows retained from the rectangular shape of those in the incorporated walls of the old seventeenth-century house.[21] This classical-Gothick mix was typical of his work:[22] internally, he created new classical sequences on these main southern fronts. The northwest wing was altered to provide a new staircase and picture gallery; meanwhile the old part of the castle survived for the moment in the north-east wing.[23]

That summer the Duke wrote from Belvoir to the Duchess at Cheveley Park, their house near Newmarket, that 'Since dinner we have been examining every part of the improvements, and I had no conception or idea that so much could have (been) done in such as space of time. As I know our ideas widely differ upon this subject, and probably never will agree, I shall not persevere on it, or upon the beauties of this place at this time; which even in its present rude state, are very great…'[24] In response she said she was sure they would one day agree: 'indeed I hope some day or other, to find a very comfortable and pleasant place, and I flatter myself, I shall spend many happy days there with you…'[25] Writing from her holiday at Yarmouth the following summer, she said: 'I am so glad to hear the building goes on so fast, I shall be anxious to see it.'[26] At last Elizabeth was interested and involved in her acquired family home. By the summer of 1803 the Duke was writing to her about the terrace round from the barn, the new plantations and 'laying the fields together'.[27] From a holiday that year at Ramsgate she longed to hear how much the trees had grown, and 'how the sweet briars look'.[28] He reported that 'the battlements appeared…to be completed on the tower and the buttresses are also far advanced. The whole clock side of the castle is laid low and now presents one grand aperture, to repair which little I fear will now be done this year.'[29] The aperture was the gap for the new projecting round tower, in which round headed windows in the classical manner were to be created. This was later named the Regent's Tower. Two days later he wrote: 'I cannot yet satisfy all your expectation concerning the Castle…the battlement certainly gives the tower a most magnificent appearance.'

At the same time, the Duchess made improvements to Cheveley Park. She was rather nervous about them, and about spending her husband's money, which he seemed to control fairly tightly. Due to these periods of enforced separation, and long days alone even when he was at home, the Duchess was becoming tougher, gaining independence in a way that the Duke had perhaps not envisaged. He carried on in his normal manner with his horses, dogs and men friends, and planned to bring guests to Cheveley for early partridge shooting when she had hoped they would have a week alone. She lamented: 'I know you do not like tête a tête with your wife quite so well as I do…I could almost <u>cry</u> at the idea of finding people at Cheveley.' However, she had become judicious, in the same letter admiring his shooting ability and giving him praise and support: 'I believe you to be one of those people who can do, and do <u>well</u> anything they undertake…' Elizabeth was emerging from being the 'dear little miniature' of their early letters to a young woman making her own arrangements.

She was also a dutiful and affectionate mother; her children regularly played around her, and later she was very careful of their education. From the time of her birth, in May 1800, Lady Caroline was always with the Duchess on her travels. Two more daughters, Elizabeth and Emmeline, were soon born; but the Duchess had much affliction as well as much joy over her children. In 1804 little Caroline died. Distraught, the Duchess expressed her grief in verse:

> My Child! My Infant! Sweet yet faded Flow'r!
> Snatch'd by — heavens interposing pow'r!
> From the cold chilling, dreary wintry blast,
> And plac'd, where living and eternal last.
>
> Can I regret that thou art freed from pain?
> And when thou'rt happy do I dare complain?
> Yet not regret thee / – Ah it cannot be
> This heart no comfort knows bereft of thee![30]

The couple's early letters often mentioned their surviving 'dear little girls', known as Bibbi and Emmi, later to be joined by Katherine and Adeliza. Over two decades the Duchess bore five daughters and six sons, of which the daughters mostly came first. Her first son died as a very young baby in 1807; a second longed-for heir, named George like his brother, finally arrived in August 1813.

During these years building proceeded apace at Belvoir Castle. The young Edward Wyatt, James' nephew, designed and carved the capitals of the castle's Gothic columns with foliage and animals, closely following medieval prototypes.[31] The house was almost complete by 1813, the year in which James Wyatt suddenly died in a road accident. The quadrangular castle sat almost lozenge shaped, following the format of the original King John keep, on which both the Tudor and the Restoration house were based, making the naming of the wings very confusing. The main approach arrived at the corner of the north-west and southwest façades. The new suites of rooms were first used on a grand scale when the Prince Regent made a visit to Belvoir in 1814, with his brother, the Duke of York. On the Duke of Rutland's birthday, 4 January, the Prince and the Duke of York acted as sponsors at the baptism of the little Marquess of Granby in the newly completed long gallery on the southwest front, 'which has been recently fitted up for the reception of his royal highness, in a state of elegance, splen-dour, and magnificence, perhaps not to be surpassed in Europe'.[32] Before leaving on 7 January, the Prince named the new southwest tower the 'Regent's Tower' and the adjacent new gallery was also given his name.

Tragically, like his elder brother, the little boy at the centre of all the attention died, on 15 June 1814. Letters between Elizabeth and the Duke in 1814 show how especially afflicted she was after the death of her son. While admiring 'the extreme delicacy & sensibility of that mind, which is to me a treasure of such value', the Duke hoped after only a few weeks that the time had come to turn a corner.[33] Aware of her struggle, he assured her that 'my spirits are mainly dependent upon yours and my happiness completely interwoven with yours',[34] and appreciated 'the existing circumstances of distress & misery in which we are both placed'.[35] He pointed out that they seemed to have some kind of serious affliction every single year. Each had come to make generous allowances for the other.

Elizabeth was effectively running the estates at Belvoir by now, and had settled to country life, with children, dogs and builders; as a prac-tical farmer she won prizes and medals. She was good with staff, and when she later made an emergency will after a difficult childbirth, she showed especial care for them: 'Do not part with Miss Goody, she will I am sure be a second mother to those poor dear girls, make it worth her while to remain with them.' Of a Mrs Griffin she instructed, 'when she grows old, make her comfortable'; and even at a time of such dis-comfort, she mentioned several other little pensions for her servants.[36] She also watched events abroad and in 1814, after the sad death of her second son, was grateful of an opportunity to visit Paris. On 26 July, the Duke and Duchess embarked for France, having waited two days for a wind before they could sail.

The journal of their trip to Paris[37] was largely written by the Duke, who had earlier kept industrious accounts of visits he had made in England and Wales in the 1790s; he was also to be a prolific diarist in his later years.[38] The influence of the trip was crucial for Elizabeth. Following the imprisonment of Napoleon on Elba, it was a time of national rejoicing among Britain and her allies, in which visiting Paris meant a chance to see the royal palaces and collections for the first time in almost a generation. On their arrival, after three days' difficult travel, the Duke and Duchess began their time in the city by visiting the Pantheon and much admiring the tapestries at the Gobelins. The Duke commented in his journal that the 1740s tapestries were the finest; indeed he and the Duchess bought some *Don Quixote* tapestries made in the 1760s, woven from earlier designs by Coypel.[39] At the Louvre they found the newly created Grande Galerie very tiring and too long. The next day they walked through the royal palace of the Tuileries, destined to be destroyed by fire in 1870: symbolically, it was now slept in by Louis XVIII, but they saw everywhere 'the emblem of the usurper'. Later that week they drove past the glorious Les Invalides and the fine Ecole Militaire to visit the royal palace at St Cloud, and on the following day, in a party of nine, they travelled out westwards again, this time to the porcelain factory at Sèvres and to Versailles, visiting the Grand Trianon and the Bassin d'Apollon. Here too they saw the Galerie des Glaces and the War and Peace Drawing Rooms, and admired Marie Antoinette's private mirrored boudoir, behind her bedchamber, 'by which she escaped naked' only twenty-five years earlier. Their own purchases in Paris included fine French furniture from the reigns of Louis XIV and Louis XV,[40] notably some Boulle items now in the Regents Gallery. The next year, 1815, the Duke went on to Paris alone. By then Elizabeth had another young baby son, Charles, the future 6th Duke. From Paris, after fourteen years of marriage, her husband wrote to her every two days.

On 26 October 1816 between 2 and 3 a.m., while the Duke and Duchess were away at Cheveley Park, fire broke out at Belvoir, by the main entrance. Two of the wings were destroyed. A plan drawn by the Duchess was to show exactly what was lost, but in an accompanying letter to the Duchess of Somerset[41] she described her great thankfulness that the five children had been saved. The flames had come to within two rooms of the nursery at the centre of the southeast front, where two of the youngest had been sleeping: 'their preservation is

Saltram House, Devon, from the southeast.

Saltram House: proposed design for Lady Catherine Parker. This may have been intended to face east.

Theresa Parker with her son, John,
later 1st Earl of Morley, by Sir Joshua
Reynolds, 1772–5.

Saltram House: some of Theresa's
collection of black basalt vases.

Saltram House: the Saloon, or Great Room. Theresa's full-length portrait by Reynolds
is seen at the far end of the room. The carpet is by Thomas Whitty of Axminster.

Jane, Duchess of Gordon, in Elizabethan costume, by Sir Joshua Reynolds, *c.* 1775.

Gordon Castle, Morayshire, showing the early central tower and extensions around it, engraving.

Jane, Duchess of Gordon with her son, George Marquess of Huntly, by George Romney, 1778.

Kinrara, the house built by Jane, Duchess of Gordon for her own occupation.

Belvoir Castle, Leicestershire.

Fire at Belvoir
Castle, English
School.

Elizabeth, Duchess of Rutland, at Belvoir Castle, by George Sanders, *c.* 1817–20.
Part of the rebuilt Castle is shown through the window.

Elizabeth, Duchess of Rutland, at Belvoir, by George Sanders and John Ferneley, *c*. 1820. Her favourite view of the Castle is shown beyond.

Lancaster House, The Mall, London.

Belvoir Castle: the Elizabeth Saloon.

such a blessing that everything else appears almost nothing...'[42] The Duke was similarly philosophical, writing to his wife: 'Our loss is great, but that you will bear, as our Children are safe.'[43] The whole 'family' or staff was also safe.[44] The Duchess further described their losses to her friend, pointing to the fact that 'the whole of the old part of the Castle' had been destroyed, shown on her plan as the northeast wing. They had still been building on the northwest front, losing 'the New Staircase, and entrance Hall, which they were just finishing, and the new Picture Gallery which certainly was most beautiful...'[45] About a third of the castle's fine paintings were also lost, having been insured for far less than their real value. Everyone had rallied to save the castle, and by bricking up the door into the blazing northwest wing, the Regent's Gallery was miraculously saved. The Duchess wrote to thank the Duke's chaplain, the Revd. Sir John Thoroton, for all his care in safely removing the children to an inn, 'without their even getting a cold'.[46]

It was Sir John who would play an important part in the rebuilding of the northern sections, which began in March 1817. He was in fact a member of the family, his mother being the natural daughter and ward of the 3rd Duke. Even after her marriage to Thomas Thoroton MP she had spent most of her life with her father, either at Belvoir or in London. Sir John had therefore spent his own childhood at Belvoir,[47] and his family relationship was reinforced when he married a grand-daughter of the 3rd Duke; he had received a knighthood at the visit of the Prince Regent. Whereas the guiding hand for the new interiors was Elizabeth's, Sir John contributed to designs for the exterior, including eventually the great porte-cochere on the northwest entrance front. Elizabeth, while controlling the building works, remained concerned for her husband's good opinion of them, especially Sir John's new tower on the northeast front: '...the first thing is that you, should be pleased', she wrote in May.[48] For the moment, however, she was too busy having babies to see all of the project carried through herself. Three more sons were born, in 1817 (Adolphus), 1818 (John, the future 7th Duke) and 1820 (George). Although work at Belvoir was proceeding fast, Elizabeth had to spend extra time at Cheveley in 1817 after the difficult birth of Adolphus on 10 November. Sickly and jaundiced, the baby sapped his mother's strength. The Duke departed a few days later, and reported on building progress to her from Belvoir, saying that the scaffolding was off the new tower[49] and that while out hunting he could see 'beautiful peeps of the Castle' and that the tower 'looks handsome everywhere'.[50] The great integral tower was being built so that a new drawing room could project out into it: externally it showed the distinctive but rather amateur hand of Thoroton, with its angular buttresses and extraordinary Norman-style window. The Staunton tower, which was square, was heightened on the southeast side at the time, while the southernmost, rectangular tower, which housed the Duchess's private apartments, had already been built out by James Wyatt on the old foundations.

During Elizabeth's absence, the house was dead. Above all, the Duke wanted her to come home: 'Have you ascertained when...Belvoir Castle is truly to be Blessed with the presence of her, without whom everything around it affects to stand still?'[51] On 15 December he reported: 'Your Rooms are ready at this moment, the Curtains in the Staunton Tower Breakfast Room will be up tomorrow.' Windows were fixed, the fireplace in the Breakfast Room had been tried, all the fires had been lit and would remain so until her arrival for Christmas.

In the internal building works Elizabeth decided to emphasise that Belvoir had once been an ancient seat. Thoroton's main staircase is a delightfully effervescent piece of Gothick, while another staircase leads up to the fine Gothick Grand Corridor or Ballroom, which he designed from various parts of Lincoln Cathedral. From the landing, above the central pier the arms of Manners impaling those of Howard announce the Ballroom as well as standing out high at the far end of the room in stained glass and in two other high central locations. Parallel, on the outer side of the castle, a bedchamber and dressing room with Chinese wallpaper also show the Duchess's hand. The cornice moulding in a long acanthus leaf reveals the Wyatt workshop, which continued to supervise the construction under the direction of Wyatt's eldest and second sons, Benjamin Dean and Matthew Wyatt, with the later addition of Philip.[52] Edward Wyatt did carving, gilding and model making, and Thoroton organised the open and corridor areas, while the Wyatts were assigned actual rooms; but Thoroton also had a design role in the furniture for the Great Dining Room, which was being restored in 1820, with the bill paid to Gillows for monumental sideboards in 1824.[53]

The rebuilding at Belvoir took the rest of Elizabeth's life. The three

so-called King's Rooms above the entrance front were decorated with
exotic hand-painted wallpapers in anticipation that the Prince Regent
might again come to stay. These comprised a suite of reception room,
bedchamber and dressing room, together with a bathroom next to the
bedchamber, reached by a narrow passage that appears to have been
specially recessed to allow for the Prince's great bulk. The rooms were
decorated in the fashion promoted by the Regent, with bedcovers and
upholstery in strong colours.

Elizabeth was still learning and growing: letters between her and
Colonel Frederick Trench, a close family friend, show the Colonel
commending her on Latin translations and discussing music with
her.[54] In 1819 she accompanied the Duke on another foreign tour, this
time to Brussels and the Rhine. By then she was especially interested in
cathedrals and churches, commenting on the architecture with assurance in Tournai Cathedral, where she disliked the mixture of Gothic
and Grecian, and admiring that at Ghent. In Courtrai she was independent enough to set out on her own to visit churches. Clearly Gothic
was her preference: in Brussels she thought that John Nash, the great
classical architect of the Regency period, 'should certainly be sent here,
to get some better ideas in his Head, how to improve London'. In
Namur she thought the Jesuit church 'as usual...is spoilt by modern
bad taste'. She admired lustres and vases in an ormolu factory and
commented on the different weavings of carpets in another manufac-
tory, both at Tournai.

Elizabeth was also a talented watercolour painter. The Duke had
encouraged her to illustrate his diaries of the 1790s with sketches, this
being seen as a task suitable to a young wife in her early married years;
the diaries were subsequently published.[55] As was the custom of the
day, Elizabeth's sketches were often completed by a professional watercolourist. In 1821, completing a batch from the 1819 tour,[56] she wrote:
'I have a Dozen Drawings, perhaps Mr Holworthy may do two or three
more.' She was modest about her artistic achievement: 'I can only take
the credit for the original sketches as I cannot bear to be praised for
what I do not deserve. Mr Holworthy has the whole merit of the finished drawings therefore they may put sketched by Elizabeth, Duchess
of Rutland.'[57]

When Sir John Thoroton died in 1820, Elizabeth was devastated: 'I
cannot express how much I feel the loss of my poor dear good, old

friend, I wander about…crying all the way I go, for <u>everything</u> I see recalls him to my imagination; the roads…the gardens, the Farm, the Plantations, he understood so well the Castle which he took <u>such delight</u> in…in short his uniform kindness to me, in doing everything I could wish, or desire, all he could, to gratify and please me…so useful or kind a friend never existed.'[58] A new *arbiter elegantium* emerged in the receiver of the letter, Colonel Frederick Trench. She called him her 'active agent'.[59] From his London home, he was to help Elizabeth through her greatest crisis, one which she sailed through with remarkably little concern about anyone else's opinion or feelings. In about 1822 Elizabeth became very close to Frederick, Duke of York. A letter from the Duke of Rutland in this year to Colonel Trench was to be one of the few surviving documents to address the subject. In it he referred to Elizabeth as Venus, perhaps a new code name between him and the Colonel for the amorous Duchess. Pleased with a recent three-day visit to Belvoir, he said: 'I must say no Person ever strove to make themselves more delightful than Venus. I could observe how strong has been the tension upon a certain Chord, whenever I touched it, and how thoroughly all her Feelings have been lately called into Action – There is more of Romance in the events of the last two months (to which you have been privy) than I could conceive possible in the Events of actual Life.'[60] There is an aura of mystery in this deliberately obscure document: clearly Colonel Trench was party to the affair. Ever loyal to his master, he was sending on to the Duke private letters received by him from the Duchess.

In 1822 Elizabeth evidently had other admirers. Harriet Arbuthnot, a lively and attractive young married woman, who was the mistress of the unhappily married Duke of Wellington, recorded: 'I dined at a grand dinner at the Duke of Wellington's to meet the Duchess of Rutland, who had all her lovers and seemed to give preference to George Anson.'[61] The latter must be the suitor of whom Colonel Trench complained two years later, causing the Duchess to protest: 'No you are <u>not right</u>, and I will give you a proof of it; I suppose if you are in <u>Love</u> with a person, you like to <u>see</u> as <u>much</u> of them as you <u>can</u>, now I might have ask'd George, to have come <u>here</u> to shoot, I might have ask'd him to come to Cheveley, but I have done neither one; or the other; – it will be a long time before I see him again, and you will allow at least, that is not encouraging it either in myself or in him; if he is so foolish to be in love with me, what can I do.' In the same letter she came clean about her real inclinations: 'The real fact is, I have never been in love but twice in my life, the first time with his Grace, which began when I was fifteen, and the other you <u>know</u>.'[62]

'The other' was the Duke of York, about whom she had already written to Colonel Trench, worried on the royal Duke's behalf that he had not enough money to be free of his royal brother the King so that he could have his own house. In 1825 Harriet Arbuthnot described the continuing affair: 'The Duke (of York) is most absurdly in love with the Dss of Rutland. In that day at dinner he spoke to no other creature, &, tho' he had the Dss of Wellington on the other side of him, he never so much looked at her, nor the Dss at the Duke of Wellington who sat on her other hand. They sat together in the drawing-room till past eleven o'clock.'[63] On a second evening in June at Carlton House, the King's own fabulous home designed by Nash, there was a grand dinner, after which the normally antisocial Duke of York stayed until the Duchess arrived, sitting at her side until 1 a.m.[64] In July, Harriet Arbuthnot dined with the Rutlands and the Duke of York, who was expected elsewhere for dinner, but simply did not bother to go.[65] Three days later, Harriet dined there again and concluded: 'To be sure, that house goes on in an odd way. The Duke of York, as usual, had neither eyes nor ears for anyone but the Dss of Rutland; they are like a boy and girl 17 & 15, when one recollects that the one is 62 and the other an old grandmother, it is really disgusting.'[66] In fact Elizabeth was still a very lively and glamorous forty-four: only two years earlier she was seen dancing at a New Year's Eve ball in Stamford until half past four in the morning.[67]

Elizabeth's love life was to lead her into a more sophisticated architectural project. With the help of Colonel Trench she set about creating a magnificent house on the Mall for the Duke of York, for which the plans 'even to the most minute particulars, were formed under her immediate direction'.[68] Planned in 1823, York House, nowadays known as Lancaster House, was to be built on the site of the Duke's existing home at Godolphin House. Without substantial capital, the Duke had to ask permission from the Lords of the Treasury in order to build. Prompted by the Duchess and the Colonel, he managed to secure a loan, which his brother the King then disallowed. It was a long, hard fight. The artistically minded King disapproved of the first plan by the architect Robert Smirke, as indeed did the Duchess. She encouraged Benjamin Dean Wyatt to produce alternative proposals under her own supervision and managed to orchestrate Smirke's replacement. Philip Wyatt was also involved.[69] On 17 June 1825, the Duchess laid the foundation stone. Models of elevations were submitted for her approval. She kept a close eye on the plans, trying to prevent the northern portico from projecting too much, and commenting to Benjamin Wyatt on the shade of scagliola *verde antico* columns.[70] By late November the ground floor was complete.

Elizabeth's increasing interest in architecture and in the urban landscape coincided with the period of a great classical revival. In London the family's home was Rutland House, a small but ravishing classical house at 16, Arlington Street, looking onto Green Park, which had been built by James Gibbs for Mary Shireburn, Duchess of Norfolk. Elizabeth's numerous letters of 1824–5 to Colonel Trench show that she was obsessed by a project for the new embankment on the north side of the Thames between Charing Cross and Blackfriars, for which they were trying to raise money through shares by subscription, seeking the support of the Government. The scheme was launched by the Duke of York in July 1824, with Elizabeth sitting at his side in a barge on the river. The Duchess made many suggestions for subscribers and thought of little else: '…it is in my thoughts by day, and my dreams by night…'[71] She also hoped to build some houses in the adjoining streets that would obliterate some of the older 'ugly buildings'.[72] She told Trench: 'Pray take the <u>greatest</u> <u>care</u> that Mr Wyatt's Buildings for the Quay are <u>quite</u> correct and <u>Classical</u>, that no-one, if he comes hot, from Rome, —– Italy can find a <u>single</u> <u>fault</u>, that all the ornaments are bold and well relieved, so as to look well as a <u>distance</u>, the great fault of our Architects, is making every thing small, and frippery.'[73] Classical architecture was her new passion: 'Do not again I beseech you mention the word Gothick, it is very beautiful in its way for Churches and cathedrals, but not in the least appropriate for Quays…'[74] She had a further ambitious idea: 'I am more enchanted than I can express at the idea of the Center Building being a National Gallery, for Pictures and Statues…'[75] Philip Wyatt made plans and drawings and when the petition was presented to a parliamentary committee in March 1825 the scheme was unanimously adopted. However, it looked as if the quay, a long arched viaduct raised on Doric columns, would only have a chance of being built without the houses. There was no question about who considered herself in charge of the project: Elizabeth told Trench that 'you ought to have asked my leave' before agreeing to take the houses out.[76] She was eager to commence building that year, because 'we may all be dead by next'.[77]

At a time when no new royal palace had been built since the amendments to Charles II's old Whitehall, Elizabeth and Colonel Trench also spent much time on suggestions for a suitably noble edifice for her friend the King.[78] This was to be in Hyde Park, aligned approximately to the middle of Park Lane, with two ceremonial routes running from it, to Westminster and to St Paul's Cathedral.[79] She even completed a number of 'very beautiful' designs for an entrance to Hyde Park Corner.[80] In the event George IV increasingly looked towards enlarging Buckingham House, for which he required enormous sums of money. Elizabeth's worry was that funds for his palace would mean there was nothing for the quay.[81]

Meanwhile, Harriet Arbuthnot recorded the latest achievements of the Duchess at Belvoir.[82] When she had first met Elizabeth at a dinner given by Wellington in November 1822, she commented: 'She is said to be the proudest woman in England, but she was very good-natured & did not show off her pride. She is very handsome.'[83] In January 1823 Harriet stayed at the castle, with the Duke of Wellington: 'Nothing can be more magnificent & princely than Belvoir Castle; its situation on a very high hill commanding the whole county for 40 miles round has often been considered second only to Windsor. The Castle has been built from the present fortifications by the present Dss who has made the place, the Duke taking no part in the improvement of the place.' She said that the house had 'great faults' because of there being 'no regular suite of rooms', but felt that 'as a whole it will, I think do honour to the architectural taste of the present age'.[84] Elizabeth was also much involved in landscaping the grounds. In 1823 she was busy writing to Colonel Trench about 'my new lake', which was to the southeast[85] and 'my bridge',[86] declaring in late 1824: 'My Bridge, and my Lake look beautiful.'[87] This view from the south towards the Castle was her favourite, and after her death George Sanders painted it into the background of his portrait of the Duchess on her white mare. At this time Elizabeth was also maintaining a gloriously happy family home: 'Belvoir is a much better place when we have music dancing and hunting in the house, as they turned the Duke out today and ran him round the house.'[88] The good-natured Duke of Rutland, still in his mid forties, was quite happy to play the fox for his young and lively off-spring.

In 1824 work was beginning in the Saloon at Belvoir, which Elizabeth had ordered should precede all other undertakings. Her decision to create a French interior in the Louis Quatorze style was especially remarkable as, despite the King's passion for French porcelain and furniture, it was England's first complete interior in this style, to be followed in London in 1827 at Crockford's Club in St James's, by Benjamin Dean Wyatt, evidently working under her influence.[89] Elizabeth was a major influence in spreading the French Revival style in England. She had entrusted the decoration of the room to Matthew Cotes Wyatt, but took a close interest in it herself. Indeed, she found that Wyatt was not particularly forthcoming with ideas, although he did buy *boiseries* for the room, in Paris as a job lot for 1450 guineas.[90] At this time many such items were being sold off, having been stripped out of various châteaux after the revolution. Elizabeth's *boiseries* were supposedly from the château at Maintenon near Chartres from which Louis XIV's mistress and morganatic wife had taken her title. As with many items later misnamed in these re-creations, they were in fact from the time of the subsequent king, Louis XV, and may therefore have come from the château after a later refurbishment, or from a Parisian town house dating approximately from the 1730s. Elizabeth told Colonel Trench firmly: 'It will be quite right to take all the Carving', although there was a delay owing to the cost. She also enquired about the floor: 'Will you ask Mr Wyatt if I may take the Pattern of the inlaid Floor, to Belvoir, to show Mr Turner. I conclude Mr Wyatt will be soon able to inform us whether the Floor at Paris will do for us – of course when we live in the room we shall have carpets down.'[91] A fine carpet incorporating peacocks was woven in the Savonnerie style[92] at Tournai in Belgium, where the Duchess had admired such work in 1819.

Elizabeth was especially concerned about the chimneypieces to be used at the castle: 'Make the two Chimney Pieces in the Drawing Room as handsome as you please, perhaps you could send me a rough drawing of the largest and best, which Mr Wyatt has got, they should be of a good size to suit the room as it is large...' Of Voltaire's chairs, the sale of which had been proposed to her, she said: '...by your account the Chairs are not handsome, and as I am not in love with Voltaire, I am not so anxious to have <u>his</u> Chairs tho' I admire his tragedies.' She also worried about the windows: 'I do not know what to say about them, how will they look <u>outside</u>, the windows being <u>Saxon, outside</u>, we must not be laugh'd at.' She wanted the room to be a surprise: 'We will <u>shut</u> the <u>doors</u> and not let any one see the room till it is finished, and I promise not to say one word of the expence.'[93] The cost seemed to be rather a surprise to her husband too: she often asked Colonel Trench how he would find the money to pay for it.[94] While she understood the necessity for economy, commenting that dukes never had any ready money, and was prepared to use less expensive marble from their own works at Bakewell, such was Elizabeth's confidence in her own taste that invariably she ended by paying out.

In January 1825 the Duke and Duchess visited Chatsworth in Derbyshire. She described the landscape lyrically:

'Derby Sh, tho' in winter was beautiful, such lovely gleams of light and Sun, the distant Moors so dark and Blue, and the air so fine and bracing, one or two beautiful Sun Sets, we all agreed who would be in London!!'[95]

Elizabeth was looking at other houses for architectural details: from nearby Burghley, the home of the Marquess of Exeter at Stamford, she was thinking of copying a chimneypiece.[96] Throughout this busy year, there could be no suspicion of how it would end. When writing at Belvoir she was often surrounded by her three noisy little boys, 'Granby', 'Johnny' and 'Georgy', or during the evening joined in playing a game, 'making out words, which bothers my head'.[97] In March she visited Croxton Park Races with the Duke of York, travelling home with him in the carriage to Belvoir: 'I ride out with him every afternoon he expresses himself to be more happy than ever he was before, in <u>all</u> his <u>life</u>, which I rejoice at, as he well deserves to be so; and there is no harm in reflecting that I am the innocent cause of his happiness.'[98] In April she was still asking about the floor, the 'woods' or *boiseries* and the chimneypieces for her Saloon.[99] By August materials for Belvoir were beginning to be resolved: Wyatt was trying to get the insurance office to pay up, so that the carvings 'will immediately March for the Chateau' as Trench wrote. 'Everything is in good Train

& I hope to see – the Drawing Room in a Blaze of Splendour at Xmas,' he reported.[100] On a day spent visiting a country house near Belvoir, she spent a happy afternoon with the Duke of York pruning branches from trees in order to create views to the nearby river for her host.[101] In October the Duke of York was with her for a fortnight at Cheveley Park.[102] Meanwhile York House posed its own building problems, and plans for the quay continued to ebb and flow: Colonel Trench reported that the King was impressed by it, '& says you are an <u>extraordinary</u> woman'.[103] In November Elizabeth was back at Belvoir: 'We went into the Drawing Room yesterday, the Floor is quite finished, they have begun to Gild the Cornice.'[104] This was Wyatt's elaborate gilded entablature to set off his ceiling, the frieze depicting peacocks, the Manners family emblem. The aim was to open the drawing room for the Duke of Rutland's birthday on 4 January.[105]

Suddenly, with two magnificent building projects growing apace, and only days after her forty-fifth birthday, Elizabeth was dead. It was 29 November 1825. She had been ill at Belvoir for only a couple of days, dying of a burst appendix.[106] Both her dukes were inconsolable, the Duke of York rushing from Brighton to Belvoir to be with her husband. Lady Williams Wynn commented: 'the disconsolate Duke of York has been passing a fortnight with the disconsolate Widower, mingling…their sighs and regrets over the Ecarte table, and with their united tears making a pool in the middle.'[107] Sardonically, she told her daughter: 'The Duke (of Rutland) is in the deepest affliction, but will, I should think, not remain in his widowed state longer than is necessary, as he seems to be one who could not live without female Society.'[108] The two men were soon joined at Belvoir by their friend the Duke of Wellington, making a ducal triumvirate. The heartbroken Duke of York laid the first stone for Elizabeth's mausoleum at Belvoir on 1 March 1826. According to Mrs Arbuthnot, this caused him to catch a chill: in May he 'looked very ill, scarcely spoke & ate nothing' at a dinner. He was heavily in debt because 'he has had the folly, by the persuasion of the poor Dss of Rutland, to build a house that will cost him £100,000'.[109] In January 1827 he died at Elizabeth's home in London, in a room looking out onto the park, attended by her widowed husband. The Grand Old Duke of York had 'never been himself since her death'.[110]

In the next few years John, Duke of Rutland worked tirelessly in Elizabeth's memory. Work continued on the Elizabeth Saloon, still in the intended style of a Parisian salon of the period. Following the Restoration of the Bourbon monarchy in 1814 and encouraged by George IV's admiration for French interiors, the Parisian style was soon to be fashionable. Divided into one circular and three semicircular compartments, Matthew Wyatt's exotic and entirely personal Saloon ceiling depicted the story of Jupiter and Juno, with Juno representing the Duchess. She (Juno) appears with her chariot at the centre of the ceiling, the lunette flanked by real-life portraits of the Duke and Duchess. There does not seem to be an applied moral to the tale, but in mid ceiling above the entrance door the Duke of York is painted with a beard (possibly to disguise him) as Jupiter, while in another lunette it is the Duke of Rutland who, as King of the Gods, accompanies his Juno. In each corner are their children, those that had died shown as cherubs with wings. The Manners peacocks in the frieze were reflected in the Tournai carpet. The suite of gilded furniture in the French manner was made for the room by one Mr Hume. It comprised two round and four oblong tables, with four chaises longues and fourteen chairs, eight of which were set across the room in a row with footstools, while six were placed round the tables. While being symmetrical, the arrangement was thus relatively informal, designed for separate groups of people to converse or play at cards. Three little items now in the room were especially personal to the Duchess: these were the elaborate silk-lined workbox, the gilt music box and the George IV giltwood table cabinet, which she partly painted herself.

Accompanied both by her husband and by the Duke of Wellington, Harriet Arbuthnot customarily went to Belvoir every year after Christmas for the Duke of Rutland's birthday celebrations. In 1829 she described the opening of the new drawing room, three years later than intended, for the Duke's birthday: 'It is the most magnificent room I ever saw, fitted up in the style of Louis 14th in pannells of blue silk damask & the most beautiful carving and gilding. At the end of the room, in front of an immense looking glass, is a marble statue of the late Duchess, excessively like her. It is very proper to have her there for she was the builder of the castle, & Belvoir is indebted to her for all its beauty & decorations. She certainly was a woman of extraordinary genius & talent mixed up with a great deal of vanity & folly.' The Duke also showed Harriet the mausoleum, built by Benjamin Dean Wyatt in

Elizabeth's honour, in which he proposed to join his wife. The sarcophagus was to sit at the top of the aisle; the decoration, carved by Matthew Wyatt, was to be emotive: 'Over it is to be a marble statue of the Dss ascending to Heaven.'[111] The Norman-style mausoleum, set in a grove of yew trees at the time already a hundred years old, today sits with its own beautifully tended garden, facing the castle from the south, its ornate doorway looking up towards Elizabeth's own private apartments. This was the view that Elizabeth loved best, glimpsed through 'peeps' in the trees in a way that is so special to Belvoir.

At one end of the Elizabeth Saloon, by the inner wall from the window, stands Matthew Wyatt's fine Carrara marble statue of the Duchess, reflected in a mirror. While today this sculpture is an integral part of the room, it is a sad reminder that Elizabeth did not live to use the Saloon she had so lovingly begun. In the Grand Dining Room, Wyatt's extraordinary virtuoso marble pedestal, representing a cloth over a table, was also commissioned by the Duchess. The Duke of York's biographer called her 'the presiding genius of the place', saying that all the plans for the castle, as well as those for the grounds, villages and roads, were due to her 'elevated taste'.[112]

A revealing contemporary view of the Duchess was offered by Harriet Arbuthnot's diary: 'The poor Duchess of Rutland has died very suddenly...I am very sorry for her and she will be a most dismal loss to her husband. She managed all his affairs for him; he did nothing himself, and his estates, his horses, his family, everything was under her rule. She had all the follies & weaknesses of a beautiful woman, but she had great & redeeming qualities, a masculine strength of mind, an elevated taste & pursuits in planting & farming which were essentially beneficial to her husband's estates and to the poor and dependent around her.' Harriet showed the Duchess as a task-driven woman, uninterested in trivia: 'She was hated by all the fine ladies of London because she was far above them; conscious of her high rank, a Howard & a Plantaganet, she scorned all the petty arts & nonsenses of fashion...She had very few female friends, but to those few she was most constant and affectionate. She is a great loss to the Duke of York, who I understand is very unhappy.'[113]

An obituary circulated among the tenants at Belvoir emphasised the Duchess's qualities of mind: 'In this distinguished lady were united the attractive softness of the most perfect grace and beauty, with a vigour of understanding, and a clearness of intellect, seldom equalled in either sex. Her taste was pure and refined; she excelled in every elegant female accomplishment; and by her own spontaneous efforts, in the midst of gaiety and pleasure, had stored her mind with much solid knowledge.' Elizabeth's religious faith was also emphasised, as helping her to overcome the many afflictions of her life, especially the losses of three sons and her eldest daughter. She had demonstrated that, given the means and the encouragement, a talented aristocratic woman could make something exceptional of her life, while helping those around her: 'Unostentatious, but persevering in her efforts to improve the whole country around her, she gradually and imperceptibly accomplished her well-formed plans, by a judicious application of the ample means, which, the indulgence of the kindest and most affectionate husband, placed at her disposal.'[114]

Elizabeth Howard, Duchess of Rutland, was mourned and wept over by both her Dukes, but her memorial lives on, both at Belvoir Castle and in the fine exterior at what is now Lancaster House in the Mall, with its four beautifully orchestrated façades. At her funeral her hearse was drawn by six black horses, with coachman and postilion, the family arms richly emblazoned on the door. It was escorted by four pages each side on foot, bearing staves tipped with silver, and preceded by a huge procession, including her riderless favourite white mare, caparisoned in black. Although she herself was considered unostentatious, her funeral cortège was unrestrainedly theatrical, as befitted her rank and her remarkable career as the mistress of Belvoir Castle and as a great patroness of architecture.

CONCLUSION

The traditional eighteenth-century arrangement of the man as provider and the woman as his supporter was not necessarily stifling for either marriage partner. In an age when to be a spinster had little status and less glamour, a husband provided social acceptability, family, a sense of purpose and often the added advantages of love, affection and companionship. Women of the time were sensibly strategic in their marriages, knowing they might have no alternative but to tolerate a difficult husband's behaviour as the price of avoiding financial hardship or social insignificance. However, many married aristocratic women gained extraordinary freedom, socially and financially. This was especially so at the domestic level, and was often reflected in the imaginative arrangement and complex organisation of their homes. If the resulting efforts enhanced a great house, it was likely to benefit the husband's own image as a gentleman of property or even as a political host.

Although aristocratic women had a bevy of nursery helpers, it is noticeable from their diaries how much time they spent with their children, playing and reading with them, and directing their education. Many of those who did not have children poured a great deal of energy into building and collecting. In creating two palatial houses, the achievement of Elizabeth, Duchess of Rutland, is all the more remarkable because she had so many children. Many other women, with and without children, undoubtedly spent time and resources on their houses: unfortunately, if no diaries, paintings, letters or accounts exist, their work may often be unrecorded.

'It is a fine thing for a great house whose history has been preserved...Generally the women of the house keep up its memories, not the men.'[1] Many women felt that their aim in life was to do just that. They would display the family traditions through portraits and picture arrangements, and through monograms and coats of arms on frames and furniture, on textiles and tiny snuff-boxes. Women were often as preoccupied with the future of their dynasties as were men: those without children frequently spent extra time concerning themselves with the inheritance of their successors, ensuring that the right nephew was properly groomed for his future responsibilities in caring for a great house and its estate.

Much of what we think of eighteenth-century women was obscured until recently by our perception of the Victorians. It was assumed that because our more recent predecessors had been so apparently subservient to their husbands, and so limited in what they were allowed to do, that the same had been the case in the previous century. It was wrongly thought that the path towards greater freedom for women was one of slow but steady progress. Although this is far too big an historical subject to tackle in a closing chapter, it would seem that in terms of women's lives, the Victorians took a step backwards. Life was far more stifling for Victorian women than for their grandmothers: under the obsessively conjugal Queen Victoria, women at all levels bowed increasingly to the wishes, whims and demands of their men and to the requirements of social respectability. With their vibrant physical and intellectual energy, the great chatelaines of the eighteenth century have much more in common with their modern counterparts than either has with the aristocratic wives of the Victorian era.

NOTES

All dates have been modernised. The spelling and punctuation in quotations have been retained as originally written.

Author's Preface

1 Mark Girouard, *Life in the English Country House* (Yale, 1978), chapter 1
2 Christina Hardyment, *Behind the Scenes, Domestic Arrangements in Historic Houses* (The National Trust, 1997)
3 Christopher Hibbert, *The Marlboroughs* (Viking, 2002); Ophelia Field, *The Favourite: Sarah, Duchess of Marlborough* (Hodder & Stoughton, 2002); Julius Bryant, *Mrs Howard. A Woman of Reason 1688–1727*, Catalogue for the Exhibition at Marble Hill (English Heritage, 1988); Trevor Lummis and Jan Marsh, *The Woman's Domain* (Viking, 1990, Penguin, 1993); Christopher Simon Sykes, *Private Palaces* (Chatto & Windus, 1985); Eileen Harris, *The Genius of Robert Adam: His Interiors* (Yale, 2001)
4 Rachel Trethewey, *Mistress of the Arts: The Passionate Life of Georgina, Duchess of Bedford*, Review, 2002
5 Peter Smith, 'Lady Oxford's Alterations at Welbeck Abbey, 1741–55', *Georgian Group Journal* (2001)
6 Especially; John Cannon, *Aristocratic Century. The peerage of eighteenth-century England* (Cambridge University Press, 1984); Laurence Stone, *The Family, Sex and Marriage in England 1500–1800* (London, 1977); John Brewer, *The Pleasures of the Imagination. English Culture in the 18th Century* (London, 1977)

Chapter 1: The Feminine Touch

1 John Martin Robinson, *Temples of Delight: Stowe Landscape Gardens* (The National Trust, 1990), chapter 1
2 Francis Haskell, 'The British as Collectors' in G. Jackson-Stops (ed.), *The Treasure Houses of Britain: Five Hundred Years of Private Patronage and Art Collecting* (Yale University Press, 1985), p. 50
3 Charlotte Gere and Marina Vaisey, *Great Women Collectors* (Philip Wilson, 2000)
4 Carola Hicks, *Improper Pursuits: the Scandalous Life of Lady Di Beauclerk* (Macmillan, 2001), p. 45
5 Well summarised by Trevor Lummis and Jan Marsh, *The Woman's Domain* (Viking, 1990)
6 Information from Christine Hiskey at Holkham Archives: H/Inv 1, 2, 7 & 8
7 Arthur Young, *A Six Weeks Tour...* (London, W. Nicoll, 1768)
8 Ralph Dutton, *English Court Life* (Batsford, 1963), pp. 220–1, quoting Horace Walpole
9 R. Blunt (ed.), *Mrs Montagu 'Queen of the Blues', her Letters and Friendships from 1762 to 1800* (London, 1923), vol. 2, p. 61

10 E.g. Belvoir Castle: Conversation with Lady Ursula d'Abo (Manners), 2000

Chapter 2: Love and Strategy

1 Act II, scene vi
2 Maureen Waller, *1700: Scenes from London Life* (Sceptre, 2001). The history of eighteenth-century aristocratic marriage is well documented in Lawrence Stone, *The Family, Sex and Marriage in England, 1500–1800* (Weidenfeld & Nicolson, 1977). Amanda Vickery, *The Gentleman's Daughter* (Yale University Press, 1998), feels the study makes some over-generalisations. Marriage is also finely measured in John Cannon, *Aristocratic Century* (Cambridge University Press, 1934). G. E. Mingay, *English Landed Society in the Eighteenth Century* (Routledge and Kegan Paul, 1963), p. 28 and p. 78, points out that because of other limiting factors, the main path for advancement for the families who subsequently had the greatest wealth was through marriage
3 Robert Halsband, *The Complete Letters of Lady Mary Wortley Montagu* (Oxford University Press, 1965), vol. 1, p. 134, to Edward Wortley Montagu, 26 July 1712
4 Quoted by Adrian Tinniswood, *Belton House* (The National Trust, 1992), p. 7
5 Cannon, pp. 74–5
6 Robert Halsband, *Lady Mary Wortley Montagu* (Oxford, Clarendon, 1956), p. 175, referring to Lady Henrietta Herbert, widowed daughter of the Earl of Waldegrave, who married the singer John Beard
7 R. Brimley Johnson, *The Letters of Lady Louisa Stuart* (The Bodley Head, 1926)
8 Both quotations from Alnwick Castle, Diaries of the Duchess of Northumberland, 121/5A, 15 March 1766
9 Mary Astell, *Some Reflections upon Marriage* (1700, publ. 1706), quoted by Bridget Hill, *Eighteenth-Century Women: An Anthology* (Allen & Unwin, 1984)
10 Quoted by R. Huchon, *Mrs Montagu and her Friends, 1720–1800, An Essay* (John Murray, 1907), p. 40
11 Carola Hicks, *Improper Pursuits: the Scandalous Life of Lady Di Beauclerk* (Macmillan, 2001), pp. 60–3
12 Malcolm Elwin (ed.), *The Noels and the Milbankes. Their Letters for Twenty-Five Years, 1767–1792* (Macdonald, 1967), pp. 32–3
13 Vere Foster (ed.), *The Two Duchesses* (1898), the Earl of Bristol to his daughter Lady Elizabeth Foster, 1 August 1796
14 Quoted by Dr D. Doran, *A Lady of the Last Century (Mrs E. Montagu)* (Richard Bentley & son, 1873), p. 126, Sarah Scott to her brother in Rome, September 1762
15 Hampshire Record Office, 26.M.62/F/C17, to his brother George, undated but 1812–15
16 Rachel Leighton (ed.), *Correspondence of Charlotte Grenville, Lady Williams Wynn & her three sons, 1795–1832* (John Murray, 1920), p. 19, to her son Henry, 22 April 1819
17 Leighton
18 Leighton, p. 75, to Charles, 11 December 1801
19 Leighton, p. 164
20 This was sensibly pointed out by Amanda Vickery in her discussion of upper middle-class marriages, *The Gentleman's Daughter* (Yale University Press, 1998)
21 British Library, Microfilm, Northumberland 292, Reel 13, f. 144, Lady Pomfret to Frances, Countess of Hertford, 7 February 1740
22 Stone, pp. 282–7; he sees society as generally hostile to romantic love as a basis for marriage before 1780, but accepting it from 1780–1820, largely due to the influence of the novel

23 Stone, p. 283. It was further thought at the time that it was over-romantic novels that actually caused young people to behave foolishly

24 Lucy Moore, *Amphibious Thing* (Viking, 2000), p. 206; A. Calder-Marshall, *The Grand Century of the Lady* (Gordon & Cremonesi, 1976), pp. 119–27 for the full story of each

25 Stone, pp. 282–7: he himself also sees the dangers of too much emphasis on romance. Hicks also states, surprisingly categorically, possibly based on Stone, that the new type of ideal companionate marriage led to more divorce. Amanda Vickery, *The Gentleman's Daughter*, disputes these findings

26 *Diary and Letters of Madame d'Arblay*, edited by her niece Charlotte Frances Barrett (Henry Colburn, 1842–6), vol. 1, p. 255

27 Norma Clarke, *Dr Johnson's Women*, (Hambledon & London, 2000), p. 14

28 John Busse, *Mrs Montagu, Queen of the Blues* (London, 1928)

29 Doran, p. 31; Cannon, p. 73

30 An attitude confirmed by Cannon, pp. 77–81 and 90

31 The tolerant acceptance of illegitimate offspring by the upper classes is confirmed by Stone, who points out that well-born illegitimate boys suffered less than girls, as they were well educated and made their own way in life; girls could only hope for a good marriage (pp. 532–3)

32 Closely documented by Cannon, p. 77

33 Cannon, p. 83

34 *An Essay on Man*, Epistle IV, written 1730–2, published 1733–4

35 BL, Add. Mss. 51352, Lord Holland to Lady Susan O'Brien, 10 April 1766

36 BL, Add. Mss. 51352, Lady Holland to Lady Susan O'Brien, 8 May 1766

37 BL, Add. Mss. 40663, Mrs Montagu to Mrs Robinson, 15 March 1785

38 Figures are provided in Cannon, p. 83

39 The Duchess's poem to her deceased child is reproduced on p. 238

40 Jennifer C. Ward, *The English Noblewoman in the Late Middle Ages* (Longman, 1992), chapter 2, p. 34

41 Waller, p. 35

42 Ralph Dutton, *English Court Life* (Batsford, 1963), p. 205

43 Clarke, pp. 146–7

44 Waller, p. 35

45 The Duchess of Northumberland, *A Short Tour made in the Year 1771* (printed London 1775) (Collection of Charles Sebag Montefiore)

46 National Gallery, London

47 Antonia Fraser, *The Weaker Vessel* (William Heinemann, 1984)

48 Elizabeth's father, the Revd. Dr Carter, saw that she was given the same education as her brothers, while Catherine Talbot's foster father was successively Dean of St Paul's, Bishop of Oxford and Archbishop of Canterbury

49 W. Bingley (ed.), *Correspondence between Frances Countess of Hartford and Henrietta Louisa Countess of Pomfret, between the years 1736 and 1741* (Richard Phillips, 1805), p. 349: the Countess of Pomfret on visiting her in Brussels, 5 August 1741

50 Caroline Chapman and Jane Dormer, *Elizabeth & Georgiana: The Duke of Devonshire and his two Duchesses* (John Murray, 2002)

51 *Diary and Letters of Madame d'Arblay*, vol. 1, p. 160. This was in the 1770s

52 Fraser, p. 37; 'He "hath not only taken care of her education to his own liking but provided her a competent fortune".' She was also given a parcel of land and a string of pearls as a dowry (Trevor Lummis and Jan Marsh, *The Woman's Domain* (Viking, 1990), pp. 35–6)

53 Halsband (1965), vol. 3, p. 24, 28 January 1763

54 Hicks, pp. 51–2

55 Emily J. Climenson, *Elizabeth Montagu, Queen of the Blue-Stockings: Her Correspondence from 1720–1761* (John Murray, 1906), vol. 1, p. 155

56 BL, Add. Mss. 40663, f. 39

57 Quoted by Ronald Fletcher, *The Parkers at Saltram: Everyday Life in an Eighteenth-Century House* (BBC, 1970), p. 130

58 The acceptability of women knowing how to do accounts because they had to run estates is mentioned in Ingrid Helen Tague, 'Women and Ideals of Femininity in England, 1660–1760' (Ph.D. thesis, Brown University, USA, 1997)

59 The portrait is at Dalmeny House, Scotland (Earl of Rosebery). In his book *Ladies of the Grand Tour* (Harper Collins, 2001), Brian Dolan concentrates too much on women who went abroad for personal reasons connected with love affairs, and not enough on the real women 'grand tourists' of the second half of the eighteenth century

60 Quoted in Debrett's *Stately Homes of Britain*; also Lucy Moore, *Amphibious Thing: The Life of Lord Hervey* (Viking, 2000), p. 15

61 Gladys Scott Thompson, *Life in a Noble Household: 1641–1700* (Jonathan Cape, 1937)

62 Halsband (1965), vol. 3, p. 22, 28 January 1753

63 Johnson, p. 10

64 Blunt

65 Sylvia Harcstarck Myers, *The Bluestocking Circle: Women, Friendship and the Life of the Mind in Eighteenth Century England* (Oxford, Clarendon, 1990), p. 41

66 *Diary and Letters of Madame d'Arblay*, p. 37, 1778

67 *Diary and Letters of Madame d'Arblay*, pp. 116–17

68 *Lady Mary Wortley Montagu*, quoted by Hicks, p. 52

69 Climenson, vol. 1, p. 155, Sandleford, 26 July 1743, to the Duchess of Portland

70 Quoted by Fletcher, p. 130

71 Johnson, p. 10

72 The delights of London and the growing importance of women in the arts area are brilliantly documented by John Brewer in the *Pleasures of the Imagination* (Harper Collins, 1997), chapter 2

73 R. W. Ketton-Cremer, *Norfolk Assembly* (Faber & Faber, 1957), pp. 188–92

74 Ketton-Cremer, pp. 181–3

75 Elwin, p. 177

76 Brian FitzGerald, *Lady Louisa Conolly, 1743–1821: An Anglo-Irish Biography* (London and New York, Staples Press, 1950), p. 97

Chapter 3: Ritual, Routine and Obligation

1 Venetia Murray, *High Society: A Social History of the Regency Period, 1788–1830* (Viking, 1998), pp. 48–57

2 Rachel Leighton (ed.), *Correspondence of Charlotte Grenville, Lady Williams Wynn & her three sons 1795–1832* (John Murray, 1920), to Charles Williams Wynn, 20 March 1801

3 For information on tea-drinking, see the display in the new British Galleries at the Victoria & Albert Museum, also Pippa Shirley's chapter in Philippa Glanville and Hilary Young (eds.), *Elegant Eating* (V&A Publications, 2002), pp. 108–11

4 Malcolm Elwin (ed.), *The Noels and the Milbankes. Their Letters for Twenty-Five Years, 1767–1792* (Macdonald, 1967), p. 92, Elizabeth Noel to her aunt Mary, 24 February

1778

5 Elwin, p. 31

6 Claire Tomalin, *Mrs Jordan's Profession* (Viking, 1994)

7 Clare Baxter, unpublished exhibition notes on Elizabeth, Duchess of Northumberland, June 1996

8 Count Frederick Kielmansegge, *Diary of a Journey to England in the Years 1761–1762* (Longmans, 1902)

9 Emily F. D. Osborn (ed.), *Political and Social Letters of a Lady of the Eighteenth Century (the Hon. Mrs. Osborn), 1721–1771* (Griffith Farran & Co., 1890), p. 10

10 Quoted by Simon Houfe, 'Antiquarian Inclinations: The Diaries of the Countess of Pomfret – II', *Country Life* (31 March 1977). This was the widow of the 3rd Earl of Essex. Her daughter-in-law, Frances, daughter of Sir Charles Hanbury Willliams, was active in taking over the house

11 British Library, Add. Ms. 40663, Mrs Montagu to her brother, 9 June 1777

12 R. Bayne Powell, *Housekeeping in the Eighteenth Century* (London, John Murray, 1956), p. 102

13 BL, Add. Mss. 48218, Theresa Parker to her brother Frederick Robinson, 3 May 1773

14 West Sussex Record Office, Goodwood Ms. 1170, f. 45

15 Alnwick Castle, Diaries of the Duchess of Northumberland, 121/19, 14 October 1766

16 Essex Record Office, D/DP/213/18

17 At least in 1740 and 1749

18 Frederick Pottle (ed.), *Boswell's London Journal 1762–1763* (Heinemann, 1950), p. 104, Sat 25 December 1762

19 Belvoir Castle, *Correspondence of John, Duke of Rutland and Elizabeth his wife*, vol. 1, no. 95, 25 December 1799

20 Lionel Lambourne's section in *Elegant Eating* (p. 120)

21 Kielmansegge

22 Bayne Powell, p. 101

23 Gilly Lehmann, food scholar, unpublished notes, 2001

24 Gilly Lehmann, unpublished notes, 2001, quoting from M. Meade-Fetherstonhaugh and O. Warner, *Uppark and its people* (George Allen & Unwin, 1964), pp. 58–9

25 Emily J. Climenson (ed.), *Passages from the Diaries of Mrs Philip Lybbe Powys of Hardwick House, Oxon AD 1756 to 1808* (Longmans, 1899); Some incidents recorded by Bayne Powell, pp. 103–5

26 Sheffield Record Office, MD 3398, *Book of Accounts for Housekeeping, Lady Mary Howard*

27 Gilly Lehmann, unpublished notes, 2001

28 Leighton, p. 12

29 A. Calder Marshall, *The Grand Century of the Lady* (Gordon & Cremonesi, 1976), p. 20

Chapter 4: House Beautiful

1 Notebook viewed courtesy of the Trustees of Weston Park

2 Quotations from Christopher Hibbert, *The Marlboroughs, John and Sarah Churchill, 1650–1744* (Viking, 2001)

3 Destroyed by fire in 1785

4 *Letters to & from Henrietta, Countess of Suffolk and her second husband, the Hon. George*

Berkeley from 1712–1767 (John Murray, 1824)

5 Details and quotations from Julius Bryant, *Marble Hill, Twickenham* (English Heritage, 2002)

6 Quoted by John van der Kiste, *The Georgian Princesses* (Sutton Publishing, 2002), p. 67

7 Quoted by John Martin Robinson, *Royal Residences* (Macdonald & Co., 1982), p. 107

8 It still stands, now the home of the Royal Ballet School. The avenue on the Richmond side is called the Queen's Ride in her memory

9 Five can still be seen at Kensington Palace

10 Geoffrey Beard, 'William Kent's Royal Patrons', *Country Life Annual* (1970)

11 Marble Hill

12 Emily J. Climenson (ed.), *Passages from the Diaries of Mrs Philip Lybbe Powys* (Longmans, 1899), p. 116, 23 March 1767

13 This does not survive

14 Richard Hewlings, 'Women in the Building Trades, 1600–1850: a Preliminary List', *The Georgian Group Journal*, vol. 10 (2000)

15 Robinson, pp. 127–31

16 Climenson, p. 116, 23 March 1767

17 Major Francis Skeat, 'The Eighth Duchess of Norfolk', *Stonyhurst Magazine*, nos. 256 & 257 (1925), traces all the arguments as to whether or not they married

18 Charles Butler, *Historical Memoirs of the English, Irish and Scottish Catholics since the Reformation* (John Murray, 1802); John Martin Robinson, *The Dukes of Norfolk* (Oxford University Press, 1983), p. 150

19 Lancashire Record Office, Preston, DDSt Box 120, f. 9

20 LRO, DDSt Box 120, f. 1

21 LRO, DDSt Box 120, f. 2

22 LRO, DDSt Box 120, f. 1

23 Public Record Office, CP43/686 m14: the will is 22 April 1749

24 LRO, DDSt Box 94, f. 3, 8 August 1750

25 LRO, 94, f. 3, Codicils to Theresa, 8 August 1750, £1000; 12 March 1753, £5000; 23 August 1754, £1000

26 This is suggested by Deborah Gage, Curator of Firle Place

27 Horace Walpole, *Anecdotes of Painting in England*, ed. R. Wornum (London, 1849), vol. 3, p. 780

28 Michael I. Wilson, *William Kent: Architect, Designer, Painter, Gardener, 1685–1748* (Routledge & Kegan Paul, 1984), pp. 229–34

29 Simon Houfe, 'New Light on Ampthill Park', *Country Life* (21 October 1971)

30 W. S. Lewis et al. (eds.), *Horace Walpole's Correspondence*, 48 vols. (Yale University Press/ Oxford University Press, 1937–83), volumes 32–4 comprise their correspondence. This quotation from a letter to Mann, 14 May 1761, when she was still Duchess of Grafton; introduction to vol. 32, p. xxix

31 Lewis et al., Walpole, 1756, on his only visit to Welbeck, quoted by David Souden, *Wimpole Hall* (The National Trust, 1991)

32 Lewis et al.

33 See also Giles Worsley, 'What's in a "K"', *Country Life* (21 April 1994)

34 It was destroyed in the 1930s

35 Lewis et al., vol. 20, p. 389, to Mann, 21 July 1753. Quoted by Simon Houfe in the second of two excellent articles, in *Country Life*, both on the dowries of the Countess of Pomfret: 'A Taste for the Gothic' (24 March 1977) and 'Antiquarian

Inclinations' (31 March 1977)

36 Quoted in Houfe, 'Antiquarian Inclinations: the Diaries of the Countess of Pomfret – II', *Country Life* (31 March 1977)

37 Illustrated in David Watkin (ed.), *A House in Town* (B. T. Batsford, 1984), p. 129

38 Temple Newsam, West Yorkshire; it was probably made by William Hallett

39 Quoted by John Cornforth, 'A Countess's London Castle', *Country Life Annual* (1970)

40 Tapestry Drawing Room, Goodwood

41 Metropolitan Museum of Art, New York. Help with this information from Annabel Westman

42 Natalie Rothstein, *Spitalfields Silks* (V&A, HMSO, 1975)

43 For information on wallpapers, see John Fowler and John Cornforth, *English Decoration in the Eighteenth Century* (Barrie & Jenkins, 1974), pp. 136–9

44 W. Bingley (ed.), *Correspondence between Frances Countess of Hartford and Henrietta Louisa Countess of Pomfret, between the years 1736 and 1741* (Richard Phillips, 1805), vol. 3, p. 6, 19 February 1741

45 Bingley, vol. 3, p. 280, 14 May 1741

46 Lewis et al., vol. 9, pp. 20–1, from George Montagu, 28 July 1745

47 Quoted by Fowler and Cornforth, p. 139

48 Avray Tipping, 'Saltram, Devonshire I', *Country Life* (23 January 1926)

49 Liza Picard, *Dr. Johnson's London* (Weidenfeld & Nicolson, 2000), p. 249

50 Definitions by Annabel Westman. Rare fabric of this early type can be seen at Knole in Kent; late seventeenth-century mohair in the King's Closet, and early eighteenth-century caffoy in the Crimson Drawing Room

51 Quoted in R. Bayne Powell, *Housekeeping in the Eighteenth Century* (London, 1956), p. 39

52 Quoted by Picard, p. 248

53 J. Brewer, *The Pleasures of the Imagination* (Harper Collins, 1997), p. 29, referring to Von Archenholtz

54 Quoted by Historic Royal Palaces, at Kensington Palace, from Daniel Defoe, *A Tour through the Whole Island of Great Britain and Ireland 1724–1726*, ed. G. D. H. Cole (London, 1927)

55 Nicolaus Pevsner, *Northamptonshire*, 2nd edn, revised by Bridget Cherry (Penguin, 1973)

56 Lewis et al., 1763, quoted by Cornforth, 'Drayton House, Northamptonshire – IV', *Country Life*, 3 June 1965

57 Petworth House

58 Christopher Rowell, *Petworth House* (The National Trust, 1997), p. 72

59 Quoted by Picard, p. 249

60 Malcolm Elwin (ed.), *The Noels and the Milbankes: their Letters for Twenty-Five Years 1767–1792* (Macdonald, 1967), pp. 157, 219–21

61 Lewis et al., quoted by Bevis Hillier, *Pottery and Porcelain, 1700–1914, England, Europe and North America* (Weidenfeld & Nicolson, 1968), p. 281

62 This quotation and some details of curiosities from Charlotte Gere and Marina Vaizey, *Great Women Collectors* (Philip Wilson, 1999), pp. 79–80

63 Lewis et al., vol. 35, pp. 279–80, to the Countess of Upper Ossory, 4 December 1775

64 British Museum

65 Edward Croft Murray, *Decorative Painting in England* (Country Life Ltd., 1962), vol. 1, pp. 68 and 247

66 Both quoted from Julius Bryant, *Marble Hill* (English Heritage, 2002), p. 29

67 Quoted by Picard, p. 235

68 Brian FitzGerald, *Correspondence of Emily, Duchess of Leinster (1731–1814)* (Dublin Stationery Office, 1953), vol. 2, pp. 146–57, Lady Sarah Bunbury to Duchess of Leinster, Castletown, 10 September 1775

69 This was a corruption of the Italian name Frascati, which name the area now bears

70 FitzGerald, vol. 2, p. 174, Lady Sarah Bunbury to Duchess of Leinster, Goodwood, 21 April [1776]

71 *Diary and Letters of Madame d'Arblay (1778–1840)* edited by her niece Charlotte Frances Barrett (Henry Colburn, 1842–6), vol. 1, p. 170, 1779. Also, p. 322, 1780: Miss Bowdler 'could not bear to cross the circle'

72 Quoted in Christopher Simon Sykes, *Private Palaces* (Chatto & Windus, 1985), p. 160; Walpole to the Earl of Hertford, April 1765

73 R. Brimley Johnson, *The Letters of Lady Louisa Stuart* (The Bodley Head, 1926), pp. 257–9

74 *Diary and Letters of Madame d'Arblay*, vol. 1, p. 170, November 1779

75 *Diary and Letters of Madame d'Arblay*, vol. 2, p. 303, 1784, at Mrs Vesey's: it was 'a very full meeting', with Mrs Vesey herself in an inner room or boudoir

76 William Roberts, *The Memoirs of the Life and Correspondence of Mrs Hannah More* (London, R. B. Seeley and W. Burnside, 1834), vol. 1, p. 62

Chapter 5: Louise de Keroualle, Duchess of Portsmouth

There are many letters between Louis XIV and his various ambassadors and ministers in the Archives Nationales in Paris: these have been used through secondary sources.

There are four main biographies, plus manuscripts and articles as listed: Henri Forneron, *Louise de Keroualle, Duchess of Portsmouth*, with preface by Mrs Crawford (1887); Mrs Colquhoun Grant, *Brittany to Whitehall: Life of Louise de Keroualle, Duchess of Portsmouth* (London, 1909); Jeanine Delpech, *The Duchess of Portsmouth*, tr. A. Lindsay (Elek, 1953); Brian Bevan, *The King's French Mistress* (Hale, 1972). The anonymous *Secret History of the Duchess of Portsmouth*, published in London and Paris in 1690 and 1734, and again in Paris in 1805, is regarded by all biographers as deliberately scandalous and is not quoted.

Forneron draws thoroughly on French archives, always emphasising Louise's avarice and over-importance, but also admitting her help to Louis XIV. His translator, Mrs Crawford, is vitriolic about Louise. Mrs Colquhoun Grant uses only diaries and documents available in England, such as St Simon and St Evremond and never quotes directly from sources. She relies too much on hearsay, and her narrative is strung out by descriptions of Brittany and of Louise's ancestors. She is not scholarly and is therefore rarely quoted in the endnotes. However, she does have an interesting judgement of Louise. Jeanine Delpech seems the best source, obviously using Forneron. Bevan draws heavily on Delpech, but makes some worrying changes that may or may not be errors, such as that Charles II rather than Louise put the Garter ribbon over the Duke of Richmond's shoulder. He often does not cite his sources.

An article in the Goodwood files by Comte Antoine de Vogüé (tr. Frank Haill), *The Duchess of Portsmouth* (undated but c. 1970), makes use of West Sussex Record Office documents as well as of those at La Verrerie, Aubigny. Those documents in the WSRO are royal and family letters in the collection of Louise's descendants, the Dukes of Richmond. They now include the newly discovered legal document listing household expenses for Louise, Duchess of Portsmouth, Paris, 18 August 1714, countersigned in fifteen places (acquired from Mellors & Kirk, Nottingham, lot 686, 14 February 2003).

All are reproduced by kind permission of the Trustees of the Goodwood Collection. There are seven letters by Louise in Nottingham University Library: see note 95.

1 Brian Bevan, *The King's French Mistress* (Hale, 1972), pp. 13–14, says it was the Duke of Beaufort, Admiral of France, and also M. de Chaulnes, Governor of Brittany. Jeanine Delpech, *The Duchess of Portsmouth*, tr. A Lindsay (Elek, 1953), p. 12, says it was the Duke of Beaufort
2 Bevan, p. 2, quoting Madame de Bregis at the French Court
3 Ian Dunlop, *Louis XIV* (Chatto & Windus, 1999), pp. 109–15
4 Jean Lemoine and André Lichtenberger, 'Louise de Keroualle, Duchesse de Portsmouth', in *Revue des Deux Mondes* (date unknown), tr. Frank Haill, bound off print in French in the Goodwood Library
5 Both Delpech and Bevan suggest that this stung her deeply. Delpech, followed by Bevan, says that she received the attentions of the Comte de Sault, but it was not serious, as he would only look for a dowry. Mrs Colquhoun Grant, *Brittany to Whitehall: Life of Louise de Keroualle, Duchess of Portsmouth* (London, 1909), p. 43, says the admiration of the Comte was quoted by Mme de Sévigné, Louvois and Saint Simon, and later used against her
6 Delpech, p. 37. She implies, but without evidence, that the king wooed Louise throughout the trip. The source for that idea may be Henri Forneron, *Louise de Keroualle, Duchess of Portsmouth*, with preface by Mrs Crawford (1887), p. 56. Colquhoun Grant, p. 65 and Bevan, p. 28 also suggest that he was smitten early on
7 Authors differ in their views but peritonitis is now widely accepted
8 Delpech, p. 42 suggests she was not behaving like a possible novice: Bevan, p. 31 said that she played with the idea but had no real vocation
9 Delpech, p. 45; Bevan, p. 38, also quoting letter from Colbert de Croissy to Louvois, 8 October 1670, about how the King shared at her card table 'never letting her want for anything'
10 Forneron, p. 21, quoting Ms. *Affaires Etrangères, Angleterre*, vol. 137, f. 400, 'Relation de la Cour d'Angleterre'
11 Quoted by Lemoine and Lichtenberger
12 Charles Marguetel, Seigneur de Saint-Evremond, *Oeuvres III: Problème à l'invitation des Espagnols*, addressed to Mademoiselle de Queroualle. Quoted by Bevan, p. 40
13 Quoted by Colquhoun Grant, Colbert de Croissy to Louise, 8 October 1761
14 Bevan, p. 32
15 Colbert de Croissy: 'Having got it into her head that she could become Queen of England'; 'Taking every opportunity of discussing the Queen's indispositions as if they were fatal'. Quoted by Delpech, p. 70
16 Delpech, p. 61
17 Bevan, p. 42, quoting William Bray (ed.), *Memoirs and Correspondence of John Evelyn*, (Colburn, 1819), vol. 2, p. 350; Catherine MacLeod and Julia Marciari Alexander, *Painted Ladies: Women at the Court of Charles II* (National Portrait Gallery, 2001), p. 139, quoting E. S. de Beer (ed.), *The Diary of John Evelyn* (Oxford, Clarendon Press, 1955), vol. 3, pp. 589–90, 10 October 1671
18 Delpech, p. 82; Bevan, p. 43
19 West Sussex Record Office Goodwood Ms. 1427, n. 15, to Sir Joseph Williamson from Charles II, shows that the King may have changed his mind over the name
20 Including Frances Teresa, Duchess of Richmond and Mrs Middleton
21 Letters of Thomas Stamford Raffles, 19 December 1674, quoted by Colquhoun Grant, p. 127

22 *Lettres de Madame de Sévigné, de sa famille et de ses amis* (Paris, Hachette, 1862), vol. 4, pp. 128–9, to her daughter, the Comtesse de Grignan, 11 September 1675, vol. 5, p. 128, quoted by Colquhoun Grant, also by Constance, Lady Russell, *The Rose Goddess and Other Sketches of Mystery and Romance* (Longmans, 1910), p. 19

23 Colquhoun Grant, p. 135; Bevan, p. 64

24 C. Russell, p. 24, quoting from Louis XIV's letter as reported in Walckenaër's *Memoires sur Madame de Sévigné*, vol. 3

25 Anon., *The Duchess of Portsmouth*. Article in the Goodwood files that makes good use of WSRO and Aubigny documents to chart the history of Louise in relation to Aubigny. See p. 2: in December 1673, she was granted the land with 'all its rights, appurtenances and dependencies'. The local tax officers at Bourges still claimed it for the throne, and it was not until a new decree was signed on 15 January 1675 that they stopped these demands. Letters patent confirming Louise's complete possession did not arrive until 26 January 1692

26 Forneron, p. 253: she provided herself with letters from the King and Barrillon to this end

27 Delpech, p. 170, quotes Charles II's request to Louis XIV 'to raise the estate of Aubigny to a Duchy for Madame de Portsmouth and later for her son'. Forneron, p. 275, says the letter was from Barrillon, who thought she had gone too far; however, Louis agreed by return

28 Comte Antoine de Vogüé *The Duchess of Portsmouth*: Louis signed the decree in January 1684 to establish the Seigneurie of Aubigny as a Duchépairie for her, to be succeeded by her son and his male heirs

29 In the list of household expenses, WSRO, Goodwood Ms. (unnumbered: new acquisition February 2003), Paris, 18 August 1714, she signed herself 'L duchesse de porstmouth et daubigny' probably because it was for a legal document made in France; her will is also signed in this way, WSRO, Goodwood Ms. 4. Her letters from France to William Bentinck, 1st Earl of Portland, 1698–1700, Nottingham University Library, PwA 700–706/1, are all signed 'L Duchesse de Portsmouth', as are those to her family, WSRO, Goodwood Mss. 4 (transcripts) and 8

30 Bevan; Forneron, p. 67

31 Colbert to Louvois, 8 October 1671, vol. 101, f. 167, quoted by Forneron, p. 67

32 Delpech, p. 81 and Bevan, p. 61

33 Delpech, p. 84

34 Bevan, p. 50 quotes Henry Ball, an official at Whitehall, writing to Sir Joseph Williamson

35 British Library, Add. Mss. 27588, f. 54: see Bevan, p. 51, and Forneron, p. 205, who interprets it rather differently; both, however, point to the immense detail and extravagance

36 Simon Thurley, *The Whitehall Plan of 1670* (London Topographical Society, 1998). Plan C (Society of Antiquaries) shows this area. Plan A (Museum of London, illustrated), engraved from an original by George Vertu in 1747, shows that a long, large house just south-west of the palace, right on the river, had been built for Charles Stuart, 3rd Duke of Richmond of the earlier creation by 1666. On his death in 1672 it passed to his widow, Frances Teresa, Duchess of Richmond, and on her death in 1702 presumably to the 1st Duke of the new creation, who inherited all her assets except for Lennoxlove in Scotland. He is known to have had a house on the site: this was demolished by his son, Charles, 2nd Duke of Richmond, whose famous Richmond House by Lord Burlington was built in its place. It was destroyed by fire in 1791: Richmond Terrace and the Department of Health now stand on the site. For

Louise's rooms see Simon Thurley, *Whitehall Palace: An Architectural History of the Royal Apartments 1240–1698* (Yale, 1999), map facing p. 106; p. 142

37 Thurley (1999), p. 125

38 Colbert to Louvois, 8 October 1671, quoted by Forneron, pp. 67–8

39 Public Record Office, Work 5/19 364 ff. and Work 5/20 340 ff., quoted by Thurley (1999)

40 de Beer, vol. 4, p. 74, note

41 From 1675 the Queen lived much of the time at nearby Somerset House

42 Quoted by Delpech, p. 78: see also Bussy Rabutin's comment that 'Madame's death has made Madame de Keroualle's fortune; without it I do not think she would have found in France a lover like the one she has now'

43 de Beer, vol. 4, p. 74; 10 September 1675

44 E. Alfred Jones, 'The Duke of Rutland's Plate at Belvoir Castle', *Country Life*, vol. 91, p. 851. The cistern was later melted down

45 R. Russell, *Letters of Lady Rachel Russell* (Longman, 1853), vol. 1, p. 24, Lady Vaughan to Mr Russell, 11 February 1675

46 Forneron, p. 162, quoting Courtin, 2 November 1676

47 de Beer, vol. 4, p. 74; Delpech, p. 144

48 Bevan, p. 106, quoting Barrillon's letter to Louis XIV

49 de Beer, vol. 4, p. 343, 4 October 1683

50 Colquhoun Grant, photo facing p. 13. A marquetry chest once owned by Louise and subsequently in the Ranfurly collection in Ireland must have come from Whitehall

51 de Beer, vol. 4, p. 343, 4 October 1683: also quoted by Forneron, p. 277, who adds the mention of inlay and of desks and stands, and Bevan, p. 129

52 The set in the Galerie des Glaces must date from *c.* 1680, but he presumably had some before that

53 Bevan, p. 128

54 Bevan, pp. 71–3

55 de Beer, vol. 4, p. 343, 4 October 1683

56 Forneron, p. 120

57 In his diary Evelyn twice goes as far as to suggest that they were actually pulled down and rebuilt to please her no less than three times: de Beer, vol. 4, p. 343, 4 October 1683; vol. 5, p. 47, 10 April 1691

58 Bevan, p. 131

59 Forneron, p. 249: authorised by Louis in document of 26 October 1681

60 Bevan, p. 128

61 Bevan, p. 50: as early as 1673 she gave a ball at Barn Elms, supposed to be outdoors but confined to a barn because of all the spectators. This is not really relevant to her collecting but does smack of the Versailles outdoor summer lifestyle

62 Courtin to Pomponne, 21 September, 1676, quoted by Forneron, p. 153

63 Forneron, p. 148

64 Colquhoun Grant

65 Delpech, p. 147

66 Forneron, p. 282

67 Narcissus Luttrell, *A Brief Historical Relation of State Affairs from Sept. 1678–April 1714*, 6 vols, (Oxford University Press, 1857), p. 288, 11 November 1683; Lucy Norton (ed.), *St. Simon at Versailles* (Hamish Hamilton, 1980), p. 196

68 Delpech, p. 46

69 Forneron, p. 196

70 Forneron, p. 197

71 H. N. Williams, *Rival Sultanas* (Hutchinson & Co., 1915), p. 277, quotes Burnet as saying that Louise supported the exclusion because she hoped her son would reign

72 BL, Add. Mss. 28094, f. 54

73 The original is in the Getty Museum, the version in an English private collection

74 Goodwood and Deene Park, Northamptonshire

75 The painting is at Goodwood

76 J. M. Alexander's idea

77 Both at Goodwood

78 MacLeod and Marciari Alexander, cat. no. 53. Documents reveal that Louise was very fond of her black page, and this same affection towards the girl is advertised in the way that she has her arm on her shoulder and that the child leans confidently against her mistress. The servant is richly dressed, at Louise's expense, in a robe with embroidery and a gold clasp, and wears large pearls. She serves to emphasise Louise's exotic taste, as well, perhaps, as her humanity.

79 An article on the portraits of Louise de Keroualle is in preparation by the author

80 Both at Goodwood

81 These portraits were in the Holland House picture gallery

82 Luttrell, p. 328, 9 February 1685

83 Forneron, p. 286, quoting Barrillon's letter to Louis, 8 March 1685

84 Forneron, p. 285

85 Forneron, p. 290

86 Luttrell, p. 440: she returned to England on 24 June and, p. 461, on 17 September

87 Forneron, p. 297, says she was informed that her apartments 'with all her sumptuous furniture' had been burned: Delpech, p. 198, says she lost some precious furniture. Bevan does not mention her collection

88 Bevan, p. 171, says she was very distressed, but gives no source

89 de Beer, vol. 5, p. 47

90 Delpech, p. 189, but giving no sources for the details. She quotes that Louise got the francs 'forthwith on the death of the king'

91 Luttrell describes the fire on p. 206; quoted by Thurley (1999), p. 142

92 WSRO, Goodwood Ms., new acquisition, February 2003; Louise, Duchess of Portsmouth, legal document listing household expenses, Paris, 18 August 1714

93 WSRO, Goodwood Ms. 4

94 Forneron, p. 298

95 She arrived on Monday 15 August 1688 and departed on 16 February 1689. Seven begging letters written by her, 1698–1700, to William Bentinck, 1st Earl of Portland, are in Nottingham University Library, PwA 700–706/1

96 Luttrell, p. 431, 27 September 1698

97 WSRO, Goodwood Ms. 21, f. 5, Anne, Duchess of Richmond to her husband, Charles, 1st Duke of Richmond, London, 15 July 1713

98 *The Complete Peerage*, vol. 4, pp. 406–7, note (e), tells of a meeting between three royal mistresses attached to this visit in 1715; that when Catherine Sedley, the Countess of Dorchester, met Louise and the Countess of Orkney at a Drawing Room of George I, she exclaimed: 'Who would have thought that we three w[hores] should have met here!'

99 C. Russell, p. 65

100 WRSO, Goodwood Ms. 3, n.d.

101 Quoted in Delpech, p. 170

102 Quoted by Stella Tillyard, *Aristocrats* (Chatto & Windus, 1994)

Chapter 6: Elizabeth Murray, Countess of Dysart and Duchess of Lauderdale

As Ham House inventories have been so well researched and published by Peter Thornton and Maurice Tomlin, they are used entirely through their publication in *The Journal of the Furniture History Society*. The family history has also been thoroughly researched by Evelyn Pritchard, and original documents are quoted from her book.

1 Peter Thornton and Maurice Tomlin, 'The Furniture and Decoration of Ham House', *The Journal of the Furniture History Society*, vol. 16 (1980): this chimneypiece was probably moved from the Great Dining Room; Cleyn decorated these two rooms. All unannotated quotations are from these published inventories

2 Quoted by Evelyn Pritchard, *Ham House and its owners through four centuries, 1610–1948*, revised edn. (Richmond Local History Society, 1998), p. 6

3 The date of the creation is disputed between 1643 and 1646. See Pritchard, p. 4

4 Ham House

5 Both from Pritchard, p. 7

6 Gilbert Burnet, *History of My Own Time* (first published posthumously, 1723); see abridged edition by Thomas Stackhouse (Dent, 1979), p. 98, but the fuller version as given here is more usually quoted

7 Pritchard, pp. 13–14 explains the impossibility of the legend concerning Cromwell

8 Pritchard, p. 11

9 Surrey Record Office 58/2/4/1

10 Thornton and Tomlin suggest that Elizabeth began to refurnish the house from the mid 1650s, but they admit there is no evidence other than the 'hair styles' on one pair of caryatids. These could anyway be 1660s. It is now suggested that most of her acquisitions were post Restoration: see Christopher Rowell, with Cathal Moore and Nino Strachey, *Ham House*, revised edn (The National Trust, 1999)

11 The dates when the arrangement of the room was being amended are suggested by other works. See also Gervase Jackson-Stops (ed.), *The Treasure Houses of Britain: five hundred years of private patronage and art collecting* (Yale University Press, 1985), p. 157, cat. no. 84, by John Hardy

12 National Trust Guidebook: all these items are known to have been in the Green Closet since the late 1670s, and very possibly before. As it was granted at the height of the Civil War, the title was probably never confirmed to Elizabeth's father under the Great Seal, and was never legal: her mother was known as Mistress Murray. Elizabeth gave up the title and then obtained a new one from the King

13 A pair of sideboards was listed in the Great Dining Room in 1655, but this may have been a different pair. It is possible that the tops are much later and that the stamping is a workman's way of pretending that the whole item is early when putting a new top on an old base

14 Pritchard, p. 16; Edward Tollemache, *The Tollemaches of Helmingham and Ham* (W. S. Cowell, 1949), p. 62 (where the letter is printed in full)

15 All details of their Scottish building from John G. Dunbar, 'The Building Activities of the Duke and Duchess of Lauderdale, 1670–82', *Archaeological Journal*, vol. 132 (1975)

16 Pritchard, p. 30

17 Louvre, Paris

18 John Cornforth, 'Ham House Reinterpreted', *Country Life* (29 January & 5 February 1981), rightly lambasted the use of inadequate fabrics as copies

19 Peter Thornton, 'Magnificence in Miniature – the Ham House Model', *Country Life* (26 January 1978)

20 Cornforth, quoting the 1683 inventory

21 As a friend of the Queen, it might have been practical to have Lady Maynard nearby, but as the room is not known to have been called this until 1679, it is not certain that this was part of the plan. Margaret may anyway have had the room as a child

22 Conversation with Evelyn Pritchard, who has information surrounding the 1671 visit

23 Thornton and Tomlin, chapter 3

24 This deduction is the author's own: Thornton and Tomlin are rightly very cautious in their interpretation of the inventories, but some colour visualisation is needed. One simply cannot imagine the green scheme, especially with the fringes, in juxtaposition with the blue and yellow; once the details are perused to see if the latter could have been a replacement, the lists make much more sense. Often an inventory is overwritten in a later hand: a 1679 additional note could have been made right up to the 1683 list

25 Thornton and Tomlin; it is just possible that this arrangement was vice versa

26 E. S. de Beer (ed.), *The Diary of John Evelyn* (Oxford, Clarendon Press, 1955), vol. 4, pp. 143–4

27 British Museum, Add. Ms. 32540 ff. 26–7, quoted by Dunbar, p. 228

Chapter 7: Caroline Lennox, Baroness Holland

The sources used are both published letters and manuscripts in the British Library (BL), as well as the Catalogue of the Holland House Sale in 1775.

1 Quoted by Princess Marie Liechtenstein, *Holland House* (London, 1875), Charles Hanbury Williams to Henry Fox, 9 May 1744

2 W. S. Lewis et al. (eds.), *Horace Walpole's Correspondence*, 48 vols. (Yale University Press/ Oxford University Press, 1937–83), vol. 18, p. 450, to Horace Mann, 29 May 1744

3 Stella Tillyard, *Aristocrats: Caroline, Emily, Louisa and Sarah Lennox 1740–1832* (Chatto & Windus, 1994), p. 16

4 In November, 1766. Quoted by Tillyard, p. 256

5 In 1767. Tillyard, p. 257

6 Charles, 2nd Duke of Richmond, 26 March 1748, Whitehall, to Lady Caroline Fox, quoted by Liechtenstein

7 Goodwood

8 Earl of Ilchester, *The Home of the Hollands 1605–1820* (John Murray, 1937), chapter 3

9 Tillyard, p. 46

10 Leslie Mitchell, *Holland House* (Duckworth, 1980)

11 Earl of Ilchester, *Holland House* (George Allen & Unwin, 1914)

12 Tillyard, p. 147

13 Thomas Faulkner, *History and Antiquities of Kensington* (London, 1820), quoting *King James, Progress*, vol. 1

14 Tillyard, p. 47

15 This was acquired through his marriage to the heiress Elizabeth Strangways Horner. See Lucy Moore, *Amphibious Thing: A Life of Lord Hervey* (Viking, 2000), pp. 203–4, 208, 209. For Redlynch in Somerset, pp. 23–4

16 Ilchester (1937), reporting Lord Carlisle, 1841

17 Brian FitzGerald (ed.), *Correspondence of Emily, Duchess of Leinster (1731–1814)* (1949), vol. 1, p. 18, to her husband, the Earl of Kildare, 15 May (1755). (Where the year is given in brackets it is not written on the original letter, but has been attributed by the editor)

18 Details gleaned from the Christie's sale catalogues of the Holland House Sale, which took place a year after Henry and Caroline's deaths, and following the death of their eldest son Stephen. The sale of furniture and household items commenced on Monday 20 November 1775, and lasted twelve days. The sale of books began on Monday 11 December 1775, and lasted seven days. It is always possible that some items were added or removed by Caroline's daughter-in-law, who together with her husband Stephen Fox owned the house for a few months in 1774, but it is unlikely that she changed much as her husband was an invalid, and she had always been very compliant in family schemes. The library furnishings were sold on the third day of the first sale, pp. 13–14

19 Faulkner, p. 94, where it is described (1820) in its 'unaltered state'. It was by now the Breakfast Room

20 Photos, 1939. For plan see: *Royal Commission on Historical Monuments*, vol. 2 (*West London*), 1925, p. 74. The pedestals are in a private collection

21 Holland House Sale, Day 5, p. 22

22 Photographic record, pre-war, private collection. Other photos at RIBA

23 Faulkner, p. 92. Later the Journal Room

24 FitzGerald, vol. 1, p. 111, Emily, Marchioness of Kildare to her husband, 3 September 1761. Also quoted by Tillyard, p. 48

25 FitzGerald, vol. 1, p. 12; to her husband the Earl of Kildare, 10 May 1755

26 FitzGerald, vol. 1, p. 425; Caroline to Emily, 20 December (1764). It was ready in 1759

27 In the location of the later Yellow Drawing Room

28 FitzGerald, vol. 1, p. 298, Caroline to Emily, 24 October (1760)

29 FitzGerald, vol. 1, p. 425; Caroline to Emily, 20 December (1764)

30 FitzGerald, vol. 1, p. 425; Caroline to Emily, 20 December (1764)

31 This later became the Crimson Drawing Room

32 FitzGerald, vol. 1, p. 546, 6 October (1768)

33 All details from Holland House Sale, Day 5, p. 24

34 FitzGerald, vol. 1, p. 425; as described to Emily, 20 December (1764); also Sale, Day 5

35 All from Christie's, 20 November–1 December 1775, Holland House Sale, Day 6, p. 28

36 Lewis et al., vol. 32, p. 279, to Lady Ossory, 4 December 1775

37 FitzGerald, vol. 1, p. 238, to Countess of Kildare, 28 June 1759

38 Holland House Sale, Day 8, p. 35

39 Holland House Sale, Day 8, p. 36

40 Holland House Sale, Day 7, p. 31

41 Holland House Sale, Day 4, p. 19

42 Holland House Sale, Day 4, p. 19

43 Holland House Sale, Day 7. p. 30

44 FitzGerald, vol. 2, p. 153, Lady Sarah Bunbury to Duchess of Leinster, 10 September 1775

45 Quoted by Tillyard, p. 48

46 FitzGerald, vol. 1, p. 327; 23 May (1762)

47 FitzGerald, vol. 1, p. 409; Caroline to Emily, 8 September (1764)

48 FitzGerald, vol. 1, p. 362; letter to Emily, 21 March 1763

49 FitzGerald, vol. 1, pp. 338–9; Caroline to Emily, written from Kingsgate, 5 September 1762

50 G. Trevelyan, *The Early Life of Charles James Fox* (Longmans, Green & Co., 1880), p. 41, quoted by John Fyvie, says that for the birth of Charles James she moved to Conduit Street to get away from 'the noise of carpenters and bustle of upholsterers'

51 Quoted by Tillyard, p. 48

52 Lewis et al., vol. 19, p. 397, to Horace Mann, 5 May 1747

53 Liechtenstein, p. 213

54 Lewis et al., vol. 37, p. 352, 5 May 1753

55 FitzGerald, vol. 1, p. 223, Caroline to Emily (May 1759)

56 Faulkner

57 FitzGerald, vol. 1, p. 417, Caroline to Emily, 30 October (1764)

58 Holland House Sale, Day 4, p. 20

59 Faulkner, p. 107

60 It went to Castletown and was sold at Sotheby's, 13 November 1996. This is said to have been a version: The original may have been lost in the Richmond House fire of 1791, unless there was only ever one version

61 Now at Melbury, Dorset, the Ilchester home. A good version is at Goodwood

62 FitzGerald, vol. 1, p. 336, 8 September 1762, Caroline requests a 'head' of Cecilia from Emily

63 FitzGerald, vol. 1, p. 339, 5 September 1762, Caroline requests a half length from Emily: p. 452, 9 June 1766, Caroline says that she is very pleased with the copy of Emily's but does not think that it is quite as good as the original. See also p. 330, 14 June 1762, Caroline asks Louisa for a copy of her picture by Ramsay, 'when I have settled what size it should be'

64 Confusingly, photographs at the NMR show apparently seventeenth-century overmantels when the room was later converted into a library. These must have been moved there, or remade

65 FitzGerald, vol. 1, p. 205, Caroline to Emily, 26 March 1759: '...indeed, my dear siss, she does you honour'

66 FitzGerald, vol. 1, p. 330, 14 June 1762. Although Caroline asks Louisa for a copy of her picture by Ramsay, this one is a superb prime version (private collection). It is still in its thin frame, designed to be inset

67 FitzGerald, vol. 1, p. 336; Caroline to Emily, 8 August 1762

68 FitzGerald, vol. 1, p. 228, Caroline to Emily, June 1759

69 FitzGerald, vol. 1, p. 178; Caroline to Emily, 26 August 1758; also p. 206, 7 April 1759

70 FitzGerald, vol. 1, p. 238, Caroline to Emily (probably from the Pay Office), 28 June (1759)

71 FitzGerald, vol. 1, p. 239, Caroline to Emily, 5 July 1759

72 The handbill for the performance is still at Goodwood

73 Ilchester (1937), quoting Walpole's *Letters*

74 Ilchester (1937)

75 FitzGerald, vol. 1, p. 119; the Marquis of Kildare to his wife Emily, 20 April 1762

76 Ilchester (1937), quoting *Letters of Lady Sarah Lennox*, vol. 2, p. 291

77 Ilchester (1937)

78 FitzGerald, vol. 1, p. 118, the Marquis of Kildare to his wife Emily, 20 April 1762

79 BL, Add. Mss. 51444, 1 May 1764: '...came to my New house in Picadilly for the first time...', but it was purchased in 1762

80 BL, Add. Mss. 51444, 'Memorandum book, begun 1764 on my return from France where I had been for a Year'

81 BL, Add. Mss. 51657, An Account of Holland House by Sir James Mackintosh

82 FitzGerald, vol. 1, p. 408, Caroline to Emily, 4 September (1764)

83 BL, Add. Mss. 51444, the first pages of her 'Memorandum book'

84 BL, Add. Mss. 47470, Caroline to her son Charles James Fox, 24 July 1767

85 The house was destroyed by fire in 1774

86 J. A. Home (ed.), *The Letters and Journals of Lady Mary Coke* (Edinburgh, 1889–96), new edn, 1970, p. 100

87 BL, Add. Mss. 51444

88 Quoted by Tillyard, p. 287

89 Home, p. 99, Thursday 17 July 1772

90 Ilchester (1937), p. 62

91 Tillyard, p. 17

92 Tillyard, p. 17

93 Faulkner, p. 92

94 R. Blunt (ed.), *Mrs Montagu 'Queen of the Blues': her Letters and Friendships from 1762 to 1800* (London, 1923), vol. 2, p. 123

95 Home, p. 384, Sunday 24 July 1774

96 John Fyvie, *Noble Dames and Notable Men of the Georgian Era* (London, 1910), p. 173

97 Fyvie, p. 179, quoting Samuel Rogers, *Recollections of the Table Talk of Samuel Rogers*, ed. A. Dyce (London, 1856), p. 275

98 Fyvie, pp. 176–82: the quote is from Thomas Moore, *Memoirs, Journal and Correspondence of Thomas Moore* (London, 1853–6), vol. 4, pp. 313–14

99 Fyvie, quoting Sir George Trevelyan Bt., *The Life and Letters of Lord Macaulay* (Longmans, Green & Co., 1909), p. 151, letters to Hannah More Macaulay, 30 May 1831

Chapter 8: Mary Blount, Duchess of Norfolk

Edward, 9th Duke of Norfolk destroyed his wife's correspondence rather than let the heir, who she disliked, inherit it. Inventories for Norfolk House are at Arundel Castle, as well as other contemporary material. Those for Worksop are in the Norfolk papers at Sheffield Record Office (SRO). All are reproduced by kind permission of the Duke of Norfolk.

1 John Holland, *The History, Antiquities and Description of the Town and Parish of Worksop in the County of Nottingham* (Sheffield, J. Blackwell, 1826), p. 162

2 Alexander Pope, *Letters of Mr Pope and Several Eminent Persons* (London 1735), p. 181, 27 November 1717: 'we' includes his mother

3 Pope, pp. 183–4, 3 October 1721

4 Pope, pp. 189–90, 2 June, 1725

5 Pope, p. 181, 3 October 1721

6 Devon Record Office, Exeter, QS 76/36, 8 October 1717

7 William Rees-Mogg, 'Annabella's recipe for a truly good life', *The Times* (4 August 1997)

8 His elder brother, Thomas, 8th Duke of Norfolk, interceded for him and hostile witnesses did not appear at his trial. *The Complete Peerage* reports that he was again arrested for being part of a plot to restore the Stuart Pretender in 1722, and that

after six months in prison he was released on bail, but documents at Lancashire Record Office show it was Thomas who was in prison, as Dr John Martin Robinson believes

9   Sheffield Record Office, ACM WD 662–665. One sister became a nun, having injured herself in childhood, and probably did not receive a big dowry

10 Sir Alexander Croke, *General History of the Croke Family, formerly le Blount* (John Murray, 1823), vol. 2

11 John Martin Robinson, *The Dukes of Norfolk: A Quincentennial History* (Oxford University Press, 1982), p. 154

12 Lady Irwin, January 1733, quoted by Robinson, pp. 154–5

13 Charles Butler, *Historical Memoirs of the English, Irish and Scottish Catholics since the Reformation* (John Murray, 1st edn 1802), vol. 3 (Alnwick Castle)

14 Rees-Mogg

15 Robinson, p. 157

16 Arthur Oswald, 'Norfolk House, St James's Square', *Country Life* (25 December 1937), says that while the main façade was onto the new square, the courtyard probably faced Pall Mall

17 Butler

18 *The Times*, 1738, mentions the Duke's journey from Arundel Castle to 'his House at Poland Street.'

19 Arundel Castle, vol. 1, G 2/3, Newspaper Cuttings 1716–1906

20 See Michael Snodin, 'English Rococo and its Continental Origins', in *Rococo, Art and Design in Hogarth's England*, Exhibition Catalogue, Victoria & Albert Museum (1984), pp. 29–33; also Gervase Jackson-Stops, *Rococo Architecture and Interiors*, p190

21 Discovered by the Duke of Norfolk's librarian, Dr John Martin Robinson, at Arundel Castle

22 Arundel Castle, unnumbered

23 Snodin, p. 27

24 Arundel Castle, MD 18/3, William Edwards' Carpenters and Joiners Bill, 1755

25 The room is now gloriously redisplayed in the British Galleries at the Victoria & Albert Museum. A cypher entwining the Duke and Duchess's names over the original entrance door in the east wall was inserted later, as homage to their authorship. For reasons of museum design, the entrance door is not now in its original location. The doorway, on the outside, is one of the two by G. B. Borra retained from the Great Room

26 Brian FitzGerald, *The Norfolk House Music Room* (HMSO, 1973), pp. 48–9, Appendix A: Letter by William Farington, Surrey Street Strand, 18 February, 1756 (henceforth called Farington)

27 W. S. Lewis et al. (eds.), *Horace Walpole's Correspondence*, 48 vols. (Yale University Press/ Oxford University Press, 1937–83), vol. 37, p. 438, to Henry Seymour Conway, 12 February 1756

28 Farington

29 Farington

30 Arundel Castle, MD 18/2, Account of Joseph Metcalfe

31 Arundel Castle, Inv. 5, Inventory of furniture in St James's Square when rebuilt and new furnished, *c.* 1753

32 In 1778 Elizabeth Noel described one room as 'hung with white Sattin, & velvet flowers upon it'. As this was after Mary's death, it could arguably be the next Duchess's paper: or could it be that the Flowered Velvet Room was not completely crimson at all, but a much more novel white and red? See Malcolm Elwin (ed.), *The*

Noels and the Milbankes: Their Letters for Twenty-Five Years, 1767–1792 (Macdonald, 1967), p. 92, Elizabeth Noel to her aunt, 24 February 1778

33 Arundel Castle, Inv. 5
34 Farington
35 Elwin, p. 92, Elizabeth Noel to her aunt, 24 February 1778
36 Arundel Castle, MD 18/2
37 Arundel Castle, MD 18/2
38 Arundel Castle, York Bedroom
39 Farington
40 Sold at Christie's, now in a private collection
41 Some items survive at Arundel Castle and have recently been returned to view in the public rooms
42 Dr Tessa Murdoch attributes the tables to Cuenot: notes on her visit to Arundel. The pier glasses are known to be by him
43 All Arundel Castle, Drawing Room
44 The pier glasses are at Arundel Castle, Dining Room
45 Arundel Castle, Corridor
46 Arundel Castle, East Drawing Room
47 Arundel Castle, Little Drawing Room. The French furniture in this room was also at Norfolk House, but apart from the bergères the chairs look rather small for the grandeur of the original scheme and may have been acquired in the nineteenth century
48 Arundel Castle, MD 18/1. Many of the glasses do not survive
49 One settee is at Arundel Castle, Victoria Bedroom
50 Aspinall-Oglander, Brigadier Cecil, *Admiral's Widow, being the life and letters of the Hon. Mrs Edward Boscawen from 1761 to 1805* (1942), October 1770, p. 29
51 Farington
52 Illustrated in J. M. Robinson, *The Dukes of Norfolk* (Oxford University Press, 1982); collection of Lord Stafford
53 Arundel Castle, Dining Room
54 Arundel Castle, staircase
55 Farington
56 One is now in the Victoria & Albert Museum, the other in the Metropolitan Museum, New York
57 Lewis et al., vol. 37, p. 438, to Conway, 12 February 1756
58 Farington
59 Arundel Castle, MD 18/1
60 Arundel Castle, Newspaper Cutting
61 Philadephia Museum
62 David Howard, *Chinese Armorial Porcelain, Volume II* (Heirloom & Howard, 2003): see also his vol. 1 (1974), p. 836
63 Quoted by Simon Houfe, 'A Taste for the Gothic, Antiquarian Inclinations: the Diaries of the Countess of Pomfret – I', *Country Life* (24 March 1977)
64 All quoted by E. Beresford Chancellor, *The Private Palaces of London, Past and Present* (Kegan Paul, 1908), pp. 320–1, from letters by Mrs Delany
65 Marcus Binney, 'Worksop Manor, Nottinghamshire – I', *Country Life* (15 March 1973). His scheme dated 24 March 1737/8 is in Essex Record Office
66 Arundel Castle, Library
67 Alnwick Castle, Ms. notebooks of the Duchess of Northumberland
68 SRO, W 125, Inventory of household goods etc. at Worksop Manor on the death

of Edward Duke of Norfolk, December 1777

69 SRO, W 125, Inventory, 1777

70 Arthur Young, *A Six Month Tour through the North of England* (W. Strahan, 1770), vol. 1, pp. 366–75

71 Lewis et al., vol. 37, p. 572, to Conway, 19 September 1758

72 Lewis et al., vol. 37, p. 579, Conway to Walpole, 15 October 1758

73 Arundel Castle, MD 18/3, 15 September 1753

74 Arundel Castle, MD 18/3, 10 July 1755

75 Lady Llanover (ed.), *The Autobiography and Correspondence of Mary Granville, Mrs Delany* (Richard Bentley, 1861–2), vol. 3, p. 440, Mrs Delany to Mrs Dewes, Welbeck, 14 September 1756

76 Arundel Castle press cutting; *Life and Leisure* (April 1982), letter found in Lindrick Close Worksop, Duchess to Capt. Brand, 8 May 1766

77 SRO, W 125, Inventory, 1777

78 *Gentleman's Magazine* (May 1761)

79 Holland, p. 141

80 Binney

81 Lewis et al., vol. 37, p. 566, Henry Seymour Conway to Walpole, 17 September 1758

82 SRO, W 123, A Description of Worksop Manor before the fire

83 SRO, W 123

84 SRO, W 123

85 Lewis et al., vol. 9, p. 397, to George Montagu, 24 October 1761

86 Both quoted by Holland, p. 161: see *Gentleman's Magazine*, vol. 31 (November 1761), pp. 531–2

87 Arundel Castle, Acc. 104/8; Mary, Duchess of Norfolk to Mr Sympson at Worksop in Nottinghamshire, by express from Bath, 24 October 1761

88 Peter Leach, *James Paine* (London, Zwemmer, 1988), p. 216

89 Leach, p. 217

90 Young, p. 366

91 Binney; Leach pp. 77–9

92 Marcus Binney, 'Worksop Manor, Nottinghamshire – II', *Country Life* (22 March 1973)

93 Leach, pp. 216–17

94 Worksop Manor Plan, Worksop

95 Binney (22 March 1973)

96 Leach, p. 216

97 Holland, p. 161

98 *The Times* (15 February 1763): from its inception the project was regarded as a glorious undertaking

99 The dates are given by James Paine, *Noblemen's and Gentlemen's Houses* (1767), vol. 2

100 Arundel Castle, Newspaper Cuttings, 1764

101 Holland, p. 162

102 Arundel Castle, AD 38, Plan Book for Worksop Manor

103 SRO, W125, Inventory, 1777

104 SRO, W 125, Inventory, 1777

105 Robinson, p. 163, from Worksop 1777 Inventory

106 SRO, ACM W 12L Worksop Manor – System Proposed for furnishing the New Building, May 1766

107 SRO, W 125, Inventory, 1777

108 Arundel Castle, AD 38
109 Arundel Castle, AD 38
110 SRO, System Proposed, 1766
111 SRO, System Proposed, 1766
112 SRO, System Proposed, 1766
113 SRO, System Proposed, 1766
114 A number of these can now be seen at Arundel Castle
115 SRO, System Proposed, 1766
116 SRO, System Proposed, 1766
117 SRO, W 125, Inventory, 1777
118 SRO, System Proposed, 1766
119 SRO, System Proposed, 1766
120 Leach, p. 217
121 Holland, p. 162
122 Leach, p. 217
123 Lewis et al., vol. 5, p. 361, to Mme du Deffand
124 Butler
125 From James Paine, quoted by Holland, p. 162 n.

Chapter 9: Elizabeth Griffin, Countess of Portsmouth

Letters are in the collection of the Barons Braybrooke at Essex Record Office (ERO).

1 Essex Record Office, D/DBy C1, John Sanderson to Richard Aldworth, September 1740
2 Quoted by William Addison, *Audley End* (J. M. Dent & Sons, 1953), p. 88
3 Addison, p. 88; Berkshire Record Office, D/EN F21
4 Quoted by Addison, p. 89
5 ERO, D/DBy C42, included in volume of letters to the Countess of Portsmouth, James Scott, at Worksopp [sic] Manor to the Earl of Suffolk, 23 February 1745
6 ERO, D/DBy C42, Lord Hervey to the Countess of Portsmouth, 30 April 1745
7 Addison, p. 79
8 Kate Jeffrey (ed.), *Audley End* (English Heritage, 1997), p. 33
9 Addison, p. 82
10 ERO, D/DBy C42, Vachell to the Countess of Portsmouth, 6 June 1751, 14 July 1751
11 ERO, D/DBy C42, Lord Hervey to the Countess of Portsmouth, 2 May 1751
12 ERO, D/DBy C42, Countess of Portsmouth's draft response to Lord Hervey, 1751
13 ERO, D/DBy C42, William Vachell to the Countess of Portsmouth, 8 March 1752, enclosing Lord Howard of Effingham's letter of agreement
14 ERO, D/DBy C42, Lord Hervey to the Countess of Portsmouth, 11 March 1752
15 ERO, D/DBy C42, 18 June 1752, Countess of Portsmouth, draft letter
16 ERO, D/DBy C42, Vachell to Lord Hervey, 1 September 1754, and 21 September 1754; Hervey to the Countess of Portsmouth, 21 September 1754; Hervey's refusals to pay, to Vachell, 21 and 22 September 1754
17 ERO, D/DBy C42, Countess of Portsmouth to Lord Hervey, 6 October 1754
18 ERO, D/DBy C42, William Vachell to the Countess of Portsmouth, 24 December 1757
19 ERO, D/DBy A364, Loose bills for demolition and repairs carried out at Audley End for the Countess of Portsmouth

20 ERO, D/DBy F31, John Phillips to the Countess of Portsmouth, 18 August 1753
21 ERO, D/DBy F31, John Phillips to the Countess of Portsmouth, 18 August 1753
22 Count Frederick Kielmansegge, *Diary of a Journey to England in the Years 1761–1762* (Longmans 1902), p. 41
23 Quoted by Addison, p. 88, Countess of Portsmouth to Richard Aldworth, 9 October 1740
24 Kielmansegge, p. 41
25 ERO, D/DBy T11/1
26 All quotations from Addison, pp. 95–6, ERO, D/DBy C2/7, 14 August 1762
27 Addison, pp. 96–7, ERO, D/DBy C2/8, 21 August 1762
28 Addison, p. 95, ERO, D/DBy C2/7
29 Quoted by Jeffrey, p.34

Chapter 10: Elizabeth Seymour, Duchess of Northumberland

Letters and diaries of Elizabeth Duchess of Northumberland are at Alnwick Castle reproduced by kind permission of the Duke of Northumberland. The letters are also on microfilm at the British Library, viewed by special permission only.

1 Brian Masters, *The Dukes* (Pimlico, 2001), p. 211
2 Gerald Brenan, *A History of the House of Percy from the Earliest Times down to the Present Century* (London, Freemantle, 1922), vol. 2, p. 422
3 Edward Barrington de Fonblanque, *Annals of the House of Percy, from the Conquest to the Opening of the Nineteenth Century* (London, privately published, 1887), p. 524
4 *Correspondence between Frances, Countess of Hartford and Henrietta Louisa, Countess of Pomfret between the Years 1738 and 1741* (Richard Phillips, 1805), vol. 1, introduction, p. xii
5 Horace Walpole, *Memoirs of King George III*, ed. G. F. Russell Barker (London, Lawrence & Bullen, 1894), vol. 1, p. 332
6 All quoted by Brenan, pp. 426–8
7 Details and quotes from Brenan, pp. 422–8. This letter 14 January 1739/40, Sir Hugh to Lady Hertford
8 British Library, Northumberland Microfilm 292, reel 13; 9 January 1739/40
9 Sibylla Jane Flower, *The Stately Homes of Britain* (Book Club Associates, 1982), p. 178
10 Quoted by Brenan, p. 428
11 Masters, p. 211
12 James Greig, *The Diaries of a Duchess: Extracts from the Diaries of the First Duchess of Northumberland (1716–1776)* (Hodder & Stoughton, 1926), from foreword by Duke of Northumberland, p. v
13 Quoted by de Fonblanque, vol. 2, p. 525, 27 September 1744
14 Flower, p. 177
15 Lewis et al. (eds.), *Horace Walpole's Correspondence*, 48 vols. (Yale University Press/ Oxford University Press, 1937–83), vol. 20, p. 341, to Mann, 28 October 1752
16 Lewis et al., vol. 20, p. 341, to Mann, 28 October 1752
17 Brenan, p. 436
18 Alnwick Castle, Diaries, 121/391772
19 Clare Baxter, unpublished exhibition notes on Elizabeth, Duchess of Northumberland, Alnwick Castle, June 1996, item 4
20 Baxter
21 Alnwick Castle Guidebook; source uncertain

22 Alnwick Castle, Diaries, 121/4, 25 July 1760
23 Colin Shrimpton, *The Historical Development of Alnwick Parks, Parkland and Woodland*, Alnwick Castle, pending publication, p. 17
24 This now faces inwards, which was not the original intention
25 P. W. (Peter Waddell), *Alnwick Castle, described and illustrated with drawings by P. W.* (1785), private copy at Alnwick Castle
26 Quoted in Eileen Harris, *The Genius of Robert Adam* (Yale University Press, 2001), p. 85
27 Harris, p. 86
28 The visit was on 1 August 1772: quoted in Dr D. Doran, *A Lady of the Last Century (Mrs E. Montagu)* (1873), p. 140
29 Alnwick Castle, Diaries, 121/2, 1755–8
30 Alnwick Castle, Diaries, 121/63, p. 15, *c.* 1773
31 Alnwick Castle, Diaries, 121/3, 1759
32 Lewis et al., vol. 21, p. 88, to Mann, 5 May 1757
33 Count Frederick Kielmansegge, *Diary of a Journey to England in the Years 1761–1762* (Longmans, 1902), p. 144, 6 November 1761
34 It was only covered with Bath stone by the 3rd Duke some fifty years later
35 Alnwick Castle
36 Alnwick Castle, 121/9
37 Alnwick Castle, Diaries, 121/63, pp. 26, 324
38 Lewis et al., vol. 21, p. 191, to Mann, 14 April 1758
39 Lewis et al., vol. 10, pp. 34–5, to Montagu, 8 June 1762
40 Kielmansegge, p. 144, 6 November 1761
41 Kielmansegge, p. 236, 20 January 1762
42 Frederick Pottle (ed.), *Boswell's London Journal 1762–1763* (Heinemann, 1950), p. 70, Tues 7 December 1762
43 Boswell, p. 70, Tues 7 December 1762
44 Quoted by R. Bayne Powell, *Housekeeping in the Eighteenth Century* (John Murray, 1956), p. 100
45 Lewis et al., vol. 38, p. 401, to Lord Hertford, Fri 8 June 1764
46 Lewis et al., vol. 38, p. 401, to Lord Hertford, Fri 8 June 1764
47 Lewis et al., vol. 20, p. 49, to Horace Mann, 3 May 1749
48 Lewis et al., vol. 38, p. 235, to Earl of Hertford, 17 November 1763
49 Lewis et al., vol. 31, p. 125, to Lady George Lennox in Paris, 8 September 1766
50 Earl Bathurst (ed.), *Letters from Three Duchesses of Richmond, 1721–1761* (privately printed, 1925), p. 80, Mary Duchess of Richmond to Lady George Lennox, 29 September 1761
51 Confirmed by Norroy and Ulster King of Arms. Women did not usually use courtesy titles, so she was never known as Baroness Percy
52 Lewis et al., vol. 32, p. 211, to Lady Ossory, 27 October 1774
53 Brenan, p. 451
54 All references from Baxter, exhibition notes, items 9–14; sale of 5 and 6 June 1765
55 Horace Walpole, *Memoirs of the Reign of King George III*, ed. G. F. Russell Barker (London, Lawrence & Bullen, 1894), vol. 1, p. 333–4
56 All references from Elizabeth, Duchess of Northumberland, *A Short Tour made in the Year 1771* (London, 1775) (Library of Charles Sebag Montefiore)
57 Such as Collaert, Galle, Goltzius, Sadeler and Stradanus: see below
58 Baxter, exhibition notes, items 23–9
59 Alnwick Castle, Diaries 121/31A, 4 February 1770

60 Alnwick Castle, Diaries 121/31A

61 Waddell

62 Alnwick Castle, 121/92, Alnwick House Book, p. 3: 1768. These were already mentioned in the rooms listed as 'Library Chapel & Closet', suggesting a slightly earlier date for them than is usually recognised

63 Alnwick Castle, Diaries 121/63; Baxter, item 20

64 One section now survives in the Victoria & Albert Museum British Galleries

65 John Summerson, *Georgian London* (Penguin, 1962), p. 143

66 His illegitimate son, James Smythson, left over £100,000 to found the Smithsonian Institute in America, for 'the increase and diffusion of knowledge'

67 See A. P. Stanley, *Westminster Abbey* (London, 1869), for the crowds and chaos at her funeral

68 Malcolm Elwin, *The Noels and the Milbankes: Their Letters for Twenty-Five Years 1767–1792* (Macdonald, 1967), p. 247, Judith Milbanke to her aunt Mary Noel, 20 October 1784

69 Elwin, p. 110, to her aunt, 28 June 1778

70 Quoted by Harris, p. 93

Chapter 11: Elizabeth Robinson, Mrs Montagu

A number of Mrs Montagu's letters are in the British Library, some in an album of letters to her family and others in the Hardwicke and Lyttleton collections. There is also a group of twenty-six letters in the University of Nottingham Library, in the papers of Margaret, (2nd) Duchess of Portland. The largest collection, of some 3000 by her, with 3000 more letters written to her, is in the Huntington Library in California. Much has been gleaned from that collection through published editions. A selection of her letters was first published in two volumes by her nephew Matthew Montagu in 1809, with two further volumes in 1813. Some 'hitherto unpublished' scripts were printed by Dr Doran in 1875. The fullest edition is the work of 1906 by her great-great-niece, Emily J. Climenson, which was completed at her request by R. Blunt in 1923. A research assistant helpfully looked through a selection at the Huntington; various extracts from that collection are published here for the first time. Mrs Montagu's letters are mostly about literature, philosophy, the antique, people and travel, and are not always about anything material, but while she was building her two great houses she kept both Elizabeth Carter and Elizabeth Vesey well informed.

All letters are by Elizabeth Montagu unless otherwise described.

1 Quoted by Dr D. Doran, *A Lady of the Last Century (Mrs Elizabeth Montagu)* (Richard Bentley, 1873)

2 Huntington Library, MO 6393, to Mrs Vesey, London, 2 February 1768

3 Illustrated in an engraving, Emily J. Climenson, *Elizabeth Montagu, Queen of the Bluestockings: her correspondence*, 2 vols. (London, 1906), facing p. 8

4 R. Huchon, *Mrs Montagu, 1720–1800: An Essay* (John Murray, 1907), p. 35

5 W. S. Lewis et al. (eds.), *Horace Walpole's Correspondence*, 48 vols. (Yale University Press/ Oxford University Press, 1937–83), vol. 15, p. 305; quoted by Sylvia Harcstarck Myers, *The Bluestocking Circle: Women, Friendship and the Life of the Mind in Eighteenth-Century England* (Oxford, Clarendon, 1990), p. 27

6 Myers, p. 28, quoting Matthew Montagu, *The Letters of Mrs Elizabeth Montagu* (London, 1809–13), vol. 1, pp. 3–4

7 Huntington, MO 1551, 17 August 1742; Myers, p. 28

8 Montagu, vol. 2, p. 202; Myers p. 28

9 'Anecdotes Relating to Dr Conyers Middleton', in Lewis et al., vol. 15, pp. 291–2 nn. 3 and 4; Myers p. 27

10 Huntington, MO 4756, 1737

11 Huntington, MO 4707, 1737; Myers pp. 31–2

12 Myers, p. 34, quoting William Gilpin, *Victorian History of the Counties of England*, vol. 32, pp. 187–91

13 British Library, Add. Ms. 70493, copies of letters in the handwriting of the 2nd Duchess of Portland, from originals written by Elizabeth Robinson, 1740–1

14 Huntington, MO 4716, 12 December 1740; Myers p. 95

15 Climenson, vol. 1, pp. 42–3, to the Duchess of Portland, 25 January 1740

16 Montagu, quoted by Rebecca Warner (ed.), *Original Letters...* (London, 1817)

17 University of Nottingham Library, Ms. PC PwE 52. Some of the undated but early letters in this collection especially suggest this dread, notably PwE 54 and 55

18 Quoted by Doran p. 33, 6 August 1742

19 Quoted by John Busse, *Mrs Montagu, Queen of the Blues* (London, Gerald Howe, 1928), p. 13

20 Myers, p. 96

21 Doran, p. 39, October 1742

22 Climenson, vol. 1, p. 150, to her sister Sarah at Dover Street, 1743

23 Climenson, vol. 1, p. 159, Dover Street, 30 August 1743

24 Climenson, vol. 1, p. 211, Allerthorpe, 29 September 1745

25 Climenson, vol. 1, p. 117, Dover Street, her first letter to her mother after her marriage, 10 August 1742

26 Doran, p. 35, to the Duchess of Portland

27 Doran, p. 34, to Mrs Friend. Doran dates this letter first

28 Climenson, vol. 2, p. 136

29 Huntington Library, in London, to her husband, preparing to join him at Denton, MO 2603, 21 April, and MO 2608, 30 April 1766

30 Huchon, p. 51

31 Reginald Blunt (ed.), *Mrs Montagu, 'Queen of the Blues': her Letters and Friendships from 1762 to 1800* (London, 1923), vol. 1, p. 164, 1767

32 Climenson, p. 149

33 Between 1193 and 1202: there had been a religious building on the site since 1180

34 First by the Pitt Rivers family from Stratfield Saye and then by William Cradock

35 BL, Add. Ms. 40663, f. 41, to Mrs Robinson, 1773

36 Sybil Wade, *Sandleford Priory: The Historic Landscape of St Gabriel's School Grounds* (1997), p. 16

37 Climenson, vol. 1, p. 155

38 Doran, p. 41

39 Climenson, vol. 1, p. 229

40 The very survival of the house, with two of its original ceilings, has recently been discovered by the author. The Zephyr ceiling was previously only known from the letters. In her article, 'The Painted Rooms of Athenian Stuart', *Georgian Group Journal*, vol. 10 (2000), pp. 167–9, Kerry Bristol rightly asserted that the scheme was at Hill Street, not at Sandleford or Portman Square, as suggested by earlier commentators, but she did not realise that the house is still in existence

41 Doran, pp. 79–80, n.d.

42 Climenson, vol. 1, p. 271, to Sarah, 3 January 1750

43 Madame du Bocage, *Recueil des Oeuvres de Madame du Bocage* (Lyon, 1762), vol. 3

(*Lettres sur l'Angleterre*), p. 12, Seconde Lettre, 8 April 1750. Madame du Bocage had earlier published Milton in French. On 25 May, p. 40, she reported, again to her sister, that Mrs Montagu had sent her a wonderful present, the superb and new edition of Milton of 1748

44   Climenson, vol. 2, p. 203, to Mrs Boscawen. Assembly on 23 and letter on 24 December 1752

45   Climenson, vol. 2, p. 30, to her husband, 3 May 1753

46   Norma Clarke, *Dr Johnson's Women* (Hambledon & London, 2000), p. 64, quoting *Letters from Mrs Elizabeth Carter to Mrs Montagu between the Years 1755 and 1800: Chiefly upon Literary and Moral Subjects* (London, 1817), vol. 1, p. 154

47   Huntington Library, to Elizabeth Carter, 31 December 1765

48   'You will wonder I should condemn the taste I have complied with [in the Chinese room at Hill Street], but in trifles I shall always conform to the fashion.' Doran, p. 80: n.d.

49   Eileen Harris has pointed to SRO 4927, a letter from John Adam in Rome to his sister, 20 February 1762: 'Bob's Mrs Montagu was a relation of ours being also a Robertson or Rather a Robinson…'

50   Later he also created them at Derby House (1773) and at Apsley House, Home House and Osterley (all 1775). These were all Etruscan; one for Lady Watkins Williams Wynn at 20, St James's Square (1772) incorporated Wedgewood tablets in the chimneypiece, an idea that came from her husband rather than herself: Eileen Harris, *The Genius of Robert Adam* (Yale University Press, 2001), p. 7

51   Harris, the ceiling illustrated in colour, p. 6; Damie Stillman, *Decorative Work of Robert Adam* (London, Tiranti, 1973), plate 128, Design for a Ceiling, Hill Street, London, 1766, and plate 129, Design for a Carpet, Hill Street, London, c. 1766 (both Sir John Soane Museum, II: 200)

52   Huntington Library, MO 5331, Sarah Scott to Mrs Montagu, June 1766

53   Huntington Library, MO 5840, to Sarah Scott, 17 July 1766

54   Huntington Library, MO 1, Robert Adam to Mrs Montagu, 11 October 1766

55   Huntington Library, MO 5846, to Sarah Scott, 8 January 1767 (see Blunt, p. 153)

56   Blunt, vol. 1, p. 152

57   Doran, p. 273, to Lord Kames, n.d.

58   David Watkin, *Athenian Stuart: Pioneer of the Greek Revival* (Allen & Unwin, 1982), pp. 23 and 35–8. Georgiana, Countess Spencer, was the daughter of Mrs Montagu's friend Stephen Poyntz

59   Huntington Library, MO 1394, to Lord Lyttleton, 15 January 1760

60   Huntington Library, MO 1302, Lyttleton to Mrs Montagu, Hagley, 15 October 1762; MO 1421, to Lyttleton, Sandleford Priory, 21 October (1762)

61   Huntington Library, MO5339, Sarah Scott, at Bath, to Mrs Montagu, 6 December 1766

62   Huntington Library, to Mr Montagu, 21 April 1766

63   Huntington Library, MO 4994, to Leonard Smelt, Hill Street, 3 November 1767

64   All from Lady Llanover (ed.), *The Autobiography and Correspondence of Mary Granville, Mrs Delany* (Richard Bentley, 1861–2), vol. 4, p. 508, 28 May 1773, Mrs Delany's letter to her niece, Mary Dewes

65   Busse, p. 48; see also Brigadier Cecil Aspinall-Oglander, *Admiral's Widow, being the life and letters of the Hon. Mrs Boscawen from 1761 to 1805*, Hogarth, 1942

66   See Clarke, p. 22

67   William Roberts, *Memoirs of the Life and Correspondence of Hannah More* (London, R. B. Seeley and W. Burnside, 1834), pp. 52–3; Busse, p. 50

68 Roberts, pp. 62–3, 1776
69 *Diary and Letters of Madame d'Arblay*, edited by her niece Charlotte Frances Barrett (Henry Colburn, 1842–6), vol. 1, 1780, p. 307
70 *Diary and Letters of Madame d'Arblay*, vol. 2, p. 8, Mrs Thrale to Fanny Burney, 7 February 1781
71 Quoted by Clarke, p. 2
72 Quoted by Wade, p. 13
73 Climenson, vol. 1, p. 189, to the Duchess of Portland, 9 August 1744
74 Quoted by Wade, p. 14
75 BL, Add. Ms. 40663, f. 10, 4 December 1766, to Mrs Robinson
76 His essay *On the Sublime and Beautiful* had been published in 1758
77 BL, Add. Ms. 40663, to her sister Sarah Scott, Hill Street, 19 November 1770
78 Both quoted by Huchon, p. 40
79 BL, Add. Ms. 70493, to Mrs Donnellan, 17 October 1740
80 BL, Add. Ms. 70493, f. 21, to Mrs Donnellan, 11 January 1740, ending 'to refresh herself in my airy mansion'
81 Wade, p. 13
82 *Diary and Letters of Madame d'Arblay*, vol. 1, 1778, p. 97
83 *Diary and Letters of Madame d'Arblay*, vol. 1, 1780, p. 318
84 Henry B. Wheatly (ed.), *The Historical & the Posthumous Memoirs of Sir Nathaniel William Wraxall 1772–84* (Bickers, 1884), vol. 1, p. 102
85 *Diary and Letters of Madame d'Arblay*, vol. 1, 1778, p. 91
86 R. Brimley Johnson (ed.), *The Letters of Lady Louisa Stuart* (The Bodley Head, 1926), p. 256
87 Mr and Mrs Montagu believed these were the monks' fish ponds, but Wade, in her survey pp. 6–7, suggests that they may have been later, Tudor or Stuart
88 Wade, p. 16. The chestnuts were planted in 1757
89 HL, MO 3156, to Elizabeth Carter, 9 October 1765
90 HL, MO 3156, to Elizabeth Carter, 9 October 1765, also quoted by Wade
91 Later she wrote about her tours to Scotland at length
92 Wade, p. 16, summer 1752
93 HL, MO 5845, Mrs Montagu to Sarah Scott, 23 November 1765
94 BL, Add. Ms. 40663, f. 42
95 Sir William Forbes, *An Account of the Life and Writings of James Beattie* (Edinburgh, 1806), vol. 1, p. 342, 21 June 1773
96 HL, MO 5137, April 1777
97 Blunt, vol. 2, p. 18
98 HL, MO 6005, to Sarah, 6 July 1777
99 HL, MO 5377, Sarah Scott to Mrs M, 23 August 1777
100 Blunt, vol. 2, p. 61
101 HL, MO 6053, to Sarah, 26 December 1778
102 HL, MO 55024, to Leonard Smelt, 16 April 1779
103 Doran, p. 253
104 HL, MO 6049, Mrs M to Sarah Robinson Scott from Sandleford, 22 November 1778
105 HL, MO 6049, Mrs M to Sarah Robinson Scott from Sandleford, 22 November 1778
106 Doran, 9 July 1782
107 Kerry Bristol, '22 Portman Square. Mrs Montagu and her "Palais de la Vieillesse"', *British Art Journal*, vol. 2, no. 3 (2001), pp. 78, 80
108 HL, MO 5025, to Leonard Smelt (Bath), 25 April 1780
109 HL, MO 5026, to Leonard Smelt, 26 April 1780; quoted in Blunt, pp. 82–4

110 Blunt, vol. 2, p. 103

111 All references from Kenneth Quickenden: Birmingham Central Library, Matthew Boulton Papers. The first enquiry was on 8 April 1776 from Hill Street; it was delivered in January, February and March 1777, with designs for cutlery sent to her in 1778

112 All references from Kenneth Quickenden: Birmingham Central Library, Matthew Boulton Papers

113 HL, MO 6085, to Sarah Scott, 27 September 1780

114 Bristol (2001), pp. 74–8; full details of the glazing history

115 HL, MO 6086, to Sarah Scott, 2 October 1780

116 Bristol (2001), p. 80

117 Blunt, vol. 2, p. 112

118 HL, MO 4070, Hill Street, to Sir William Pepys, 3 November 1781

119 HL, MO 6568, to Elizabeth Vesey, 12 December 1781. The letter to Mrs Carter quoted by Kerry Bristol as being the first was written three days later

120 HL, MO 3499 (Hill Street), to Elizabeth Carter, 6 July 1780

121 Blunt, vol. 2, p. 111

122 BL, Add. Ms. 40663, f. 156, 10 January 1788

123 HL, MO 6574, to Elizabeth Vesey, 18 and 22 June 1782; Blunt, vol. 2, p. 119, 1782

124 Doran, p. 318, to her sister-in-law Mrs Robinson, 26 November 1783. She also says: 'I make it a rule never to dine from home'

125 HL, MO 1133, to Mrs M, 4 November 1780

126 Blunt, vol. 1, p. 9; Lewis et al., vol. 29, p. 184, to the Rev. William Mason, 14 February 1782

127 Busse, p. 16. Presumably he saw the house before its destruction in 1941

128 Watkin, p. 47. The only record is a set of eight photographs taken by Bedford Lemire in 1894: National Monuments Record

129 The latest book on Kauffman, Wendy Wassing Roworth (ed.), *Angelica Kauffman: A Continental Artist in Georgian England* (The Royal Pavilion Art Gallery & Museums, Brighton, 1992), disputes this claim, in the chapter on Decorative Work by Malise Forbes Adam and Mary Mauchline. They say that Chancellor's statement that Fanny Burney wrote in her diaries of Kauffman's involvement at 22, Portman Square cannot be substantiated. They infer that Sykes simply followed on from this. Although she was very skilled in portraying subjects from Greece and Rome in a decorative way, she stayed mostly in her studio in London and most paintings in decorative schemes attributed to her are by copyists. She did do 'mechanical paintings', which Boulton produced between the mid 1770s and 1782 as a cheaper way of acquiring wall decoration, and some of which he supplied to 22, Portman Square. In the chapter on the Print Market, David Alexander suggests that some of these printed paintings in the house were therefore by her

130 Peter Meadows and John Cornforth, 'Joseph Bonomi, Decorator', *Country Life* (19 April 1990), claim that the room was designed by Bonomi, who they believe advised on more than just the Great Room. Bristol sees the coffering as a favourite motif of Stuart

131 Peter Meadows, 'Drawn to Entice', *Country Life* (28 April 1988), says that Bonomi also produced designs for this

132 BL, Add. Ms. 40663, f. 138, *c.* 1784, to Mrs Robinson

133 Doran, p. 335

134 Blunt, vol. 2, p. 201, 1786

135 Blunt, vol. 2, p. 258, to Elizabeth Carter, 27 June 1791

136 *St. James's Chronicle*, 11–14 June 1791, quoted in Lewis et al., vol. 29, p. 290

137 *St. James's Chronicle*, 11–14 June 1791, quoted in Lewis et al., vol. 11, p. 290, n. 6

138 Busse, p. 16

139 Watkin, p. 49

140 All from HL, MO 4069, Sandleford, to Sir William Pepys, 14 August 1781

141 RIBA, SA5/3/3 (1782). RIBA, SA5/3 (1–9) and SOS/A/10 are ten drawings by Bonomi. Kerry Bristol believes the design to be Bonomi's scheme entirely, not in collaboration with Stuart. Other drawings at RIBA were thought for a time to relate, but are now believed to be for another house: they are illustrated in Charles Saumarez Smith, *Eighteenth-Century Decoration: Design and the Domestic Interior in England* (Weidenfeld & Nicolson, 1993), p. 348, nos. 346, 347, 348

142 RIBA, SOS/A/10

143 Bonomi even sketched Mrs Montagu a Corinthian capital life size: RIBA, SA5/3/9

144 Although Chancellor and Sykes attributed them to Cipriani, he had died in 1785. The original description from *St. James's Chronicle*, 11–14 June 1791 is the most likely to be correct for the centrepiece

145 Blunt, vol. 2, pp. 241–2, says that they were for the Great Room, quoting a letter from Mrs M's nephew Matthew Montagu, showing them to his friend Thomas Ryder. This is confirmed in Peter Meadows' use of the letter, *Joseph Bonomi Architect 1739–1808: Catalogue of an Exhibition of Drawings from Private Collections* (Royal Institute of British Architects, 1988), p. 20. Schemes for overdoors appeared in Bonomi's 1790 design. Busse, p. 17, wrongly said that they were for the Feather Room, but there was no evidence of this kind of decoration in there

146 Meadows, *Drawn to Entice*

147 *St. James's Chronicle*, 11–14 June 1791

148 Christopher Simon Sykes, *Private Palaces* (Chatto & Windus, 1985), p. 223: Lewis et al., vol. 11, p. 290, to Mary Berry, 14 June 1791

149 Quoted by Blunt, vol. 2, pp. 257–8, to Elizabeth Carter; Meadows, *Joseph Bonomi* (see endnote 145), pp. 19–20

150 BL, Add. Ms. 40663, f. 158, December 1788

151 BL, Add. Ms. 40663, f. 154, 8 February *c.* 1787

152 Sykes, pp. 223, 227

153 HL, MO 4069, to Sir William Pepys, 14 August 1781; Blunt, vol. 2, p. 111

154 HL, MO 3478, (London) to Elizabeth Carter, 7 July 1779

155 Quoted by Doran, 9 July 1782, p. 313

156 HL, MO 6564, to Elizabeth Vesey, 14 July 1781

157 HL, MO 3513, to Elizabeth Carter, 26 July 1781

158 HL, MO 6565, to Elizabeth Vesey, 31 July 1781

159 HL, MO 3531, Sandleford, to Elizabeth Carter, 23 July 1782

160 HL, MO 6565, to Elizabeth Vesey, 31 July 1781; Wade, p. 20

161 Quoted by Wade, p. 20

162 HL, MO 3545, to Elizabeth Carter, 11 June 1783

163 Wade, pp. 20–1

164 HL, MO 6572, to Elizabeth Vesey, 18–20 March 1782

165 Doran, p. 313, 9 July 1782

166 HL, MO 3531, to Elizabeth Carter, 23 July 1782

167 HL, MO 6579, Denton Hall, to Elizabeth Vesey, 27 September 1783

168 Richard Wendorf and Charles Ryscamp, *A Blue-Stocking Friendship: The Letters of Elizabeth Montagu and Frances Reynolds*, in the Princeton Collection, Princeton University Library Chronicle (1980), p. 197, to Frances Reynolds, 28 July 1783

169 HL, MO 6096, to Sarah Scott, 25 June 1784: 'The piece of water has a fine effect'
170 BL, Add. Ms. 40663, f. 155, to Mrs Robinson, 14 July 1787: to make 'a piece of water down to the river from the water on the side of the wood'
171 BL, Add. Ms. 40663, f. 138, to Mrs Robinson at Denton, 3 November 1784
172 HL, MO 3530, to Elizabeth Carter, 11 July 1782
173 HL, MO 3532, to Elizabeth Carter, 6 August 1782
174 HL, MO 3547, Sandleford, to Elizabeth Carter, 28 June 1783
175 HL, MO 3569, to Elizabeth Carter, 19 June 1784
176 HL, MO 6586, to Elizabeth Vesey, 25 August 1784
177 All quotations from BL, Add. Ms. 40663, f. 139, full description to Mrs Robinson at Denton, 3 November 1784. See also HL, MO 6587, to Elizabeth Vesey, 24 October 1784
178 HL, 6579, Denton Hall, to Elizabeth Vesey, 27 September 1783: 'The Front of the House & the approach to it remain as yet just as when you were at Sandleford'
179 Doran, p. 31
180 Warner
181 Doran, p. 331, to her sister-in-law Mrs Robinson, 26 November 1783
182 Diary and Letters of Madame d'Arblay, vol. 1, p. 97, 1778
183 Diary and Letters of Madame d'Arblay, vol. 2, p. 9, Fanny Burney writing to Mrs Thrale, 8 February 1788
184 Wraxall, vol. 1, full description pp. 100–15
185 BL, Add. Ms. 40663, f. 138, to Mrs Robinson at Denton, 3 November 1784
186 Busse, p. 46
187 Clarke, p. 200, quoting Wraxall, 1776: 'a very thin velvet glove over a steel hand'
188 Lord Bath had a close four-year friendship with her when she was in her forties and he an octogenarian. It was almost an affair, but perfectly correct
189 BL, 3562, f. 15, Mrs Montagu to Lord Hardwicke, n.d.
190 Busse, p. 2; Doran, p. 322
191 Johnson, p. 256

Chapter 12: Theresa Robinson, Mrs John Parker

The Parker-Robinson correspondence is divided between:

1. The Parker papers in the West Devon Record Office at Plymouth, where John Parker's cash book (still at Saltram) is on microfilm.

2. The Morley papers in the British Library (BL) (Add. Ms. 48218), comprising Anne Parker's correspondence with both her brothers; Theresa Parker's correspondence with her brother Lord Grantham (ff. 105–71b); Theresa Parker's with her brother Frederick, 1771–5, (ff. 172–218b). The brothers were located abroad, from 1771 in Spain. All letters used are from this collection unless otherwise indicated.

3. The Grantham letters among the Vyner papers in the West Yorkshire Archive Service.

4. The Lucas papers in the Bedfordshire Record Office (the 2nd Lord Grantham married Mary Jemima, daughter of Philip Yorke, 2nd Earl of Hardwicke and Jemima, Marchioness Grey).

All Vyner and Bedfordshire Record Office papers are as quoted by Eileen Harris, The Genius of Robert Adam (Yale University Press, 2001).

Papers relating to Robert Adam:

According to Harris, p. 3, Robert Adam made fair drawings for the client, followed by duplicates or triplicates with the same or variant colouring for the office. These were used as samples for other patrons, and by craftsmen, such as Rose, to make estimates. It is most of the office material that is now in the Soane Museum. Fair drawings were the property of the client who commissioned them and paid for them, whether or not they were executed.

1 British Library, Add. Mss. 48218, Theresa to her brother, Lord Grantham, 26 May 1769
2 A separate article is in preparation by the author on Lady Catherine's work
3 Avray Tipping, 'Saltram, Devonshire – I', *Country Life* (23 January 1926), gave c. 1750 for the Front Hall. National Trust Guidebooks have since suggested the 1740s, but it would be very rare for it to have been completed this early in remote Devon. Norfolk House in London, whose rococo decoration commenced in 1752, was a possible influence: the Duchess of Norfolk came from nearby Blagdon in Devon, and her sister, Lady Clifford of Chudleigh, lived thirty miles away at Ugbrooke Park. The Morning Room ceiling, with its musical decoration, may even have been influenced by the Norfolk House Music Room although trophies of musical instruments were seen elsewhere in England before this date
4 Ceri Johnson, *Chinese Wallpapers at Saltram*, article for the Devon Buildings Group, 1997
5 Eileen Harris, *The Genius of Robert Adam* (Yale University Press, 2001), p. 233
6 Anne Robinson to Frederick, 8 December 1771
7 Quoted by John Cornforth, 'Saltram, Devon – II', *Country Life* (4 May 1967)
8 Lord Grantham, at Aranjury, to Theresa, 25 May 1772
9 Henry Stapleton, *Heirs without Title. A History of the 1st Earl of Morley & his Natural Children* (published by the author, Skelton Rectory, York, 1974), p. 5, says that Theresa was thirty-four when she died. This would make her date of birth 1741. However, other evidence suggests that she was twenty-four when she married, making her date of birth 1745, and this is what is usually given. The latter is marginally more likely, otherwise she would have married at twenty-eight, which was relatively old. Although the average marriage age was twenty-six, it was much younger for the aristocracy
10 Theresa to Lord Grantham, 31 July 1774
11 Theresa to Lord Grantham, 3 February 1774
12 Theresa to Lord Grantham, 3 February 1774
13 Anne to Frederick, Whitehall, 4 April 1773
14 Harris, p. 234 suggests that this may have been at the recommendation of Lord Shelburne, who was employing Adam at Bowood and Landsowne House. There may also have been a contact through John Parker's neighbour in Devon, Lord Clifford of Chudleigh, at whose home at Ugbrooke Park, Adam worked from 1763 to 1768. On p. 239 Harris points out that the bookcases for the library at Saltram were similar to those designed only about a year earlier for Ugbrooke
15 It may even have been Lady Catherine's 'Salloon' on her courtyard plan, still at Saltram, details of which are to be published by the author separately
16 Saltram, J. Parker I's leather cash book, 1768
17 Sir John Soane's Museum: First ceiling design, not executed, dated 1768, SM 2:253. Second design, as executed, SM 2:254, 255 (reproduced by Harris, p. 236)
18 Harris, p. 234, quoting *Catalogue of the Pictures, Casts and Busts belonging to the Earl of Morley at Saltram* (Plymouth, 1819): *Diana* in the centre, the *Seasons* in the corner

roundels, *Venus and Adonis* on one side, the *Death of Procris* on the other, and the *Triumphs of Neptune* and *Thetis* opposite one another in the cove below

19 He was paid a total of £434. John Parker II's cash book (May 1770–August 1778); September 1770 and 31 January 1772

20 Harris, p. 236, West Yorkshire Archive Service Vyner papers 6160/6013/14476; Theresa to Frederick, 17 September 1769. John Parker's cash book, 8 September 1770: 'Mr Parker left with Mr Robinson to pay for ye Genoa Damask £300'

21 Cornforth

22 Harris, p. 15

23 The drawing is in the corridor at Saltram. The present curtains are too small: the originals would have had proper drops

24 Harris, p. 234, BRO, L 30/14/333/63, Frederick Robinson to Lord Grantham, n.d.

25 Harris, p. 238, BRO, L30/14/333/61, Frederick to Lord Grantham, 11 September 1770

26 The payment was on 31 March 1772: John Parker's cash book. See SM 17:11, illustrated Harris, p. 236, for the design that was probably the source of a sketch seen by Perfetti

27 28 March 1771: it does not say to whom

28 National Trust Guidebook, p. 13

29 1 May 1771, £40, and 30 July 1771, £20. John Parker's cash book.

30 SM 50:67, illustrated in Harris, p. 238

31 Quoted by Harris, p. 240, WYAS Vyner papers 6160/6013/14476, Theresa to Frederick, 17 September 1769

32 John Cornforth, 'Saltram, Devon – III', *Country Life* (11 May 1967)

33 SM 50:66

34 Confirmed by Cornforth (11 May 1967)

35 Harris, p. 240

36 Harris, p. 6 (Introduction)

37 St John Gore, 'A Patron of Portrait and Landscape. The Picture Collection at Saltram House, Devon', *Country Life*, 2 June 1966

38 Cornforth (4 May 1967)

39 Earl of Bessborough (ed.), *Georgiana, Excerpts from the Correspondence of Georgiana, Duchess of Devonshire* (John Murray, 1955), p. 54

40 Theresa to Lord Grantham, 23 August 1771

41 Theresa to Lord Grantham, 2 April 1772

42 Theresa to Lord Grantham, 2 April 1772. It was paid for at the time; on 1 April 1772, £63.00: John Parker's cash book

43 Theresa to Frederick, 1 Sept 1772

44 Theresa to Lord Grantham, Sackville Street, 11 March 1774

45 Theresa to Lord Grantham, 5 May 1775

46 Theresa to Lord Grantham, 10 July 1775

47 Ellis Waterhouse, 'Reynolds, Angelica Kauffmann and Lord Boringdon', *Apollo*, vol. 122 (October 1985)

48 Anne Robinson to Frederick, London, 3 March 1772

49 Anne Robinson to Frederick, London, 3 March 1772

50 Theresa to Frederick, 12 March 1772

51 Theresa to Lord Grantham, 2 April 1772

52 Theresa to Lord Grantham, 20 October 1772

53 Lord Grantham to Theresa, 16 November 1772

54 Theresa to Lord Grantham, 15 June 1773

55 Theresa to Lord Grantham, Sackville Street, 5 March 1773
56 Cornforth (4 May 1967)
57 John Parker's cash book, 16 May 1771 and June 1772
58 Waterhouse
59 National Trust Guidebook, p. 47
60 Theresa to Lord Grantham, 23 August 1771
61 See Library and Morning Room
62 J. V. G. Mallett, 'Wedgwood's Early Vases. The Collection at Saltram House, Devon', *Country Life* (9 June 1966). Mallett suggested that a few items may have come via Montagu Parker, but he did not have access to the correspondence showing Theresa's love of the ware
63 Nicholas Goodison, *Ormolu: the Work of Matthew Boulton* (Phaidon, 1974), pp. 159–62
64 Theresa to Frederick, 9 April 1772
65 Goodison, p. 160
66 Theresa to Frederick, 9 April 1772
67 Theresa to Frederick, 1 September 1772
68 National Trust Guidebook, p. 47
69 Theresa to Lord Grantham, 20 October 1772
70 Lord Grantham to Theresa, 14 December 1772
71 Theresa to Lord Grantham, from Sackville Street, 5 March 1773
72 Theresa to Lord Grantham, 2 September 1775
73 Theresa to Lord Grantham, 2 September 1775
74 John Parker's cash book, 17 August 1772, £80
75 Theresa to Frederick, 3 June 1774
76 Theresa to Frederick, 24 August 1775
77 Theresa to Lord Grantham, 2 June 1775
78 Theresa to Frederick, 1 September 1772
79 Theresa to Lord Grantham, 15 June 1773
80 Theresa to Lord Grantham, 20 October 1772
81 Theresa to Lord Grantham, November 1774
82 Ann to Frederick, 8 December 1771
83 Theresa to Frederick, quoted by Ronald Fletcher, *The Parkers at Saltram 1769–89* (BBC, 1970), p. 13
84 Theresa to Lord Grantham, 23 August 1771
85 Theresa to Frederick, 13 September 1771
86 Theresa to Frederick, 29 November 1771
87 Theresa to Frederick, 4 June 1773
88 Lord Grantham to Theresa, 13 September 1773
89 Theresa to Lord Grantham, June 1775
90 Theresa to Grantham, 2 June 1775
91 Lord Grantham to Mr Parker, 19 October 1775
92 Theresa to Frederick, 20 October 1775
93 Waterhouse, p. 273
94 BL, Add. Ms. 48252
95 BL, Add. Ms. 48252
96 Written in 1809, quoted by John Cornforth, 'Saltram, Devon – I', *Country Life* (27 April 1967)
97 BL, Add. Ms. 48252

Chapter 13: Jane Maxwell, Duchess of Gordon

J. M. Bulloch was a very thorough family historian in the early twentieth century. George Gordon in 1980 also gave good coverage. There have been many rather general books, also much legend, perpetuated by two novels; *The Forgotten Duchess* by Angela Petron (Scotforth Books, 1991), and *Island of the Swans* by Ciji Ware (Bantam Books, 1998). Petron's story about the 4th Duke of Gordon and Jean Christie is largely imagined, on the basis of their actual relationship. Ware did some very good research, but fact and fiction are inextricably mixed. There are 8 tons of Gordon documents in the Scottish Register Office, including accounts and inventories, of which collection most of Jane's letters came to West Sussex Record Office in Chichester to be available to her Richmond descendants at Goodwood. There are some letters in the National Library of Scotland and a few at King's College, Aberdeen. There is an interesting memoir by her hairdresser and valet, Matthias Damour.

1 No source discovered for this, but it is much quoted
2 This story is first recounted in J. W. G. (J. Wyllie Guild) (ed.), *An Autobiographical chapter in the life of Jane, Duchess of Gordon (Letters to F. Farquharson)* (privately printed, Glasgow, 1864). It also seems to have been passed down orally: it was reported by Lady Maxwell's brother-in-law and recounted in W. Wilmott Dixon, *Dainty Dames of Society* (Adam & Charles Black, 1903), p. 95
3 George Gordon, *The Last Dukes of Gordon and their Consorts 1743–1864* (Aberdeen, 1980)
4 This is based on oral tradition, handed down to Major Robin McLaren, the present owner of Kinrara. Fraser's actual identity is unknown. In her novel, *Island of the Swans* (Bantam Books, 1988), Ciji Ware suggested that the young man was called Lieutenant Thomas Fraser of Struy, that he was a cousin of the Frasers of Lovat, that Simon Fraser was his guardian, and that he and Jane knew each other as children. Although this is based on clever research from army lists, combining those of 1766 and 1776, these additions to his identity are fictitious: conversation with Ciji Ware, 2002
5 Gordon, chapter 1
6 The story that at the last minute before the wedding they discovered that her fiancé was still alive but did not tell her is entirely fictitious. Conversation with Ciji Ware, August 2002
7 All details of this sequence from George Gordon. The report, including the timing of the news of his death and the appearance of the letter after the marriage, including the swoon, is based on oral tradition, and seems to have been in existence for a long time, well before the Ware novel
8 Scottish Register Office, Catalogue entry for GD 44/55/1/226; William Maxwell from Mertoun to Jane, 26 September 1767: West Sussex Record Office
9 SRO, Catalogue entry for GD 44/55/1/227; Henry Home Lord Kames to Jane, 1 November 1767 and 229, 1768: neither letter located
10 SRO, Catalogue entry for GD 44/55/1, letters 228, 20 November 1767 and 229, 5 February 1768, Jane to Lord Kames: neither letter located
11 Sir Nathaniel Wraxall, *The Historical & Posthumous Memoirs of Sir Nathaniel William Wraxall 1772–84*, ed. Henry B. Wheatly (Bickers, 1884), vol. 4, p. 458
12 Wraxall, p. 458
13 Elizabeth Grant of Rothiemurchus, *Memoirs of a Highland Lady: The Autobiography of Elizabeth Grant of Rothiemurchus 1797–1827*, ed. Lady Strachey (John Murray,

1898), p. 251
14 Wraxall, p. 458
15 Pryse Lockhart Gordon, *Personal Memoirs; or Reminiscences of Men and Manners at Home and Abroad during the last half century* (H. Colburn & R. Bentley, 1830), p. 37
16 Constance Russell, *Three Generations of Fascinating Women, and other Sketches from Family History* (Longmans, 1904), p. 216
17 Gordon gives a clear family tree, showing the mothers
18 Rachel Trethewey, *Mistress of the Arts: The Passionate Life of Georgina, Duchess of Bedford*, Review (Headline, 2002), p. 9
19 WSRO, Goodwood Ms. 1170 f. 69, Diary of Events at Gordon Castle, December 1765–December 1776
20 SRO, GD 44/49/16/1, Memorandum for Mr Salisbury Architect, April 1783
21 SRO, GD 44/49/15/1, Inventory of Plaster and Stucco Work at Gordon Castle, 24 November 1779
22 SRO, GD 44/49/16/2, Measure by John Baxter, 1779
23 WSRO, Goodwood Ms. 1171, f. 42, Jane to Lord Kames, 28 February 1779
24 SRO, GD 44/49/15/5, Copy of account of plaster work at Gordon Castle, 1779, Philip Robertson
25 SRO, GD 44/49/13/4, Inventory of Table Linen, Gordon Castle, 26 March 1774
26 WSRO, Goodwood Ms., f. 80, 19 January 1769
27 Trethewey, p. 19
28 Margaret Forbes, *Beattie and his Friends* (Archibald Constable & Co., 1904), p. 163, 27 May 1780
29 Grant of Rothiemurchus, p. 91
30 Russell, p. 217
31 SRO, GD 1/479/15, all from letter of 4 November 1774, to Lady Frances in Edinburgh
32 WSRO, Goodwood Ms. 1171, f. 47, to Dr James Beattie
33 WSRO, Goodwood Ms. 1170, f. 69, Diary of Events at Gordon Castle, December 1765–December 1776
34 WSRO, Goodwood Ms. 1171, f. 45, to Lord Kames
35 WSRO, Goodwood Ms. 1171, f. 49, Jane to Dr James Beattie, 20 December 1779
36 WSRO, Goodwood Ms. 1171, f. 49, Jane to Dr James Beattie, 20 December 1779
37 WSRO, Goodwood Ms. 1171, f. 63, Lord Kames to Jane, September 1782
38 WSRO, Goodwood Ms. 1171, f. 32, declining an invitation to stay there, 2 September 1777
39 Moyra Cowie, *The Life and Times of William Marshall 1748–1833. Composer of Scottish Traditional Music & Clock Maker* (privately printed with the assistance of Moray Council, 1999)
40 Elizabeth Rose of Kilravock, who lived at Kilravock Castle near Inverness
41 My assumption for the reason they moved there
42 Mrs Grant of Laggan, quoted by Trethewey, p. 21
43 The painting by C. M. Hardie of one such evening is a Victorian historicising work, dating from 1887 (Burns Museum, Ayrshire)
44 Mrs Alison Cockburn, quoted by Trethewey, p. 21
45 R. Brimley Johnson (ed.), *The Letters of Lady Louisa Stuart* (John Lane, The Bodley Head, 1926), p. 76
46 T. S. Surr, *A Winter in London* (London, Richard Phillips, 1806)
47 Wraxall, vol. 4, p. 459; Grant of Rothiemurchus, p. 102
48 Originals in the Huntington Library

49 Gordon, p. 66

50 Castalia, Countess Granville (ed.), *Lord Granville Leveson Gower (first Earl Granville): Private Correspondence 1781 to 1821* (John Murray, 1916), p. 68, Lady Stafford to Granville Leveson Gower, 13 August 1793

51 The marriage was at the Duke's house in Piccadilly in 1797

52 Documented by Trethewey (Author's Note)

53 H. S. (ed.), *A Souvenir of Sympathy* (Aberdeen Journal Office, 1900), p. 60

54 Trethewey, p. 57, quoting the Russian ambassador, Markoff, from the *Private Correspondence of Lord Granville Leveson Gower, 1781–1821*

55 Granville, p. 376, Lady Bessborough to GLG, 15 December 1802

56 *The Times*, 23 June 1803

57 Gordon, p. 107

58 J. W. G. (J. Wyllie Guild), p. vi

59 The Marquess of Huntly, *The Cock o' the North* (London, Thornton Butterworth, 1935), p. 191

60 Gordon, p. 86, tests the veracity of the 'kissing' story, which had been denied by Lady Madelina, and concludes that it was true. J. M. Bulloch, *The Gay Gordons* (Chapman & Hall, 1908), pp. 196–201, doubted it, saying that it was not recorded until 1901 by Colonel Greenhill Gardyne in *The Life of a Regiment*: 'It is told how she gave a kiss to the men she enlisted...' However, Bulloch has to concede, p. 198, one contemporary verbal source, documented in H. S. (ed.), *A Souvenir of Sympathy* (Aberdeen Journal Office, 1900), as from a writer who averred that his ninety-seven-year-old grandmother described how she saw the Duchess wave at a 'fine young fellow' and after a little talk gave him a sovereign from between her teeth. There is also a charming poem in this anthology, p. 67, called 'The Gordon Plaid', written as if by the sweetheart of a Highlander, who has kissed the Duchess to get his Shilling

61 Quoted by Bulloch, p. 195

62 Angus Fairrie, *The Northern Meeting, 1788–1988* (Scotland, Pentland Press, 1988), quoting G. Yates

63 The Female Jockey Club, 1794, quoted in the *Complete Peerage*, vol. 6

64 Jean Christie has variously been called the housekeeper, the daughter of the housekeeper (who was known from housekeeping books to be one Mrs Christie), a housemaid, or, in the most recent turn, the daughter of a tenant farmer (Trethewey). In her novel *The Forgotten Duchess* (Scotforth Books, 1991) Angela Petron suggests that she was offered a position at the castle soon after the Duke became interested in her, but refused it. This is probably fictitious

65 Gordon, p. 77

66 Pryse Lockhart Gordon, p. 397

67 SRO, GD 51/9/213/2, Omans Hotel, to Dundas, n.d.

68 Grant of Rothiemurchus, p. 34

69 Painting of it at Goodwood: date of commencement from Goodwood Ms. 1170, f. 69, Diary

70 Grant of Rothiemurchus, p. 94

71 The farmhouse is shown in a print of 1801. A little cottage, with outbuildings, still stands on the site. It may be the central part of the original, but restored. Elizabeth Grant's memory that the new house was built between the old farmhouse and the Doune is probably incorrect: she was very young at the time, and very elderly when she wrote her memoirs. It would make the original farmhouse to the west of the big house, but there is no suitable knoll-like location. The print must show

what she called 'the real old farmhouse'. The landscape corresponds to that of the more eastern location

72 Grant of Rothiemurchus, p. 35
73 Grant of Rothiemurchus, p. 36
74 Grant of Rothiemurchus, p. 37
75 J. W. G. (J. Wyllie Guild), letter II, from 'The Cottage of Kinrara', 10 October 1804
76 J. W. G. (J. Wyllie Guild), letter III, 2 November 1804
77 J. W. G. (J. Wyllie Guild), also letter V, 15 June 1805
78 J. W. G. (J. Wyllie Guild), p. 10, 15 June 1805
79 J. W. G. (J. Wyllie Guild), 8 July 1805
80 SRO, WD44/34/56
81 SRO, WD44/34/53/1, Receipt No. 4, 18 January 1808
82 SRO, WD44/34/53/1, Receipt No. 3, 14 November 1809
83 SRO, WD44/34/57/12–13, 19 January 1811, Edinburgh, letter from James Gibson, saying that the house can neither be sold nor let in its present state and that perhaps she should try to get Mr Maxwell to sell it to her (he does not say what she can then do with it). It seems to have been one of those arrangements where the son had inherited the house but leased it to the women of the family
84 SRO, WD 44/34/53/3, Accounts paid for her while staying in Dumbucks Hotel, Edinburgh, 1809–11, especially No. 55, lodging 23 November 1808 to 13 April 1809
85 SRO, GD 44/34/53/1, January 1808, paid February
86 SRO, WD 44/34/53/3/34, 14 February 1809, Receipt by Alexander Laing for £10 10s.
87 SRO, GD 44/34/53/3, No. 28, 13 January 1809
88 SRO 44/34/53/3, No. 59, Account paid to The Caledonian Company, Inverness, 1809
89 SRO, 44/34/53/3, No. 56
90 SRO, GD 44/34/53/3, No. 51, Receipt for furniture and upholstery, 12 April 1809
91 SRO, GD 44/34/53/3, No. 53, 13 April 1809
92 SRO, GD 44/34/53/1, Receipt No. 25, January 1808, Gow & Shepherd, Edinburgh
93 SRO, GD 44/34/53/3/58, 25 July 1809
94 SRO, GD 44/34/53/3/57
95 Letter of Lord Gower, S&Q Series 2, vol. 8, p. 147, quoted by Gordon, p. 137
96 Revealed by a survey map 1867–9, engraved by Major General Sir Henry James RE, FRCS, published 31 December 1874
97 Cowie, p. 45
98 Dr Peter H. Reid, 'Some Observations on the Dukes and Duchesses of Gordon', Aberdeen University Lecture (January 1998)
99 David Mannings, *Sir Joshua Reynolds. A Complete Catalogue of his Painting* (Yale, 2000), no. 745
100 John MacCulloch, *Highlands & Western Isles of Scotland. Diaries of Annual Journeys between the years 1811 and 1821...in letters to Sir Walter Scott Bart.* (Longmans, 1824), vol. 1, pp. 396–7

Chapter 14: Elizabeth Howard, Duchess of Rutland

All correspondence is at Belvoir Castle, unless otherwise stated, and between John, 5th Duke of Rutland and Elizabeth, unless otherwise stated: the last section is between Elizabeth and Colonel Trench. It is reproduced by kind permission of the Duke of Rutland.

1 Belvoir Castle, *Correspondence of John, 5th Duke of Rutland and Elizabeth his Wife*, vol. 1, 1799, file 23, no. 1, 23 February 1799

2 No. 4, 26 February 1799

3 No. 23, 16 March 1799

4 No. 40, 20 May 1799

5 No. 99, 28 December 1799

6 No. 101, 30 December 1799

7 No. 3, 26 February 1799

8 Probably in the southeast and southwest fronts, but it is not known to what height; the Regent's Gallery has exactly the same proportions as the narrow southwest wing of the Webb house. Also in the northeast front, where the Duchess later mentions that 'all the old part of the castle was burnt'

9 No. 164, 22 November 1800

10 No. 164, 27 November 1800

11 No. 169, 3 January 1801

12 No. 174, 29 January 1801

13 No. 103, 30 March 1800, and 136, April 1800

14 No. 188, 27(?) April 1801

15 No. 137, 14 June 1800

16 No. 175, 30 January 1801

17 Family tradition and all modern commentators concur in this view

18 Revd. Irvin Eller, *The History of Belvoir Castle* (London, Robert Tyas, 1841), p. 126; 'ample preparations' had been made during his minority; Christopher Hussey, 'Belvoir Castle, Leicestershire – I: The Regency Apotheosis', *Country Life*, CXX (6 December 1956), dates these as 1782. Pevsner, revised by Elizabeth Williamson with Geoffrey K. Brandwood, *Leicestershire and Rutland*, The Buildings of England (Penguin, 1984), gives 1789, but this seems to be the date of Brown's survey, after the Duke's death

19 Quoted by Eller, p. 132: it was written on 10 March 1817 and placed as a memorial after the fire in one of the foundation stones of the centre tower on the northeast front

20 Hussey

21 Pevsner, pp. 95–101. A good description is given of the extent to which the old castle is incorporated

22 Neither the Wyatt designs nor letters exist: they may have perished in the 1816 fire

23 See the Duchess's drawing after the fire, which refers to one 'old part all burnt', suggesting that some of the old rooms had been retained in their 1800 rebuild, at least on the northeast side. Her accompanying letter also says that the 'whole of the old part' was burnt

24 No. 182, 18 July 1801

25 No. 186, 21 July 1801

26 No. 201, 6 September 1802

27 *Correspondence of John, 5th Duke of Rutland and Elizabeth his Wife*, vol. 3, file 25, no. 216, 6 August 1803

28 No. 217, 6 August 1803

29 No. 218, 7 August 1803

30 *Miscellaneous Correspondence of Elizabeth, Duchess of Rutland*, blue box file, 2/22/1, Letter on the death of her first child Lady Caroline Manners, November 1804. There are two more verses

31 John Martin Robinson, *The Wyatts. An Architectural Dynasty* (Oxford University

Press, 1979), p. 158

32 Eller, p. 125

33 *Correspondence of John, 5th Duke of Rutland and Elizabeth his Wife*, vol. 4, file 28, no. 561, 8 July 1814

34 No. 563, 10 July 1814

35 No. 565, 12 July 1814

36 No. 578, November 1817

37 *Journal of A Trip to Paris by the Duke and Duchess of Rutland, July MDCCCXIV* (British Library, manuscript version at Belvoir Castle)

38 Many at Belvoir Castle

39 The engravings by Coypel of his own paintings date from 1723–34

40 Robinson, p. 107: the receipts are in the Duke's papers

41 *Miscellaneous Correspondence of Elizabeth Duchess of Rutland*, 5 November 1816, to the Duchess of Somerset, responding to her letter of commiseration to the Duke and enclosing the plan

42 *Miscellaneous Correspondence of Elizabeth Duchess of Rutland*, 5 November 1816, to the Duchess of Somerset

43 Farington's Diary, vol. 14, p. 4916, Friday 1 November 1816: the Duchess shows Colonel McMahon the letter she has received from the Duke

44 Memorial note, 1817, quoted by Eller, p. 133

45 *Miscellaneous Correspondence of Elizabeth Duchess of Rutland*, 5 November 1816, to the Duchess of Somerset

46 *Miscellaneous Correspondence of Elizabeth Duchess of Rutland*, Cheveley Park, 29 October 1816

47 He may well have helped the child Duke in his minority, but I have found no evidence

48 *Correspondence of John, 5th Duke of Rutland and Elizabeth his Wife*, vol. 6, file 28, no. 584, 29 May 1817

49 No. 581, 22 November 1817

50 No. 585, 25 November 1817. Although he calls it the 'North West' tower, he must be referring to the one on the northeast, which had earlier been mentioned by the Duchess. Although he was unlikely to make an error, he referred to the northwest entrance front as the west, so perhaps he was casual about the orientation. The only alternative is that he was referring to the much smaller tower on the corner of the two façades, but this is unlikely as it follows the larger tower in design and is not substantial. He also says the tower looks 'very handsome' in no. 581.

51 No. 587, 26 November 1817

52 Robinson, p. 107

53 James Yorke, 'Belvoir Castle. Leicestershire – I', *Country Life* (23 June 1994)

54 *Correspondence of the Duchess of Rutland and Sir Frederick Trench*, vol. 1, no. 1, 15 May 1816

55 John Henry Manners, 5th Duke of Rutland, *Travels in Great Britain, with engravings from drawings by the Duchess of Rutland: Journal of a Tour round the Southern Coasts of England* (publ. 1805), *through North and South Wales, the Isle of Man* (publ. 1805), *to the northern parts of Great Britain* (publ. 1813) (British Library)

56 John Henry Manners, 5th Duke of Rutland, *A Tour through part of Belgium and the Rhenish provinces (with plates from sketches by E. Manners, Duchess of Rutland)* (British Library)

57 *Correspondence of the Duchess of Rutland and Sir Frederick Trench*, vol. 1, no. 12, 15 December 1821

58 No. 11, 23 December 1820, to Colonel Trench

59 No. 25, 17 February 1823, to Colonel Trench

60 *Correspondence of the Duke of Rutland and Sir Frederick Trench*, blue file, no. 21, 1822

61 F. Bamford and the Duke of Wellington (eds.), *The Journal of Mrs Arbuthnot*, vol. 1, p. 167, 25 June 1822

62 *Correspondence of the Duchess of Rutland and Sir Frederick Trench*, vol. 1, no. 39, 23 August 1824, to Colonel Trench

63 Bamford and the Duke of Wellington, vol. 1, p. 402, 16 June 1825

64 Bamford and the Duke of Wellington, vol. 1, p. 403, 16 June 1825

65 Bamford and the Duke of Wellington, vol. 1, pp. 406–7, 6 July 1825

66 Bamford and the Duke of Wellington, vol. 1, pp. 406–7, 9 July 1825

67 Bamford and the Duke of Wellington, vol. 1, p. 201, 31 December 1823

68 Eller, p. 137

69 James Yorke, *Lancaster House, London's Greatest Town House* (Merrell, 2001); Bamford and the Duke of Wellington, vol. 2, see Editor's note for 31 May 1826

70 For his recommendation on scagliola to her, see James Yorke, 'Better than any Original', *Country Life* (1 April 1993)

71 *Correspondence of Elizabeth Duchess of Rutland with Sir Frederick Trench*, vol. 1, no. 65, 21 or 28 November 1824

72 No. 69, 5 December 1824

73 No. 43, 10 October 1824

74 No. 48, 23 October 1824

75 No. 58, 20 November 1824

76 No. 112, 18 March 1825

77 No. 111, 19 March 1825

78 Eller, p. 137

79 Information from John Martin Robinson

80 Eller, p. 136, and letter 64, 27 November 1824

81 No. 145, 6 October, and 150, 21 October 1825

82 Bamford and the Duke of Wellington, vol. 1, p. 167, 25 June 1822

83 Bamford and the Duke of Wellington, vol. 1, p. 196, 11 November 1822

84 Bamford and the Duke of Wellington, vol. 1, p. 201, 12 January 1823

85 *Correspondence of Elizabeth Duchess of Rutland with Sir Frederick Trench*, vol. 1, no. 26, 7 March 1823

86 No. 28, December 1823

87 No. 56, 19 November 1824

88 No. 20, January 1823

89 Robinson, p. 107

90 Robinson, p. 107: receipt at Belvoir Castle. James Yorke, 'Belvoir Castle. Leicester-shire – II', *Country Life* (30 June 1994), cites the first letter mentioning these; the Duchess to Col. Trench, 13 July 1824: 'I should like to see the Madame de Maintenon furniture'

91 All from no. 45, 14 October 1824

92 A bill for a large carpet was dated 19 January 1826, from Messrs Castellain, Shaizi and Co. of Tournai (Duke's account book), for £145 with charges of £27.6s. A large carpet was also supplied by M. Lefevre: it was probably the same item, perhaps with a further charge for him providing the French style design to the factory. Account details from James Yorke

93 All from no. 45, 14 October 1824

94 No. 62, 25 November 1824; no. 76, 23 December 1824

95 *Correspondence of Elizabeth Duchess of Rutland with Sir Frederick Trench*, vol. 2, no. 86, 30 January 1825
96 No. 82, 20 January 1825
97 No. 84, 23 January 1825
98 No. 122, 31 March 1825
99 No. 124, 9 April 1825, and no. 128, 25 April 1825
100 No. 136, 15 August 1825
101 No. 138, 19 August 1825
102 No. 149, 18 October 1825
103 No. 141, n.d.
104 No. 166A, 20 November 1825
105 John Watkins, *A Biographical Memoir of his late Royal Highness Frederick, Duke of York and Albany* (London, 1827), pp. 529–30
106 Eller, p. 135, said that it was in her bowel, but it is now believed to have been peritonitis
107 Rachel Leighton (ed.), *Correspondence of Charlotte Grenville, Lady Williams Wynn and her Three Sons 1795–1812* (John Murray, 1920), p. 337, 10 January 1826
108 Leighton, p. 331, 11 December 1825
109 Bamford and the Duke of Wellington, vol. 2, p. 71, 8 January 1827
110 Bamford and the Duke of Wellington, vol. 2, p. 72, 8 January 1827
111 Bamford and the Duke of Wellington, vol. 2, p. 230, 11 January 1829
112 Watkins, p. 530
113 Bamford and the Duke of Wellington, vol. 2, p. 430, 20 December 1825
114 Eller, p. 136

Notes to Conclusion

1 Sir Walter Besant, quoted in Lady Margaret Maria Verney, *The Verney Letters of the Eighteenth Century from the Mss. at Claydon House...*, 2 vols. (London, Ernest Benn, 1930), vol. 2, p. 257

SELECT BIBLIOGRAPHY

The following list gives the main books consulted. For reasons of space, it has not been practical to include all relevant books on eighteenth-century history, art and architecture. Books used just for one brief section together with scholarly articles, especially from *Country Life*, exhibition catalogues, house guidebooks and obscure publications are referred to in full in the notes to the individual chapters. Important articles that have not been endnoted are included in their own section of this list.

GENERAL

Bayne Powell, R., *Housekeeping in the 18th Century*, John Murray, 1956.

Brewer, John, *The Pleasures of the Imagination. English Culture in the 18th Century*, Harper Collins, 1997.

Bryant, Julius, *Mrs. Howard. A Woman of Reason 1688–1767*, English Heritage exhibition catalogue, 1988.

Bryant, Julius, *Marble Hill*, English Heritage, 2002.

Cannon, John, *Aristocratic Century. The Peerage of Eighteenth-Century England*, Cambridge University Press, 1984.

Chapman, Caroline, *Elizabeth and Georgiana. The Duke of Devonshire and his Two Duchesses*, John Murray, 2002.

Clarke, Norma, *Dr. Johnson's Women*, Hambledon & London, 2000.

Croft Murray, Edward, *Decorative Painting in England*, Country Life Ltd, 1962.

Dolan, Brian, *Ladies of the Grand Tour*, Harper Collins, 2001.

Draper, Marie P. G., *Marble Hill House and its Owners*, GLC, 1970.

Dutton, Ralph, *English Court Life*, Batsford, 1963.

Foreman, Amanda, *Georgiana, Duchess of Devonshire*, Harper Collins, 1999.

Fowler, J. and Cornforth, J., *English Decoration in the 18th Century*, Barrie & Jenkins, 1974.

Fraser, Antonia, *The Weaker Vessel: Women's Lot in Seventeenth-Century England*, William Heinemann, 1984.

Friedman, Terry, *James Gibbs*, Yale University Press, 1984.

Girouard, Mark, *Life in the English Country House*, Yale University Press, 1978.

Glanville, P. and Young, H., *Elegant Eating: Four Hundred Years of Dining in Style*, V&A Publications, 2002.

Goodison, Nicholas, *Ormolu: The Work of Matthew Boulton*, Phaidon, 1974.

Halsband, Robert, *Lady Mary Wortley Montagu*, Clarendon, 1956.

Hardyment, Christina, *Behind the Scenes: Domestic Arrangements in Historic Houses*, National Trust, 1997.

Harris, Eileen, *The Genius of Robert Adam: His Interiors*, Yale University Press, 2001.

Harris, Frances, *A Passion for Government: The Life of Sarah, Duchess of Marlborough*, Clarendon Press, 1991.

Hicks, Carola, *Improper Pursuits: The Scandalous Life of Lady Di Beauclerk*, Macmillan, 2001.

Hillier, Bevis, *Pottery and Porcelain, 1700–1914*, Weidenfeld & Nicolson, 1968.

Hill, Bridget, *Eighteenth-Century Women: An Anthology*, Allen & Unwin, 1984.

Kay, Frederick George, *Royal Mail. The Story of the Posts in England from the Time of Edward IV to the Present Day*, Rockliff, 1951.

van der Kiste, John, *The Georgian Princesses*, Sutton Publishing, 2000.

Leach, Peter, *James Paine*, Zwemmer, 1988.

Little, Bryan, *The Life and Work of James Gibbs 1682–1754*, Batsford, 1955.

Lummis, Trevor and Marsh, Jan, *The Woman's Domain: Women and the English Country House*, Viking, 1990, Penguin, 1993.

Macaulay, James, *The Gothic Revival, 1745–1845*, Blackie, 1975.

McClain, Molly, *Beaufort: The Duke and His Duchess, 1657–1715*, Yale University Press, 2001.

Mingay, G. E., *English Landed Society in the 18th Century*, Routledge & Kegan Paul, 1963.

Moore, Lucy, *Amphibious Thing: The Life of Lord Hervey*, Viking, 2000.

Murray, Venetia, *High Society: A Social History of the Regency Period, 1788–1830*, Viking, 1998.

Picard, Liza, *Dr. Johnson's London*, Weidenfeld & Nicolson, 2000.

Robertson, Una A., *Coming Out of the Kitchen: Women Beyond The Home*, Sutton Publishing, 2000.

Robinson, John Martin, *Royal Residences*, Macdonald, 1982.

Robinson, John Martin, *The Wyatts: An Architectural Dynasty*, Oxford University Press, 1979.

Robbins, Alice, *A Book of Duchesses: Studies in Personality*, Andrew Malone, 1913.

Russell, Constance (Lady), *Three Generations of Fascinating Women*, Longmans, 1904.

Saumarez Smith, Charles, *Eighteenth-Century Decoration: Design and the Domestic Interior in England*, Weidenfeld & Nicolson, 1993.

Stone, Lawrence, *The Family, Sex and Marriage in England 1500–1800*, Harper Collins, 1977.

Sykes, Christopher Simon, *Private Palaces*, Chatto & Windus, 1985.

Tillyard, Stella, *Aristocrats: Caroline, Emily, Louisa and Sarah Lennox 1740–1832*, Chatto & Windus, 1994.

Vaizey, Marina and Gere, Charlotte, *Great Women Collectors*, Philip Wilson, 1999.

Vickery, Amanda, *The Gentleman's Daughter: Women's Lives in Georgian England*, Yale University Press, 1998.

Worsley, Giles, *Classical Architecture in Britain: The Heroic Age*, Yale University Press, 1995.

PRINCIPAL CONTEMPORARY COMMENTATORS

d'Arblay, Madame, *Diaries and Letters of Madame d'Arblay*, edited by her niece Frances Charlotte Barrett, Henry Colburn, 1842.

Bessborough, Earl of, and Aspinall, A., *Lady Bessborough and her Family Circle*, John Murray, 1940.

Bingley, W. (ed.), *Correspondence between Frances Countess of Hartford and Henrietta Louisa Countess of Pomfret, between the years 1736 and 1741*, Richard Phillips, 1805.

Blake, Mrs Warrenne, *An Irish Beauty of The Regency*, compiled from 'Mes Souvenirs, the unpublished memoirs of the Hon. Mrs Calvert', John Lane, The Bodley Head, 1911.

Boswell, James, *Boswell's London Journal 1762–63*, ed. Frederick Pottle, Heinemann, 1950.

Brimley Johnson, R. (ed.), *The Letters of Lady Louisa Stuart*, The Bodley Head, 1926.

Burnet, Gilbert, *History of My Own Time*, abridged by Thomas Stackhouse, Dent, 1979.

Coke, Lady Mary, *The Letters and Journals of Lady Mary Coke*, ed. J. A. Horne, Kingsmead Reprints, 1970.

Damour, Matthias, *Memoirs of Mr Matthias Damour*, Paul Rogers, 1834.

Defoe, Daniel, *A Tour Through the Whole Island of Great Britain and Ireland*, ed. G. D. H. Cole, London, 1927.

Elwin, Malcolm (ed.), *The Noels and the Milbankes: their Letters for Twenty-Five Years 1767–1792*, Macdonald, 1967.

Evelyn, John, *The Diary of John Evelyn*, ed. E. S. de Beer, Clarendon Press, 1955.

Farington, Joseph, *The Diary of Joseph Farington*, ed. Evelyn Newby, Yale University Press, 1998.

FitzGerald, Brian (ed.), *Correspondence of Emily, Duchess of Leinster (1731–1814)*, 1949.

Forbes, Sir William, *An Account of the Life and Writings of James Beattie Lld*, Edinburgh, 1806.

Greig, James (ed.), *The Diaries of a Duchess. Extracts from the Diaries of the First Duchess of Northumberland (1716–1776)*, Hodder & Stoughton, 1926.

Halsband, R. (ed.), *The Complete Letters of Lady Mary Wortley Montagu*, Oxford University Press, 1965.

Leighton, Rachel (ed.), *Correspondence of Charlotte Grenville, Lady Williams Wynn & her three sons 1795–1832*, John Murray, 1920.

Lennox, Sarah, *The Life and Letters of Lady Sarah Lennox 1745–1826*, ed. Countess of Ilchester and Lord Stavordale, John Murray, 1901.

Lewis, W. S. et al. (eds.), *Horace Walpole's Correspondence*, 48 vols., Yale University Press/ Oxford University Press, 1937–83.

Llanover, Lady (ed.), *Autobiography and Correspondence of Mary Granville, Mrs Delany*, Richard Bentley, 1861–2.

Luttrell, Narcissus, *A Brief Historical Relation of State Affairs from Sept 1678–April 1714*, Oxford University Press, 1837.

Northumberland, Duchess of, *Castles of Alnwick & Warkworth, &c from sketches by C. F. Duchess of Northumberland*, privately printed for the Duchess, London, 1823.

Pope, Alexander, *Letters of Mr Pope and Several Eminent Persons*, London, 1735.

Reresby, Sir John, *Memoirs and Travels 1634–1689*, London, 1734 and 1813.

Suffolk, Henrietta H., *Letters To and From Henrietta, Countess of Suffolk, and Her Second Husband*, ed. J. W. Croker, London, 1824.

Wraxall, Nathaniel, *The Historical & Posthumous Memoirs of Sir Nathaniel William Wraxall, 1772–84*, ed. Henry B. Wheatly, Bickers, 1884.

Young, Arthur, *A Six Weeks Tour Through the Southern Counties of England and Wales*, W. Nicoll, 1768.

Young, Arthur, *A Six Month Tour Through the North of England*, W. Strahan, 1770.

ARTICLES AND CATALOGUES SUPPLEMENTARY TO THOSE MENTIONED IN THE NOTES

Bolton, Arthur T., 'James Stuart at Portman House and Spencer House', *Country Life* (1 May 1915), p. 8.

Bryant, Julius, 'Deciphering Palladian Decoration', *Country Life* (19 April 1990).

Bulloch, John Malcolm, *The Duchess of Gordon as Recruiter. Her Company in the Fraser Highlands*, privately printed, 1908.

Cornforth, John, 'Drayton House, Northamptonshire, I, II, III, IV', *Country Life* (13, 20, 27 May, 3 June 1965).

Dunbar, John G., 'The Building Activities of The Duke and Duchess of Lauderdale, 1670–82', *Archaeological Journal*, vol. 132.

FitzGerald, Brian, 'The Norfolk House Music Room', *HMSO* (1973).

Gore, St. John, 'A Patron of Portrait and Landscape: the Picture Collection at Saltram House, Devon', *Country Life* (2 June 1966).

Hunter, Jean E., *The Eighteenth-Century English Woman*, Samuel Stevens, Hakkert, 1976.

Myers, Evelyn Elizabeth, *A History of Sandleford Priory*, privately printed.

Smith, Peter, 'Lady Oxford's Alterations at Welbeck Abbey, 1741–55', *The Georgian Group Journal*, 2001.

Strangways, Henry Edward Fox, afterwards Earl of Ilchester, *Catalogue of Pictures belonging to the Earl of Ilchester at Holland House*, privately printed, 1904.

Worsley, Giles, 'On Tour with Adam', *Country Life* (16 April 1992).

Louise de Keroualle

Bevan, Brian, *The King's French Mistress*, Hale, 1972.

Colquhoun Grant, Mrs, *Brittany to Whitehall: Life of Louise de Keroualle, Duchess of Portsmouth*, London, 1909.

Delpech, Jeanine, *The Duchess of Portsmouth*, tr. A. Lindsay, Elek, 1953.

Forneron, Henri, *Louise de Keroualle, Duchess of Portsmouth*, London, 1887.

Macleod, Catherine and Alexander, Julia Marciari, *Painted Ladies: Women at the Court of Charles II*, National Portrait Gallery, 2001.

Lauderdale

Pritchard, Evelyn, *Ham House and its owners through four centuries 1610–1948*, Richmond Local History Society, 1998.

Thornton, Peter and Tomlin, Maurice, 'The Furniture and Decoration of Ham House', *The Journal of Furniture History Society*, vol. 16 (1980).

Tollemache, Edward, *The Tollemaches of Helmingham and Ham*, W. S. Cowell, 1949.

Tollemache, Lionel, *Old and Odd Memories*, Edward Arnold, 1908.

Holland

Faulkner, Thomas, *History and Antiquities of Kensington*, London, 1820.

FitzGerald, Brian, *Lady Louisa Connolly, 1743–1821, An Anglo-Irish Biography*, Staples Press, 1950.

Fyvie, John, *Noble Dames and Notable Men of the Georgian Era*, London, 1910.

Ilchester, Earl of, *The Home of the Hollands 1605–1820*, John Murray, 1937.

Liechtenstein, Princess Marie, *Holland House*, London, 1875.

Mitchell, Leslie, *Holland House*, Duckworth, 1980.

Norfolk

Clifford, Hugh, *The House of Clifford from Before the Conquest*, Philimore, 1987.

Holland, John, *The History, Antiquities and Description of the Town and Parish of Worksop in the County of Nottingham*, J. Blackwell, 1826.

Robinson, John Martin, *The Dukes of Norfolk: A Quincentennial History*, Oxford University Press, 1982.

Portsmouth

Addison, William, *Audley End*, J. M. Dent & Sons, 1953.

Braybrooke, Richard, Lord, *The History of Audley End to which are appended Notices of the Town and Parish of Saffron Walden in the County of Essex*, Samuel Bentley, 1886.

Northumberland

Brenan, Gerald, *A History of the House of Percy from the Earliest Times down to the Present Century*, Freemantle, 1922.

de Fonblanque, Edward Barrington, *Annals of the House of Percy, from the Conquest to the Opening of the Nineteenth Century*, London, privately published, 1887.

Montagu

Aspinall-Oglander, Brigadier Cecil, *Admiral's Widow, being the life and letters of the Hon. Mrs Boscawen from 1761 to 1805*, Hogarth, 1942.

Blunt, Reginald (ed.), *Mrs Montagu, 'Queen of the Blues': her Letters and Friendships from 1762 to 1800*, London, 1923.

Busse, John, *Mrs Montagu, Queen of the Blues*, Gerald Howe, 1928.

Clarke, Norma, *Dr Johnson's Women*, Hambledon & London, 2000.

Climenson, Emily J., *Elizabeth Montagu, Queen of the Bluestockings: her correspondence*, John Murray, 1906.

Doran, Dr. D., *A Lady of the Last Century (Mrs Elizabeth Montagu)*, Richard Bentley, 1873.

Montagu, Mrs Elizabeth, *The Letters of Mrs Elizabeth Montagu*, ed. T. Cadell and W. Davies, London, 1809.

Myers, Sylvia Harcstarck, *The Bluestocking Circle: Women, Friendship and the Life of the Mind in Eighteenth-Century England*, Clarendon, 1990.

Watkin, David, *Athenian Stuart: Pioneer of the Greek Revival*, Allen & Unwin, 1982.

Parker

Fletcher, Ronald, *The Parkers at Saltram, 1769–89*, BBC, 1970.

Gordon

Bulloch, J. M., *The Gay Gordons*, Chapman & Hall, 1908.

Dixon, W. Wilmott, *Dainty Dames of Society*, Adam & Charles Black, 1903.

Foster, Vere, *The Two Duchesses*, Blackie & Son, 1898.

Gordon, George, *The Last Dukes of Gordon and their Consorts 1743–1864*, Aberdeen, 1980.

Grant of Rothiemurchus, Elizabeth, *Memoirs of a Highland Lady: The Autobiography of Elizabeth Grant of Rothiemurchus 1797–1827*, ed. Lady Strachey, John Murray, 1898.

Guild, J. Wylie, (ed.), *An autobiographical chapter in the life of Jane, Duchess of Gordon (Letters to F. Farquharson)*, privately printed, Glasgow, 1864.

Huntly, Marquess of, *The Cock o'the North*, Thornton Butterworth, 1935.

Trethewey, Rachel, *Mistress of the Arts: The Passionate Life of Georgina, Duchess of Bedford*, Review, 2002.

Rutland

Bamford, F. and the Duke of Wellington (eds.), *The Journal of Mrs Arbuthnot, 1820–32*, 1950.

Cornforth, John, 'Stafford House Revisited', *Country Life* (14 November 1968).

Eller, Revd. Irvin, *The History of Belvoir Castle*, Robert Tyas, 1841.

Hussey, Christopher, 'Belvoir Castle – Leicestershire': 'I The Regency Apotheosis', 'II The Norman, Tudor and Caroline Castles', 'III Resplendent Phoenix' and 'IV Pictures and the Picturesque', *Country Life* (6, 13, 20, 27 December 1956).

Watkins, John, *A Biographical Memoir of his late Royal Highness Frederick, Duke of York and Albany*, London, 1827.

Yorke, James, *Lancaster House: London's Greatest Town House*, Merrell, 2001.

Relevant Houses Open to the Public

In approximate order of chronology to match the women discussed. Some of these were their homes, while others house the remains of their collections.

Weston Park, Shropshire	Lady Wilbraham
Goodwood House, Chichester, Sussex	Louise de Keroualle; Caroline West Holland; Duchess of Gordon
Château de la Verrerie, Aubigny, France	Louise de Keroualle
Ham House, Richmond, London	Duchess of Lauderdale
Thirlestane Castle, Berwickshire	Duchess of Lauderdale
Petworth House, West Sussex	Duchess of Somerset
Knole, Kent	Lady Betty Germaine
Marble Hill, Twickenham, London	Countess of Suffolk
Firle Place, West Sussex	Mary Shireburn, Duchess of Norfolk
Arundel Castle, West Sussex	Mary Blount, Duchess of Norfolk
Ugbrooke Park, Devon	Mary Blount, Duchess of Norfolk
Uppark, West Sussex	Sarah Lethieullier, Lady Fetherstonhaugh
Audley End, Essex	Countess of Portsmouth
Syon Park, Brentford, London	Duchess of Northumberland
Alnwick Castle, Northumberland	Duchess of Northumberland
Castletown, Ireland	Lady Louisa Conolly
Saltram House, Devon	Theresa Parker
Belvoir Castle, Lincolnshire	Duchess of Rutland

INDEX

Academy of Ancient Music, 27

Acland, Elizabeth, 8

Adam, Robert: asked to renovate Audley End, 146; designs for Mrs Montagu, 178–9, 182, 190, 192; designs for Northumberlands, 147, 155, 159, 165–7; designs for Saltram, 201–3; staircase at 10 Portman Square, 52; style appeals to patronesses, 16

Adams, Samuel and Sarah: *The Compleat Servant*, 40

Addison, Joseph, 31, 103

Ailesbury, Diana, Countess of (*née* Grey), 52

Albemarle, Anne, Countess of (*née* Lennox), 108

Allen, Ralph, 34

Allerthorpe (estate), Yorkshire, 174

Almack's Assembly Rooms, King Street, London, 26

Alnwick Castle, Northumberland: Elizabeth, Duchess of Northumberland's designs and rebuilding at, 3–4, 147, 152–9, 165–7; estate management, 38; Hertfords at, 148; ivory collection, 164; Northumberlands visit, 25; Salvin redesigns, 168; servants, 166

Amelia, Princess, 52

Ampthill Park, Bedfordshire, 52

Anne, Queen, 42–3, 81

Anson, George, 244

Arbury, Warwickshire, 54

Arbuthnot, Harriet, 232, 244–5, 247, 250–2

Argyll, Elizabeth, Duchess of (*née* Tollemache; Duchess of Lauderdale's daughter), 88, 91, 98

Arlington, Henry Bennet, 1st Earl of, 68–71

Arlington, Isabella, Countess of, 68

Arlington Street, London, 50–1, 54; *see also* Rutland House

Artima, Baldassare, 93–4

Arundel Castle, Sussex, 121

Arundel House, Strand, 122

Assembly Rooms, 31

Astell, Mary, 7

Aubigny (France), 65, 70, 81

Aubigny, Charles Stuart, 3rd Duke of Richmond, 12th Seigneur of, 70–1

Audley End, Suffolk, 44, 139–46

Audley, Sir Thomas, 140

Augusta, Princess of Wales, 48, 113, 159

Austen, Jane: *Pride and Prejudice*, 11–12, 20, 176

Aviemore, Scotland, 225

Aycliffe Heads, Co. Durham, 22

Badminton House, Gloucestershire, 5

Ballin, Claude, 79

balls and dancing, 31

Barlaston Hall, Staffordshire, 129

Basildon Park, Berkshire, 176

Bath, William Pulteney, Earl of, 169, 196

Batoni, Pompeo Girolamo, 109–10

Baxter, John, 217

Beattie, James, 182, 195, 218–19

Beauchamp, George, Viscount, 148, 150

Beauclerk, Lady Diana (*née* Spencer; then Bolingbroke), 10, 60

Beaufort, Elizabeth (Betty), Duchess of (*née* Boscawen), 7, 38, 195

Beaufort, Henry Somerset, 5th Duke of, 7, 12

Beaufort, Mary, Duchess of (*née* Capel; *then* Lady Beauchamp), 5

Beaulieu, Hampshire, 176

305